What Do You Say?

What Do You Say?

Autism with Character

Tyler Lagasse and Deborah Lagasse

Library of Congress Control Number:		2015904862
ISBN:	Hardcover	978-1-5035-5684-3
	Softcover	978-1-5035-5683-6
	eBook	978-1-5035-5685-0

Print information available on the last page.

Rev. date: 04/08/2015

To order additional copies of this book, contact:
Xlibris
1-888-795-4274
www.Xlibris.com
Orders@Xlibris.com
536367

CONTENTS

Introduction

WHAT YOU ARE ABOUT TO read is an accurate account of a life of one individual living in two worlds: the so-called real world and one that is as far from orthodox as you can possibly get. It's a long story, but it is better when it's long as it wouldn't be complete if it weren't. So far, my story has lasted twenty-five years, and during that time, I have lived through enormous highs and excruciating lows. I've lived with the hope that there is no limit to what I can accomplish and that anything is possible. Even my mother said that I am destined for greatness. I even overheard my mom classify me as a god during a conversation with someone. I am complicated yet talented. I am sensitive yet exceptional. I am mysterious yet bright. I am unusual yet punctual. I am awkward yet smart. I am more gifted than you will ever know. I am Tyler Hollis Lagasse.

Throughout this book you will see sections printed in italics. These are insertions that are written from a different perspective—the view through the lens of Tyler's mom, me, Deb Lagasse. I don't doubt for one minute that everything Tyler has written is his full experience. However, experiencing autism from the other side lends itself to a vastly different experience. Tyler started journaling during his senior year in high school. That was when he took over documenting various events in his life. However, journaling about Tyler is nothing new to this family. Journaling, taking notes, documentation, or whatever else you want to call it became a part of my life for so many years. I started taking "mental notes" on Tyler when he was about two years old. I knew deep down that he was different about three months after his birth. Tyler didn't respond to stimuli the same way his brother, Clint, did. He didn't seem to enjoy cuddling. He didn't seem to settle in to nurse. He never really played with toys the way other children did. I found it difficult to console him when he cried. He seemed to prefer to be left alone and in his baby carrier. It sounds foolish now, but I thought he was just a content baby who knew how to settle himself down. I ignored the inner voice inside telling me something else was going on with my baby. I struggle with using the words "something's wrong" because in some ways, autism has been a gift to me. Don't get me wrong. It is challenging to raise a child with autism, but now that he is getting older, I find myself thanking God for allowing me to give birth to such a unique, thoughtful, caring, and inspiring human being. I've been asked, if I could have chosen a different road for myself, would I have taken it? Because of the wonderful people that we have come to know and trust, I can honestly say that I wouldn't choose a different road, but I would make sure I have a four-wheel drive!

My pregnancy and delivery with Tyler was quite normal and uneventful. He was welcomed into this world on November, 17, 1986. He weighed 8 pounds, 6 ounces. He was born three years after our first son, Clint, was born. Within six months, I began to notice differences between Tyler and Clint. Clint liked being held and cuddled. As I mentioned previously, Tyler preferred to be left alone, in his swing or baby carrier. I chalked that up to the possibility that maybe the fact that his brother was a toddler had something to do with it. He hit all the milestones that infants and toddlers did: rolling over, crawling, walking, etc. However, he didn't really like playing all the infant games that most children do: peekaboo, pat-a-cake, etc. He never really sought out my comfort when he was distressed. He didn't seem to react to pain the same way that his brother did. Things that shouldn't bother him appeared to be tremendously painful, such as certain types of clothing or shoes. Yet things that should really cause a reaction, such as falling or getting a scrape or a bug bite, didn't seem to affect him. I thought that was so strange.

He never enjoyed children's television shows, such as Sesame Street *or* Mister Rogers. *In fact, he would cry when the Count from* Sesame Street *would stop counting at 20! He would scream out, "21, 22, 23," and so on. He was fixated on the logo for MTV. I cannot count how many papers we would fill out with the logo written on it. He would hand us a different kind of crayon for each line of each letter. It seemed as if that was the only way to get him to calm down. He also has strange phobias of certain TV personalities. The sight of Bill Cosby could send him into orbit. His entire body would shake, and he would bang his head against the floor. Even his older brother knew that if Bill Cosby would come on the TV for one of his Jell-O commercials, it would be imperative for us to run and change the channel to avoid the outburst. Remember, this was during the late '80s and early '90s, when* The Cosby Show *was rated number 1!*

Connie Chung was another trigger for Tyler's outbursts. We still don't understand why Tyler was petrified by these two individuals. Tyler was also afraid of closed-captioned television. I remember one time trying to go to a department store and shopping in the electronics section. I never noticed that most of their television monitors had closed-captioning turned on. Tyler would throw a tantrum, but he was still unable to have a conversation at that point, so I didn't know what was setting these tantrums off.

Tyler had a fascination with letters and numbers. He was obsessed with writing. We soon learned that it was necessary to always carry a pencil or pen and a notepad whenever we wanted to go anywhere outside the house. He didn't play with toys the same way other children did. He would line up the toy cars to spell various words. If he didn't have a pencil handy, he would use his index finger and spell words in the air. It seemed as though no one else but I noticed that he wasn't really playing with toys. He was using them as a tool to satisfy the need to spell words.

As you will see throughout this book, we have two very different concepts of what was happening at any given point in time. In fact, if I had known what Tyler was going through, maybe as a parent I might have reacted totally different. As they say, "Hindsight is 20/20." I find it interesting that Tyler believes he lives in two worlds. It must be tremendous work to try to make sense of both of these worlds. I know that he prefers life to be predictable, and when it isn't, he is somewhat unsettled. "Unsettled" for you and me can be a nuisance. But for Tyler, "unsettled" brings him to a halt. He has to regroup and use the tools and therapies that he has been taught in order to proceed. He does that with lightning speed now, but in the beginning, it was a long, drawn-out process. Hopefully, this book will not only enlighten you and inspire you to reach out to people with various disabilities but also make you pause, reflect, and celebrate each and every moment of your life and value every experience that has made you the best person that you can be. I can honestly say that much of my success in life has been the willingness to learn from my challenges.

This book is about what it took for me to get this far. It's about how I've used my autism to my advantage rather than as an excuse. As of right now, I feel that I have done an amazing job with my life with all the stuff that's happened to me. How it got to that point is certainly fascinating in every sense of the word, I guarantee it. The details of my first twenty-five years on earth will inspire you.

1986–1999: The Childhood Years

MY FATHER'S NAME IS RONALD Wilfred Lagasse. He was born in Lowell, Massachusetts. He was the only son of Lorraine and Edmond Lagasse, my *memere* and *pepere*. They were both working-class parents of French Canadian descent. Dad lived in the Pawtucketville section of Lowell throughout his childhood until moving to Tyngsboro in 1970 after the home they lived in was taken over by what is now the University of Massachusetts–Lowell. Dad went to Tyngsboro High School, where he met my mother. My mother's name is Deborah Lee "Bell" Lagasse, daughter of Harold and Christine Bell. She was the sixth child born out of seven siblings (one brother, five sisters) in her family. My mom was everything—I mean, Scottish, Swedish, Dutch, English, and two Native American tribes, Choctaw and Cherokee. Mom lived in Tyngsboro almost all her life. Ronald and Deborah got married on June 19, 1977.

For the first six years of their marriage, they lived in the Centralville section of Lowell. Dad got an office job at Digital in Salem, New Hampshire. Meanwhile Mom went to a hairdressing school in downtown Lowell and pursued her career goal as a hairdresser. Later on, she decided to teach cosmetology at Greater Lowell Technical High School in Tyngsboro. Mom and Dad had their first child together, a son named Clint Adam Lagasse, on October 15, 1983. Two months after Clint was born, they moved right next door to Memere and Pepere's house in Tyngsboro, where they built an addition and turned their house into a duplex. Three years after moving back to Tyngsboro, Ronald and Deborah would welcome another son to the world. Weighing in at 8 pounds, 6 ounces and measuring in at 20 inches long, a bright future was in store for this boy. I happened to be this boy.

My full name is Tyler Hollis Lagasse. I was born at Emerson Hospital in Concord, Massachusetts, on November 17, 1986. As far as I can remember, my first memory was getting my picture taken with relatives from my mother's side of the family during the holiday season of 1986.

In our home, we have many family pictures hanging on walls. One of these pictures was taken when Tyler was only six weeks old. That picture hung on the wall outside his bedroom for several years. I am sure that he doesn't have a memory of having his picture taken for that photo, but this is where the "autism factor" kicks in. It is difficult for Tyler to separate actual memories and pictures, videos, and conversations that involve him.

In the first couple of years of my life, my parents noticed strange behavior from me. As soon as I could walk, I would find myself opening the refrigerator to take out some eggs. I wanted to see what would happen if I dropped one to the floor. I thought it was cool to see the egg turn into something else once it cracked. I kept on dropping the eggs until Mom or Dad caught me doing it. They didn't just get mad at me. They went absolutely ape and punished me. I don't know what the punishment was, but it was bad.

The punishment would be to send him to his room. I am sure that I probably raised my voice as well, but that would be the extent of the harshness of his punishment. His perception of punishment would certainly feel severe because any change or interruption in his routine was a traumatic experience for him.

Another thing that I did that got my mom upset was when we would go shopping and I would come upon babies. There were times when I would go up to them and give them a nudge. My mom remembers this more vividly than I do. After I pushed them, they bumped their heads, and it made them cry, and I would laugh out loud—or LOL in computer terms. I didn't do it because I was an evil or stupid person. I did it because I was curious, perhaps too curious for my own good. I didn't treat them like people. I treated them like toys.

This particular habit was really difficult for me. I was so embarrassed that Tyler would run up to a child and knock them over. Luckily, this phase didn't last too long. It lasted for about six months. I had many discussions with Tyler's therapist regarding this and many other odd behaviors. We came to the conclusion that Tyler had an intense need for every facet of his life to be predictable. As such, babies can be quite unpredictable. Think about it—they sometimes walk, sometimes crawl, laugh, and then they cry. All of these actions occur within seconds of one another. For someone like Tyler, a person who needs time to process everything around him, this can be quite unsettling. To compensate for this unpredictability, Tyler would simply knock the toddler down. He knew with certainty this child would cry, their parent would come and pick that child up to console them, and I would react with a loud voice and punish him. All these things would happen each and every time he knocked a toddler down. It's not as if we allowed him to do this. He would do it so quickly. He wouldn't hit, scratch, bite, or punch. He would simply knock them gently as if they were part of a building block that he was playing with. I must admit, I found this habit both frustrating and embarrassing.

When I was a toddler, I would draw the MTV logo. I even read *Reader's Digest* out loud on a monitor so that my parents could hear. My photographic memory was so hard to fathom. Somewhere up until I was five years old, my parents would eventually figure out what was causing my perplexing behavior. After visiting with several doctors, they had come to this startling conclusion of what exactly was happening to me. My problem could only be described by the one word that would alter the Lagasse family landscape forever: *autism.*

Specifically I have pervasive developmental disorder (PDD), but autism in the general sense is a neurological disorder that affects the brain's ability to function normally. Back when I was born, autism was so rare and so unknown. Today there is more awareness of this dreadful intellectual disorder. According to today's figures, 1 out of less than 100 people has autism, and the chances of boys having autism are greater. Nobody knows for sure what causes this problem, and what's more frightening about it is the fact that there is no cure for this dreadful disorder at all. To many parents of children with autism, it is literally a jail sentence with no chance at parole—in other words, you are trapped and confined to care for this person and his disability for the rest of your life or his or hers. Autism is not contagious the same way influenza is, where you spread it from one person to another. Still there are more and more people living with autism now than ever before, so it seems like an epidemic.

I find it so sad that Tyler sees autism as a jail sentence. He is correct when he says that only he knows what it is like living with autism. For the past several years, Tyler has been giving speeches about living with autism.

Even though I have sought out the advice of every expert I can find, the real expert is Tyler. He is able to teach us what it feels like to live with this diagnosis. As he matures and gains new experiences, he is able to let us share a part of the inner workings of his thought process. Each year that passes brings with it a new piece of information and understanding of the complexities of living with autism.

Living with autism or being a mother or father or sibling of a person with autism could not be more challenging. It's like playing the same song over and over and over again inside your head, and you can't turn it off or at least turn down the volume. It's extraordinarily hard to describe my autism, and it is especially hard to live, deal, and cope with it. Nobody can vividly describe my autism but me. My type of autism, which is PDD, is high functioning, second highest to only Asperger's syndrome in the autism spectrum disorder—meaning that I can do most basic things, such as speaking, while someone with a different type of autism may not speak at all. There is nothing that my family and I can do about it right now. But the least that my family can do is to help and support other families of children with autism and let other people know that autism can no longer be ignored and that it must be taken care of. The least I can do is tell them about my life with autism in my own words.

I liked to watch television when I was a child. I would watch MTV back when they did music videos, and I got hooked on them instantly. The videos on MTV and VH1 described the music very well, too well perhaps. It had a profound impact on my childhood. There was also a time when I insisted on watching game shows like *The Price Is Right, Wheel of Fortune, Jeopardy!, Press Your Luck, Sale of the Century, Family Feud,* and many, many others. I didn't know all the answers to every question because back then I was too young. I watched Nickelodeon back in the day, and I could not go through a whole day without *Rugrats, Doug,* or any other Nicktoons. I may have watched too much television, probably more than anybody else. By the time I became a teenager, I would grow out of them.

The true fact is that Tyler did not watch as much television as other children. He liked to write. The problem was that he liked to write the same thing over and over and OVER! We never went anywhere without a pen or pencil and a pad of paper. From time to time I would put a children's video on the television, and interestingly enough, Tyler would refuse to be in the room the first few times it would play. Eventually, he would come into the room and watch the video, but it seemed as though he had an intense need to listen to the sound of the video first. Then he could watch the video once he knew what it would sound like. To this day, he is not fond of going to the movie theater. I suppose it is due to the fact that the movie is too loud, and he would also have to contend with the various sensory inputs from the other viewers and such.

From the day I was born to pretty much the end of my childhood, I couldn't go through a whole day without crying. The 1980s was hard for me because I was struggling through toddlerhood. Mom and Dad back then couldn't understand why I kept on crying. It was the only way I could communicate to them because I barely knew how to use my own words. Every time we passed a nearby McDonald's, I would cry. I would beg Mom and Dad to take me there. They couldn't take me shopping all the time because they were worried I might scream so loud for everybody to hear. My parents knew very well that I was a world-class screamer. They couldn't watch TV with me all the time because every time I saw Bill Cosby, I would cry. I know for sure that it wasn't the person per se that scared me, and I know for sure that it was a certain face he made that set me off. I had a hard time getting that mental image out of my head. Not only did I have a very uncanny photographic memory, I even had outstanding hearing back then. There were certain sounds that I also had big trouble getting out of my head. Sometimes the sounds were so bad that I tried to scream them out. Mom or Dad wanted me to stop, but I couldn't listen to them as I kept trying desperately to clear the sounds out completely.

I remember vividly how frustrated Tyler was during this time in his life. It was equally frustrating for me. I knew something was wrong when I couldn't console him. We had to avoid roads because if we drove past a McDonald's, Tyler would have a tantrum. He would cry hysterically, and even if we stopped, we couldn't get him to stop crying long enough to go in and order something. His fear of Bill Cosby or Connie Chung was unexplainable. It took us a little while to figure out why he was hysterical whenever a Jell-O commercial came on or the evening news. All I know is that he was deathly afraid of both of these individuals. It was so peculiar. We also had a hard time if we went to any store that had a television department. Tyler was and probably still is afraid of closed-captioning.

Many stores put their monitors on closed-captioning, and that would stop Tyler in his tracks. He would cry hysterically whenever a television was set on closed-captioning.

They knew something was up with me. They just didn't know what exactly. My parents wanted to know what was wrong with me, so they took me to my doctor in Billerica. If that wasn't helpful enough, they took me to Boston. It was then that they found out I had pervasive developmental disorder. Two years after I was born, there was a movie called *Rain Man*, starring Tom Cruise as Charlie, an impatient young car salesman, and Dustin Hoffman as Charlie's big brother Raymond, who is a middle-aged man with autism and lived in an institution. Charlie and Raymond never knew each other, and while they were traveling on this road trip from Cincinnati to Los Angeles, they bonded with each other. Mom and Dad were now faced with a grim scenario. They were going to learn how to bond with their autistic son, me.

Early on I had reservations and concerns with Tyler's development. I had mentioned them to my pediatrician. It must have sounded strange at the time because I was saying that something was wrong, but yet here I had a son that could read and write by the age of three! He could easily count to over one hundred before he was three years old. We always had to have a pen or pencil and a pad of paper with us so that he wouldn't have a tantrum in public. I remember bringing him with me to his older brother Clint's nursery school. He didn't look around at the kids or the toys. He would run over to the wall and play with the wooden blocks shaped in the letters of the alphabet and begin spelling words and phrases. He would get so mad when he ran out of letters! The preschool teachers told me not to worry, that he would be fine when it was his turn to go to nursery school. Deep in my heart, I knew it wouldn't work. But I had to try.

When the time was appropriate, my parents let me attend Little Angels, located near the old Littlefield Library in the center of Tyngsboro.

I remember dropping Tyler off at nursery school. I was sure I had made the wrong decision, but I buried that fear deep inside my head and hoped for the best. I can remember driving off, and by the time I left the parking lot of the nursery school, I was already crying. I couldn't explain why I was crying. I just knew he wouldn't be safe at that school. Of course they would keep him physically safe, but it was more than that. I just knew that something was wrong and this wasn't the right setting for Tyler. When I went to pick him up at the end of that first day, I found his teacher holding Tyler in her lap and looking exhausted! The owner of the school met me at the door and told me to write a letter to the head of the special education department in our town and request an evaluation. I drafted that letter and mailed it off. Life hasn't been the same since! As part of the initial evaluation, it was required that our pediatrician have input. While we were waiting in the exam room for the pediatrician to come in, Tyler was writing on a pad of paper. That was a normal occurrence for him. He always wrote whenever he could. Just as our doctor entered the exam room, Tyler handed him a piece of paper. Tyler had written, "Here is your life. OUT OF CONTROL!" He handed that piece of paper to the pediatrician. The doctor looked at it and said, "How long has he been able to write like this?" I told him that he had been able to write things like this for well over a year. It was so frustrating because I had been to his office and mentioned that I thought that Tyler was different from other kids and I was concerned. It wasn't until the nursery school referred him that anyone took my concerns about Tyler seriously. At that point, the pediatrician referred us to Tuft's Floating Hospital in Boston, Massachusetts, for further evaluation. Specifically, we went to a clinic inside the hospital called the Center for Children with Special Needs. It took several months for the evaluations to be completed. We saw many specialists. They all came to the same conclusion: PDD-NOS with autistic-like characteristics. Many people want specific diagnoses. However, I have come to realize that any type of diagnosis within the autism spectrum is more important to the professionals than the parents involved in raising the children. I really don't care to take the time to argue about how "severe" Tyler's autism is.

Sometimes it would take over two months to actually get the typewritten report from the various specialists. I found that so frustrating! How could we develop a plan on how best to deal with Tyler's challenges without actual documentation and recommendations from the professionals? While we waited for the evaluations, my husband and I felt that Tyler should remain in some kind of school setting. Therefore, I attended nursery school with Tyler. I decided to accompany him for two reasons: safety (because he could bolt out of any room) and to collect information on his development. I observed Tyler's reaction to his peers, teachers, and other adults. I also watched how the other children reacted to the same stimuli. It was both rewarding and challenging for me to witness the differences between Tyler and the other children. I must admit it was helpful to collect this information and share it with the professionals that would be making recommendations for Tyler's educational future.

After Little Angels, I went to Winslow School, also in the center of town. A nice old lady named Carol, who worked for SP&R Transportation, was my first cabdriver, and she would pick me up and take me to school and then take me home. My teachers at Winslow School were Gail Semonian and Joelyn Riley. There was this speech therapist named Marge Peabody, and once in a while I would have sessions with her. Once a week I would have this thing in my classroom called "gym with Jim." A gym teacher named Jim Tansey would come into my classroom to have us practice some ski pulls or ski tucks. I liked going to Winslow School, I liked my teachers, and I liked my classmates.

The public school system completed an initial educational evaluation. Several specialists from the public school evaluated Tyler in the following areas: speech and language, occupational therapy, developmental, and psychological. My husband and I decided to combine the information that the school had learned from their evaluations with the information from the evaluations conducted by the Center for Children with Special Needs at New England Medical Center in Boston, Massachusetts. In the meantime, Tyler would attend an integrated preschool four mornings a week. Twice a week, "typical" students would attend the preschool with students that had special needs. The other two days, the class would be smaller because only the students that had special needs would attend. Normally an Individual Education Plan (IEP) would be written and developed, then implemented for each student. We didn't feel comfortable writing an IEP based solely on the recommendations of the public school system. Therefore, with the advice of one of my friends, who happened to be a special education liaison in a neighboring community, we agreed to develop a diagnostic IEP. Typically, a diagnostic IEP is used for about two months while the "team" gains further information needed to develop a more comprehensive IEP that would remain in effect for the entire school year. Interestingly enough, Tyler's diagnostic IEP kept getting renewed and was in effect for two years. During that time, we would have short-term goals to determine the effectiveness of each goal and the best course or action to meet Tyler's unique needs.

The team—consisting of Ron and myself, the building principal, a preschool teacher, a paraprofessional, a speech therapist, an occupational therapist, and the school psychologist—would meet approximately every two weeks to amend or support each goal on the diagnostic IEP. We were also very fortunate that our public school system hired some of the evaluators that we used in Boston to attend these meetings and offer suggestions that would help Tyler. These meetings would last all morning. We learned so much about Tyler and about the limitations and expectations that were possible within the public school. It got to the point that I felt so bad that our meetings would go on for so long that I began to cook lunch in a Crock-Pot and bring it in for the staff for us to have a "working lunch." One of the recommendations from our independent evaluation was for Tyler to attend a full-day preschool program with an extended school year. We were very fortunate that our town created a full-time program. Many other parents were grateful as well. The following year, Tyler went to the public school full-time (well actually, four days). After that second year, it became obvious that we were "creating the wheel." Our consultant mentioned that we should look at private schools for Tyler. To be honest, I didn't know that schools for children with special needs existed. I knew that there were schools where children lived, but I didn't realize that there were schools within driving distance that specialized in children like mine. We got recommendations on several schools. There are so many factors to consider when trying to decide which school is best for your child. I was hoping that I would be able to find a school that was located within one hour driving distance from our house. I visited several schools. Most of the time, I felt hopeless. I know that these schools were known for excellence in the field of special needs. However, I just couldn't wrap my head around the fact that MY SON would need to be in a school like this. Some of the schools had children with much more challenging behaviors and circumstances than Tyler. It was difficult to picture Tyler attending these schools. On many occasions, I would sit in my car and cry before I could begin to drive home. I knew that he needed something more than my town had to offer, but it was certainly not the schools that I was visiting. Just when I had practically given up hope, I was directed to the Community Therapeutic Day School in Lexington, Massachusetts. The school itself was a historical colonial home that had been converted into a school. There were only thirty students attending this school. The age range was three years old to twelve years old. They had small classrooms in what would normally have been a bedroom. Students were in classes in what would be considered the dining room and living room. There was a huge barn on the property, which would later be renovated and turned into some therapeutic rooms and a large area to have gatherings in and things of that nature. I must admit I was skeptical upon arrival. That feeling vanished once I stepped inside and met the directors and various staff members. They were so welcoming and appeared to be genuinely concerned about what was best for Tyler. We shared our reports from the various experts as well as all the reports from our public school. We had a meeting for almost two hours, and I left feeling full of hope and acceptance. The thing that I was most impressed with was the fact that this school was embracing the entire family, not just Tyler.

Naively, I thought that if Tyler had intensive therapy for a year or so, his "problem" would disappear. I wasn't quite ready to give up on public school at this point. My original thought was maybe I could have the experts from this school come out to the Winslow School in Tyngsboro and observe Tyler and the staff in Tyngsboro, and just maybe they could make recommendations to the public school program and VOILA! Looking back, it was a crazy plan! We were able to have Alan Shapiro from CTDS come out to Winslow School and observe Tyler in his school setting. He spent the morning there observing things that even I didn't notice. It was at that point that I knew Tyler needed a more intense approach to his education.

However, Mom and Dad felt that the Winslow School wasn't the right place for me, nor was it the best place for me. By the time I was five years old, they knew I wasn't making enough progress. During the 1991–1992 school years, they set out to look for a new school best suited for my disability. In the end, they found a place in Lexington called the Community Therapeutic Day School. I didn't want to go to Lexington to go to school. I wanted to stay at Winslow School in Tyngsboro and be with my friends there. It was not up to me though, but it was for my own good and for the greater good that my parents sent me to CTDS.

I first went to CTDS one day a week starting in February of 1992 and started going there full-time in September of that year. In my first few years going to CTDS, I had to learn how to get used to the following: The commute on the way to the school was usually a nightmare. Routes 3 and 128 heading southbound would be slow every God-given morning. I was so used to going fast that I hated going slow. I even had to get used to the routine and the rules of CTDS. The teachers at CTDS were tougher on me than those at Winslow. I had Laura and Patti as my teachers in my first year. If I broke their rules—for example, if I didn't pay attention to my teachers or if I got lost in my head or if I did something that was not appropriate to my teachers—I would sit in a chair. My teachers called it a *time-out*. If time-out wasn't enough, I would get held or wrapped up by one of the teachers. Being held was the worst punishment. I remember one time in my first year when I tried to fight my way out of being held. It was no use. Eventually it would be over after they had punished me enough. Being good at CTDS was wicked hard for me.

As I mentioned previously, I was not quite ready to give up on public education. Therefore, I recommended that Tyler go to CTDS on Wednesdays when he was off from school in Tyngsboro. I also recommended that a teacher or therapist from Tyngsboro go to CTDS and observe what was going on so that they could replicate what was happening at that school and continue to provide that type of therapy back home in the public school. I must admit it was a very odd request. I was fortunate that both my public school and CTDS agreed to try this novel idea. Thus began a new chapter for Tyler's education. Each week, a different teacher, an aide, a speech therapist, or an occupational therapist would go to CTDS on Wednesday and observe various therapeutic techniques employed. This went on for several months. I noticed a vast improvement regarding Tyler's eye contact and "connectedness." It was at this point that I felt a glimmer of hope. This back-and-forth education lasted for the remainder of the school year. All the while we would continue to have monthly meetings to discuss Tyler's progress. By the end of the year, it was decided that Tyler would benefit from attending CTDS full-time. I remember feeling so anxious making this decision. It's not easy for the public school system to agree to pay tens of thousands of dollars for an out-of-district placement. I was struggling with the guilt of adding a financial burden to the school system. I had to put those thoughts out of my head and push for what was best for my child. I will say that Tyngsboro Public Schools did support our decision with very little resistance. Tyler began attending CTDS full-time that summer.

My CTDS classmates did not specifically come from Lexington. They came from all over Eastern Massachusetts. Each class usually had up to seven students, two teachers, and an intern. Each classroom was like a family of some sort. My new school had Friday morning music sing-alongs, meetings, art, snack time, nature walks, gym, and rest time. My favorite part of CTDS was park time. CTDS called their playground on top of the hill the Park. The Park had a basketball hoop, where I would play some basketball. I would ride a three-wheel toy bike on the paved surface of the park and play on this wooden structure with a slide, monkey bars, and a metal pipe. My least favorite part of CTDS was the meetings. I didn't find most topics to be interesting and appealing, so I didn't listen. If I didn't listen, I was in big trouble. It wasn't my fault I wouldn't listen, but every day, my teachers were there to help me listen and to make sure I was with my class.

Once in a while, I would have special time with Alan Shapiro. He did his best to help me with my problems and to figure out what was going on inside my head. If there was one speech therapist that I disliked the most at CTDS, it was Elizabeth. She was harder on me than anybody else. Every Thursday, my class would have speech group with Elizabeth. She would make us listen to her instructions at all times. She would force me to look at her when I wasn't paying attention. She would always say, "Be here in speech group!" She would get on my case every time I did a thing that seemed peculiar to her. Nobody punished me more than Elizabeth. For the first three and a half years, she was there to reach out to me and to keep me in line. I may have hated her guts when I was little—I don't remember saying that to her—but she helped me become a better person.

I owe an immeasurable amount of gratitude to everyone at CTDS. I often say that Alan Shapiro is the one person that truly taught me how to be a mom to my son Tyler. He has always been there for EVERYONE in my family. He didn't just focus on Tyler. He and everyone else at CTDS are concerned on the entire family. The philosophy at this school is that everyone plays a role in the life of the child with the disability. Each person needs to be nurtured and valued. The directors of this school, Nancy Fuller and Dr. Bruce Hauptman, created an environment for their staff that truly puts the child's and the family's needs in the forefront of every decision. When I thought about education, my initial thoughts were about the academics—reading, writing, and arithmetic. I wasn't really giving any consideration to life skills—such as critical thinking, decision making, and self-awareness—as things that would need to be taught in a very specific, comprehensive way. CTDS taught the "whole" child.

Every day during every school year for seven years, my mom and my teachers would write to each other in a black composition book. They did an outstanding job in keeping track of my progress from day 1. By the time I left CTDS, fourteen books would be written over the course of seven years. My parents were not writers, and neither were my teachers. Yet they covered every day of my mental growth process and did it with complete accuracy.

That black book became my lifeline toward learning how to parent Tyler. It wasn't as if I could get any feedback from Tyler on how his day went. Without that black book, it wouldn't have been possible to continue working on the things that were essential for Tyler to integrate into our world. As I look back on those books, I notice that my handwriting reflects the level of frustration and joy that I was feeling on any particular day. I was always happy to see Tyler when he got off the van upon arriving home, but I would be lying if I didn't confess that I was just as happy to open that black book and see what was going on in Tyler's world when I wasn't around. I continue to look back on the writings from those books to remind myself of how far we've come. For me, those black books symbolize growth, strength, courage, wisdom, and, most of all, acceptance.

Communication was the central focus of that school. Learning to communicate for our children and communicating between the staff and the parents of the children were clearly defined in the communication books as well as weekly calls between teachers and parents. Every week at a specific time, the phone would ring, and I would spend thirty to forty-five minutes discussing Tyler's progress with his teacher. His teachers were my window into his world. They helped me through struggles with understanding Tyler's complex needs. There's no other way to describe what they did, except to say they made it bearable to raise a child with such unique challenges. They listened with keen ears as I cried. They celebrated with joy at all of his accomplishments. In short, they gave me hope.

In my last year at CTDS in 1999, Michael B. was my only classmate from my first year at this school that was also in my current classroom. Michael was like my twin brother at CTDS. In my first three years at this school, there were times when I would cry every time Michael would cry. It bothered me to look at him cry. I couldn't stand it. I even went to time-out for it because my teachers thought I was making fun of it when I really wasn't. Back in the day, I was too worried and scared to admit it to my teachers and my parents because I would feel embarrassed that they might make fun of it. I think that's why we were separated for two years.

I love the fact that Tyler considered Michael a brother! I wasn't sure if Tyler understood the concept of friendship or even missed me whenever I was gone. He didn't seem to react when I would leave to go to work and come home. My experience with my older son was that he was glad to see me return from wherever I had been. Tyler never seemed to notice!

I went to the Community Therapeutic Day School for seven long years. Even though going to and from CTDS was never my taste, I somehow learned to respect other people and respect nature. Once a week when the weather was suitable, I would go on nature walks with Sara Arshad. She said trees have feelings just like humans. She really taught us firsthand about respecting nature the same as respecting other people. I grew to love nature thanks to Sara. CTDS played a huge role in the making of me.

CTDS held summer programs in July. After the CTDS Summer Program was over, I would be overjoyed because I did not have to deal with long rides and school for a month. In 1992 I went to Cape Cod with my family. I did not like it there because a couple of times it would rain so bad that I feared that we would drown to death. Just to be safe, I went right to bed to protect myself from the rain.

When Tyler says he went right to bed, he is making an understatement. The fact is he "checked out." He basically went to sleep for several hours of the day and slept through the night. It was so peculiar how a rambunctious young boy could basically shut down. I knew he was afraid of the rain, but it was surreal to see his reaction to several days of rain. I finally discovered that it wasn't really the rain that he was afraid of. Tyler didn't like changes. Weather changes caused a sensory overload for him. He really didn't like snow either. Cloudiness wasn't a real issue, unless the cloudiness led to storminess.

The next summer in 1993, we went up to New Hampshire's White Mountains, and I had a better time there. In 1994 we drove all the way down to Virginia to stay at a resort with my relatives who happened to live there.

It was easier to try to stick to the same routine when going on vacations. When we went to Virginia, we stayed at a resort that my sister used frequently. I asked her to send me pictures of the resort so that Tyler could familiarize himself with the surroundings. These pictures were not your typical postcard pictures of rooms and scenery. They were specific in nature. She took a picture of the sign entering the resort. She took a picture of the actual cabin we would be staying in. She took a picture of the bathroom that Tyler would be using. It was so helpful and lowered the anxiety level for Tyler.

In 1998 I went with Mom, Dad, Clint, and his friends Josh and Zack Trearchis to Springfield, Massachusetts. We all visited the Basketball Hall of Fame, Riverside (now Six Flags New England) in Agawam, and the Holyoke Mall. Just days after that, I went with my family and our friends the Reaults to Cape Cod. When my family didn't travel and stay at other places, we would go to Water Country in Portsmouth, New Hampshire, or visit the beaches in the Seacoast Region of New Hampshire. Sometimes my brother Clint would let me hang out with his friends to play Wiffle ball, ride bikes, play rundown, bocce, flashlight tag, and swing off a tire swing into Lake Mascuppic. In the summer of 1996, Clint and I attended the same wrestling camp together at Tyngsboro High.

I have often said that sometimes it felt like we were raising two "only children." However, it's nice to see that Tyler doesn't see it that way. We tried to do everything that any "normal" family would do. We just needed to be a little less spontaneous and stick with our plans. We are so blessed to have friends and family who include Tyler in all their activities and actually ask us what they can do to make each experience as comfortable as possible for him.

When I was at CTDS, goodbyes were never easy, transitions were never easy, and changes were never easy. All three of these things were inevitable and out of my control. Every time when the CTDS school year wound down in the month of June, a goodbye book would be made for each class. I went through seven goodbye books before my last year. Each and every one of these goodbyes was sad. Each class was like a tight-knit family. We looked out for each other, we helped each other out, and we were together almost constantly from September to June. Then when the school year ended, all those feelings kicked in. For seven years, I saw many teachers and interns and students and therapists come and go. I grew very close to some of them. It was always hard for me to say goodbye to them.

Finally came a time for me to say goodbye to CTDS. I had mixed feelings myself. I was happy that I was leaving CTDS, but I was also sad. Of course I was not going to stay at CTDS forever because all students have to leave by the time they reached twelve years old. Each student who was leaving in 1999 was given their own personal goodbye book. My goodbye book had drawings from my classmates and notes from my teachers Janet and Olivia and my intern Leann.

Janet's note went like this:

Dear Tyler,

I have loved working with you at CTDS. You have learned so much! You worked hard at being a good friend and at becoming a better sportsman. I love your sense of humor and the very funny and clever things you say. You have done a good job trying to talk about your feelings instead of going in your head. I will miss teaching you math. You were an excellent math student! I will miss you very much! You are ready to leave CTDS. Good luck at the Gifford School!

Janet

Olivia's note went like this:

Dear Tyler,

You are truly a very special person, and you have taught me so much about your world. I am so proud of how hard you worked this year and how you're always trying to pay attention to people. You are an incredible athlete, writer, and musician. I will miss you so very much and you will always have a special place in my heart.

Olivia

Finally, there was Leann's note:

Tyler,

I have enjoyed getting to know you this year. I will miss your witty personality. You were a joy to have in reading and I was proud of the work you accomplished. You will do great at your new school. Remember: Changes can be good. Good luck, I will always remember you!

Love, Leann

I remember my last day at CTDS, July 30, 1999. I remember almost everybody waving goodbye to me as Mom and Dad took me home. I got two books on my last day. One was my own goodbye book with pictures of me at CTDS dating back to my first year and notes of "good luck" from the people who were there for me all those years. The other book was a program from the 1999 Major League Baseball All-Star Game, which took place at Fenway Park. The year 1999 was definitely a year of goodbyes for me. Not only did I say goodbye to CTDS, but in April I also said goodbye to my grandpa Harold O. Bell Jr., who passed away of complications from diabetes. The world was saying goodbye to not only a decade, not only a century, but a millennium.

Even though the new millennium didn't begin until January 1, 2000, I was taking the next step in my life. I was going to turn thirteen in November of 1999. This meant that my childhood days were giving way to a tougher part of life called adolescence, or teenage life. The two years after CTDS were the hardest, if not the most challenging, times of my life. For the next two years after CTDS, I had to learn how to put up with things that didn't make sense. I never imagined that it would be like this until I entered through the door to the next phase. The next phase was my own two-season-long reality series called Gifford School.

I grew up in the small town of Tyngsboro, Massachusetts, near the New Hampshire border, less than an hour's drive from Boston. At a young age I had a fond interest and passion for the four major professional Boston sports teams (Red Sox, Celtics, Bruins, Patriots), and I still do to this day. I have a good memory of going to my first Red Sox game. My mom, my dad, my big brother Clint, and I went to Fenway Park to see the Red Sox play the eventual World Series Champion Toronto Blue Jays on a Sunday afternoon in August of 1993. Roger Clemens was pitching for Boston that day. Fenway Park was unlike any place I've ever seen before. Even before major renovations took place a decade later, the place was a pure baseball field, with the big wall in left field, called the Green Monster, and those distinctive dimensions separating the seats from the field. Each area in and around Fenway Park had its own character to it.

As you can see, Tyler focuses on facts and mostly facts. He can describe in detail events that make sense to him. What he tends to lack is the emotion surrounding the events. I guess that's why he loves sports so much. To him, they are extremely predictable. He lives his life with a lot of structure and seems to need rules or boundaries for every aspect of it. Our family enjoys sports, but not to the extent that Tyler seems to "need" them.

As a young boy, I was lost inside my own world dreaming up a million things at once. My mind was always occupied with future events. I used to keep on thinking about weekends, my next baseball game, visits with friends and family, and trips to the mall and more stuff like that. I had a deep fascination of cars when I was little, and my grandparents Harold and Christine Bell would take me to Auto Village in Nashua, New Hampshire, to check out some of the latest vehicles. I especially looked forward to such holidays as Halloween, Thanksgiving, Memorial Day, and Easter. The two holidays I looked forward to the most were my birthday and Christmas. However, when things were changed or postponed, even cancelled due to the weather or other unforeseen circumstances, I would get upset.

As his mom, I had no idea that he knew anything about the concept of a holiday. Those days seemed to stress him out the most. I dreaded going to someone else's home for any holiday. That meant that I would have to keep a keen eye on Tyler and not really get to visit the relatives. Tyler seemed to have this intense need to explore each and every room of the house that we were visiting. It was so embarrassing to see him sneak away and open doors that he shouldn't be exploring. I now know that he was having a sensory overload and needed to understand the layout of the home in order to settle down. It was also difficult to see the disconnection between Tyler and our relatives. When he was just at home with our immediate family, his odd behavior didn't seem as noticeable. I can remember many birthdays and holidays where he would not participate. He didn't even seem to notice that we were celebrating. He would go off on his own and write or would try to be in another room, away from the noise.

I can remember feeling a loss because Tyler never gave us any indication that he understood the concept of Santa Claus, the Easter Bunny, or the tooth fairy. We went through the motions, but each holiday seemed to pass with little or no emotion from Tyler to indicate that he believed in Santa or anyone else. His favorite gifts to receive were pencils, markers, or crayons and paper. He seemed obsessed with writing all the time.

In the winter of 1995–1996, I went to my first Celtics game at the place then known as the Fleet Center. It was the Celtics' first season away from the legendary Boston Garden. I remember seeing myself on the Jumbotron that night as they were about to get beaten by the Los

Angeles Lakers. In March of 1999, I went to my first Bruins game, a Sunday afternoon game against the New York Rangers. I have gone to three New England Revolution soccer games, twice at old Foxboro Stadium in the '90s and once at Gillette Stadium in the spring of 2004. As of 2011, I have yet to go down to Foxboro to see the Patriots play.

Back in the 1990s, the only organized sports I played as a young boy in Tyngsboro were baseball, soccer, and basketball. My parents would not let me play football or hockey, although I loved watching them and I wanted to give them a try. The first sport that I played back then was baseball. I admit I was never a great hitter in baseball, but every time I hit that ball, it felt so good. It bored me to move the base runner along or to hit sacrifices—I wanted to get the big hit. On defense, I was very good at first base, as a catcher, and in the outfield. Every time I was on that pitcher's mound, I wanted to throw a no-hitter, although I never did. I do recall throwing ten strikeouts in four innings while I was playing for the Cubs as an eleven-year-old in 1998.

In soccer, I was never on any winning team, and I wasn't that good until my final season in 2001. There were times when I would throw tantrums when my team gave up a goal or lost. My most thrilling soccer moment came in the summer of 1994 when I was at a soccer camp run by some gentleman named John Smith and I got a water bottle for winning a one-on-one competition. Afterward I had my picture taken with John Smith. Later on in my life I would find out that he had made a game-winning field goal for the New England Patriots in the snow back in 1982.

In basketball, I wanted to make a shot at the buzzer. There was this one time when I made two buzzer beaters at a pair of pickup games on the same night with some friends my age at Tyngsboro High School. Every time I beat the buzzer, I felt like I was on top of the world. There was this one bad time when I was twelve and playing in an intramural youth basketball game at Tyngsboro High. I wrapped an opponent around trying to get the ball, and I got elbowed in the mouth, losing one baby tooth in the process. My dad was refereeing that game, and he failed to blow the whistle when I had that kid wrapped up. I insulted him and then gave him the middle finger. When I came back, I tried throwing my elbow at one of the opponents. It was a very upsetting moment for me. My team was losing, my team was undermanned, and I sort of let them down by making an already bad situation worse.

I was a terrible sport when I was a kid because I wanted to win all the time, but most of the time, I was not good enough to win. That did not stop me from trying however. I did not care what I was playing. Whether it was Wiffle ball with my older brother Clint and his friends, Ping-Pong with my friend and schoolmate Michael B., or the many board games I had at home, I wanted to win. There were times when I would get upset when my team lost or if I didn't play well or if I made a mistake. I have had more downs than ups as a kid playing baseball because I wasn't on a champion team, and I did not win a trophy for finishing first, second, or third. It was rough on me not getting what I wanted, and sometimes it definitely got to me.

One time I threw my helmet toward my team's dugout after I struck out during a Little League baseball game as a ten-year-old. I was thrown out of the game. It was my first and luckily my only ejection in any baseball game. The next year, in the final inning of the last game of the season on the same baseball field, I was the catcher, and the pitcher threw a wild pitch. I tried to get the ball and make a play to the plate, but it was too late. The winning run scored, and my team lost. I was totally upset when the game ended the way it did, and it was understandable. Just seconds after the run scored, I chucked the ball out of frustration, unaware of where that ball went. The next thing I knew, I noticed the kid that scored was down on the ground. I hurt him. One person in the stands said, "That was intentional!" even though I did not know what I was doing. I was treated like a criminal, and I never felt more humiliated while playing in a sport. I felt just as bad hurting that kid as I did losing the game, even though losing the game hurt a bunch. I know that nobody is perfect, not even myself. I tried very hard at being a good sport, and my parents always stressed good sportsmanship over winning even to this day.

My older brother Clint has always been considered the athlete of the family. In the '90s he excelled in baseball, soccer, and basketball. Just like me, he too hated losing and wanted to win. Sometimes it would take him twenty-four to forty-eight hours to get over a loss. Every time I played against him, he would always beat me. Actually, he wanted to beat me so bad that it wasn't funny at all. Funny thing, I would feel bad for my childhood tormentor every time his team lost or if he didn't play well. He would give everything he had against his opponents and give some more. My brother was better than most athletes his age. People think his best sport was soccer, but the fact is he was just as good at any other sport that he focused on.

Sports have played an integral role to help teach Tyler right from wrong. The major problem for Tyler is the fact that he treats every sporting event as if it were the World Series, the Stanley Cup, the World Championships, the Super Bowl, or the Olympics. Most of us view sports as entertainment for the most part. Tyler pours his heart and soul into each event, even Little League games. He is so conflicted when his team makes a bad play. It might be cute when you are eight or nine years old. But believe me, it gets pretty old when you are still struggling with this issue when you are twenty-five. It's downright embarrassing! When he has an outburst at a college hockey game, not only am I embarrassed, humiliated, and angry. I am fearful that someone may come up and start a fight with him. At this point it not only becomes a social issue. It becomes a safety issue. We continue to work on this issue and have left a game midstream if he doesn't follow the rules of behavior in any given situation. For that reason, both Ron and I accompany him to all sporting events. On rare occasions, he can go with one of our relatives, but even then, we are uneasy sending him without one of us to make sure his emotions remain in check.

I liked to listen to music when I was a kid, and I still do to this day. My favorite band back in the day was Hanson, that trio of youngsters from Oklahoma. At first I couldn't stand them, when my brother and his friends were playing "MMMBop" over and over again. But when I first saw their music video, I could envision myself playing with that band. If those kids can make music and do so well at it, I thought to myself, *Why can't I?* When I was nine years old, I started taking piano lessons. I was so good at it that everybody wanted to see me play. For whatever reason, I lost interest in the piano and ultimately quit playing when I was thirteen years old. I felt that I was better off listening to music than playing it. As I got older, I started to get into some classic rock or some of the music that my dad grew up listening to. To this day, classic rock and alternative are still my favorite genres of music.

Tyler has an uncanny ability to remember the most remote facts regarding many topics. He can remember almost any fact about any major sport, musician, president, or highway in America. It's really a unique gift. He has a fascination for road maps. He loves to read the road atlas. He doesn't go right to the page for a city, state, or town. He reads the atlas from cover to cover. It's almost as if he is a scanner and he is putting a visual picture of each page into his brain. I can remember going on a vacation to Virginia when he was very young. It was no problem driving from Massachusetts to Virginia. My husband and I just sat in the front seat, and Tyler gave us the directions to where we were going! He was more accurate than the AAA TripTik that we had as a reference. He would give us a warning as to which lane to get into before the exit so that we wouldn't have to worry about missing the turnoff. This was before the Internet or smart phones were available and even before GPS was a household name.

Piano playing seemed to come easy to Tyler. I wouldn't say he was "really good" at it. He seems to think that he is really good *at most things. Self-esteem does not seem to be a problem for him! When I signed him up for piano lessons, my intention was to give Tyler the opportunity to meet new people and have to follow instructions and things like that. The focus was not really on learning piano. I wanted him to practice the skills he was learning each day in school and transfer those skills in various social experiences. For me, I am always trying to give Tyler opportunities to engage with people in the "real" world. By providing those types of opportunities for Tyler, I can see firsthand if all the therapy that he has received is actually working. It also affords me the opportunity to see what skills we need to work on for him to move forward into living an independent life. I guess in some ways, I see every opportunity as an evaluative tool for him. I know this is exactly what I do, but to put it into words seems exhausting! Sometimes I think,* **Maybe I'm the one with the real issues!**

One of the many things that I looked forward to when I was a kid was playing miniature golf. Miniature golf to me was very special and fun. I asked Mom and Dad to take me miniature golfing at any place or town where they had a miniature golf course. As I grew older, I grew into hitting a bucket of golf balls with real clubs at Max's Driving Range in Tyngsboro. Before I knew it, I was ready to start playing some real golf. By the time I was ten years old, once I had been given my first set of golf clubs, my dad took me to a place off Route 110 in the nearby small town of Westford called Kimball's. Kimball's was best known for their ice cream, but they had a driving range and a pitch-and-putt par-3 golf course. That is exactly when my old man and I started taking up golf together (it was also the place where I had my first summer job in 2003). Later that year, Dad and I started golfing at Tyngsboro Country Club, located just two minutes from my house.

So many years have passed since I've started golfing, and I can tell you that this one sport has helped me become a better human being on and off the golf course. Back when I started playing the game, I never thought I would even write about all this. It never crossed my mind at all. I dreamt about being lots of things, but being a golfer or writing about me being a golfer was not what I had in mind.

Golf has been one of the most therapeutic influences in Tyler's life. I would have never guessed that just hitting a little white ball into a small hole could have such an impact on Tyler's day-to-day life. It began very innocently. For me it was just another activity to expose him to.

Things turned out more different than what I had wished for when I was going to school at the Community Therapeutic Day School in Lexington or Gifford School in Weston or Cotting School in Lexington.

After Cotting School, I decided to take my writing seriously, so I wrote some journal entries from a composition book that I got for my senior year at Cotting. Originally it was going to be about the summer of 2005, but I've kept on writing in my journals and haven't stopped since I graduated from Cotting. By the year 2010, I would complete five journals. That's over one thousand pages worth. I never thought for once that I would even become a writer as well as a golfer.

Tyler is a very eloquent writer. It's always interesting to see how he uses his words in print. He is so expressive when writing. When he was much younger, he had the hardest time speaking to both Ron and me. Sometimes when he was really frustrated, I would tell him to write down what he was trying to tell me. He was always better at writing his emotions down as opposed to telling me what he was feeling. Currently, Tyler is writing a golf blog for our local newspaper. He also writes all his own speeches. It's almost comical when he delivers a speech with passion, emotion, and sincerity, because after he delivers a speech, people usually assume he can have a one-on-one conversation with them. As soon as someone approaches him after his speech, he responds with one-word answers and very little eye contact and almost comes off aloof.

The Bell Family portrait taken on Christmas 1986. The baby on Mom's (Deborah's) lap is me.

The 1st Christmas featuring all four members of the Lagasse Family. Clockwise from top left: Mom (Deborah), Dad (Ronald) holding me, and Clint.

The first ever photograph of my older brother Clint holding me.

A very little version of me hanging onto monkey bars while attending Winslow School.

One of the earliest bits of evidence of my writing and drawing prowess. My parents would have to go out and get me new Magna-Doodles in case I wore out ones such as this one.

Showing off my love of sports without a single regard for which kind. This was me on my 7th birthday 1993.

This is the first such "Black Book" used to describe my progress at CTDS. Now this was before the era of e-mail.

Summers were so much fun for me. This one in Cape Cod in 1998 was no exception. (Left to Right: brother Clint, Mike Reault, Alyssa Reault, and me deep in the hole we all dug into.)

Gifford School

As soon as I was twelve years old, Mom and Dad had to look for a new school after CTDS. We looked at two places. One was Willow Hill in rural Sudbury, where one of my old classmates went, and the second was Gifford School, which was west of Boston. I knew a couple of people from CTDS who went to Gifford. The most notable was Elia Veloso, who had just spent two years at the Gifford School. We were in the same cab together because I lived just down the road from her. In my last two years at CTDS, Lillian Paquette would drop off Elia at Gifford before 8:30 a.m. and then drop me off at CTDS before 9:00. In the afternoon, Lillian would pick me up from CTDS, then shuttle to Gifford to pick up Elia.

Gifford School was big. It had a small baseball field near the entrance, two basketball courts—one was indoors inside the Fenn Center where lunch was served, and one was outdoors where tennis could be played—and a big field behind the Fenn Center, where football can be played. I thought I was going to fit right in with all the students there—one reason I chose Gifford. I thought the people were going to be just as nice, just as helpful, and just as different as CTDS. This was supposed to be *the* place where I could fit right in with the students there. I would later find out that this wasn't the place for me after all. I would also have to face the everyday trials and tribulations from the students of this school.

By the time September came in 1999, I started my first day of school at Gifford. Gifford School was divided into three areas: lower school, middle school, and high school. The lower school was brand-new at the time. I thought I was going to the lower school, but the teachers there said I graduated early, so they took me to the middle school to find my homeroom teachers. My first teachers were named Jenn and Abby. My new homeroom classmates were all boys.

My new school was an hour longer than CTDS. School started at eighty thirty with classes starting at nine, and it ended at two thirty. There were no half days on Mondays like in CTDS. In Gifford School, every student had a point sheet. There were ten periods in a whole school day. At the end of each period, a teacher or staff member would determine how many points I had earned. Each period had six parts. The most points I could get in one part was 3 for following two school year–long goals all the time. I got 2 points if I showed that behavior most of the time, 1 point some of the time, and 0 points none of the time. The most points I could get in one period is 18, while the most points I could get in one day is 180. If I got anywhere between 170 and 180 points, I would be in Level 4. I would be in Level 3 if I were in the 160s, Level 2 if I were in the 150s, and Level 1 if I were anywhere under 150. The lowest level Gifford had to offer was DR, or desk restriction. Desk restriction meant that I needed an escort to take me to my classes. If I was in Level 4 three times a week for a certain number of weeks, I earned a field trip for a very impressive performance at school. The Gifford School calls these trips VIP trips.

The Gifford School had this homework program where I needed twelve homework credits so that I can earn one homework certificate. I needed three homework certificates to earn a homework reward trip. Gifford's homework assignments went like this. Monday's homework was science, Tuesday's was math, Wednesday's was reading, and Thursday's was social studies. Social studies was my favorite subject, followed by math, then science and reading. I loved social studies because I wanted to learn all about the world and what was happening to it. I loved math because I was good with numbers. My least favorite subject was reading because I didn't find the books I read to be interesting. I read *The Giver*, *The Pigman*, and *Walk Two Moons* while I was at Gifford.

The one thing I hated most about Gifford was the bad language that some of the kids used. For example, I would hear the F-word at least ten times a day on average. I was startled to hear thirteen- to fourteen-year-old kids use those words. They made *Scarface* sound PG rated. My second day of school at the Gifford was pretty hard. It was science class, and one of my classmates was acting out and used the F-word in front of the students. Unable to get that word out of my head, I broke down and cried at my desk in a very loud and hysterical screaming manner because it sounded so terrible in my ear. My science teacher, Cheryl, had me leave the room and go see someone. It wasn't the only time I cried after hearing the F-word. I cried again upon hearing it after group activity or gym class later that day. That's the way it was going to be the rest of my first year at Gifford. As the season went on, I would be able to get used to it.

I first heard the F-word in the movie *Rain Man* but didn't pick it up until I was almost nine. The F-word in my opinion is the worst word in the English language. The second worst is a four-letter word resembling fecal matter. Those are the two words that have no place on television unless it is rated TV-MA or if you have HBO. I knew that every time I said that stuff, I would get into trouble. Not too often, but occasionally, I would use those words, but that was before I came to Gifford School. Mom and Dad were very strict about bad language when I was younger than twelve. My punishments would range from two minutes of time-out to a slap on the wrist to having my mouth washed out with liquid soap. Believe me, those punishments were not pretty. Mom and Dad would be most upset if I used them during sporting events, either the ones I played or the ones I watched. They threatened to banish me from watching or playing sports if I kept on swearing. There was a time when I felt like doing so after the Red Sox gave up the game-winning run, when the Patriots turned the ball over, when the Celtics gave up a game-winning shot at the buzzer, or when the Bruins or Revolution gave up a game-winning goal. As time went on, I learned how to keep my cool when the going got tough.

Unfortunately I was in a place where those students were not afraid to drop F-bombs or go out of line with their superior. Luckily I wasn't one of those kinds of people. In 1999, there was this TV show that came out on the air at the same time I joined Gifford, called *Freaks and Geeks*. That show featured some of today's great actors, such as Seth Rogen, James Franco, and Jason Segel. It would have been a great show, but it lasted just one whole season, and I would not watch any episodes of it for ten years.

You know, today we have reality TV all over the place, compared to 2000. There are at least seven *The Real Housewives* shows all over America. If you were to make a reality show about my time at Gifford

School, I would call that show *The Real Freaks and Geeks of Massachusetts*. For two years I was living that reality show. I labeled the ones who acted out and swore in class the *freaks*. I remember a couple of instances during lunch period at the gym. There was this little lower-school child that could not have been any older than ten who would run across the gym, avoiding his teachers and making insults toward them. He would later make his way onto the stage. He then started shouting, "F——— you! F——— you!" to his teachers and waving his middle fingers at them. It was the damnedest thing I have ever seen. It was priceless. Can you believe the ratings if that show made television? Good thing there was no YouTube back then. That was something you didn't see every day, if not at all, because I never saw anything like it before, and that made me sick.

Then of course there were the smart kids, the quiet kids, those who played Pokemon cards and Phase 10—you know, those who stayed out of trouble, called the *geeks*. I was one of the geeks because I fit right in with them, because I was smart enough to stay out of trouble, and I knew that I was going to be in trouble if I broke one of the rules at Gifford. If I were to do those things, it was going to cost me some precious points out of my point sheet. I worked really hard at trying to be a good student for my teachers. I was the kind of person who didn't want to let other people down. I followed my point sheet more religiously than any of my classmates. As a result, I found myself in Level 4 for nearly my entire first school year.

Again, Tyler had to go by the rules. The only issue I had with this point system was the fact that it played into Tyler's weakness—collecting data and getting fixated on it. I believe he was focusing on earning points more than learning anything else. That issue is the main reason I chose a psychotherapeutic school instead of a behavior-based school in the first place. As it turned out, Gifford School was not the right setting for my son. I am sure that it is an excellent school for most children with all kinds of challenges. However, for our son, it was not the right setting for his specific needs.

I was lucky enough to be in a homeroom mostly made up of smart and even-tempered classmates—in other words, I was in a room consisting primarily of *geeks*. I got along with them extremely well. I got along nicely with my teachers as well. My social studies teacher was named Don. Don, who had a slight resemblance to the

Unabomber, came from the state of Oklahoma. He taught us ancient world civilization topics—such as the Middle East, Egypt, Japan, India, China, and South America. I also studied the early humans, the Fertile Crescent, and the feudal system of the Middle Ages. Once a week, Don would take me and my homework group to the back of the school for an archeological dig when the weather was suitable. Don even let me look at his Mickey Mantle calendar. I found out that he was a switch hitter who was capable of hitting a baseball some five hundred to six hundred feet, and I even learned that Mickey was born in Don's home state of Oklahoma. Thanks to Don's guidance and way of teaching, I was able to win the Geography Award at the graduation ceremonies for the high school on the last day of my first school year. As for my other homework teachers, Cheryl was my science teacher; Jen, my homeroom teacher, taught me math; and Gala was my reading teacher.

All teachers at Gifford School are recognized by their first names the same way as my teachers at CTDS. There were a few teachers in my first year at Gifford who were really cool. The one that stood out as the coolest was a man in his late twenties named Rory. Rory was a redhead who usually came out for group activity and participated in some games with the students most of the time. The games I played at group activity were football, basketball, softball, capture the flag, and ultimate Frisbee, to name what I know. My favorite sport to play at Gifford was football, touch or flag. I loved it even better when it snowed. I didn't care if my clothes were a little wet from the snow. I was more than happy to enjoy it.

In October of 1999, I went on a school hiking trip to Mount Monadnock near Jaffrey, New Hampshire. I've been on hikes before, but this was not an ideal day for a little hike, let alone a big one. It was raining all day up there, and I have never hiked Monadnock before, so I didn't know what to expect. After leaving Gifford School and traveling up Routes 128 and 2, we took some secondary roads because there was no major highway access to the mountain. There was a healthy rainfall at the base of Mount Monadnock when we arrived. The first part of the hike was easy, a wide dirt pathway with a slight incline leading up to the hard part. The hard part was a steep, rocky climb up to the midway point of Monadnock. Compounding matters was the rainfall that would not stop. The midway point was an open, flat rocky area. With the rain not letting up and the fog getting wicked dense since we were in a cloud and time becoming a factor, we went back down the mountain. On the way down, one of the students sustained a broken leg. I did get to the base but wound up getting separated from my group. I did manage to find my people, get in the van, and head back to Gifford. My clothes were soaking wet and a little dirty from being out in the rain all day. When I look back now, I think of that hike as one of the best moments I've ever had while at Gifford School.

My highlights from the 1999–2000 school years include going to a movie theater to see *The World Is Not Enough* (the last movie I would ever see in theaters for quite some time), going to Lake Cochituate in Natick, starring in a small role at the beginning of a middle school play called *Romeo and Juliet*, and winning the Gifford School Geography Award at the end of the school year. I went to two plays at the Merrimack Repertory Theater in Lowell with the Gifford School: *Avenue X* and *Defying Gravity*. *Avenue X* was about life in 1960s Brooklyn, and I was shocked to witness the kind of bad language used in the play. *Defying Gravity* was a more appropriate play as it was based on the real-life story of local teacher-turned-astronaut Christa McAuliffe, with a twist, as Monet the artist was in that play. I also went to Boston with the school to see the play *Our Town*, about a love story that takes place in a fictional small town in New Hampshire.

I really enjoyed playing this new card game called Phase 10, which was similar to Uno. I played in a Ping-Pong tournament with the middle school. I went to Papa Gino's in Wayland a few times in my first year for the VIP trip. I made a lot of friends and learned new things in my first year there. I did those things while having to experience some circumstances that didn't make much sense. A couple of teachers in the middle school left, but a couple of new teachers joined to replace them. There were lots of changes going on at Gifford School—from teachers moving on to different departments or leaving the school altogether to students leaving the school. As it later turned out, this was just the beginning. There were going to be more changes in store for the 2000–2001 school years.

I attended the 2000 Summer Program at Gifford School. I didn't have the same teachers that I had in my first year there. Once a week during the Summer Program, I would go with my group to Lake Cochituate to go swimming or fishing off the dock or play out in the field. I spent most of my time there fishing with friends. It was the place where I caught a three-pound fish. One time during the program, I went to Duxbury Beach on the south shore of Massachusetts. I remember playing football along the shoreline with a few boys from my group. When the Summer Program was drawing to a close, I had won the Junior Counselor in Training of the Day Award on July 24, 2000, in recognition of my being a positive team player and for my sportsmanship. Three days later, I was given a certificate of recognition for All-Around Excellence throughout the Summer Program.

When I came back to Gifford School for the 2000–2001 school year, the whole school was much different from last year. The middle school coordinator was gone, the library where town meetings were held on Fridays had undergone a makeover, and a new art building was finished to replace the one that had turned into the principal's office. Half the middle-school students from last year either moved up to the high school or left Gifford entirely. Elia had moved up to the high school, while I was still in the same homeroom with an entirely different class. I was going to a noticeably changed Gifford School. Some changes there were good, and some were not so good. But the things that didn't change in my second year were the point system, the Gifford way of teaching, and of course the students' incessantly bad behavior. Cheryl, Don, and Gala returned to teach me science, social studies, and reading. I continued to make new friends, work hard at being a good student, and gain my teachers' respect. My goals for my second year were asking a teacher for help when I needed it and focusing on my assignment or activity. I went for a hike up to the Blue Hills Observatory south of Boston with the middle school because there was wet weather in Mount Monadnock.

My second year at Gifford School wasn't much better than the first. In fact, it was worse. Lillian Paquette was still my cabdriver, and every year she became more and more of a control freak. She always kept telling me to sit up straight, turn down my headphones, and stop babbling to myself. I don't know if it was her fault or mine that she was bossy. Either way, Lillian and I just didn't get along after six years of being in her cab. Then all of a sudden in February 2001, Lillian got sick, and just a week later, she passed away. It was very shocking to hear about her death because I didn't see it coming. The last time she dropped me off, I must have felt angry over her rules. I don't think I've ever said goodbye. I did attend her wake and paid my last respects to her. For the rest of the school year, I would have a couple of different drivers to take me to and from school.

Meanwhile back at Gifford, I was feeling more miserable and more uncomfortable by the day. Teachers and students were still coming and going as if it were going out of style. I kept on having trouble trying to adjust to the ever-changing atmosphere that was Gifford. While I was doing my best to maintain my good behavior and keep my grades above par and of course getting my hard-earned VIPs, I was growing less and less comfortable behind my desk at school. My teachers for some reason came to this conclusion that my homework class was making me feel miserable. So they switched me to another homework class, thinking that it might make me feel better, but it only did the opposite.

Midway through my second school year, a new kid among the many new kids coming to Gifford School in 2000–2001 arrived. This new kid had a strong resemblance to the rapper Eminem, with his short bleached blond hair. He joined my homework group at about the same time I joined. He was a rotten kid—no, he was the worst kid I had ever witnessed at Gifford School. Of all the freaks that came to Gifford, that kid was the most volatile of all. He was a total sociopath who never listened to his teachers, always undermined their authority, and made most classmates around him very uncomfortable. And yes, he used bad language time and time again.

Finally on Friday, March 2, 2001, during the free-time part of my math class, everything came to a head. The kid went into his nuclear fits and just wouldn't stop. I went to the cabinet, took out a ruler, and told him to stop it or I was going to hit him with the ruler. Then the kid called me something that I would never forget, and it would hurt my feelings in the worst possible way. He called me a "f——ing faggot" right to my face in front of several students and my teacher. I would have tackled that kid right away and beat the living crap out of him, but I didn't and I couldn't because I knew I'd get in trouble for doing it. So I did the one thing I've always done when the going was at its toughest. I walked away and went outside to keep myself safe, out of trouble, plain and simple. I could still hear him shouting obscenities and personal insults. I tried to get back inside and say a few words to him, but the door closed on me, and I threw a wild conniption in the small patch of snow outside the room and screamed so loud that the whole middle school could hear me. That was the last straw. I didn't want this anymore, I had enough of the insults, and I had had it up to here with them. I didn't deserve to be treated the way I was in March of 2001. No one would. Rarely would I see instances at Gifford where students would fight each other and some students had to be restrained by the faculty, but those two words that he said to me were the last two words that I would ever think about saying to another human being. I'm not the kind of person who insults people for who they are. If I did, my parents would ground me.

I hear some people say that words can't hurt you, but believe me, *words do hurt*. What I mean is that words can hurt your feelings, and I certainly had my feelings hurt when I was insulted. I never felt more emotionally hurt in all my life. My psyche was damaged, and I had a hard time getting over this incident. I wasn't what that kid said I was. He did apologize for making that chastising reference to me, and I apologized to him for threatening him with a ruler. He didn't set foot at the Gifford School for a whole month. He did come back for one week, but he went back to his cursing fits and never went back to the Gifford School again.

My parents thought it was best for me to take at least one day off per week before the school year ended. They agreed that Gifford was no longer the right school for me. So in March we looked at one school—Cotting School in Lexington. It was actually located about a mile from CTDS. It was a huge building that housed the lower school, the middle school, and the upper school. Cotting School was for students who either were handicapped or had physical or intellectual disabilities. Some students there use wheelchairs to get in and around the school, whether they turn the wheels by themselves or use motorized ones or have one of the nurses push them. There were some students who couldn't speak or who have speech impediments there. I had some mixed feelings about going there because I wasn't used to being around those people. Mom and Dad took me there for a visit anyway.

The first faculty member I met at Cotting School was Janine Brown-Smith. Janine showed me how things are at Cotting. She assured me that there were nice people in the building. It had a ramp for people in wheelchairs so they could get around from top to bottom or vice versa. The bottom floor had the lower school, a physical/occupational therapy room, a nurses' office, a dental office, a desktop publishing room, and an industrial arts room, or wood shop. The top floor had the middle school, the upper school, the library, an eye exam office, a kitchen for home economics, and a computer room. She then took me to a classroom across from the computer room, where I met my future classmates. Then we went to the gymnasium, where gym class was being held. The gym had a nice basketball court, a little smaller than the one at Gifford. At the gym I said hello to a CTDS alum and old classmate, Matt W. I was going to be reunited with some of my old friends at CTDS. Finally we went to the cafeteria to finish the tour. My parents and I started to think that the Cotting School was the right place for me. Everything was mellow, the people were kind and friendly, and the classes and programs they had were impressive. I felt that I could get along better with the students and staff there than at Gifford. The staff at Cotting School was looking forward to having me at their school in September. I was looking forward to going there as well.

I had to finish the last three months of school at Gifford, and finish I did. During a softball game at group activity, I hit a home run in my last at bat, just like Ted Williams did. The one thing I was going to miss most about Gifford was group activity. When June arrived, it was time to say goodbye to all my classmates, my teachers, and the rest of the middle school. They wished me the best and said goodbye. The last words I heard when I came out of the school were "peace out" from one of the students. For two years, I had to work really, really hard at being good in a rotten environment. I had to stay true to my goals all the time to please my teachers. When I look back now, the Gifford School was trying to unlock my potential by setting some goals not just during school but for after it. I learned a lot about setting goals in my time with Gifford. The two most challenging and confusing years of my life were over, and now I could finally move on.

Besides Elia Veloso, I never kept in touch with any of my old classmates and teachers at Gifford School. I've never spoken to or contacted any of my old Gifford classmates since I left. I didn't attend the Gifford School Summer Program in 2001, so I spent most of June and all of July and August at home. This was the longest I had ever spent away from school at the time. During my longest summer, I got a PlayStation 2 game console; visited Hampton Beach, New Hampshire, with my aunt Lauri and cousin Chantelle; played some golf with my dad;

helped Pepere out in the backyard; and visited the White Mountains of New Hampshire.

I got to see two Red Sox games in August. The first one was against the Texas Rangers on August 6. My dad got the tickets from his job at Compaq. Before we entered Fenway Park, I saw a partially disguised Derek Lowe jogging right past me. I sat with Mom and Dad in the bleacher section a couple of rows behind the bull pens against the blazing hot sun. A few days before the game, I made a sign that said, "Tyngsboro loves Jerry and NESN." Jerry Remy is the color commentator for Red Sox games. I brought it with me to the game, which featured Hideo Nomo as the starting pitcher for Boston (Nomo threw a no-hitter at Baltimore in his Red Sox debut during Boston's second game of the 2001 season). Scott Hatteberg, the Red Sox catcher who hit into a triple play earlier in the game, would hit a grand slam not far from where I was sitting to give the Red Sox the lead for good. Before the ninth inning began, when I was holding up my sign, I was on television. I spent every break in the action holding up my sign to get on NESN. I didn't know I was on television until Clint called to say he saw me. Clint's friends also said that they saw me as well. I had a tape of the game. I went and watched it to see myself. I had never been on TV before. It was probably my biggest highlight of 2001, holding the "Tyngsboro loves Jerry" sign for five seconds on NESN. The Red Sox went on to win that game.

I went to another Red Sox game later in the month of August against the Baltimore Orioles. Jaret Foley got me the tickets to that game, and Dad took me there. This time I didn't bring my sign. Instead of driving down to Fenway Park, Dad and I took two subway lines. Dad and I got out at Boston Common because Dad couldn't stand the subway. I didn't enjoy the subway ride too, so we took a taxi from the Common to Fenway Park. We arrived just a little after the first pitch. Midway through the game, it started to rain. Dad and I decided to leave because we had to golf the next morning.

For almost three summer months, I spent that time trying to forget the bad memories of Gifford until it was just a memory. It was a gradual process, but in time I felt much better about myself as the summer progressed. I kind of wished that this summer would last forever. Unfortunately, the summer of 2001, not unlike every summer, had to end in the month of September, and it was time for me to get back to school. I wasn't going back to Gifford for the 2001–2002 school years. No sir! I was returning to good old Lexington, Massachusetts. I wasn't going back to CTDS, but I was going to pass my old school pretty much every day. I was going to a place that was just down the road from CTDS. I was not just looking for a fresh start. I was going to take the next step.

Cotting School

I WAS FOURTEEN YEARS OLD when I took the next step in my life on Tuesday, September 4, 2001. It was my first day of high school at Cotting School in Lexington. It was also the first day of school for Elia at Cotting after spending four years at the Gifford. I remember my dad taking me and Elia to Cotting School that Tuesday morning in early September. There was a path that led to the entrance to the school. Once I got inside, a lady named Janine took me to the second floor and introduced me to my new classmates. Some of my classmates were as old as twenty years old, old enough to be college sophomores. Most students who attend Cotting School can stay there until the age of twenty-two. My classmates in my freshman year were Joe, Paul, Dana, Carolyn, Andonia, and Sarah. Elizabeth would come to my homeroom later in the school year switching places with Sarah. My first teacher actually got married in November. It was the first time that I recognized my teachers by the last names rather than their first names. My first Cotting School class was computer class across from my homeroom. I knew this was the right crowd for me. I knew I was going to enjoy my first year at Cotting and many more years afterward.

In the fall of 2001, Clint was on his way toward becoming the MVP of his school's soccer team. He was a senior at Greater Lowell Technical High School and had already established himself as a three sport star there, excelling at soccer, swimming, and track and field, but soccer to me was his specialty. His team—also known as the Gryphons—began the season on a tear with a 7–2–1 start, and during that stretch Clint had two 4-goal games and one 5-goal game. There were times when his team would win by scores of 7–0, 9–0, even 11–0. On October 12, just three days before his eighteenth birthday, Clint was in a local newspaper called the *Lowell Sun*. An article was written about him along with a couple of pictures of him in soccer attire. My name was mentioned in the article. In Clint's freshman year in 1998, he was in the paper after having one of his big games. As for his Gryphons in the fall of 2001, they would falter in the second half of the season to finish with a 9–7–3 record. He would later finish the season with twenty-eight goals and fourteen assists for 42 points and was on the *Lowell Sun* First-Team All-Star Soccer Team.

While Clint was having his best soccer season yet, I was having my best soccer season yet. I played on a semitravel team for the Tyngsboro Youth Soccer Association. I was never always good at soccer, I never scored a ton of goals, I was never great at defending or preventing goals, and I never always understood the game. But that didn't mean I never kept on trying. I had to learn how to play the game before I got good at it. I worked very hard at my game during soccer practices before the season started. I just wanted a fresh start because I never felt good about myself the last couple of years playing the game. I had been on losing soccer teams every time I played. But in 2001, it was all going to change.

My first game of the 2001 season was on Saturday, September 8, at Bridge Meadow soccer field in Tyngsboro. I think we were playing a team from Lowell. The first time I had the ball, I took a shot and it went in the goal. Then on my next shot attempt, I scored again. The previous season I only scored two goals, one in the first game of the season and one in the last game of the season, both miss-hits. The two goals I scored this time were good shots. Then later in the first half, I took a pass from a teammate on a 2-on-1 break, shot the ball and scored. I had a natural hat trick, meaning I had just scored three straight goals in one half of play. My team would go on to win the game. All of a sudden, I had become the best player on my team while Clint was the best player on his team.

As the season progressed, so did my team. I started to feel confident in my soccer ability, something I've never felt before. For the first time ever, I was the leading scorer on my soccer team at the same time I was on a winning soccer team. On the last game of the season against a team from Tewksbury, I scored two goals in the second half. The last goal I scored was from the middle of the field on a free kick that went over the goalie but stayed below the crossbar to go in the back of the net. It was the longest goal I've ever made and definitely the biggest goal of my life. Sadly, the game was marred with questionable officiating going against the Tewksbury side. The Tewksbury coach got really upset over inadvertent whistles going Tyngsboro's way. It was my last competitive outdoor soccer game for me and it ended because a coach complained over inadvertent whistles. I didn't want that season to end that way. I played my best soccer ever that fall. Clint and I had reached our pinnacle of our soccer playing careers in 2001. Together, Clint and I combined to score at least 35 goals this year.

I never realized how similar both boys were regarding their level of competition. It is now apparent to me that I wasn't raising two "only children." Shame on me for not understanding that they had more similarities compared to differences.

In my first four months at Cotting I was trying to get used to the rules of the school. Cotting School was unlike any school I've ever been to. It wasn't the same as the Community Therapeutic day School or Gifford School. This school was extraordinarily different from any other private school in the world. Cotting School was founded in 1893 in the city of Boston, before they moved to Lexington while merging with the Krebs School. Since this school was for handicapped children and young adults and children and young adults with physical and intellectual disabilities, I had to really be friendly with them. It took a while for me to adapt to people with challenges that are different than mine. The staff and teachers there taught me how to be kind and gentle in a certain manner to everyone because many of the students are medically fragile. However, in spite of their challenges, they get an outstanding education with unique accommodations.

When Tyler joined the student population at the Cotting School, both Ron and I were so relieved to have him be part of such a calm, caring environment. This was the first time that we saw Tyler show empathy toward his fellow classmates. Up until this time, Tyler never seemed to recognize the needs of anyone else. He always seemed to be consumed with his feelings, his thoughts, his wants and his needs. However, now it seemed as if he was noticing everything around him, including the personalities and unique challenges that others were facing. It was a real awakening for me as well. It seemed as though all the psychotherapy that Tyler had been receiving for so many years would finally pay off! It was wonderful to see this maturation and his personality develop and grow into the kind, compassionate person that I knew was deep inside him.

I did my best to be nice and careful around my classmates and all the students at this school. There were a couple of times where I made fun of their disabilities. It took some time for me to get my mind right but by the middle of my first school year I learned my lesson. Other than my classmates, I made a lot of friends in my first year. In Boy's Group I got to know Marc, Joe, Josh, and Etienne. At the lunch table, I ate with Peter and Naeem who was confined to a wheelchair. In Desktop Publishing class, I made friends with Bethany, Ramona, and the late Michael Myers.

My fifteenth birthday on November 17, 2001, was once the happiest birthday of my life. That day I got an NCAA Basketball tournament bracket board and NHL 2002 and NCAA Football 2002 on PlayStation 2. Later that night I went to a Boston Bruins hockey game with my folks. I bought myself a black Bruins jacket, a yellow Bruins sweatshirt, a hat and a puck. I got this goodie bag with Fleet Center coins and a Jozef Stumpel–autographed puck. During the game I saw my name on the Jumbotron and then saw myself holding my red Compaq Bruins birthday shirt on the Jumbotron. The most disappointing moment of that night was seeing my favorite Bruin Joe Thornton get kicked out of the game. However, the Bruins did beat the Buffalo Sabres that night.

As I have mentioned before, Tyler loves to go to almost any type of professional sporting event. Whenever we are at these events, we can always say that we definitely get out money's worth out of our tickets. Unlike many children, Tyler is quite content to remain in his seat throughout the game because he is playing such close attention to the action at hand. He is not really interested in jumping up to go to the concession stand or to the pro shop. Those activities occur only before or after a game. He makes sure that he has everything he needs before he heads to his seat for the action!

By the time my soccer season ended with Tyngsboro in November of 2001, I joined Cotting School basketball team. Basketball is the most competitive sport Cotting School had to offer. It was also the school's biggest sport. Basketball at the time was my least favorite sport, but since there were no other options in the winter, I decided join the team. In my first year, I was on a team that had the size and experience to be competitive with the likes of Peter, Josh, Paul, Marc, and Joe. Kate and Kara played key roles for this team. Then there were Naeem, Kevin,

Brian, and Andonia who would help this team out as well. My coaches were Mrs. B. and Mr. T., a former Cotting student. I came to this team being the most athletic, most gifted, and most talented player. I was supposed to be playing my first game on November 30, 2001, but during school I developed pain and stiffness in my neck, mostly pain. My parents felt I shouldn't be playing with pain in my neck. I decided not to show up for the game because every time I moved my head to the left, it hurt.

I did get to play the team's next game on a Friday night in December. We were playing a team from Braintree that wore white T-shirts. I thought this was going to be an easy game for me because I thought the level of play wasn't advanced enough. There were five factors contributing to the outcome of my first Cotting basketball game:

1) I wasn't used to playing against a team full of special players.
2) The basketball court inside the gym was wicked small.
3) It was my first game, so I did not know what to expect.
4) I underestimated Braintree because they had this female player who just simply outplayed me.
5) Braintree shot lights out that night. My team lost to Braintree in my Cotting School debut.

On the last day of school before Christmas, we played the faculty. The game started after lunch during school time. It was a close game throughout. Finally with two seconds left, my team had the ball at half-court. I got the inbounds pass, drove to the basket and stuffed in the game-winning layup. No one guarded me and the basket was lower than usual. All in all, a win was a win. I had become a hero to the entire student body of Cotting School. It won my first Cotting School basketball game on the last day of school in 2001.

The basketball season at Cotting School was definitely the highlight of the school year for Tyler. We marveled at how inclusive the game was. Everyone on the team participated throughout the game. Students played alongside individuals with physical as well as cognitive challenges. Cheerleaders rooted their team on in grand fashion. These games were more than sporting events for me. It was an opportunity for fellowship with parents, students and faculty. Smiles could be seen from ear to ear each Friday night!

However 2001 will forever be defined by 9/11, perhaps the darkest day in twenty-first-century American history. Not since Pearl Harbor had America experienced something this catastrophic before. The United States was forever changed on the Tuesday morning of September 11, 2001. It was only my sixth day of school at Cotting and I was in computer class when it happened. While I was working on something, I overheard a faculty member say a plane has crashed into the World Trade Center in New York City. After Computer Class was over, I went back inside my classroom. My teacher had a stereo and the whole class listened to some disturbing developments of what was happening. We heard that two planes had crashed into both World Trade Center towers, one plane for each tower. Then one plane had just destroyed a section of the Pentagon in Washington DC. Finally one plane crash landed in a field in Shanksville, Pennsylvania. But the most startling news of the day to us was that all four planes involved in these incidents took off from Logan Airport in Boston. Everybody in my classroom gasped when they first heard about it, even my teacher gasped. When I went back home to see the images of 9/11 for the first time, I was in awe, I just could not believe what was happening. There was wall to wall coverage of the events on every channel. Who would do such a disgusting thing, and why? In the months to come following 9/11, I would eventually figure out those two questions. Five years after the attacks, I would write in my journal my side of the story about September 11, 2001, and it went as follows:

> I was never the same person I was prior to 9/11 again. Ever since that day, I thought more differently than ever before. That day changed the way I was as a person, as a friend, as a brother, as a son, as a human being. That day taught me how to grow up and be a man. That day, September 11, 2001, has, is, and will ever be a turning point in my life.
>
> It's hard to believe that there is no World Trade Center anymore, even though it gets easier by the day. We all know now who did it, and why they had done it. It was all done by humans who did it for a certain desire. They did it to intimidate us, torture us, harm us, murder us, traumatize us, and paralyze us. That day, as a result, showed us how

human we were, how humble we were. But that day, as a result, showed us how strong we were, how brave we were, how resilient we were. It was the ultimate test for just about everyone. It was one year into the new millennium, but that day just equaled one millennia.

On September 12, 2001, the United States of America, and the entire world woke up to a brand-new day, with a new resolve, and a new attitude on life. Things changed, things remained the same. We all lost everything, at the same time we gained everything. We all went back to work, back to school, back to our lives, but in New York City, Washington DC, and Shanksville, Pennsylvania, there was still some more left to do. However, we will never forget that day when everything happened so quickly, at the same time people sprang into action with such character, will, authority, vigor, pride, and heroism. September 11, 2001, was the most silent of days, but it was the most finest of days. When we think of 9/11, five years later, we think of the values we have. We become more thankful that we live in a free country founded in the year 1776. That day, September 11, 2001, we became proud to be Americans.

The timing for the attacks could not have been more perfect. I was just getting to know the people at Cotting at the time. My childhood met its end right there on 9/11. I came to Cotting School looking for a fresh start and I am ever so thankful that I made this transition, especially when America was under attack. If I went right to Cotting in 1999, my story would not have been the same.

Isn't it interesting that Tyler feels that the timing could not have been more perfect? Clearly, it was a defining moment for everyone in the United States. Reading the statement that Tyler has written about the attack of 9/11, it is clear that he had the tools to recognize the impact this attack made on not only America, but he recognizes the impact it has made on him as an individual. That just goes to show you that ALL people with or without disabilities have the same ability to think, hear, and feel, just like you and me.

In 2002, the New England Patriots won the Super Bowl in one of the biggest upsets in all of sports. The Winter Olympic Games took place in Salt Lake City that year. Afghanistan would be the site of America's longest war as they proceeded to hunt down Osama bin Laden and many others responsible for the 9/11 terrorist attacks. The year 2002 was very historic for my family as I got to be a part of at least three significant celebrations that year. I was finally getting settled in my routine at Cotting School, and later in 2002 I was about to take my gifts to the next level.

I was making good strides late in my first year at Cotting School. I did book reports on Mario Lemieux and Abraham Lincoln, crammed a report on China at the last minute on the night of the Patriots Super Bowl game, wrote sports articles for the school newspaper the *Falcon Flyer*, made signs out of wood for the Patriots and Bruins at industrial arts, and did well in math, science, computers, and desktop publishing. But Cotting School was different than Gifford School in terms of physical education. Cotting School Athletics was more limited than Gifford's because the gymnasium was a little smaller than that of Gifford's. They had a big field for Softball but it would often flood so I didn't join the softball team. They did offer track and field and golf there. I wasn't interested in track and field at the time and didn't join them. I didn't join the golf team until my last year at this school.

In spite of their limited sports opportunities, my favorite subject was gym class. Gym activities usually took place in the gymnasium, so I would shoot some hoops before gym class started. I could still play some games where running was involved. Sometimes during gym class I got to play floor hockey with foam sticks, Wiffle ball, soccer, and "messy backyard." "Messy backyard" was one of my favorites at Cotting School. The goal is to be the first team to knock down all five bowling pins with foam balls while protecting all of your pins from being knocked down.

In February of 2002, Dad found out about an athletic organization for people with disabilities known as Kids in Disability Sports Incorporated, or KIDS Inc. for short. One of my Cotting Basketball teammates had participated in basketball with the KIDS group, and my father learned about the group and then he convinced me to join them. One week after I played my last pickup basketball game at Tyngsboro High School, I joined KIDS Inc. and played basketball at McAuliffe Elementary School in Lowell. I played on the junior team for the first few weeks before joining a team of older people. Being with the older players helped me enjoy the game and helped me become a better basketball player.

Kids in Disability Sports was founded in Lowell in 1995 and incorporated four years later. Its founder and former president was Bruce Lucier. Bruce was once a star athlete for Lowell High School in the late 1960s. After finishing high school, Bruce was involved in a serious car accident that left him paralyzed. Ever since his car accident, he did all he could in helping the lives of the disabled and eventually forming KIDS Inc. This organization, which began as one basketball program, now has as more than a dozen sports programs plus dances, outings, as well as awards ceremonies. I felt pretty glad that I got to be a part of this organization and still feel glad to this day.

I helped my Cotting Basketball Team to a four-game winning streak before we lost to the Cotting Alumni Team in the season finale. Our final record in my first season was 4–3. Then in the March Basketball Tournament at Cotting School, where there were four teams of handpicked players, I helped my team win two games to win the tournament. I do recall the first game when I was heading to the basket for a layup, I got clocked in the head yet I still managed to make the basket. I had no idea what had happened after I got fouled. Then I heard a loud noise from the crowd, which meant that I scored. My team went on to win the basketball tournament, the only one I would ever win as a student at Cotting School. Each of my teammates was rewarded with their own basketball.

At the Cotting School basketball banquet in the month of May, I was named the Most Valuable Player on my basketball team. At age fifteen, I think I was the youngest Cotting School student ever to be named MVP of the varsity basketball team. I was playing on a team made up of some people who were five to seven years older than me. I wasn't the biggest player on the team. My athletic gifts earned me the Athletic Achievement Award during the school awards ceremonies on May 30, 2002, my dad's forty-sixth birthday. I also won an award for being the most original that day. Webster's dictionary defines the word original as being creative and inventive.

Tyler has a unique appreciation for the definition of words. Often he can be found scouring through the dictionary to find "just the right word" to use whenever needed. Sometimes I'll ask him what word he's looking for and his response will be "I'm just looking for new words to use in case I need them." Tyler was extremely excited to receive the awards. He has worked so hard for each and every achievement and can tell the difference between a genuine award and an award for basically just "showing up."

After one year in this school, I would move to a new homeroom for my second year, and that year was going to be more challenging for me because I nearly aced all of the assignments that I took in my opening year. My next teacher was going to take my talents to the next level, you know dig deep into my fullest potential as a student. If I was going to be in the most gifted classroom on school grounds in 2002–2003, it meant doing more homework, making more sacrifices, and being more responsible. My new class was going to be a mix of new friends at Cotting and old ones from CTDS. I was ready to take on the next challenge in my sophomore year.

It was fun for Ron and me to watch Tyler have a more typical classroom experience with homework, and a focus on academics verses behavior based learning. It seemed as if he was really coming out of his shell. He was presenting as a more "typical" individual. I found myself forgetting about the autism factor more frequently.

The year 2002 was the last year I played organized baseball. I played for the Tyngsboro Red Sox in the Babe Ruth League. My ball club was the best I've ever played on. I usually batted at the top or bottom of the batting order. I was the smallest player on the team but I led the team in infield singles. I did my best in the outfield and on the base paths. I even did some pitching for the Red Sox. In my last at bat, I struck out to a kid with one arm. Not a fitting way to end your baseball career. After the final game of the season, I knew that I wasn't going to play baseball anymore. Baseball was my favorite sport to play from when I played tee-ball when I was six years old to when I played Babe Ruth League baseball at the age fifteen. My last baseball season was my best. I never played on any real baseball team ever again.

The summer of 2002 was a busy one for the Lagasse family. Early in the summer, Clint graduated from Greater Lowell Technical High School. The graduation ceremony took place at the Lowell Memorial Auditorium where a few hundred seniors were about to take the next step in their lives. During the ceremonies, a severe thunderstorm blew through the city of Lowell but everybody inside the auditorium was safe inside. After graduation, a party was thrown at my house for Clint. I thought things were going to be different now that Clint was a high school graduate. He was accepted into UMass–Boston—perhaps play on their soccer team. But after a few days of taking summer classes he dropped out and decided to become a plumber. Instead of living in a college dorm, he still lived at home.

After my brother graduated and after I finished my first year at Cotting, a once in a lifetime celebration took place on June 19, 2002. There was a big party for my parents and grandparents at Mount Pleasant Golf Club in Lowell. Mom and Dad were celebrating their twenty-fifth wedding anniversary while Memere and Pepere, Lorraine and Edmond Lagasse, were celebrating their fiftieth wedding anniversary. Gary Browning, a family friend, was the disc jockey for the party. I got to help Gary out with his job of playing music. A lot of people showed up for this celebration, Mom's siblings and many friends and Dad's many relatives. Clint brought his new girlfriend to the party. In the middle of the party, I said something what the late sportscaster Jack Buck once said one week after 9/11. I said to the crowd, "I don't know about you, but as for me the question has already been answered. Should we be here? Yes." Mom and Dad danced and so did Memere and Pepere. The party didn't end until sometime after midnight. At the time, it was the latest I had ever stayed up not counting New Year's.

Tyler doesn't really enjoy listening to a DJ or music unless he can choose the station or select the songs. I guess we all like certain kinds of music, but his needs to be in control of the music make it difficult for him to go to dances and celebrations. Gary knew this and invited him to help with the DJ part of our celebration. Tyler always wears cotton in his ears whenever we go to a crowded place. That night was no exception. By allowing Tyler to participate in the DJ activities, it made the evening more predictable for Tyler. He would know what song was going to be played next, and that was very helpful for him.

In July of 2002, I attended the Cotting School Summer Program. I didn't want to go, but Mom and Dad said it was for my own good. Furthermore, my computer class instructor wanted me to go to Cotting in the summer so I could better prepare for the MCAS test, which was in the spring of 2003. I got to do some fun things during the monthlong program. I helped build a bench and made a downhill racer in shop class. I did a report on fishing and got a decent grade. Later in the Summer Program, I met my teacher for next year, Mrs. Dorothy Clark.

My favorite moment during the Summer Program was going on a field trip to Fenway Park. I was the one who brought up the idea of going on a tour of Fenway Park. So I went on the school van with my Summer Program classmates down there for the tour of the ballpark. We started at the left field side and walked to the area behind home plate. This was my second Fenway Park tour. Only this time, I got to visit the .406 Club, a luxury section behind home plate and below the press box. This area used to be the 600 Club because of its six hundred seats but was renamed the .406 Club after Ted Williams's 1941 batting average, because he recently passed away earlier in July. Then we went to field level, where we walked on the warning track and went into the Red Sox dugout. We stayed on the warning track and came upon centerfield, where I impersonated Fred Lynn crashing into the then-unpadded wall in game 6 of the 1975 World Series. Next, I posed for a picture in front of the Green Monster, that thirty-seven-foot wall in left field with a manual scoreboard on the bottom of it. Fenway Park turned ninety years old that year. I took lots of pictures during the tour. I was glad I took them because it was the final year before all those renovations took place in the off-season. I had such a ball going down there with my Cotting School summer class to experience the sights, the smells, the history, and the tradition of the oldest and most beloved baseball venue in the United States of America.

This is where the history buff in Tyler shines. He is able to see firsthand everything that he has learned from his reading and research and bring all that information into context. It is wonderful to see him enjoying himself in these settings. Museums are also very enjoyable for him. He loves to go anywhere that he can learn something new and exciting. Learning in general is exciting for him. It doesn't matter if the subject is sports, weather, science, history, or politics—he loves learning!

In September of 2002, I returned to Cotting School for my sophomore year in a new classroom. My new teacher was Mrs. Dorothy Clark. She was the kind of teacher that believed in old fashioned virtues and the value of hard work. Mrs. Clark brought the highest level of learning Cotting had to offer. She went to great extremes to get the best out of me. My classmates for my sophomore year were Brian M., Cotting School newcomer Jenna S., Kurt, Sarah S., and two members of the Cotting class of 2003, Ramona and Bethany. Finally, there were two students who used to go to CTDS, James S. and David N. I was being reunited with two students from CTDS whom I knew very well.

As 2002 drew to a close, I bought in to her style of teaching. I learned a heck of a lot more about history, English, and current events from Mrs. Clark than any other teacher before her. Later on in the school year, I would read *The Hobbit*, a prequel to *Lord of the Rings*. I had to read it to show Mrs. Clark that I was capable of being up to her challenges. Mrs. Clark's homework assignments were twice as hard as my first teacher at Cotting. After finishing *The Hobbit*, I read some stories from William Shakespeare. I read *Macbeth* and went to the North Shore Music Theater in Beverly, Massachusetts, to see *Romeo and Juliet* and *Taming of the Shrew*. I was on my way to the most productive school year of my life thanks to the teachings of Mrs. Dorothy Clark.

I love the fact that Tyler is so appreciative of the hard work and dedication his teachers' have demonstrated in order for him to reach his potential. I don't think enough gratitude is shown by most people for all the hard work that teachers and therapists provide for our children in this country whether or not they have learning disabilities or other challenges.

In September of 2002 I first learned that Pepere was really sick. Pepere was diagnosed with lung cancer. I heard from Memere that he had not been feeling well since August. Pepere was once a smoker but he quit smoking more than twenty years earlier. All he had to do now was hope for the best because the lung cancer was weakening his health every day.

Pepere did not go to high school because he had to work in the quarry to support his family. When he was nineteen, he married Memere and after that, he was drafted by the U.S. Army during the Korean War. He was stationed in Stuttgart, Germany for a while before coming back home. After working in the quarry, he joined CalComp & Sanders Associates. After that, he worked as a custodian for Greater Lowell Tech before retiring. Ever since he moved to Tyngsboro in 1970, he took pride into mowing the grass out in the big backyard and growing vegetables in his garden during the spring and summer months, and shoveling snow in the winter months. When I was a kid, he would take me out to my piano lessons and after that he would take me out for ice cream on Monday afternoons. He had this uncanny personality and taught me how to play cribbage, tock, and canasta. He was once a pretty good bowler in a local bowling back in the 1970s. Pepere meant a lot to me, and now time was running out on his life. He was dying and there was not much anybody can do about it.

On the same day that I heard about Pepere being sick, I went to the orthodontist about having braces on my teeth. I didn't think I needed braces but as it turned out, after looking at pictures of my crooked upper teeth, I did need to wear braces after all. One month before I had braces put on me, I had to wear spacers between my upper back teeth. Then on Veterans Day, I had braces put on my teeth. While I was on the reclining chair, I was like this deceased policeman in *Robocop*, where the doctors were turning me into a cybernetic organism. The orthodontist glued cement onto my teeth so that a metal wire can fit to move my teeth into the correct position. Then they put this metal spring in the roof of my mouth so that my tongue doesn't get bitten. My teeth and my mouth felt strange once I had those braces in me. When I was trying to have spaghetti, my teeth were very sensitive and it hurt to even take a bite. I could not chew solid food for a while because my teeth were in the process of being moved to the correct position. I would spend twenty-five more months with metal in my mouth. I wasn't the only family member who had to wear braces. My brother Clint had worn braces when he was twelve years old, and my mom wore them after she finished high school but had her braces removed for her wedding. After I was done with braces, I would have to wear a plastic retainer to keep my teeth from moving.

A few days after I had my braces, I turned sixteen years old. For my sixteenth birthday, I got a Tom Brady uniform, an Atari arcade pack on CD-ROM, and *Hoosiers* on DVD. I got to go to a Lowell Lock Monsters hockey game at the Tsongas Arena with Mom, Dad, Clint, and Beth. Before the Lock Monsters played the Saint John Flames, I saw a group of Bruins Alumni play an exhibition game. Unlike last year where I had these five seconds of fame in Boston at a Bruins game, I had a somewhat obscure sweet sixteen. My sixteenth birthday didn't have to be full of glitz, just a good time.

On December 30, 2002, Edmond Victor Lagasse, my pepere, died after a battle with cancer. He was seventy years old and left behind his two brothers, older brother Maurice and younger brother Leo, his wife, his son, his two grandsons, and many nephews and nieces. His mother, my great-grandmother, Yvonne "Old Memere" Lagasse, had passed away earlier in the month of February. This was a pretty sad year for the Lagasse's because two very significant family members passed away in 2002. But Pepere's death was more significant because he lived right next door and I would see him almost every day. I remember having Memere and Pepere being at my house every Tuesday and Thursday afternoon when I was at CTDS while Mom was working at Designs in Methuen.

The holiday season of 2002 was the least fun I've ever had because Pepere was dying. He was well enough to celebrate Christmas but it was the last time he showed any strength whatsoever. I do remember Pepere playing canasta with Memere and my parents that night. I didn't get out of the house much during my holiday break. If I wasn't at home, I was sledding with my brother at Tyngsboro Country Club, out at dinner, and at Michael Reault's house to watch the Patriots come back to beat the Dolphins in the final game of the 2002 NFL regular season. I was watching *Rudy* on DVD when Pepere died.

His funeral was on January 3, 2003. The wake was the day before and a lot of people showed up. I shook hands with every one of them. So many friends and relatives came to pay their last respects to Edmond. Memere couldn't come to the funeral because she came down with the flu. It was the second-largest funeral procession I have ever witnessed next to my grandpa Bell's back in April of 1999. I went in a limousine with Mom, Dad, Clint, and his girlfriend, from Laurin Funeral home in Lowell to St. Mary Magdalen's Church in Dracut. At the church, Mom read a wonderful eulogy for Pepere. The last sentence of the eulogy was written in French, and it meant "Be. I love you, my friend. Your love will be always be with us, my *chibidawing.*" *Chibidawing* was a made up word that Pepere would use whenever he couldn't think of the right word to use. Then we had to go all the way to St. Joseph's Cemetery in Lowell to say goodbye to Pepere forever. Just like that, Pepere was gone. I understand that it's perfectly normal and natural to lose at least one member of the family once in a while. Almost four years apart, I had lost two of my grandfathers. Once again, I had to adjust to life without a grandfather.

Pepere played a significant role in Tyler's life. He always "called it like he saw it." He never treated Tyler different because of his autism. He just worked around his challenges very naturally. He never gave up on him. He was proud of every accomplishment both boys achieved and he was the first to cheer them on to do their best at everything. He taught Tyler how to tend to the yard work. I believe Tyler got his strong work ethic from watching how his pepere committed to doing an honest day's work at any task at hand.

The year 2003 was another adjustment year for me. Now that Pepere was no longer here for us, things were going to be different. My dad was going to take over Pepere's old responsibilities. For the next three years Dad would mow the grass in our front and back yards and drive Memere to her relative's places and take her to do her errands. In late 2002, Dad got laid off from his job at Hewlett-Packard in Littleton, a job that he had for twenty-four years. He worked for his friend Rick Reault in the construction field for a while before finding work in a luxury apartment complex in Chelmsford where he became a certified maintenance technician. After a few years, Dad went back to work for Rick again, only this time Rick had opened a Beekeeping Supply Business.

In 2003, as a member of the Kids in Disability Sports Basketball Team, I played in my first ever event for Special Olympics Massachusetts (SOMA). Our team was well experienced and talented. We had size, athleticism, speed, and we could shoot. And of course there was me, the gifted player with a ball in my hand. First, we had to play in an assessment round at Milton Academy. We coasted through the qualifier and won the gold medal. It was my first Special Olympic medal.

In March of 2003, my team went to the SOMA (Special Olympics Massachusetts) Winter Games at the College of the Holy Cross in Worcester, Massachusetts. I don't remember the score of all the games we played, but I'll tell you what I know. After easily beating our first opponent, we were up against a tough opponent called the Crusaders, coincidentally the nickname of Holy Cross. In the first half, we didn't get many breaks, nothing went our way, we had a hard time putting the ball in the basket and we fell behind early. Then in the second half we were a different team as we trimmed the deficit. Finally with time winding down, I got the ball, took a shot and made the basket while getting fouled in the process. That shot proved to be the game winner, and we won the second game of the state tournament. We would win the third and final game of the tournament to finish in first place in our division. Kids in Disability Sports had just won the gold medal in the basketball tournament of the SOMA Winter Games. The gold medal I got for winning the state tournament was bigger than my first gold medal at the qualifier. The second gold medal would be a sign of things to come.

Special Olympics have provided so many opportunities for Tyler. He has participated in many different sports and met many different athletes from around the country. It has been a wonderful resource for Ron and me as well. We have met many parents that walk in our shoes each day. They provide support, encouragement and recommendations for programs, physicians, employment and other groups for Tyler to join.

As for my other basketball team, the Cotting School Falcons, I had my best season in 2002–2003. Cotting School had lost at least four players to graduation in 2002. However, the Falcons gained an all-around big man named David, my old classmate from CTDS. David would go on to win the Most Valuable Player trophy for the basketball team. Cotting School would go undefeated in 2002–2003. We only played five games that season because about two games were cancelled due to inclement weather. In the opener against the Alumni on December 6, 2002, we won 44–38. Two weeks later on the last school day before Christmas, we beat the staff 40–39. In my first game since the death of Pepere, January 10, 2003, Cotting won 52–47 against the Alumni. Then on Valentine's Day we beat the staff 45–40. On the last game of the season, February 28, against Braintree, we completed the undefeated season by winning 52–51. I never had another basketball season like that again.

The basketball team provided Tyler to have an opportunity to practice the social skills he was learning during school and in therapy. It also gave him the same experiences that his peers in our home town were having. He could have a conversation with the kids from our town and actually share their common experience. It is so important to keep the connections with the neighborhood kids whenever your child is placed in a school that is not in your town or city.

In the spring of 2003, I took the tenth-grade MCAS tests required by Massachusetts state law. I took the eighth-grade MCAS tests when I was in Gifford School in 2001 and didn't get a good score. I spent the next two years studying math and English to better prepare myself for the next tests. When spring came in 2003, it was time for me to take the MCAS. I worked like crazy on the English and math tests. I did the best I could because if I didn't pass both tests, I would not be able to graduate in 2005.

In October, I received something great from the mail. They were the results from my MCAS tests from the spring of 2003. It said that I was in the advanced level of performance in mathematics and my English language arts needed improvement. In other words, I passed math with flying colors and was at the highest level in the state. My English test wasn't great, but I was good enough to pass it. My mom was so excited about me not only passing MCAS but being in the advanced stage in math. Bottom line, I was going to graduate from Cotting School in 2005.

I remember the feeling of elation when we opened the envelope to reveal his test scores. I had tried to prepare for the fact that Tyler may not receive a score high enough to attain a high school diploma. I tried to downplay it in my head. I told myself that it's just a number. I tried to focus on all the progress that Tyler had been making. The reality was that I was trying to justify my decision for placing Tyler in "special schools." The practical side of me knew that Ron and I had made the best decision for Tyler, but the emotional side of me was still wishing that he could have gone to public school and "blended in" just like all the other kids. I didn't even realize how I had placed so much emphasis on him being successful on the MCAS testing. I really wanted Tyler to receive a high school diploma as opposed to a certificate of attendance. I knew he was brilliant and I couldn't wrap my head around the fact that the government felt that students should take an all or nothing test to determine if they knew enough to receive a high school diploma. I still to this day have concerns about all these high stakes testing that we are putting our children through each year. While we are busy having students take a pretest to see how much they know of material we are teaching, and then making them take a post test to see if they have gained any knowledge, then analyzing the test results and making curriculum changes in between, I am left to wonder, when is the real teaching and learning going to occur? Not everyone learns the same way and not everyone should be tested the same way. I just think too much emphasis on the testing does nothing more than create more stress for our students and stressed out students don't learn as well under those circumstances!

My second year at Cotting School was a success. I was voted most artistic and most athletic by my peers. On awards day in May 29, 2003, I received the Athletic Achievement Award for the second year in a row. I learned more things in one year than the last few years before that combined. I enjoyed my first year as Ms. Clark's student. She had such a way of reaching out to her students. She did an outstanding job preparing her pupils for the real world. I made a ton of sacrifices so I could get my homework done on time for her. I was glad that I did or else I was never ever going to make a name for myself in the future.

After I finished my second year at Cotting School, I didn't attend the 2003 Summer Program. Instead, I decided to take a part-time, summer job at Kimball's Ice Cream Stand in Westford. I was familiar with the place because I played on the Pitch & Putt Golf Course. When I first came to work there, a miniature golf course was built. It was an honor to work for such a nice place like Kimball's. For the first time in my life—at age sixteen—I was a working man earning real money. My job was to pick up cigarette butts in the parking lots with a broom and pan. I also made sure that the miniature golf course and the driving range were all cleaned up. When I first got my paycheck in the mail, I was ecstatic and my mom took a picture of me holding my paycheck.

The summer of 2003 was not always about work and making money. It was about enjoying the moment and sharing the moment with other people. In July, I got to visit York Beach in Maine. I had been to Maine only once before and that was at a water park and mini golf course in Saco back in 1992. The Browning's were vacationing at a cottage in York Beach and I went up there with Mom and Dad for the day. I helped Cody Browning dig a hole despite a high water table at there, threw a football around with Mike Reault, and tanned. It was nice to go back to the state of Maine to see some familiar faces.

One month after going to Maine and a whole lot of struggling hours of work at Kimball's, I went with Mom, Dad, Clint and his girlfriend, and Memere to Seabrook, New Hampshire, to spend a week at a little beach house. The place we stayed was home to a friend of Mom's. It was such a summer haven even though we were staying at a residential area with the nuclear power plant in sight. The place had a deck, a living room, a kitchen, three bedrooms, a bathroom, and a porch. No basement, no second floor, just the house within walking distance from the ocean.

Tyler takes great pleasure in all the details to each event in his life. It almost feels as if each day is such a separate event for him. It almost feels as if he doesn't realize tomorrow will be here. He pays close attention to every different sensation he experiences.

Once I was at the beach, I would build some stadiums and ballparks out of sand, work on my tan in the sun, listened to some music, threw a baseball around with Dad or Clint and did some wakeboarding in the ocean. On some nights I would go out to eat with my family at Brown's or Markey's, both seafood places. One day Clint and his girlfriend took me to Playland Arcade at Hampton Beach. Late in vacation, my dad took me golfing at Amesbury (Massachusetts) Country Club. One time we visited Newburyport, Massachusetts, for a bite to eat at a local restaurant and to check out this Life is Good store. It became apparent that Seabrook had become my favorite summer destination.

For me, it was difficult to tell if he actually had a good time on vacation. It seemed to me that he spent most of his time writing in his journal. Whenever Tyler is out of his routine, he seems to feel grounded as long as he can document everything he has done in his journal.

After Seabrook, my dad took me to Waterville Valley for a two-night stay. Dad and I began the trip to Waterville Valley with a hike up Mount Osceola. At 4,315 feet, it was the tallest mountain I had ever hiked before. It was where I first started to really enjoy nature. The White Mountains of New Hampshire is a great place to visit on a weekday in the latter stages of the summer because there are not a lot of people visiting. Dad and I stayed at the Best Western Silver Fox Inn at the valley. We enjoyed lots of activities there including mountain biking, swimming, and golfing. Waterville Valley had a brand-new golf course there. This was the place where I made my first birdie. There was a town square with shops and restaurants and we visited them any chance we got. That trip to Waterville Valley capped off a very pleasant summer of 2003.

I enjoyed that summer better than any other in my life. I got to go to two beaches, one mountain, and I worked in a real job for the first time ever. I went to four Red Sox games in 2003. I got to meet some new people and I interacted with them nicely. I learned a lot of new things from my parents this summer. I felt like a very responsible person. I was doing grown-up things for the first time ever during the summer of 2003. Then as the fall of 2003 arrived, I was only going to have my work cut out for me.

In September of 2003, at the time of my third year at Cotting School, I had a new assistant teacher named Ms. Harkins, a twenty-two-year-old who had just graduated from college. Just when I thought I was going to have an easier year than the one before, I had another thing coming. Just like Ms. Clark, Ms. Harkins brought out the best in me and pushed me to work as hard as I could ever imagine. She was not like any other twenty-year-old who had just graduated from college a couple of months earlier. NO! She was a well-focused individual who took her job seriously. She was new to teaching after graduating from college just months earlier but she was no rookie teacher. She was the most ambitious twenty-two-year-old woman I have ever met.

Most of last year's class returned for 2003–2004. Now that Bethany and Ramona had graduated, two new students had just joined Ms. Clark's class, Kimberly R. and another former CTDS student named Ruby R. This school year we learned about the United States government. Later in the school year I read and did a book report on Julius Caesar. I also learned about communism and read *Animal Farm*, a book about pigs taking over a farm from a ruthless farmer and forming a type of communist rule with pigs being the noble upper class and the rest of the animals being the working lower class.

On December 19, 2003, an event took place at the arena then known as the Fleet Center, Boston, Massachusetts. It was Special Olympics night at the Boston Celtics game against the Utah Jazz. The KIDS Inc. Basketball Team was chosen to play a halftime exhibition game. I was going to play basketball on the same sacred parquet floor that the Celtics play on. The Fleet Center, which was known at the time, was not the same as the old Boston Garden but it was the permanent home of the most storied franchise in basketball. Once I walked on that floor, it felt like a dream that came true. This was a once in a lifetime moment to me but there are some guys who do it forty times a year. Watching your sports heroes is one thing, going to the game in person is another thing, but playing the game on the same court, field, or ice rink as your favorite player, it's every kid's dream. Whether they are from Phoenix, Dallas, Los Angeles or New York City, It's every child's dream.

My team sat in the balcony area for the game. Since it was Special Olympics night, somebody with Cerebral Palsy sang the national anthem. Midway through the second period, my team and I got out of our seats and onto court level to get ready to play basketball during halftime. We were going to play a five-minute game against a team from Worcester County called Seven Hills. There was a big crowd on hand that Friday night for a game that was not too meaningful for the Celtics. After both the Celtics and the Jazz left for their respective locker rooms, we took to the parquet floor to live a dream. The floor was a heck of a lot different than on TV. I was playing in front of thousands during halftime while some of them left their seats to get food or use the restrooms. As for my game, I was trying my best out there, trying to make plays to my teammates, trying to make a shot. The Seven Hills defense made it difficult for me to play my game. On defense, I did this unintentional imitation of Dave Cowens in the 1974 NBA Finals by diving for a loose ball as it was going out of bounds. I wound up with a small abrasion on one of my arms trying to get the ball. Later in the game, I made a pass to a teammate who put up a rainbow of a shot and got nothing but net. Once that ball went into the basket, the whole Fleet Center crowd went crazy. After both teams exchanged baskets, this crowd was into it. Then my dad, who was coaching us at the time, made a substitution while the game was still in progress. This crowd was still going bananas as I was taking my seat.

While I was sitting on the Celtics bench, some big-framed man with a ring on his wrinkly finger walked in front of me. It was Tom Heinsohn, *the* Tom Heinsohn who does color commentary for Boston Celtics games, *the* Tom Heinsohn who helped his Celtics win eight NBA titles as a player and two NBA titles as a coach. He congratulated me and I shook Tommy's hand. It was the first time I've ever shaken hands with a real-life sports legend. Nothing can come close to this.

I had the time of my life on the last Friday before Christmas in 2003. Even a Celtics loss could not tarnish one of the greatest nights of my seventeen-year-old life. I was fortunate enough to be a part of this occasion and nothing can take it away. It was pretty much an early Christmas gift and possibly the highlight of a very emotional year. It took until December to find the best story of 2003, and I found it on the hallowed parquet floor of the New Garden. The year 2003 was the biggest basketball year of my life and it would never be matched or surpassed.

The year 2003 sure did end on a high note for me after beginning on a silent note with the passing of Pepere on the final days of 2002. I had my own room for the first time in years after Dad had turned a section of the basement into a bedroom for Clint. I had just entered the age of maturity thanks to being in Ms. Clark's homeroom for a second year and working at a real job for the first time ever. I was feeling so good about myself that I started to believe that anything was possible after all. I was at the top of my game in 2003 and bigger opportunities lay ahead in 2004.

Tyler is exactly on point when he says that 2002 and 2003 were extremely challenging years—both good and bad. I believe Tyler handled most of these challenges better than Ron and I did. Death is always difficult to deal with. Tyler's Pepere lived on the other half of our duplex. He was very involved in everything that happened in our household. Tyler and Pepere had a very unique bond. His cancer took us by surprise and his passing happened so quickly. Tyler had all the emotional tools to process what was going on. We are so grateful to all the people that played such an instrumental role in his life to support us during this time.

On the other hand, 2003 was a very rewarding year for Tyler. His school had arranged for him to have his job at Kimball's Farm. It's true, he felt as if he was an adult because he had a job. It is so important for employers to see the value in hiring our children. They truly can contribute to their company or business. It was truly an empowering experience for him. He learned about how to manage his money and the importance of earning a day's pay.

The year 2004 began just the same way as 2003 began. It began with a death in the family, Cotting School family that is. Kurt St. Pierre, my classmate in Ms. Clark's class for a year and a half, passed away very unexpectedly on January 10, 2004. He suffered from Muscular Dystrophy and used a wheelchair for mobility. He was very bright for his age in spite of his disability. He was a quiet kid and always did his best at school. Once the year started, Kurt didn't show up for school. He was coming down with something and his condition made it difficult for him to recover from most illnesses. Then Kurt died. He was eighteen years old and would have turned nineteen on April 19, 2004.

It never happened to me before, having a classmate like Kurt get taken away from me so suddenly. There were at least three other people from Cotting School that had died while I was attending that school. Kurt's was the biggest loss because I would see him at class a lot. In 2005, I spoke to the crowd about Kurt before presenting a bench made by the Cotting students in his honor. To me, he was too young to die in my book.

Sadly, death and illness sometimes happens more often at a school such as Tyler's. It has helped Tyler to look outside of himself and demonstrate empathy, courage and compassion on a daily basis. These are skills that all children need to practice every day.

Later in March, after earning the bronze medal in a Special Olympics basketball tournament held in Basketball City, located on top of a parking garage across from the Fleet Center in Boston, my team KIDS Inc. hosted an invitational basketball tournament at Costello Gymnasium on the UMASS–Lowell North Campus. This invitational, the first tournament for basketball run by KIDS Inc., was a flat-out success. All the teams we invited to play came. Before the games, I was practicing my three-point shots. I started making those shots to the point where I couldn't miss. During practice, I would make as many as five three-pointers in a row. I think I was shooting better than I've ever shot before that day. Then I attempted a shot from slightly beyond half-court and made it. Then we played our first game of the tournament. With time running out in the first half, I got the rebound and from beyond half-court, I let her fly. Bang! Nothing but net! Before I knew it, I was being mobbed by all my teammates. That was where I received the nickname Fly Boy for my ability to make shots from long distances. My team would go on to win that game and the next two to win the first KIDS basketball invitational. However, this day would be forever known for my half-court shot to end the first half of the first game.

Again, sports have been a catalyst for empowering Tyler in all different facets of his life. I would encourage people to volunteer to coach or sponsor a team with special needs. It seems as though everyone is so busy these days, but I guarantee the rewards genuinely make up for the commitment of your time and energy.

At industrial arts class, I created and completed the most ambitious project in my years at Cotting School. For most of the 2003–2004 school years, I spent most of the time at shop class constructing a Ping-Pong table. I wasn't going to be able to have it since there was no room in my house to accommodate the table. The table was going to have to stay inside the industrial arts room. In early spring of 2004, the Ping-Pong table was finished. During breaks or spare times at industrial arts, I would play some Ping-Pong. I had a lot of fun putting this thing together. Besides basketball, it was my biggest accomplishment ever at Cotting School.

One of the best characteristics of Tyler's autism is the fact that he feels comforted by rules and specific directions. Once he learns something, he remembers it forever. Therefore, whether he is working on the job for an employer or in the academic classroom or in the industrial arts shop, he follows each and every direction to the letter! He was taught the importance of safety whenever he is working with tools. He uses safety glasses when necessary. He uses ear protection regularly, and so on. We have found that if something came out wrong it was usually our fault for not giving him a complete set of directions. It can work the other way as well. He won't take any shortcuts. So if you want him to rush to do something, you better be prepared to be disappointed! His work will always be complete, neat and he always remembers to clean up after himself. Most of the time it is a blessing, but some of the time, it can be a curse—especially when I am in a hurry to go somewhere. He pretty much refuses to change his routine. If he is forced to change it, there are usually repercussions to deal with later. He is unsettled, unhappy and can't seem to "get it together."

By the time the school year drew to a close, it was time to say goodbye to some people who were good citizens of Cotting School. One of them was outgoing president and executive director of Cotting School, Dr. Carl W. Mores. All five members of the Cotting graduating class of 2004 were girls. One of the graduates was my longtime friend named Elia. She only spent three years at Cotting School and I was at the same lunch table with her for two years. She liked art class, and she loved to listen to Loren and Wally, local DJs, in the morning on the radio. Elia and I were voted most artistic in the superlatives of the 2003 Cotting School yearbook. I went to the same school with her since Winslow School in the 1991–1992 school year. I lived just down the road from her house and we were on the same cab when we went to CTDS, Gifford School, and Cotting School. Things were not going to be the same without Elia in the same cab as me.

The biggest goodbye for me in 2004 was Ms. Dorothy Clark. My teacher of two years was retiring from Cotting School. I learned a lot from her in two years—more than any other teacher I've ever had. Ms. Clark had made a humungous impact on my life as she got me to work my way toward my potential. I bought in to her style of teaching because I found her style interesting. She was a person that I could trust and believe in. Last but not least, she was right. She knew what she was talking about. The first thing she would say every morning when she came into the homeroom was "okay." She had this yardstick with her just in case her students were unruly. She rarely used it because her students rarely clashed with her. I don't necessarily recall a moment when one of my classmates lost its control and I am pretty sure I behaved very well. Ms. Clark was a teacher at Cotting School for a long time, longer than I can remember. It was tough to see her go. I wished that she was there to see me graduate.

Let me make this CLEAR. Ms. Clark never used the ruler for corporal punishment! I don't know why Tyler would feel that she or any of his teachers would do that. Even Ron and I don't believe in corporal punishment for our children. He must have seen or read stories about teachers hitting students years ago and believes it to be a truth of today. That is one of his problems—he doesn't know when people are exaggerating to make a point or making a joke. He believes everything someone says at face value. It can be problematic for him in so many situations in life.

For the third straight year, I was given the Athletic Achievement Award at awards day. I also got an achievement in mathematics, my first such award because I nearly aced the math portion of the MCAS exam. And finally, I received the Bob Lobel for Sportscasting Award, named after famous Boston sportscaster Bob Lobel. I was voted most athletic by my peers in the 2004 school yearbook along with David and Kate (Cotting Basketball MVPs in 2003 and 2004, respectively). Once again, I finished a Cotting school year with flying colors. Next year, I was going to be a senior, and it would be my last year at the school on Concord Avenue in Lexington.

Tyler puts a tremendous amount of pressure on himself to achieve excellence in anything he does. He makes a commitment and sticks to it until it is complete. His dedication borders on a compulsion and we have to work on that sometimes to make him understand that it's OK if he is not first in his class or doesn't score the winning basket, make the final putt for birdie or get an A for a grade on every paper that he writes.

The summer of 2004 was a repeat of the summer of 2003. I worked at Kimball's for the second summer in a row, and I got to make some money again by performing the same old tasks as last year. The more money I made there, the closer I was to earning enough for college. Once again, Merrimack Education Center (MEC) was paying me. Both

MEC and Kimball's admired my work ethic and Kimball's surely liked having me around. As a sixteen- and seventeen-year-old, I liked going there.

Also during this summer, I went to York Beach in Maine again, I went to Waterville Valley again, I went to Seabrook again, and I got to play some golf here and there again. The Summer Olympics took place in Athens, Greece that summer so I got to watch some of them at Seabrook. During my second vacation there, I went golfing with Dad at Sagamore-Hampton Golf Course for the first time ever. I shot twenty-five strokes over par for a score of 96 that morning. After golf, I went into the ocean for the first time during vacation. The weather wasn't all that great at Seabrook Beach that week. There would be two more beach days afterward. I did a few things while I was on the shoreline such as making sports venues out of sand and doing a little wakeboarding. On day 5 of vacation, I went to Playland Arcade at Hampton Beach.

Again, we stuck to our usual schedule. It is hard for Tyler to relax if we change schedules too much. That is why we tend to go to the same places each year. They do change a little, but the basic experience is the same for him and he finds that very comforting and therefore he can relax. And if he relaxes, we relax!

My three years at Cotting School went by extremely fast. The 2004–2005 school year would be my last one as I was going to graduate next June. I worked harder than I've ever had since I first walked inside the entrance of Cotting School on that Tuesday afternoon in September. I had made some amazing strides over the course of my time at Cotting. I became a model citizen for this school, got along beautifully with my peers and faculty, and got closer and closer to being my own man. I thought I could learn everything I could over those three years at Cotting School, but in my fourth year, I realized that I had a lot more learning to do.

Isn't self-actualization the real goal for all our children? In so many ways Tyler has always been far more mature than most people his age. It is such a struggle for me as a parent because his is extremely naïve in many different situations, yet his work ethic and desire to succeed is so mature.

In September of 2004, I began my fourth and final year at Cotting School. I moved to a different homeroom, which was half the size of Ms. Clark's. With Ms. Clark now retired, Ms. Harkins became my full-time teacher for the 2004–2005 school years. I was one of four members of the graduating class of 2005 and was the only senior in the homeroom. More than half of the entire homeroom was made of CTDS alumni. David, Ruby, Maura M. and I all came from CTDS, so there was this sense of reunion here at Cotting School. The rest of Ms. Harkins's class consisted of Brian, Jenna, and Sarah who left Cotting School in September and was later replaced by Becky R.

Early in my last school year, I did some research on three Olympic athletes since the Summer Olympics took place a couple of weeks before school started. I learned some interesting facts about Fanny Blankers-Koen, four-time gold medalist in track and field in the 1948 summer games in London; swimmer Gary Hall Jr., a diabetic who won ten Olympic medals; and Lance Armstrong. I did a book report on Lance, I learned that he lived with a single mother, did triathlons before focusing on cycling, and learned more about his battle with a dreadful form of testicular cancer at the tender age of twenty-five. He was one of my inspirations until his performance-enhancing drug use altered his image for the worse.

In science, I discovered more things that were interesting to me. I learned how to make this Outrageous Ooze by mixing dry corn starch and water in a big bowl. It was the coolest experiment I have ever done when I was at Cotting. This ooze can act as a liquid when you move your fingers in the ooze slowly and act as a solid when you move your fingers in it quickly. Since it was homework, I played around with my creation. I picked a handful of the ooze, squeezed it, and let it drip through my fingers. Then I rested my fingers on the surface of the ooze, let them sink down to the bottom of the bowl and pulled out my fingers fast. I wrote in my report this: "When I pulled the ooze out fast, it acted as a solid. After that it began to drip like a liquid. Eventually the ooze would dry out on my hands and become a waxy substance then it turned to powder."

This was a big experiment in many ways for Tyler. He was learning the science end of the lesson, yet for me, he was learning about the various sensations he was processing.

In my last school year with Cotting, I got into several extracurricular activities with the school such as the Circle of Friends, an afterschool group that I joined in late September. I knew some people that were a part of this group. Once a month, I would do certain things with the Circle of Friends, such as shop and eat at the Burlington Mall off

Route 128, go candlepin bowling at a place off Route 2 in Belmont, and see a Lowell Lock Monster hockey game. I was also a member of the Cotting School Golf Team. The team would go to a nearby par-3 course called Stone Meadow once a week in the fall to play some golf on the course or hit a bucket of balls at the driving range. Then in November of 2004, I went on a class field trip to the Museum of Fine Arts in Boston. I went there once before with Ms. Clark's class. I saw some impressionist paintings and some contemporary or modern art. After that we went to an art room where I made a painting of an album cover from the band Rush.

Even though I was making good strides at school as a senior, I just didn't feel all that good about myself. For a little more than a dozen years, I had to ride in a cab to get to school. My drivers from the cab company S, P & R did the best they could. I had to put up with everything, the morning commute, the music on the radio, the other people inside the cab, Lillian. Every morning and afternoon, I didn't have much of a choice but to go through my usual cab routine. Somehow, I still managed to get through those days when I was at school.

When I was aged fourteen to eighteen, not including Wednesdays, my daily routine went like this. I would wake up just shy of 6:00 a.m., then spend just one hour getting dressed, eating breakfast, brushing my teeth, washing my face, and waiting for my cab. My morning commute was an hour long. I would spend almost seven hours at school. My ride home was longer than the morning because everyone else got dropped off before me. If I was lucky, I would get home by 3:30 but normally I would get home somewhere between 3:45 and 4:00. The majority of my day would be spent away from my home and my family.

Bernie drove me to Cotting School from 2001 to 2004. For the first three years I was at Cotting, We would play this game called Punch Buggy. Every time one of us saw a Volkswagen New Beetle, we would say "punch buggy" and the color of the vehicle. We would listen to Loren and Wally in the morning on the way to school. It was funny at first but I grew out of it the older I got. Then Elia graduated in 2004 and it was just Bernie, another girl, and me.

Then early in my last year going to Cotting, Bernie told me that she was going to do another route so that she would earn more money. Bernie did not like her current route any better than me because she had to be in the cab longer than me. Bernie was the best driver I've ever had, and now she was moving on just as I was about to enjoy my final year.

I would have three different cabdrivers for the whole winter and early spring months. Each driver would bring their own child along for the ride. There were several occasions when that child would throw crying fits and tantrums for whatever reason. There was this one three-year-old boy from my first driver after Bernie who would go crazy after waking up from having bad dreams. I remember him going on screaming rampages at least three times in the month of November alone. His tantrums would last at least thirty minutes. It only made my ride to and from school all the more uncomfortable. Still, I had to put up with it, I had no choice. And yet, how can one tolerate such repeated screaming and wailing? Lucky for me, I would not have to ride in the minivan to and from school as much in my last year at Cotting. Bernie eventually came back to be my cabdriver again for the last month of my last school year in time before my graduation.

I know that most people think it's a great deal to have a van come to your house to pick your child up and bring them to school. And don't misunderstand. I really do appreciate the fact that we had reliable transportation for Tyler. In reality, I was envious of all the kids and their families that were able to send their kids off to school on the "regular" bus. I knew how unhappy Tyler was riding in the van for such a long day and I also knew that the other kids in the van had just as many challenges as Tyler. I also knew that there was no way that Ron or I could do the daily commute an hour away each day and be able to earn a living at our jobs. I've struggled with the guilt of knowing how hard that was for Tyler each day.

After the Thanksgiving break, I asked Mom and Dad if I could have a co-op job, which meant going to work part-time all the while still being able to go to school. Merrimack Education Center, the group that got me the summer job at Kimball's, took care of that. I visited two places in the Lowell area to see what jobs were available and what jobs were the right ones for me. One was CVS Pharmacy near the Lowell Connector, and the other was Lowell General Hospital. I chose Lowell General Hospital because it was nearby and I felt that this was a good working environment for me. One day MEC took me inside the copy center/mail room at the hospital. There I met Paul S., the head of the copy center and Kevin, a student from MEC. My job at Lowell General was going to be the mail clerk. The mail clerk's duties were to sort and deliver mail to various offices in and around the hospital. I would go out and deliver mail once in the morning and once in the afternoon.

And so a meeting was held at my school. I would work at Lowell General Hospital on Mondays, Tuesdays, and Wednesdays and go to school on Thursdays and Fridays. It was a six-hour-a-day, eighteen-hour-a-week job that would run from December to the middle of June, when the school year ends. I was sacrificing some schoolwork but I was still going to graduate in June 2005. I was hoping it would lead to greater job opportunities in the long term because I needed a job after graduating high school. It turned out to be a great decision because if I had not worked there, I would not have enough money to pay for college or be able to do something that I loved to do. I will get to that something later.

The co-op job was a fantastic experience for Tyler in so many different aspects. To begin with, the hospital is about two miles from our home. This helped Tyler to have a break from riding in the van for so long. Each day he worked, he would hop in the car with me and go to the school that I worked at before it opened. From that point, he would take the city bus to Lowell General Hospital for work. He would reverse that process to get home. It worked out splendidly. The work at the hospital was fantastic for someone with Tyler's strengths. It was a fairly quiet setting. He never gets lost, so he was able to deliver the mail with speed and accuracy. He never gets sidetracked, so he was extremely efficient. He was polite and cordial with all the employees and they had a genuine respect for him. I, too, wished that this job would have led to a permanent position. However that is not how it works. Once you leave the school, the co-op position goes to the next person that needs a job experience.

Boston had reason to celebrate in 2004. Football's New England Patriots and Baseball's Boston Red Sox won their championships that year. The more significant of the two was the Red Sox as they had to wait eighty-six years to go all the way. The Boston area was first city to have two major sports champions in the same calendar year in a quarter of a century. I was not with my dad when the final out was made for fear that I might jinx my favorite baseball team. I came downstairs from my room to the living room where my dad was to witness the celebration take place. It was almost midnight and I only stayed with Dad to see them celebrate for only half an hour since it was a school night.

That was a big night for all of the Boston area. Still, Tyler needed to keep to his routine as much as possible. This is where having autism works out well sometimes and doesn't work out well sometimes. If the Red Sox had lost, the world would have felt like it came to an end for Tyler. He overreacts to losses at sporting events. His highs are super highs and his lows are super lows. There are no in between emotions.

For Christmas that year, I got a whole bunch of Red Sox merchandise. I got a new Red Sox jacket, two hooded sweatshirts, one set of 2004 Red Sox baseball cards, two Red Sox DVDs, and a new hat. I even got *Believe It*, a book of articles from the Boston Globe chronicling the 2004 Red Sox. I also got a program of the 2004 World Series and a Beckett magazine commemorating the 2004 Boston Red Sox. And I got a new MP3 player with FM radio and enough space in it to hold up to two hundred songs.

During Christmas break, just before the New Year, I got my braces taken off. During my twenty-five months with braces on, I also had to wear a palate expander and then elastics, and I had to rinse every night before going to bed. After the orthodontists took them off, I could feel my teeth again, something I have not experienced since 2002. My teeth were free again, with just one exception. The orthodontists said I had to wear plastic retainers so that my teeth wouldn't go back to where they were before I had my braces put on me. I still rinse after I brush and still go to sleep with plastic in my mouth ever since I had my braces removed from me.

That is clearly an understatement! I mentioned earlier that Tyler is a creature of habit. Oral care is no exception. He uses a timer to make sure that he rinses for the appropriate amount of time. He also uses a timer to make sure he brushes his teeth for the allotted time as well. Then he flosses twice a day. I do admire this, however, when I need to get going in a hurry, there is no deviation from this routine. It can be tremendously frustrating when I am in a hurry!

The year 2004 was pretty emotional and confusing for me because I was eighteen years old, had a driver's permit, and was working three days a week at the hospital, so I was given more responsibilities than I've ever had. I was to graduate from Cotting School next summer and I had no idea what to expect after that. I had come very far from being this fourteen year old who first walked down the path to Cotting School and being the youngest in my classroom. Now the year 2004 was about to become 2005. I was in my final year at Cotting School, and I was going to miss this place and miss it more now that I was working part-time in the mail room at Lowell General Hospital.

For the longest time, we felt that Tyler wouldn't miss anything or anyone as long as he had a routine. It is nice to know that he genuinely had personal connections to people and not just events.

In February of 2005, just a day after the Patriots won their third Super Bowl, I went on the Cotting School Ski Trip to Mount Sunapee in New Hampshire. More than a dozen students and a few teachers came to the ski trip. The ski trip was supposed to last for four days but it lasted three days because of a threat of heavy snow. Everybody on the trip stayed at the Best Western Hotel, located just a couple of minutes from the base of the mountain. On the first day of the trip, I visited the New England Handicapped Skiing Association (NEHSA) Lodge to try on some ski accessories and equipment. I brought my own ski stuff with me to the trip. During my stay, I shared a room with my fellow senior Joe.

Tyler had never gone on an overnight trip with anyone but family. He was anxious to say the least. We talked to him the first night of the trip and we could hear the stress in his voice. We knew this trip was an essential part of growing up for him. It was all I could do to not hop in my car and go "rescue" him! I must admit, I didn't sleep well that night thinking about how uncomfortable he was. I never felt that he was homesick in the traditional way. I just felt that he was on sensory overload and he really wanted his routine to be the way it normally was. His roommate was a nice classmate with a wonderful personality. I knew Tyler would survive, but I was still worried.

On day 2 of the trip, I was actually doing some skiing. I was more advanced at skiing than any other students who came to Mount Sunapee because I've been doing this since I was six. There were some students on the trip who have never or rarely skied before. I started skiing at the beginner area and later went down from the summit of Mount Sunapee. I met a few nice instructors up there. They taught me how to ski like a professional, do some 360-degrees on skis, extend my arms and keeping my head tucked in, and do the slide, plant, and turn technique on the moguls and had a good time doing so.

After skiing, I went with the group to dinner. I had some clam chowder and a sandwich there and later went downstairs to the game room. I played this Off-Road arcade game in the game room and played air hockey with my classmate Brian. Then while we were walking to the hotel, Brian hunched over for some reason. I thought he was throwing up but he was choking on a toothpick. He got that piece of wood out of his mouth and he felt okay afterward.

The third day of the trip was the last day because of the risk of a snowstorm. I was nonetheless happy to ski for at least one more day. Mom and Dad were up at the mountain for some skiing of their own that day and they were glad to see me. However, I was gladder to see them than they were to see me. I showed Mom and Dad the tricks I learned during the trip. I no longer felt alone when my parents showed up. After skiing, I checked out of my room and headed to the NEHSA banquet. I was awarded with a certificate, pin, and a poster of Mount Sunapee. I thanked the people of NEHSA for helping me become a better skier.

Tyler lit up and came over very quickly and gave us the biggest hug when he saw us at the mountain! It felt as if he hadn't seen us in a year! I never knew he cared about us that much! Imagine—it took eighteen years for us to get the feeling that Tyler really cared about our parent-son relationship. Maybe I'm wrong on that assessment, but I'm sticking with that version because I'll never forget that moment and how it felt so different for him to seek us out for comfort and a hug!

As the winter seasons of 2004–2005 were coming to a close, I met a lot of people while working at Lowell General Hospital. I got to know Andrea and Linda, the ladies that run the volunteer department at the hospital. I learned a lot from my boss Paul, and coworkers Kevin and Travis, the latter two who were at least a couple of years older than me. There was this girl named Jessica who would come by once in a while to take care of the in-house mail. Then there was a courier who would bring in the in-house mail for us to sort to various offices and rooms in and around the hospital. I got to know some workers over at general stores, the area adjacent to the loading dock and the mail room/copy center.

I would do two routes during my typical work day, one in the morning and the other in the afternoon. In the morning, the courier would come in with the mail. Then I would sort out all the mail with a little help from Travis or Kevin or Paul if necessary. Once all of the mail was sorted out, I would put it all in my cart, in the slots where the mail is supposed to go. Then I would go deliver the mail to the offices and rooms in the hospital. If I had any mail for the places I was assigned to go, I delivered to them. If I didn't, I would just move on to the next room. Once I finished my route, I would bring all the interoffice mail and outgoing mail back to the copy center. After getting all the interoffice mail sorted out, I would take a lunch break at the cafeteria. The LGH cafeteria had better lunches there than at Cotting School. It had a soup section and a salad bar and served different lunches every day.

After lunch I would go back to the copy center to resume my workday. I put the sorted mail in my cart and then would start my afternoon run. The afternoon run was longer than the morning run because I had to go to more places in the hospital. I had to go deliver mail to the offices in the School of Nursing such as Public Relations and Continuity of Care on the west side of the hospital where the volunteer office is located. Then I delivered to the ground floor offices where orthopedics, the emergency room, and the sleep lab were located. Then I went up to the first floor to deliver to IMC or Intermediate care, ICU or Intensive care, ACU or the Ambulatory Care Unit, Nursing Administration, and Administration. Then I would go to the other side of the building on the same floor to deliver to Patient Service Center, Admitting, Human Resources, and Medical Records.

Then I moved upstairs to the second floor to deliver to Pediatrics. Then I went up to the third floor to deliver to MP3 or Mansfield Pavilion third floor and Delivery room. Then I moved on to the fourth floor to deliver to the computer room and Maternity. Then I went back down to the third floor and into another building in the hospital to deliver to MS3, an area with rooms for the patients. Next, I went down to the second floor to deliver to TCU or the Transitional Care Unit, patient advocate and the library. Then I would go back to the ground floor to deliver mail to the lab, the cardiac catheterization lab, and the X-ray lab. Then I would make my way through a long tunnel, which led to the Medical Office Building, to deliver mail to certain doctors' offices. Finally I took both crates of in-house and out-side mail back to the copy center to sort them all out. This was how my average day at the hospital was.

Details, details, details . . . and so goes his life!

The 2005 Cotting School Senior Class Trip

On May 3, 2005, I went on a plane ride for the third time in my life. The first time I have ever been on a plane was when I flew out of Manchester, New Hampshire, to Baltimore-Washington International for a cousin's wedding in Virginia in 1999. I didn't like flying the first time around because I had a hard time hearing once I got off the plane. Then on Memorial Day weekend 2001, I had to go on a plane to my brother's soccer tournament with his club Lazio FC in Virginia. This time I flew with my parents out of Logan Airport in Boston to Dulles Airport in Northern Virginia. The second time around worked out much better.

Any guess as to why the second time flying was a better experience for Tyler? You guessed it—he had already had the experience. Therefore, he was able to draw on that experience and make sense of it. We all get anxious when we try new things. However, Tyler can't process new experiences efficiently. As a result, he takes a long time to get over these transitions.

Unlike the first two flights, the third was my first flight since the September 11 terrorist attacks changed the way airport security was in America and the world. Logan Airport was much different than when I last came there. The airport was much nicer in 2005 as the terminal I flew out of looked like a mall with a sports bar and several restaurants. I went on the Cotting School Senior class trip to Disney World in Florida with my fellow seniors Etienne, Joe, and Franny, and three Cotting faculty members, Mrs. Birmingham, Mr. Moran, and Mr. DeAngelis. This would be the farthest and longest I have ever been away from my parents. I flew Song Airlines to and from Florida with my group. Unlike my first two flights, this flight had TV screens on the backs of every seat on the plane. You could watch TV, see a movie, listen to music, and look at the airplane's present location and where exactly it is headed. I elected to listen to my MP3 player on the way to Orlando.

Tyler had expressed to us that he didn't really want to go on the senior class trip to Florida. Ron and I felt he needed to have the full experience of being a senior in high school. We were pretty firm with our decision that he would go on this trip. He was able to do a fair amount of prep work regarding where he would stay. He knew his classmates and teachers very well. We knew he would be safe throughout the trip.

Once I first saw Florida, it was flat, no hills at all, just swampland. The airport in Orlando was nice, had a Nathan's hot dog stand and a lot of shops. We took a big taxi bus from the terminal to the entrance where our bags were located. After we all got our bags and things, we took a Disney bus from the airport to the All-Star Sports Resort, the place we were going to call home for four days and three nights. On the way to the resort, I saw Florida firsthand. There were new houses being built outside the highway connecting the airport to Disney World where swampland once ruled. Then we arrived at the All-Star Sports Resort. This place was gigantic because All-Star Sports was connected to All-Star Music and All-Star Movies resorts. The main building had an airport-sized lobby, a big Disney store, an arcade, and a giant food court. Outside between the hotel rooms and the main building were an outdoor pool, a picnic area, and a football field display. Mr. Moran was documenting the whole trip with his camcorder. I was going to share a room with Joe and Etienne. While they slept on real beds, I used one of those folded spare beds that did a number on my back. Once I came inside my hotel room, I used my calling card to call Mom and Dad. It was the only time I called them while at Disney World.

Joe and Etienne were of bigger stature than Tyler. That is the reason for Tyler ending up on the spare bed. He would have complained no matter which bed he was sleeping in due to his sensory overload issues.

On our first full day of the trip we took a bus from our hotel to go to Magic Kingdom. Behind the entrance was Main Street, USA. Straight ahead down the road was the Cinderella Castle. I didn't go inside the castle but I went inside other places. I visited Fantasyland where I saw Mickey Mouse's PhilharMagic. The showing was in 3-D and once I tried to adjust my 3-D glasses, they broke. I had to watch the show holding my glasses and since it was loud I had to block my ears. I later went on this Small World boat ride, where they were singing, "It's a small world after all." After that, I rode this Haunted Mansion ride, where Snow White characters were being displayed.

Then we marched through Liberty Square and into Frontier Land where Splash Mountain was located. I decided not to go on this ride because I'm not a fan of roller coasters and rides like this one. I then moved on with them through Adventureland where the Pirates of the Caribbean were as was the Swiss Family Robinson tree house. There I had my pictures taken with a couple of Disney characters, Captain Hook, and Chip and Dale. Then we crossed the center of Disney World past the statue of Walt Disney to Tomorrowland where I rode a go-kart along Tomorrowland Indy Speedway. Once I finally got to ride, it was not that much fun to tell you the truth. I did not admit it to the people that attended Senior Class trip, but I was feeling disappointed while at "the Happiest Place on Earth."

Tyler has never been a fan of amusement parks. He likes a more predictable setting. The "randomness" of all the sights, sounds, and movements put Tyler on "sensory overload."

Later after lunch, I went aboard this Walt Disney World Railroad. We rode once around Magic Kingdom with stops at Frontierland and Mickey's Toontown Fair. After the train ride, we went to Main Street, USA to catch the parade of Disney stars. During the parade, the sky opened up with authority, and it started to rain. While it was raining, it was coming down in torrents, the parade still went on. I took a few pictures of this parade that not even Mother Nature could dampen the spirit of the characters marching down Main Street, USA. After the parade, it was time for us to go back to the resort, and I was glad that the day was over. Later that night, Etienne, Joe, Mr. Moran, Mr. DeAngelis and I watched the Red Sox beat the Tigers in Detroit.

Tyler had overcome his fear of rain by this point in his life. He still didn't like it, but he could tolerate it. The teachers made a wise decision to allow Tyler to watch the Red Sox game that evening. It gave Tyler a chance to decompress.

Day 3 of the trip was Cinco de Mayo and after we had our breakfast at the food court, we went on the Disney bus to go to Animal Kingdom. This place was much bigger than Magic Kingdom without a doubt. While we were there, we saw a member of the Cotting School class of 1999. Past the entrance was the Oasis area, which included rare animals from all around the world. Then we went through Discovery Island with its main attraction being a big tree to the Africa area. In the Africa area, I got to go on this safari through the Harambe Wildlife Reserve. I went inside this vehicle where it would take me to this land of such beauty and wildlife. I took some pictures of certain animals such as giraffes, rhinoceroses, lions, and more. It's too bad that they didn't come out that good because they got ruined while my camera was going through the X-ray at the security checkpoint at the airport the next day.

After that we went back to Discovery Island to check out that big tree. The big tree was not really a natural tree but it was a nice work of art overall. Inside the big tree was a theater. We went inside there to see a 3-D showing of *It's Tough to Be a Bug!* This time my 3-D glasses didn't break, and I got to see the show without holding my glasses. The show appeared entertaining, and the characters were in your face. Just like at PhilharMagic, it was loud and noisy and unkind to my ears.

Unpredictable loud noises are actually painful for Tyler. He can be at a stadium to watch a sporting event, because he understands the sport and is prepared for the loud noises associated with the game or match.

After the show, we visited DinoLand USA. Next to DinoLand USA was the construction of a new area called Expedition Everest, which was going to be located in the Asia section of the park. In DinoLand USA, we saw Dino-Sue, the largest *Tyrannosaurus rex* ever discovered, at forty feet long and thirteen feet tall at the hip. Then we went inside Dinosaur, an indoor thrill ride. Dinosaur was the first and only real thrill ride I've ever gone on during the trip to Disney World. I waited in line with my group while I learned the hard truth about dinosaurs. Next, I got to take my seats with the group on the ride where we traveled back 65 million years in time to rescue dinosaurs from extinction. Sometimes the ride was dark. At times the ride was scary, noisy, and exciting and fast and bumpy. The Dinosaur ride was all right nonetheless. After the ride, we all checked out the gift shop where I got this Dinosaur clearance card. After Dinosaur we left DinoLand USA to eat lunch at Discovery Island. For the first time on the trip, the sun was shining after being so cloudy for most of the day and entire trip.

Tyler made the best of this situation because he has such an intense need to learn. He doesn't really like to be entertained as much as he likes to learn something.

After lunch we had to go to Camp Minnie-Mickey. Inside the camp there was this spacious wooden structure, and inside this spacious wooden structure was the Festival of the Lion King. This festival was a circus act in tribute to the movie *The Lion King*. At the beginning of the show, the crowd made some animal sounds, I made a giraffe noise with the audience in the section that I was seated in. It was pretty interesting to see all those performers and acrobats dressed in flashy and festive colors. Simba the lion was there, as was Timon and Pumbaa, my favorite characters from the movie. The show was a half hour long, and it ended on a high note as did the trip to Animal Kingdom. Before we left for the hotel, I bought a hat at the outpost near the entrance/exit. I wore the hat for the rest of the trip.

After Animal Kingdom we went back to the All-Star Sports Resort to take a dip into the outdoor pool. This was definitely not ideal pool weather because the clouds made the pool a lot less fun. This was the only time I got wet during the trip unless I count being in the monsoon during the parade the day before. Later in the day we went to visit Downtown Disney. This place was downright beautiful I admit it but I could not find any places that were my cup of tea. I sat on the banks overlooking Village Lake while my group was pondering about what we should do here. Next, we went to dinner where I had some steak, the best meal I had on the trip. Finally, it was time for us to go back to the resort.

This vacation really took its toll on Tyler. He had to stay present and focused all the time. He was basically in "survival mode" for the trip.

Thursday, May 6 was the fourth and final day of the Cotting School Senior class trip. We were supposed to go visit Epcot Center that day but it did not happen. We were going to leave in a few hours so the teachers took us on a tour of the entire All-Star Resort. Like I said before, the All-Star Resort consisted of three areas: movies, music, and sports. We ran into some nice places to have pictures taken of all four seniors, Joe, Etienne, Franny, and I. After probably the most tranquil part of the trip, we packed our bags, checked out of our rooms and said goodbye to the resort. Before we left, I got to play in the arcade for a while and won some prizes. Then we all went outside to enjoy some Florida sunshine. It was the only time on the trip when the sun was hot because every day it was mostly cloudy with instances of rain. The bus came to pick us up and take us to the airport. Once I was at the airport, I had a couple of hot dogs at Nathan's. Then I went to the gate where our flight bound for Logan Airport. I just couldn't wait to get back home.

I was more than glad to see my parents again when I first saw them at the baggage claim area at Logan Airport. I was also glad to be home in the state of Massachusetts because until the Senior Class trip, I've never been this far from home without my parents. I didn't go directly home from the airport because I had to go to CTDS in Lexington to attend their alumni picnic. This was my sixth alumni picnic since my last day of school there in 1999. I got to see most of my old teachers and friends from back in the day. I told them about my trip to Disney World, and I'm sure they found it interesting. After the picnic, I went back home to good old Tyngsboro, Massachusetts, for the first time since last Tuesday.

Just to be honest, I thought the trip to Disney World would be fantastic, but in the end it was anything but. The weather wasn't all that good, and I didn't like the food because it wasn't healthy. I just felt overwhelmed with all those attractions, all those tourists, all the children crying. But at least I was man enough to keep my cool and behave myself. I realized how far I have come from the little child I was. That trip to Florida in 2005 showed me that I was not a boy anymore. In less than a month I was no longer going to be a high school student. I was going to set foot in the real world.

Tyler was MORE than glad to be finished with the trip. I still believe (especially after reading what he mentioned above) this trip was a necessary tool for him to use the skills he has learned and have a more mature experience, knowing that he can manage without Mom and Dad.

Goodbye Cotting

SINCE I GOT THE JOB at Lowell General Hospital, I did little schoolwork. In the middle of my last school year, I got a new assistant teacher named Mr. Thomas. I did manage to squeeze in some reading time in the last month of the school year to show my teacher, the then-twenty-three-year-old Ms. Harkins, that I could work hard at school while not being at school most of the time. I read three books about a boy with attention deficit disorder—*Joey Pigza Swallowed the Key, Joey Pigza Loses Control,* and *What Would Joey Do?*—all within a month before graduation. The last month of school was very special to me. There was not really that much schoolwork besides my reading, just games to play with my classmates and teachers. I did not go to the Cotting School prom after saying that I was going to. Instead I attended to Kids in Disability Sports banquet in Dracut on the night of the prom. I knew that I missed a once in a lifetime occasion but there was one place where I'd rather be and that was at the banquet. I do not regret not going to the prom at all. One week before my graduation, there was an end-of-school-year awards ceremony at the auditorium. For the fourth year in a row, I received an Athletic Achievement Award. I also won the Bringing Home the Bacon Award from Ms. Harkins's class. I had no idea what that award meant to me back then, but now I know that it means making money in order to feed your family. In the Cotting School basketball banquet that year, I was chosen as the team's Most Valuable Player for the second time in four years.

Ron and I knew that the prom would not be a fun experience for Tyler. He loves music, but he has to be in control of deciding each song that is played. He doesn't like the spontaneity of songs being played randomly.

He likes a specific song list. He feels better when life is predictable. We decided we would push him to attend the prom. The Bringing Home the Bacon Award really confused Tyler. This happens all the time to him. He interprets everything that is said to him in literal terms. Once he learns the inference, it doesn't bother him anymore. But it can be problematic because he doesn't always know what you are talking about if you use generalizations or inaccuracies.

My final day of school at Cotting School in Lexington, Massachusetts, was on a sunny Friday, June 3, 2005. I was saying goodbye to a place that I called a home away from home. It's strange to realize the fact that you are leaving a place where you go every weekday for four years besides holidays, vacations, and summers. Back then I could hardly imagine not going back to school anymore. During my final days at Cotting School, I brought in a picture book to show Ms. Harkins. Also in the picture book was the tour of Fenway Park with my Cotting School summer class in 2002, some images from Seabrook, and many more. Also that day, there was a little party at the cafeteria. I said goodbye to all of my classmates and the teachers that made a big impact on me, kept me in line, and made me a better human being. I learned a heck of a lot from them, did my hardest to get good grades and to have done so well at Cotting. In 2003 and 2004, I had to buy a Cotting School yearbook, but since it was my senior year I did not have to pay for one this time. This time my 2005 Cotting School yearbook, the *Torch* as it was called, had my name on it. My yearbook featured notes of encouragement from David W. Manzo, the president of Cotting School, and Dr. Michael L. Talbot, the headmaster.

There was also this small section attached to my yearbook called "New England Champions," a small memento of the highlights from the Red Sox and Patriots championship seasons in 2004 and 2005. I was voted most athletic by my peers in the school yearbook for the third or fourth straight year. I don't have a yearbook from my first year with the school. The year 2005 was remarkable for the former students of the Community Therapeutic Day School. Also in the yearbook, all four seniors including me listed their best friends, teachers, school memories, hobbies, favorite music, and future plans. My favorite memories with Cotting School include scoring a game-winning layup to win my first basketball game as a member of the Cotting Basketball Team, winning the Most Valuable Award on the basketball team in my first year at the school, and building a Ping-Pong table at Industrial arts class in the spring of 2004. I listed classic rock, heavy metal, and adult contemporary as my favorite types of music. I listed *Patton, Hoosiers, Miracle,* and *The Matrix* trilogy as my favorite movies. My future plans were for me to become a basketball player. Unfortunately as I grew older, I grew closer and closer to giving up on my basketball dreams and focused on something else instead, but I'll get to that later. I put down playing and watching sports as my hobbies. I was looking forward to my last basketball season with the Cotting School, the ski trip, and completing the mission, which meant that I was almost done with my four years at this school.

I listed David, Joe, Peter, Brian, Kurt, and Michael M. as my best friends at Cotting School. I could have put down some other best friends, but I would have run out of space. I had more teachers than friends listed in my yearbook because I looked up to them more than my friends throughout my time at Cotting. I put down a lot of favorite teachers in my yearbook, including Ms. Clark Mr. Phelan, Mr. DeAngelis, and Mr. Navaroli, who was a custodian. Just before the school year ended, Mr. Navaroli wrote this in my yearbook.

Tyler,

Always remember that the world is full of loose talk, false promises, and glitz. Courage has always been a rare virtue. At your age and time you have a chance to change it. The challenges will be great but the rewards will be greater. Character is not everything, but the only thing that matters in an uncertain world. Your job ahead is clear—be an inspiration to others. Be careful. Strive to be happy.

Sincerely,
Mr. Navaroli

I have had a lot of great support over my four years at this school from many teachers and faculty members, but the one gentleman that made the most significant impact on me in those four years was Mr. Navaroli. Once or twice a year, he would hold those impromptu classes.

He brought along some of his tapes for all of the students to listen and sheets of lyrics from the songs he was playing. Most of the songs he played were from the 1960s, the type of music I still listen to today. He would explain the meaning of character, war, and finding out "who am I?" During this session about war, he talked about the unknown soldier and the "forgotten sailor." It turned out that he himself was the "forgotten sailor," and he brought a picture of him in his navy uniform. He was an avid fan of the Boston Red Sox and the game of baseball. This guy was there to enlighten me just as Ms. Clark was enlightening me.

One time in November of 2002, he had me do a music report, and I listed whatever songs that I listened to on the radio on the way home from school and what those songs meant to me. In my report, I wrote that music makes you feel emotionally sound, and it makes you forget the hard days. After that he wrote:

To Tyler,

> *You did a great job in evaluating the different songs on 103.3 and other radio stations. You can hear a lot just by listening. Music has the power to educate us and hopefully make us into the best people we can possibly be. Always think.*

> *Sincerely,*
> *Mr. Navaroli*
> *Grade: A*

Every time I encountered him, he would always begin a conversation with me with six words: "*What do you say, Mr. La-ga-say?*" Here are some examples of what I said to him.

In 2003, the day after the Red Sox lost to the Yankees in the American League Championship Series, Mr. Navaroli asked that six-word question, and I replied to him, "It's not fair."

Then Mr. Navaroli said to me, "Life is not fair."

Then the very next year, when the Red Sox finally went all the way to win their first World Series title in eighty-six years, he asked me, "*What do you say, Mr. La-ga-say?*"

Simply put, I responded, "Now I can die in peace." I admit that Mr. Navaroli was not pleased when I said that.

My days at Cotting School were coming to an end. For almost four years, I rode to school in a minivan, through traffic every now and then, with Loren and Wally on the radio every morning. Most often I would arrive to school early and go to the Upper School library where I would spend my fifteen minutes to take refuge and read the Boston Globe before coming to my classroom. After that would be whatever the class schedule had to offer on Mondays, Tuesdays, Wednesdays, Thursdays, and Fridays. Now it was time for me to say goodbye to all that.

Just like at CTDS, and just like the Gifford School, I was going to say goodbye to everybody and everything inside and outside the school. I was going to miss a lot of good people there, the kind of people that had made an immense impact on me. I was going to miss my classmates David, Brian, Ruby, Maura, Jenna, and Becky. I was going to miss some of my basketball teammates, some nonclassmates, and many others. I was going to miss my therapists, my teachers including Ms. Harkins, my gym teachers, my basketball coaches, the headmaster Mr. Talbot, the then first-year president Mr. Manzo, and the one and only Mr. Navaroli. I was going to miss the lady who gave me my first tour of Cotting School and introduced me to my classmates before I officially became a student there, Janine Brown-Smith. Finally, I was going to miss the graduating class of 2005 Etienne, Franny, and Joe.

Then there are the ones that I knew in my first two years at this school. I was already missing my old classmates from my first three years. I was already missing nonclassmates, old basketball teammates, and old teachers as well. Then there were the two students who passed away during my years as a student there, Michael M. and my classmate Kurt. I was about to know them very well, but they were suddenly taken from the Cotting family and me. They were very young when they died but they are in a better place now.

When I first came to Cotting School, I didn't understand why some students used wheelchairs and walkers, and I didn't understand why some of them could not speak. By the time I was ready to graduate, I had a clear understanding of what their physical and intellectual disabilities were. They taught me how to treat them with the utmost dignity and respect because they were human beings, they were people and nothing else. The staff and faculty were there to keep me within the rules of Cotting School and to make me a better human being. Just think, at fourteen years old I had just overcome two of the most trying years of my life. I had certainly come a long way from that fourteen-year-old individual. At Cotting, I have never been around such nice people, such well-behaved students. I learned a heck of a lot from my teachers, and I worked my hardest to treat other students the way I would like to be treated. My four years at Cotting School went by quickly and here I was, eighteen years old and with my whole life ahead of me. Now it was time for me to move on to the next chapter in my life.

Tyler has always been more comfortable around adults as compared to people his age. He has always been interested in world and current events. He has never been particularly interested in the latest Hollywood gossip. For that reason, he seems to relate to older people as compared to his peers. I must admit, it has gotten much easier as he has grown older. He does seem to have more in common with his peers now.

Graduation

THIS WAS THE MOST IMPORTANT day of my life to date and I remember it well. It was early in the evening, Friday, June 3, 2005. It was time for me to graduate at long last. Before I left for the ceremony, I put on my 2004 Red Sox World Series Champion polo for what would turn out to be a surprise for later in the ceremony. I got a few cards of congratulations from most of my relatives. Then I went to Cotting School in the historic town of Lexington, Massachusetts, one more time. The people that came to my graduation ceremony besides Mom and Dad were my brother Clint and his girlfriend, my aunt Lauri, my two grandmothers Memere Lorraine Lagasse and Grammy Effie Christine Bell, and my godparents Terry and Roger Marion.

During the slide presentation of the Cotting School graduating class of 2005 at the auditorium, two songs "Child of Mine" and "Stand by Me" were being played. I was at the KIVA center, the room next to the gymnasium putting on my blue gown and blue hat with a golden yellow tassel to match the school colors with my fellow seniors, Etienne, Joe and Franny. As soon as we were ready, we walked to the hallway next to the auditorium and waited there until we got our cue to enter. According to the program, the class of 2005 motto was "The class of '05 is a four-star class!" During the slide presentation, there was an image of all four members of the class of 2005, Joe, Etienne, Franny, and I. In this image, I was saying, "All for one, and one for all, the class of 2005, rock on! Hoowah!"

After the slide show ended, Mr. David Manzo, the first-year Cotting School president, introduced the Cotting School class of 2005. It was our cue to enter. We entered the auditorium one by one in order of our height from shortest to tallest, Franny first, then Etienne, then me, and finally Joe. We all walked in between a row of some teachers and faculty members that have had a profound influence on me and the rest of the seniors. Then we exited out the side door of the auditorium after passing through the faculty members, and reentered the auditorium by coming up a ramp into a back room and onto the stage the same way that we entered the auditorium. Everything went smoothly because we rehearsed as much as we could up to this day. Then we took our seats by the time "Pomp and Circumstance" was done.

As soon as the audience was seated, the headmaster Dr. Michael Talbot was ready to speak about this event. He called this evening both a happy day and a sad day, happy because we seniors were ready to take the next step in their lives, and a sad day because it was the last day of our high school lives and that we were not going to be students here that much longer. In my opinion, Dr. Talbot was best known for his collection of colorful neckties that he wore to school. I think those neckties gave him plenty of character. Dr. Talbot was a kindhearted gentleman to be with and to talk to, and he showed that kindhearted attitude when he spoke to the audience that evening.

After Dr. Talbot was finished speaking to the audience, John Beach of the Board of Trustees made his way to the podium. He said the Board of Trustees' purpose to Cotting School was to help the teachers and staff. He said his congratulations and thanked the staff, the teachers, and most importantly the students and seniors for doing the best they could during our time at school. Mr. Beach called the seniors a "lucky group" and said that we were lucky to be here in this marvelous facility, lucky to have the care of our families and teachers, and also said that the Board of Trustees were lucky to be a part of our lives.

Then the senior class advisor and my math teacher, Mr. Moran, took his turn to speak. According to Mr. Moran, the seniors never had a single harsh word for one another, we never had any significant complaints about anything to each other, and that together we demonstrated a wonderfully positive attitude. After Mr. Moran was finished, the seniors took their turns speaking. Joe went first, and he talked about his friends, teachers, favorite classes, and Cotting memories and activities and thanked his mom. Then Franny came to talk about her friends, teachers, staff, and fond memories and thanked her parents. Etienne was next to mention his friends, staff, classes, and memories at Cotting School as well.

As for me, I was trying to maintain my composure throughout the ceremonies because I was the last Cotting student to speak to the audience. I typed most of my speech notes myself with the help of my mother. I began working on my graduation speech the week before the ceremony. I did all I could to keep myself from doing foolish things, such as sudden body movements, gestures, and inappropriate facial expressions in front of the cameras, because this ceremony was being taped. As soon as Mr. Moran called on me, I got out of my seat, walked to the podium, took out my speech notes, and began to speak to the crowd. Unlike the previous three speeches done by the seniors, mine was the longest any senior did that night at seven and a half minutes long. It must have been the biggest speech of the exercises. Somehow it would not be my last, but I'll get to that later.

In my graduation speech, I began by describing my first day of school on September 4, 2001. I mentioned how beautiful this place was when I first came inside it as a Cotting School student. I talked about going to my new homeroom and taking my first class there on my first day. I then went on about my favorite subjects, my favorite teachers, and my friends at Cotting, all the programs I joined—such as the Summer Program and Circle of Friends—and the trips I went on, such as Mount Sunapee and Disney World. I listed being on the basketball team as my favorite part of being at Cotting School.

Then I went on to talk about the present and how much has changed after being in this school for four years. I thanked many people that have come and gone during that time, my classmates, my friends, my teachers, everyone else at Cotting that have made an impact on me, and last but not least my parents who have guided me since the day I was born. I went on to say that it was my turn to use the tools that I have taken from Cotting and use them in the real world. I concluded my speech by saying something from the late comedian Rodney Dangerfield in the movie *Back to School*. I told the audience, "You gotta look out for #1, but don't settle for #2." The last thing I said was "Cotting School is #1. My future is as bright as it can be. Best wishes to the class of 2005."

Out of everybody who came to speak at the graduation ceremony, I must have had the longest ovation of any that night. Mr. Moran called my speech "eloquently put." He said the seniors had a well-earned sense of accomplishment getting through this school year. Mr. Moran also announced that we seniors decided to carry over the funds from our graduating class to the Cotting School class of 2006. Then Mr. Moran talked about our class gift in dedication to the memory of Kurt who died in 2004. It meant that I was not done speaking, so I went back to the podium when it was my turn. I spoke very passionately about Kurt, telling him that he was an inspiration to me and the rest of his peers. To honor his life and memory, I presented a bench made by many students at industrial arts class. The bench was finished and ready just in time for the graduation ceremony. After I was done speaking, I helped move the bench so that everybody in the audience could witness the hard work that the Cotting School students put into this project. It was an extremely nice-looking bench. Later in 2005, the bench was dedicated in honor of Kurt and was placed behind the school.

Then it was time for Joe and Etienne to play their musical instruments onstage with the instrumental ensemble in front of the stage. They were about to perform Beethoven's "Symphony No. 7," with Joe playing the dulcimer and Etienne playing the viola. Beethoven, like nearly all of the Cotting School students, had a disability at the same time he was one of the greatest musicians and composers of his time. In the beginning of the performance, Joe played a few notes on the dulcimer while the piano was being played in the background. Then it was Etienne's turn to perform. Etienne did a marvelous job playing with his viola. The majority of the song was done by Etienne, Joe did the opening and Etienne did the rest. I think Etienne, in spite of being pretty nervous early in the ceremonies, sounded wicked good throughout his performance. The auditorium crowd loved the performance, so did the people onstage, and so did I.

After the music was over, Mr. Manzo made his way to the podium to talk about his first year at Cotting School. Mr. Manzo was from the state of Connecticut, therefore he lived closer to New York City than Boston and so like most residents there, he was a New York Yankees fan. In his speech, he talked about how he spent parts of his first few weeks into his new job trying to convert all of the Cotting students from Red Sox fans to Yankee fans. That would have made Josh H. very proud because he, too, was a Yankee fan. However, after the Red Sox beat the Yankees in such historical fashion in the American League Championship Series and followed that up by winning the World Series one week later, Mr. Manzo gave up his Cotting Yankee movement. After he talked about his "massive failure," I opened up my blue graduation gown to show off my 2004 Red Sox World Championship polo shirt. I wore that shirt to the ceremonies because I thought it would be a fitting tribute to the biggest sports moment during my last school year at Cotting. I didn't expect Mr. Manzo to bring up the Yankees, but I suppose my timing was perfect. Obviously my shirt exposure was the biggest surprise of the 2005 Cotting School graduation exercises.

Mr. Manzo spoke eloquently about the seniors. He said he found tenaciousness and toughness in us and that we overcame some seemingly insurmountable obstacles to get to this point. He described his definition of graduation as taking stock of our educational and personal accomplishments. He called all four seniors "four of the most successful people in America." He made a few personal remarks to each senior starting with Joe. Mr. Manzo said that Joe taught him the rules of Cotting Soccer and kidded about the Yankees. He said that Joe had a warm personality that makes us all feel welcome. Then he talked about Etienne and his music playing. He said that Etienne's music makes the world brighter, richer, and happier, makes our lives better, and soothes our souls. Next, he talked about me and my versatile athletic abilities. He said that my athletic gift "excites all who watch you." He called me an "excellent athlete" and "more than that, a superior teammate." He also said that I make my teammates around me better players and better people. He finished by saying that he had great respect for me. Finally, he described Franny as one of the kindest people, greets everybody with a "warm" smile, and makes all of our lives richer. He said that she had the gift of being an artist and that her art brings pleasure to us all. Before he was done, Mr. Manzo said a quote that he used many a time during the Cotting School's Sunshine Breakfast. That quote was used in the play *Les Miserables*. He said, "To love another person is to see the face of God."

After his speech, he gave out the awards and scholarships to the seniors. The first one was the Edward H. Bradford Memorial Award, named after the cofounder of Cotting School, for the student demonstrating wisdom and character. I thought I was going to get that award because of that word, *character*, because I felt that I was a man of character according to one Mr. John Navaroli. That award went to Joe. Then there was the Charles E. Cotting Award for the student that demonstrated courage, industry, and dedication. Franny was the recipient of that award. Next was the Barbara D. Hardaway Scholarship to the graduate who most closely reflects the outstanding qualities of a leader and has a positive attitude, as demonstrated by former Cotting student Barbara D. Hardaway. That award went to me. The last award was the Charles H. Taylor Memorial Scholarship to the graduate with concern for the welfare of all children with disabilities and who exemplifies firm leadership, ethical standards, and calm judgment, and it went to Etienne.

After the scholarship presentations, a commencement speaker appeared and he was not like any other speaker I've ever seen before. The speaker was Dennis Heaphy, a person who held three master's degrees, one in public health, one in education, and one in divinity. He studied at Boston University and Harvard University and became a chaplain at Georgetown University. At some point during his life, he became paralyzed from the neck down after some kind of accident. His malady is similar to the one that former Boston University hockey player Travis Roy has. He gets around on his wheelchair with the same sip-and-puff technique that Roy does. Heaphy had traveled as far as Nicaragua to reach out to people with all sorts of disabilities ever since his accident.

Early in his speech, he talked about a book that he read about the soldiers from World War II and how they were also known as the "greatest generation." Dennis said that he didn't believe those people were the greatest generation. Instead he called us seniors the greatest generation. He later had a few more things to say to each of the seniors. He said Joe was the first of his family to graduate from high school. Then Heaphy made some remarks about me. He said he liked my speech, and that Lowell General Hospital was grateful for my contributions since I first worked for them last December. He said that I have already accomplished a tremendous amount. And he said that my mom, my dad, and brother Clint would be proud of me. Then he talked about Franny and how he loved her works of art. Finally, he spoke about Etienne and how he admired his music.

Dennis also explained what was happening to the disabled community in general. He said that the Americans with Disabilities Act was "under attack," disability support services were being cut, and that there was "rampant discrimination against people with disabilities." "The world needs you," he said. I believed in what he just said and I also believed that we seniors were a part of the greatest generation. He talked about his best friend named Jim, who suffers from cerebral palsy. He described Jim as "more beautiful than you want to know." He also said that every time he feels down, he doesn't call his brothers for help. He calls his best friend Jim.

Dennis said to the seniors that we are "beautifully and wonderfully made." He also used that term beautiful from a Christina Aguilera song titled "Beautiful." He admitted that Christina Aguilera was not his favorite music artist. Still, he used the main chorus of her song to describe the seniors. "You are beautiful in every single way, words won't bring you down." And he went on with the lyrics for a while. Also in his speech, he told the seniors to celebrate today as tomorrow will bring new challenges and new opportunities and that we will need everything that we have learned at Cotting to overcome them. He also said, "No matter what we do, no matter what they say, and everywhere we go, the sun won't always shine, but tomorrow will find a way." He implored to the seniors, "Know that you are beautiful, and nothing can take that away."

After Dennis Heaphy was finished with his speech, Etienne was called on to do a recital of *Lanterns on the Levee*. Before he sang, he said, "I'm dedicating this song to my mom, who has always been there for me, and I will always be there for you." Remember, he had to play Beethoven's "Symphony No. 7" on the viola. I have fond memories hearing that song many times in music class.

Finally, it was time for all the seniors to receive their Cotting School diplomas. After we all picked up our diplomas, we were no longer students, we were no longer seniors, and we were no longer the Cotting School graduating class of 2005. We were now and forever known throughout this school as *graduates*.

As soon as the instrumental ensemble started playing "Voluntary in D," the graduates stood up one at a time and went out through the back of the stage and entered the auditorium through the side door. Mr. Manzo was there to turn the yellow tassels of our blue hats from right to left starting with Joe, then me, then Etienne, and finally Franny. For some reason, Joe did not exit the auditorium like he did during the rehearsals. Instead he stayed inside the auditorium floor to find his family. I followed suit by breaking protocol to find my family. I hugged every person that I knew, my mom, my dad, my brother and his girlfriend, my grandmothers, my godparents, and my aunt Lauri. Then I was told to exit the auditorium and head for the cafeteria.

At the beginning of the reception, my fellow seniors and I shook hands with everybody who came to the graduation exercises. I had pictures taken of me. I had cards given to me. I was not only celebrating an important day in my life, I was saying goodbye one final time to my fellow seniors, my friends, my teachers, the administrators, and of course, Mr. Navaroli the custodian. He gave me two old issues of Sports Illustrated, and two Red Sox World Series championship team pictures, one from 2004 and one from 1918. He also gave me a copy of his poem called "A Bunch of Idiots" about the 2004 Boston Red Sox playoff comeback. This poem went like this:

A Bunch of Idiots
By: John L. Navaroli

On the evening of Saturday, October 16, 2004 the heart of Red Sox Nation was breaking. Our ace pitcher had previously torn up his right ankle and he looked finished for the season. The Sox were playing a very talented and solid team (with baseball's highest payroll) and were losing their third straight game by a score of 19-8. No one had ever come back from a 0-3 deficit in post-season play. Tears were shed by the faithful at Fenway and the bunch of idiots took notice. The issue now seemed how and when it would end? One last nagging question was lingering in the shadows of the souls of Red Sox Nation: "Why not us?"

There is no need to go over the details of what happened and how the Boston Red Sox made baseball history by winning eight straight post-season games. This is now baseball folklore and common knowledge. After the 19-8 loss the Sox seemed to play baseball pitch-to-pitch, moment-to-moment. Time seemed to be suspended as if in a dream like state and games ran into each other. Citizens of Red Sox Nation were sleep deprived but nobody minded it. Adults were giddy and childlike; children spoke of wisdom and insight. Terminally dying people willed themselves to live longer to witness the outcome of both series.

The team and entire ball club collectively faced themselves, their history, and found strength of character and courage and decided to charge forward to victory. The bunch of idiots defeated imaginary curses and real curses such as: cronyism, alcoholism, racism, incompetence, and irrelevance. When history is written for the 2004 season with its bunch of idiots it will paraphrase Winston S. Churchill, that so few did so much for so many, and that this was Red Sox Nations "Finest Hour."

Dr. Talbot gave me this book from Dr. Seuss called *Oh, the Places You'll Go!* Inside the book, he wrote, "Tyler, May the happy thoughts in this book come true for you! Best Wishes, Dr. Talbot." As the reception was coming to a close, it was time for me to fly like the Falcon, the Cotting School mascot and nickname. I have earned my wings after four tumultuous years. I have learned a lot during my four years there. I have touched so many lives there. I was blessed to be their best athlete every year. Now it was time to say my final goodbye to the school that I called a second home from my first day on a warm Tuesday, September 4, 2001, to my last day on Friday, June 3, 2005.

I walked out of the cafeteria, down the long hallway through the reception area, past the garden near the entrance where I entered the school for my first tour, took a right turn before passing the music room and the ramp for students in wheel chairs, took a left turn into another hallway, past the nurses and dentist offices, past the desktop publishing room, past the art room and in between the work skills room and the industrial arts room until I exited the school. I knew that I was not going back to Cotting School for quite a while. I was so used to being at school that I had no idea what it was going to be like not to go there again. When I first came to Cotting School, I was a boy with a lot of heart and potential. When I left Cotting School in my blue graduation attire on the night of Friday, June 3, 2005, I was on my way toward being a man. I was now a high school graduate that was about to enter the next phase of my life.

The graduation ceremony was magnificent. Tyler had so many wonderful experiences at the Cotting School. He matured so much during his time there. He leaned a lot about kindness, compassion and character. To this day, he mentions the influence that everyone at that school had on him, in particular, Mr. Navaroli.

My Cotting School picture from the 2001-02 school year.

Just before leaving for the double wedding anniversary celebration for my parents and grandparents on June 19, 2002. (L to R: Clint, Lorraine "Memere" Lagasse, me, and Edmond "Pepere" Lagasse)

Posing in front of the "Green Monster" on my tour of Fenway Park with students at Cotting School in July, 2002. I came up with the idea of going on a tour of Fenway with my class!

Summer work: My 1ˢᵗ paycheck from my first summer job at Kimball's in Westford back in 2003.

Summer fun: One of my hobbies during the summer in my teenage years was making sports venues out of sand. I didn't seem to copy any particular stadium or ballpark, I just wanted to have fun building something.

The Cotting School Class of 2005 during our trip to Disney World. (L to R: Franny, Joe, Etienne, and me)

The proudest day of my life to date, which was June 3, 2005, the night I graduated from Cotting School. Posing in my blue cap and gown between Mom and Dad...

... and walking toward my future.

Life after Graduation

TWO DAYS AFTER I GRADUATED, I started to do some writing in my journals. Originally, my journal entries were going to be about the summer of 2005, but after the summer was over I decided to keep on writing and I have been writing in journals ever since. Early on, my journal entries were brief and they didn't take up more than one page. I just wrote about small events such as golf outings, cookouts, work, and lazy days. As I got older, my entries became longer and the events that I wrote about in my journals became more significant.

Ron and I have found that Tyler's journaling has a tremendous calming effect on him. Whenever he is feeling really stressed or his routine has gone awry, he can usually be found quietly writing in his journal. The written expression affords him the opportunity to clear his mind and not be interrupted in his thoughts.

The first month of my life after graduation was great. I received at least twenty graduation cards on or after my graduation day from relatives, friends, classmates, teachers, and even some people at Cotting School whom I didn't know too well. Most of the cards were about wishing me the best of luck in the future. I was amazed and a little overwhelmed with all the support I got after graduation. I wrote many thank you cards to the people that wished me the best in the future. I wouldn't have my own graduation party until Labor Day weekend.

My summer of 2005 did not officially start until three weeks after Graduation as I had to finish my job at Lowell General Hospital as part of my co-op program with the Merrimack Education Center. The good news was that I had two free weekdays so that I could spend those days with Dad. During my days off from work, I would go golfing with Dad.

On one of the weekends in the month of June, I went fishing at the Tyngsboro Sportsmen's Club with the Kids in Disability Sports group. After the regular work season with MEC was over, Dad and I played forty-five holes of golf together in a span of four days—eighteen holes one day, eighteen holes the next, and then nine holes two days later.

At one point near the end of June, while I was hitting a bucket of golf balls at a driving range in Andover with the KIDS group, the strangest thing happened there. Once as I was hitting some range balls with my driver one evening, my swinging power caused the shaft of the club next to the head to snap once it hit the ground. I killed my own driver by accident. The driver was a part of a set of clubs that my dad got me. They were not even three years old, they were cheap, but they were not overused. It wasn't the first time I broke a golf club and it wasn't going to be the last. I still keep my broken driver, the shaft and the head, in the closet of my room.

The day after I broke my driver, my dad took me to Golf n' Ski Warehouse in nearby Hudson, New Hampshire, to try out a left-handed Nike driver that cost $300. It was such a great club that I was hitting range balls with both precision and power. I liked that driver but I was not willing to spend $300 on it. After passing on the Nike driver, Dad and I went farther up north to a Play It Again Sports store in Nashua, New Hampshire. They had a left-handed driver there, which I purchased for a cheap $50. It was not the best driver I've ever had, but it was a start. When I first used this driver, I was slicing the ball way to the left. It was a far cry from the Nike driver that I tried out at Golf & Ski.

We have always stressed the importance of spending your money wisely and this driver was not the wisest purchase for Tyler. We also felt it would be good for him to learn to wait for something that he really wanted. We felt that if he really wanted that driver, he would really want it in six months from now!

The beginning of July was mostly fun. On the first two days leading up to the Fourth of July, I played golf at Green Meadow and went to two cookouts. The first cookout was at Rick Reault's house down the road where I got to go swimming, hang out with friends, and enjoy some fireworks late at night. The next day, I went to a second one at my uncle Bob's campground next to a pond in North Salem, New Hampshire. There were wall-to-wall fireworks blanketing the pond later on that night. On the way home, we were stuck in traffic in nearby Pelham because some people were leaving a fireworks display outside a school. It took fifteen minutes to travel five hundred yards, but to me it felt like forever. I didn't take it that well but I managed to get through it.

The fact is Tyler reverted to some of his old ways. He was whining the same way a four year old would whine. That is not so bad when you have a four year old, but it can drive you crazy when your "child" is eighteen!

After a pretty good first month after graduation, for some reason or whatever, things took a turn for the worse in the month of July. On the day after Independence Day, I returned to work as part of this Merrimack Education Center Summer Program that ran for eight weeks. I worked at Lowell General Hospital for three days, and I worked at Kimball's for two days. In my first week I only worked four days. After that it was five days a week, every week until the program was over.

One thing I didn't like about the program was how I was transported to my job and back. My cab company would pick me up and take me to the MEC building. There were some passengers in the same cab that went to their buildings before my driver took me to my building. After that I would hang out at the MEC building for a while before the drivers from MEC took me and several others in a big van to their job sites. There were some times when I would pass my house on the way to my jobsites or to the MEC building. After coming back to the MEC building from my jobsite, I would wait until my cab company would come and pick me up at MEC and take me home. Before the driver from my cab company took me home, the other passengers had to be dropped off to their homes away from mine or their afterschool places. It was definitely a waste of time for me and it didn't make sense at all.

As the month of July progressed, it kept getting worse and worse by the day. One time in the first week of July, while I was on the way to the MEC building, we were waiting for the traffic light to turn green when one of the passengers just got out of the cab in the middle of traffic and started walking out on the street. The cabdriver didn't do anything. She just let the passenger go, and so we went to MEC without the passenger. It is none of my business but that passenger had serious behavioral problems. It was not going to be the last time in which I had to put up with unacceptable behavior from the MEC students.

I tolerated a little bit of bad behavior in the first two weeks of the MEC Summer Program, but in the third and fourth weeks, it started to get out of control. There was this one kid who sat in the front seat of the van who used the F-word many times. It bothered me very much but I didn't complain about it. There were also some girls on the van that felt insulted after they overheard some boys making some disrespectful remarks about them. It hurt me because I was overwhelmed by their attitudes. Then one time there was a hip-hop song in Spanish that was playing on the radio in the van and it further overwhelmed me. I completely lost it and yelled out loud, "Speak f——ing English!" in front of everybody inside the van. When I arrived at the MEC building from my jobsite I broke down and cried. I don't want to make any excuses but those kids in the van kind of made me want to swear out loud. I don't like to hear bad words and I am not the kind of person that would use such words. I was told by the people at MEC not to be hard on myself. I tried my best to keep my sanity for the duration of the Summer Program, but the worst was yet to come.

One time on the way to Kimball's, I took the wrong van by mistake. Instead of going to Westford, I went through Nashua, New Hampshire, and even past my house. It was the most stressful day of my summer. The ride to Kimball's took at least an hour and a half because of some traffic and the driver had to go do the drop-offs. This is coming from one who is used to rigid time schedules. I was feeling more frustrated the longer I was inside that van. The breaking point came when I kicked a window handle loose when a stoplight was about to turn red. Once again, I let my anger get the best of me. The MEC driver was trying to reach out to me by saying, "Do you want to talk about it?"

I screamed at the MEC driver, "NO! It doesn't matter. You can't change what you did!" and then I just jumped onto the next row of seats closer to the back of the van until the last passenger was dropped off. I could have handled it better, but on that day, I did not take it like a man.

After the driver dropped off the last passenger before me, I decided to go to the front of the van and have a chat while we were headed for Kimball's. My driver was trying to explain to me why I was going to arrive at my jobsite very late and why this summer has been crazy. I later understood what the driver was trying to say. I took the situation really hard but I managed to pull myself together as soon as we got to Kimball's. By the time I arrived, it was already 10:15 a.m., more than an hour later than my start time. I told my boss at Kimball's as much as I could about why I was late for work. My boss understood how I felt and let me hit a bucket of golf balls at the driving range for a while to blow off some steam. That was nice of my boss to let me erase all that stress that was put upon me. I went on to have a very good day afterward, and then a very good weekend, and then a very good month of August.

I lived through the toughest day of 2005 after a series of tough days. However, what I have endured that day is nothing compared to what some other people around the world are forced to deal with every day. I'm sure that there are certainly much worse things that can happen to a single human being than me. Somewhere in this world, there are people that don't have enough good food to eat or clean water to drink or warm clothes to wear on a cold day or medicine to take when they are sick or a place to call home. There are also some children that do not have a mother or a father to take care of them. There are some children in this world that can't go to school because they either cannot afford to go to school or have to work so that they have enough money to support their families. Some children in hostile nations that go to school have to face danger every time to get there. There are people out there that are suffering worse than me.

I am thankful that I live in a place where I have a mother and a father and a brother to take care of me, and more thankful to have a grandparent living next door. I am thankful that I have people that love me and care a lot about me. I am lucky to be able to graduate from Cotting School and have the support from my teachers and friends. I'm wrong if I say that I'm worse off than anybody else in this world, because I am better off than most people in this world. I'm lucky to be a part of the Lagasse family. I was given one tough break after another late in July of 2005, but I was eighteen years old, and I had my whole life in front of me to live.

In the month of August, things started to get better for me. I did not have to ride to the MEC building and go to my jobsites from there anymore, and I did not have to go to MEC from my jobsites and home from MEC anymore. My cab company and MEC worked something out so that my cab company could take me from home to my jobsites and back. The people that I rode with in the MEC van were not the kind of people that I want to hang around with, I didn't get along with them, and I did not believe that I fitted in with them. All they did was trigger bad memories from Gifford School. They made me feel miserable but I had to tolerate them. The first four weeks of the Summer Program were awful to say the least, but the next two leading to the vacation at Seabrook were okay.

Transportation has always been challenging for Tyler. This transportation routine was just unacceptable to us. He was spending more time in transit, than on the job. It felt as if he was riding around in circles! This was so unhealthy for him. We felt that he was slipping backward emotionally. All the work that he had done for years to enable him to have a job was falling apart by the day. The simple fact was: he was miserable!

For the third year in a row, I spent a week at Seabrook Beach, New Hampshire. My parents came, so did Memere, my brother Clint and his girlfriend. The place had a new tiled floor installed, plus new furniture and a new island with stools. Early in the vacation, I made some sports venues out of sand at the beach once again, only this time I ended up getting sunburn on my back that lasted throughout the whole vacation. On Wednesday during the vacation, Dad and I went up to Portland, Maine, to see my first Portland Sea Dog baseball game. The next day was the busiest day of the vacation. Early in the day, Dad and I got up early in the morning to go golfing at Sagamore-Hampton Golf Course several miles from our beach house. I did not play well that day as I shot 102 in eighteen holes of golf. My dad beat me by two strokes. After golf and a little lunch, I went up to Water Country in Portsmouth with Mom, Dad, Clint, and his girlfriend, where we spent the whole afternoon going on rides before closing time.

On the last full day of vacation, I had this sentimental moment at the beach. I started walking toward the ocean to get my feet wet when I found this big shell the size of a flattened softball in the water. I thought about bringing it inside the beach house until I noticed something strange about this shell. On the side of the shell, there was this goo. I showed this shell to Clint's girlfriend so that she could take a look for herself. She said it looked dead and I believed her. As I was bringing the shell back to the ocean, I was thinking about keeping it for myself. Then that goo on the side of the shell started to open up. There was something resembling a tongue that was sticking out. Something alive was in that shell! I thought it was a big, fat clam and the moment I saw that tongue stick out, I had to put the shell back into the ocean as quick as possible.

After feeling bad over putting the shell back, I picked it up, kissed it goodbye, put it back in the water, and walked away. On my way to my area in the sand, I started to cry. I was emotionally attached to this shell, because it was a living thing and it seemed fragile in the environment where it was living in to me. I walked back to the water one last time to look for that shell and to see how it was doing. I could not find the shell and then I thought to myself, the shell belongs in the ocean because it's its home. I believed that the thing inside its shell was alive and well and was ready to move on with its life.

Tyler has reflected on that moment with the shell on more than one occasion, especially when we visit Seabrook Beach each year.

The rest of August and the days leading up to Labor Day were tremendous. Late in August, I went with Dad up to the White Mountains of New Hampshire to go hiking up Mount Moosilauke. At the time, Mount Moosilauke was the largest mountain I have ever hiked at 4,802 feet. It was the most fun I've ever had hiking with Dad besides Mount Osceola near Waterville Valley two years earlier.

On the Saturday of the Labor Day weekend, my long-awaited graduation party finally came. There were many reasons why my party took place this late in the summer. Supposedly, the people who were invited to my party were not going to show up if my party took place in June, July, or August. Furthermore, I was working, I was playing golf with Dad and for Special Olympics, and I went to Seabrook. Simply put, we were just too busy.

My parents and relatives did all that they could to make my party perfect. They came up with an all-you-can-eat menu for my party. A lot of food was served such as chili, taco salad, meatballs, chicken kabobs, steak kabobs, and deep-fried turkey. There were plenty of desserts such as cookies, chocolate truffle cake, cannolis, fruit kabobs, and chocolate peanut butter cup sundaes. Many friends and relatives came to the party and I played Wiffle ball, kickball, and horseshoes with some of them. Mom and Dad held a showing of my graduation speech inside the living room. Everybody who came to witness my speech loved what I had said. I was showered with cards throughout the party. The way that they cared about me made me feel like a special person a world over. My mom asked me, "How do you rate your party from a scale of 1 to 10?"

I told Mom, "I rate this party a 10, a perfect 10!" I described my party at the time as "one for the ages." My party may have taken place in September, but it was the best day of that summer and it was saved for the end.

As soon as the summer came to an end, I returned to work at Lowell General Hospital on Mondays, Tuesdays and Thursdays and Kimball's in Westford on Wednesdays and Fridays through the Merrimack Education Center. As soon as Kimball's closed, I got a job as a librarian aide at Tyngsboro Public Library. The library job replaced the Kimball's slot on Wednesdays and Fridays. I met some nice people at the library, such as Connie who worked the children's section of the library, and Randy who became the library director in 2005. I did some simple tasks at the library such as rearranging books, videocassettes, and DVDs in the children's section and I also did the same thing at the general section of the library. It was a nice, quiet work setting and it worked perfectly for me.

The library was a perfect setting for Tyler for so many reasons. To begin with, it was right in our own town. Second, there weren't any loud noises there. And finally, he met people from his own community. He was also able to satisfy his need to learn. Whenever he was caught up with his work, he could read whatever book he was interested in. He loved working there.

It was in 2005 that I tried out road racing. I was never always a runner, and I never joined the track team at Cotting School. I did play sports that required running such as baseball, soccer, and basketball. Late in July, I tried to do some jogging on Willowdale Road and I started gasping for air after I approached the Browning's house and then I turned around for home after five minutes of running. It was wicked hard at first because my legs got tired and cramped up after every run, but running got easier the more I practiced. In September, I ran my first 5K road race. In case you don't understand road racing, a 5K race is five kilometers or 3.1 miles long. The start of the race took place at Molly Kay's Pub near the Lord Overpass in Lowell. The proceeds from the race benefited Kids in Disability Sports Inc., the sports organization where I play my basketball and golf. I didn't know what to expect since it was my first ever road race. I remember my dad telling me to run at a pace where I felt comfortable. The race went on and I started running. I didn't sprint at all at any point of the race because if I did I would be too exhausted. For all five kilometers of the road race, I struggled to maintain a comfortable pace. I was tired, I was sweaty, and my legs were aching. I never ran this far before and I never ran for this long before. I tried to finish strong in spite of the pain. In the end, my time for my first 5K was twenty-eight minutes and six seconds. It was a start. After that first run, I would go on to run in two more road races, one in Methuen in October, and one on Black Friday up in Amherst, New Hampshire.

Road races have worked out very well for Tyler. He likes to beat his previous times and he also gets to meet and interact with new people.

I've told you about my biggest moment in 2005, which was graduation, now I am going to tell you about my second biggest moment in 2005. It was November 10, one week before my nineteenth birthday. My dad took me to Lawrence for my driver's test. It wasn't my first drivers test. One month earlier I drove to the Registry of Motor Vehicles down in Wakefield with my driving instructor to take my driver's test there. I didn't pass the test the first time, because I had a hard time making my way around a place I have never been to.

This time in Lawrence during my second test, I told myself to relax, take as many deep breaths as possible, and go with the flow. I listened to the state trooper's instructions very carefully while I was driving. I said, "Yes, sir," after every instruction because I remembered what my driving instructor said about saying "yeah, man" or "I got you"—the trooper would think that I'm not following directions. I did whatever he told me to do such as changing lanes when it's safe to do so, making a three-point turn, and looking both ways very carefully. Then I pulled into a parking lot after I was done. The trooper said some things about my driving and then he said the two most important words I wanted to hear. "You passed." After he said those two words, I said to myself in relief, "Oh my god." I finally passed the road test. One week later, on my nineteenth birthday, I received my driver's license in the mail.

The first six months after my graduation was an emotional roller coaster to begin with. When I look back now, I think of the year 2005 as an historic year for me. I was not going to school down in Lexington anymore, but I had more responsibilities both at home and at my jobsites. I made the transition from Cotting School to life after graduation. If I thought 2005 was a challenging year, considering what I had gone through, then 2006 was going to be a bigger challenge for not only me, but my whole family. 2006 was the year for me to become . . .

2006: My Own Man

THE YEAR 2006 WAS ROUGH from the beginning. I started to feel down on myself and I wondered if I had made a mistake going to Lowell General Hospital in the middle of my last school year. I never once really hated my job. I liked delivering mail and saying hello to the people that I delivered the mail to. The people at the volunteer office liked me, the people in the mail room and general stores liked me, and my boss Paul was glad to have me be the mail carrier. I knew I was making money for college, I was faithfully doing my job, but still I wasn't as happy with my job like I was when I first came to work there. I still had enough heart and character to do my job. I remember what Mr. Navaroli said about character, and that kept me going when I was doing my job at the hospital and the library, and it still keeps me going today.

Meanwhile back at home, my relationship with my brother Clint was deteriorating. Then to add injury to insult, Clint tore up his anterior cruciate ligament in one of his knees while playing a pickup soccer game. The two things he was good at doing, those being plumbing and soccer, were viciously taken from him just like that. What began would be the most excruciating and agonizing recovery for Clint. In February, he had to have surgery to repair his knee followed by months of rehabilitation. Clint would need all of the support that he could get.

One Saturday night in February, a couple of days after his surgery, I was left alone with Clint. I was fixing a pizza in the oven when I heard a crashing noise in the basement steps followed by some obscenities. He fell down but got back up and as he was climbing upstairs he started banging the basement steps with his crutches. The way he banged those steps, he could've put a hole in one of them. The situation would eventually only temporarily cool down when we had our pizza. He regressed to his negative, ignorant, and self-destructive ways, and it came closer and closer to a head the more F-bombs he dropped. This was one of the most traumatic moments I've ever had to live through. He said that he was free to swear any time he wants. Then I said to him, "You can swear all you want but it will not make you a better man." I tried to reach out to him as best as I could but he would not listen to me. Every time I tried to reason with him, every time I tried to set him straight, he would change the subject and then I would say, "We're not talking about me or this or that. We are talking about you." I felt betrayed and let down every time he didn't listen to what I was saying. I just lost faith in him that night.

I could never have felt bad enough for him to see what he had to go through. But I was also upset in the way that he was handling his injury and recovery. I was frightened for him and frightened of him. Clint was twenty-two, still young, brash, out of control, and still living with his mom and his dad. He was not the soccer star that he was when he was with the Voke or Lazio FC. He was at a point where most people his age are living by themselves without parental supervision. But to have no job and not being able to get back to health for months on account of his torn ACL was painfully rough on him. It took all of 2006 for Clint to get his knee better again but it took longer for me to truly get along with Clint again.

Siblings do go through rough patches and during this particular stage in their relationship if felt as if Tyler was being the more mature person. Clint was at a low point in his life and instead of leaning on the support that Tyler was offering, he ignored it and in the process fractured their relationship. They have always loved each other. However, they had to figure out how to be brother's without Ron and I interfering and telling them what their relationship should look like.

In 2006, I set out to seek inspiration. In February I tuned in to ESPN and saw an upstate New York high school student living with autism named Jason McElwain make several three-pointers in a basketball game for his high school. After the game, Jason was carried off the court like a hero. Instantly he became an overnight celebrity and an inspiration to so many in the autism and disabled communities. Also that week I saw this special on a young man from Canada named Terry Fox who lost his leg due to cancer. In 1980, he started the Marathon of Hope, where he tried to run clear across his native country on one leg and a prosthetic leg. He didn't complete the whole run but he helped raise millions of dollars in cancer research and left indelible marks not only on Canada but throughout the world. After watching what Terry Fox and Jason McElwain had done, I decided to become an inspiration to people like me—people with autism and other disabilities—and to my family.

I did start to take my running seriously by using the treadmill inside the basement of my house to train for road races. In April of 2006, I ran a 5K in the rural town of Groton with Mom and Dad and finished the race in twenty-seven minutes and four seconds. My dad finished in just over thirty minutes, and Mom, who was running her first 5K, finished in over thirty-five minutes. It was the first time that Mom, Dad, and I ran a road race together.

Starting in November of 2005, I went to Gold's Gym in nearby Chelmsford with my dad to get my body stronger. The KIDS group started a strength training collaboration with the people at the gym. We met the owner of Gold's Gym in Chelmsford named Rick Dupuis. Rick was a member of the Team Micky running group named after champion professional boxer and Lowell native Micky Ward. The running team runs road races and competes in marathons in Boston and Chicago and they also put together road races to raise money for people in need in the city of Lowell and its surrounding areas.

When spring arrived, I joined a group of the athletes from the KIDS organization to participate in track and field activities coached by Rick Dupuis. Rick was instrumental in putting together this team and named the team after Micky Ward. We had nice green racing uniforms and warm-up jackets with both the Team Micky and KIDS logos on it. I went to track meets every Saturday morning with the KIDS group at Notre Dame Academy in my hometown of Tyngsboro. Cotting School did have a track team, and they would compete in events for the Special Olympics, but I didn't join because I wasn't that into running back then. By the month of May, I was already competing in track and field for the Special Olympics. I was running the 100-meter dash, the 200-meter dash, and the 4 x 100 relay. At the Special Olympics North Sectionals at Andover High School, I won a gold medal in each of those events I mentioned.

On Memorial Day weekend of 2006, I competed in my first five-mile road race. It was the inaugural Lowell Spinners two-mile/five-mile run. Mom and Dad ran the two-miler, and I ran the five-miler. The latter race finished inside LeLacheur Park, home to the Lowell Spinners Baseball Club. The two-mile race was followed by the five-miler. Both races started out on Aiken Street, just outside of the ballpark. More than eight months have passed since I ran my first road race in Lowell. My first four road races were 5Ks. This time around, it was going to be the toughest race yet. My strategy was the same as all of my other road races, stay at a pace where I felt comfortable.

The race began outside LeLacheur Park and the course ran along the Merrimack River and some parts in downtown. Once I made the three-mile mark I started walking for a couple of minutes to recover before I proceeded to run until the end. I went inside LeLacheur park through the left field side, ran along the warning track until reaching the finish line between the Spinners' dugout and the first base side. I finished at a time of forty-five minutes and forty-eight seconds, good enough for third place in my age division, 13–19. For the second time in five road races, I came away with a prize. I won a Spinners' drinking glass and a car wash card. I got to be on the field to receive my prizes. It was amazing to be on the playing field of LeLacheur Park to not only finish the race, but win some prizes. However, it would not be the only time in which I got to set foot on that field as I will explain later in this chapter. Two months after the Spinners' road race, I ran another five-miler through the streets of Lowell and Dracut and finished two minutes faster than last time.

The Lowell General Hospital Golf League

EARLY IN THE BOOK, I explained briefly about how I got into golf. My love of the game goes back to when I played miniature golf. I golf left-handed just as I bat left-handed in baseball. Golf was not my #1 favorite sport at the time, but I liked it. My parents would take me and my brother Clint to any miniature golf course or driving range once in a while. There was this one place in Tyngsboro called Max's Country Golf driving range. I used to love going there with my parents, my friends, my brother and his friends. My first taste of real-life golf occurred when Dad took me to Kimball's Pitch & Putt in Westford by the time I was ten years old. Tiger Woods won the Masters just as I started going to Kimball's. Then I moved up to regular nine-hole golf at nearby Tyngsboro Country Club soon after.

Golf is a sport where you use a club to hit a small white ball with many circular dents around it. The object of the game of golf is to hit the ball into the hole and finish the round—whether it is nine holes or eighteen—by making the fewest strokes possible. I try to make as many pars as I can and to stay as close to par as possible. The scoring format for golf is different from any other sport. Any stroke or strokes over par are listed as bogey or worse, a bogey is one stroke over par and a double bogey is two strokes over par, and so on. Meanwhile, any stroke or strokes under par are listed as birdie or better, a birdie is one stroke under par and an eagle is two strokes under par. A hole in one, one of the rarest and greatest feats in golf, typically takes place on a par-3 hole, and it counts as an eagle. A double-eagle, a feat that is just as rare as a hole in one, is three strokes under par.

For those that are unfamiliar with this sport, golf is a game that requires concentration, practice, strategy, patience, resiliency, responsibility, and character. A typical set of clubs consist of a driver, a 3-wood, a pair of utility clubs called hybrids, a set of irons and lofted wedges, and a putter. This game involves decision-making, where you have to decide which clubs to use in certain situations. For example if you need to shoot over a water hazard to reach the green, use a club (a long iron or hybrid) that will hit the ball a long distance. But there are times where you must play it safe by using a short iron or wedge so that your ball won't go in the water or any unplayable area. For many beginners, you should start by practicing with your clubs so that you can be familiar with them. To me, practice is what separates great golfers from good ones.

Getting on the green is only part of the job. Getting the ball in the hole can be a maddening task as I would figure out on my own the more I played the game. Making putts require reading greens and a good feel for the slopes of them. A hole is most likely a success or a failure on the green. In golf, finishing the hole is what matters most. You can't complete a hole unless you put the ball in it.

In golf, every stroke counts, there are no do-overs. You must accept the shot that you made. You also have to deal with failure and try to do better on the next hole. Adversity is going to happen on the course once in a while. What you do with adversity is more important. The game of golf can be ridiculously unforgiving, it is either going to own you if you let it or it is going to make you try harder and make a bigger person out of you.

Until 2006, I was lucky to play golf just once a week. Then one day in early 2006 at my job at Lowell General Hospital, I noticed an ad in the hospital newsletter about their golf league. This golf league took place at Tyngsboro Country Club every Monday afternoon from Late April to Labor Day. I showed the ad to my dad and convinced him to join the league. Dad and I each had to pay for our entry fees. I was exactly $20 short of the required amount to enter the league, so I used the $20 bill that I got from Clint's girlfriend for my eighteenth birthday in November of 2004. I was hoping to save that bill for the rest of my life to think of her but thanks indirectly to her, I was able to enter the golf league.

May 1, 2006, was the first round of the Lowell General Hospital Golf League season for my dad and me. I was inconsistent in my first time around in the golf league as I was not making good enough shots. I ended up with an 11-over-par score of 46 while my dad shot a 39. However it would be the highlight of his golf season as he failed to come even close to that number. I struggled my way through the first month and a half of the golf season as I was trying to break 45 in nine holes. My time finally came in the sixth week of the league, Monday, June 19 when I shot a 44. I followed that up the next week by shooting a nine-hole personal best 41. In the Red, White, and Blue Tournament— where Dad and I got to tee off from the red tees, white tees, and blue tees—which took place on the first Monday after the Fourth of July, I began the round with four pars, and was on my way toward another personal best with a score of 40, a score that should have been lower if I had not double-bogied the last hole.

Tyler loves to share the fact that he almost always has a better golf score than anyone else in the family! On the golf course, his autism plays to his strengths. He is able to concentrate completely. It is usually quiet on a golf course. And people usually have good manners when they are golfing. These are all things that really matter to Tyler.

I have competed in golf with the Special Olympics before, starting in 2003 at a par-3 course in Middleton. In the first three years in which I golfed for the Special Olympics, I played nine-hole tournaments. I remember competing in the state tournament in Middleton in 2003 and 2005, and I recall playing in the 2004 Special Olympics Invitational in Billerica Country Club. I got a bronze medal in my first Special Olympics golf tournament in 2003. The next year, I won a gold medal in the invitational in Billerica. In 2005, I won gold in Middleton. The highlight of the tournament in 2005 was when I made par on the eighth hole. My first shot landed on a mound in front of the green. Then on my second shot, I made a remarkable chip to get my ball within six inches of the hole and tapped in for par. I would finish the nine-hole round with a score of 36, nine strokes over par, good enough to win a gold medal.

On the Sunday afternoon of July 16, 2006, I went to Mount Hood Country Club in Melrose, located just several minutes north of Boston to compete in an eighteen-hole assessment round of golf for the Special Olympics. There I played with Keith Peabody, the son of my old speech therapist from Winslow School, Marge Peabody. I have played with him before in a couple of Special Olympic golfing events. Keith, almost forty years old at the time, recently won a gold medal at the Special Olympics

USA National Games in Iowa State. There was an article on him that made the front page of the *Lowell Sun*.

I didn't feel all that prepared for the assessment round because I showed up late and I didn't have time to practice before the round began. It was the first time I golfed in Mount Hood and I didn't know what to expect. Mount Hood was once a ski area a long time ago. The holes were treacherous, dangerous, and confusing. Every shot meant trouble because some holes were downhill, some were uphill, and some had ninety-degree doglegs going left or going right. Some holes were so hilly, that it blocked the view of the green. And on a windy day, the ball will get caught in the wind and find its way going out of bounds. My highlight of the assessment round was when I made birdie on the par-3, third hole by hitting a bad tee shot only to have my ball take a lucky bounce off a mound and on the green where I would make my birdie putt. I had three pars to go with my birdie and finished with a score of 91. I made some mistakes and had some shots that I would like to have back. I was new to Mount Hood so I had a hard time adjusting to it. I was impressed with Keith Peabody's putting and short game.

Two weeks after the assessment round, I played at Tyngsboro Country Club in the golf league. Ever since the Red, White, and Blue Tournament, I was mired in a slump in which I shot a 46 one week and a 48 the next in the last two nine-hole rounds. In 2006, I considered breaking 45 in nine holes an accomplishment. I was in this phase where I was just trying to get better every time. After my 48, which matched my highest score of the hospital golf league season, my dad said this to me, "You got to be mentally tough, grind it out, and be quick to forget about bad shots on previous holes." I've also played eighteen holes at Green Meadow with Dad three times leading up to this round at Tyngsboro. My scores at Green Meadow were 93 at the par-70 Prairie Course in June, a 92 at the par-72 Jungle Course on July 8—the week before Mount Hood—and a 93 at the Jungle two days before this round at Tyngsboro.

On the last day of July at Tyngsboro Country Club, I made history by making two birdies in a nine-hole round for the first time ever. Here is how I made those birdies. After my usual slow start, I had a chance to make birdie on hole #6 after a decent drive only to duff my second shot. But on the seventh hole, I finally made a birdie, my second birdie there, one week apart. Then on the last hole, the par-3 ninth, I hit my tee shot a little left of the green, which set up arguably the shot of the year. I was not wearing a golf glove on my right hand that I would normally wear when swinging a club. I was twenty feet away from the pin, in the rough. Once I chipped the ball, using my sand wedge, I thought I had hit it past the hole but the ball stayed in line as it rolled right at the pin and sank into the hole. I lifted my arms in amazement and let out a scream. I finished the round with a score of 43, but I called it the finish of a lifetime.

Tyler does persevere and eventually he conquers his challenges. He has enormous tenacity that serves him well in many situations on and off the golf course.

On August 6, three weeks after the assessment round at Mount Hood, I played with Keith Peabody once again, this time in the Special Olympics Invitational on his home course at Billerica Country Club. I was off to a good start on this Sunday afternoon in August at Billerica when I made four bogies and two pars in the first six holes. Then on the seventh hole, a par-3, I hit my tee shot into the water and eventually made a triple-bogey 6. After a bogey on the eighth hole, I was on my way toward beating Keith when I hit a good drive to start the ninth and last hole. But there was one problem with my tee shot. Nobody could see where my ball ended up. I figured my ball would still be in play, but after minutes of searching, nobody could find my ball. As a result, I would end up with a triple-bogey 7 and lose to Keith by one stroke. Two of the last three holes cost me, my lost ball in the water on the seventh, and the ball that got away from me on the ninth. I received a silver medal for my efforts.

The 2006 Special Olympics Massachusetts Golf Tournament

ON THE MORNING OF FRIDAY, August 11, 2006, my dad and I made a trip to a small community called Amherst in Western Massachusetts, where the University of Massachusetts–Amherst Campus is located. Back in the late 1990s, I would go there to see UMass Minutemen basketball games. But this time Dad and I went to Amherst for the Special Olympics Massachusetts August Games where I was going to compete in golf. This was my first ever Special Olympics golf tournament at the state level, and I was going to play two eighteen-hole rounds of golf—one on Saturday, August 12, and one on Sunday, August 13. The tournament was to take place at a nine-hole golf course a mile north of the Amherst Campus called Cherry Hill Golf Course. Since it was my first state tournament, I had set my expectations a little bit low and I had very few ideas on what to expect. Either way I was just glad to be there.

Dad and I went to golf nine holes there the Friday morning before the tournament so that I could get a clear idea of the course. I had nothing going my way that morning as I began the day with a triple-bogey, 8 on the par-5 first hole followed by a 9 on the par-4 second. The only bright spot that morning was a bogey and par on holes 3 and 4. I shot 55 in nine holes, but in spite of my high score, it was a productive learning experience. After that round, I came to the tournament knowing that I was not only going to do better, but put together an astonishing performance that would ultimately change the course of my future.

Dad and I stayed at a Holiday Inn Express in the nearby town of Hadley, just a minute or two from the campus. One time at the hotel, I got to use the treadmill inside the workout room while listening to the band Rush on my MP3. Across from the workout area, Dad was swimming in the indoor pool. Also that day we went to a Dick's Sporting Goods store across the street from our hotel. I got a snazzy new red Nike golf bag there. Later in the evening, Dad and I went to the campus to attend the opening ceremonies of the Special Olympics August Games.

Day 1 of my first August Games golf tournament at Cherry Hill began in the middle of the morning. My Level 5 competitor was none other than Keith Peabody. There was a shotgun start where every golfer teed off at their starting holes at the same time. My first hole took place on the par-5, five-hundred-plus yards, seventh hole, otherwise known to Marge Peabody as "the hole from hell." It started downhill, and past the halfway point it took a left turn. Then once I had the green in sight, I had no less than a hundred yard shot to carry a deep ravine with water inside. At the start of the tournament, I was struggling to make some shots. My first hole score from the hole from hell was a double bogey 7. After that double bogey, I would recover and shoot a first nine-hole score of 45.

After a lunch break between the first and second nine holes, I started the back nine on the short par-4, fifth hole. Two holes later, I was back on 7, the hole from hell. This time I used my cheap driver from off the tee. I haven't had much success with it since I bought it the year before. This time however, I hit that ball straight down the fairway. I knew that shot was good as soon as that ball left the tee box. My drive had to be at least 250 yards. It was probably the best ball I hit this weekend. Thanks in part to that great drive, I was able to make par on the most difficult hole of the course. By the time I was done, I had a back-nine score of 44 adding up to a total score of 89 for the first round of the state tournament. After not being able to break 50 in nine holes a day earlier, I broke 90 in eighteen holes. My performance in the first round of the Special Olympics Massachusetts state golf tournament was the best in 2006 to date. But I was only going to get better.

My first eighteen holes were finished, and I had eighteen more holes left to go. For the second straight day I got to pair up with Keith Peabody, who had a first round score of 97. The second round began for me and Keith on the fifth hole, a short par-4. After beginning with two bogies on two short par-4s, I returned to the hole from hell, the long par-5, seventh raring to make some noise with a 3-iron that has helped me all year. Instead my 3-iron betrayed me as I shanked my tee shot left and out of bounds. I was trying to muscle the ball off the tee that time instead of just keeping it in play. I was trying to do too much on the most difficult hole on the course. That only gave me a reason to play smart golf. I went on to score a 10, that's five strokes over par on the seventh hole. It was the only time that weekend when I felt down on myself after having a pretty bad hole.

After that disaster on #7, I moved on to the par-3, eighth hole where I played like a different golfer. The eighth hole was where I made my first par of the day. On the ninth hole, a short, elevated par-3, I made another par. I overheard Marge Peabody say that "this was the best turnaround anyone can hope for," but the best was yet to come. On the first hole, normally a par-5 but shortened for the tournament, I hit my best drive of the day, then made my best chip of the weekend, and finished with a two-foot putt for a 3. Eagle or birdie, it was my best hole of the tournament. I went on to shoot a 44 in my first nine holes of the second round of the August Games.

After a lunch between the nine holes, I started the last nine on the hole from hell. This time I fared much better as I made a bogey 6. Afterward I was making par as if it was my job to make them. I made par on the eighth, ninth, second, and third holes. I shot a 5 on the first but since the hole was shortened it could've been a bogey. According to the scorecard I made five pars in succession. I had just tied the family record for most consecutive pars with 5 set by my dad on the day that he shot a 39 in our first ever round of golf with the Lowell General Hospital Golf League.

I haven't played this much golf in such a short amount of time before (45 holes over three days). After making five straight pars, I would make back-to-back bogies on both the fourth and fifth holes, both par-4s. By the time I made the thirty-sixth and final hole of the tournament on the short par-4 sixth hole, I was a bogey or better away from breaking 40 in nine holes of golf, something that I have never done before. After a decent drive, I had a good lie from ninety yards out. It was then that my game started to fall apart on me even though I had my first gold medal in the state level secured. My second shot wound up short of the green, and then I used a putter from the rough on my third shot only to come up short of the green again. Trying to make par, I hit the ball past the hole and almost off the green. I was having a hard time getting my putter to work. When the hole was over, I ended with a quadruple-bogey 8. I felt a bit of disappointment in myself for not finishing strong, but I had a reason to be happy. I did shoot a 42 on the last nine, and for the tournament I set a new personal best with a score of 86. My best round yet was good enough for my first state title for the Special Olympics.

I played my best golf so far in my young life. I won a gold medal for finishing in first place in Level 5 golf, the highest level that I could possibly play in golf for the Special Olympics. My other Level 5 opponent Keith Peabody earned the silver medal. After leaving the golf course, I just put it all in perspective. I believed after the tournament that golf was more than winning a medal. It was a life-changing experience for me. This experience taught me for example that I could have at least one bad hole and still recover afterward. To put it eloquently, it was my best weekend of 2006. It's hard to believe that six months earlier I had to contend with my brother's agonizing pain as he was going through his most difficult time in his life. I had made my family proud. I later wrote in my journal that "this weekend is the one I'm going to remember for the rest of my life."

For the next several days, I spent some time taking it easy, relaxing, decompressing, taking walks with my family, jogging along the shore and building sports venues out of sand. One day while I was building a sand baseball park, Mike and Alyssa Reault and Cody Browning came by and congratulated me on winning the Special Olympics state golf tournament. I had a great week at Seabrook following that memorable weekend over in Amherst.

In 2006, thanks to the Merrimack Education Center, I had part-time jobs at Lowell General Hospital; Royal Crest Estates up in Nashua, New Hampshire, where I did some computer work for just a few weeks early in the spring of 2006; Bristol-Myers-Squibb in Billerica, where I worked in the mail room; and Tyngsboro Public Library. I grew really close to Randy and Connie at the library and the rest who worked there during my time working there. Randy was new when I first started working there two days a week. I enjoyed working at my hometown library, I really did, and they really liked having me around there. In August I received a certificate of appreciation from the folks at the library. The people at the library really made me feel welcome the same way the people at Cotting School did. I still have my library card in case I want to check out some books. I got to watch each inning of Ken Burns's *Baseball* on VHS thanks to the library and I enjoyed every minute of it. I am still welcome to come back to the library anytime I want to.

From April to August, I worked at Bristol-Myers-Squibb on Mondays, the hospital on Tuesdays and Thursdays, and the library on Wednesdays and Fridays. During the Summer Program with MEC, my boss at the hospital, Paul, decided to quit his job. I had to work the summer without the guidance of Paul who helped me with my route when I first came here. I really fit in with the routine and stuck with it for a year and a half. I knew what to do even without Paul to help me out. For the whole summer I had no boss and I was the only one handling the mail throughout the hospital. By the time August drew to a close, I was out of work. Being out of work was also a blessing to me because it gave me more free time than anybody would want to have. I got to spend more time with Dad as the summer was winding down. On August 30, I went hiking up Cannon Mountain with my dad and his friend Dick Brown from his old jobsite. During that hike I spotted two moose, a baby moose and possibly its mother. It was the first time that any of us saw a moose on any hike.

Two days later I went to a Red Sox game in which they beat the Toronto Blue Jays, 2–1. I went to the game via commuter rail and subway with my godparents Terry and Roger Marion and Denise Borghi. The game ended at 10:00 in the evening but we walked from Fenway Park to a crowded Kenmore Square to take the subway to North Station. Half way there we had to get off and wait for the next one because that train was switching lines. By the time we got to North Station we missed the 10:45 train to Lowell, so we had to wait until midnight for the next train to Lowell. I didn't get home until after 1:00 a.m. It was the latest I've ever stayed up at the time.

On the weekend after Labor Day, I went with Dad back to the White Mountains of New Hampshire for a one-night stay. We went to White Lake State Park up in Tamworth where we met up with one of Dad's old friends from his old work, John and Bob. On the first day of camp, Friday, September 8, we went kayaking on Lake Chocorua. It was a very peaceful setting, no jet skis or fast boats, no public beach, just four guys and the lake. After kayaking, we had some hot dogs and steak on the grill. After that I spent the night under a tent with Dad. I didn't get a good night's sleep as I was sleeping on a firm surface in a cramped tent with my dad.

The next day we went on our hike up Mount Chocorua. The beginning of the trail was located next to the famed Kancamagus Highway. A good bulk of the hike took place in the forest. Two hours into the hike, you are walking on rocky surfaces. But you see nothing but views left and right. I was the first to reach the top of Mount Chocorua. It was so windy and cool at the top that I had to put on my Red Sox hoodie. On our way down we encountered some suspense. Dad and I were alone together while our two acquaintances John and Bob turned up missing. The two pairs got separated by this turnoff between the secondary peak and the main peak of the mountain. After waiting ten minutes for John and Bob, Dad and I continued down the mountain. Dad and I made it to our vehicle at three and waited for the rest of our group. Dad and I were considering driving to the other side of the mountain to look for them if they did not show up in an hour. John and Bob would eventually make it to us.

The hike for all of us may have been finished but the suspense continued after the hike. Dad and I packed up our tent and what we needed for camping, we said goodbye to John and Bob and set out for the trip back home. Little did we know that the journey back home would turn into an adventure? While traveling down Route 25 in the area of Ossipee and Moultonborough, we encountered some dark clouds. Then the wind was starting to get noisy and I was thinking that there might be a tornado near us. Next, it was starting to rain and it was really raining. Adding to the rain was thunder and lightning. It was five by the time the rain was coming down in torrents. Once we got to Center Harbor, we saw the damage done by the storm. Two trees or its limbs fell onto the road we were traveling. The rain didn't stop until we reached Meredith. After the rain had stopped, the sun came out and after a bite to eat at a Subway near I-93 we went right home without having to encounter another thunderstorm.

Again, rain or sudden changes in weather are really unsettling for Tyler. He has a really hard time processing these changes.

On the day after the hike up Mount Chocorua and the adventure home, I ran in my second straight Micky Ward 5K in the Highlands section of Lowell. Since I was out of work, I found the time to run and of course hike. I hoped all my training would soon pay big dividends because I had no idea what to expect this time around. Last year I was new to road racing, but this year I was more experienced and ready to improve on last year. Before the race began, my dad said that I could run an eight-minute mile. When the gun was fired, I took off. I paced myself for the first few minutes of the race until I reached that hill on Sayles St. I ran up the hill as long and as hard as I possibly could. Then I had some water and paced myself once again. I went down the hill on Stevens St. and turned right. I was at the point where I felt sick to my stomach. When I heard footsteps of racers trying to pass me, I had to give my all, because the nearest racer form my age-group was catching up. I kept it going for the final half mile of the race. I couldn't run the way I would when I wasn't tired. I found myself dogging in the final two hundred feet of the course. It wasn't easy at all. I mean it was hard work. Once I got closer to the finish line, I saw the clock say twenty-three minutes and something. When it was over, I walked and caught my breath in relief.

As soon as the results came in, I went to find my name. I found out that I had finished thirty-fourth overall in the 5K at a time of 23:28. I was at least four and a half minutes faster than last year. I also managed to finish in second place in my age-group to an eleven-year-old, but I created a new personal best in a 5K road race by less than four minutes. I got my first road race trophy that day, adding to the list of accomplishments that I have made in 2006. In order to get that trophy, I had to earn it and earn it I did.

In the fall of 2006, I had no work because I graduated from the Merrimack Education Center Program and I got my high school diploma from Tyngsboro High School at age nineteen. Just because I was no longer working with the MEC program didn't mean that I wasn't busy. I would eventually find some work in my uncle's home improvement business, but it was just part-time work. In June I took self-paced fundamentals of mathematics at Middlesex Community College. Not only did I get an A in this course, but I finished the course in a couple of weeks. Then in the fall I took Algebra I in the evenings at the MCC Campus in the same building in Lowell and earned an A. Better late than never, I was continuing my education in the hope that I could land a good-paying job down the road.

Tyler enrolled in school at our local Community College. He had never really gone to public school. We weren't sure how this would work out for him. We knew he was up to the academic challenge, but we weren't sure that he could handle the social aspects of going to college. Therefore, we decided to take it one course at a time.

I went hiking again with Dad and Dick Brown, this time up Mount Tecumseh, which is part of the Waterville Valley Ski Area. At the time, September had just turned into October. It was my fourth hike in the year 2006. During the hike, we talked about a whole lot of stuff from movies to politics to sports. The top of Mount Tecumseh was tree-covered, so you didn't get a panoramic view of the White Mountains of New Hampshire. The foliage at this time of year is pretty much at its peak. We didn't go back down the way we came up. We took a trail that led to the ski area, and then we went straight down to the base lodge. We had better views going down the mountain. After the hike, we visited the Town Square of Waterville Valley. There wasn't anybody there plus it was past lunchtime and there wasn't any place for us to eat there. So we went down Route 49 and found a place off I-93. It was a great October day for a hike for Dad, Dick Brown, and me. It was also another good tune up for the half marathon.

The Half Marathon and the Duathlon

On October 15, 2006, I was about to do something extraordinary, something that no Lagasse has ever done before or since. October 15, 2006, was also the day in which my older brother Clint turned twenty-three years old. On Clint's birthday, I was in the city of Lowell running in the *Lowell Sun* half marathon. Being out of work gave me time to do some training for this half marathon and the Monster Dash Duathlon, which were both taking place in October. The Bay State Marathon was also happening and so both races started simultaneously on French Street in downtown Lowell and end at LeLacheur. The majority of the race took place along the Merrimack River. The half-marathon course would cross the river four times, twice across the Rourke Bridge on the west side of Lowell, and twice over the Ouelette Bridge right behind LeLacheur Park. Many avid runners and running fans alike know that a marathon is exactly 26.2 miles long, while a half marathon is half that distance at 13.1 miles.

At this point in Tyler's life, it was time for Ron and me to take a step back and let Tyler take some risks on his own. Up to this point, almost everything that Tyler had participated in was either supervised by us or with us in attendance. There was no way Ron or I were going to attempt a half marathon! Tyler mentioned that he wanted to give it a try and we supported his decision. I must admit, I was pretty nervous about him running this distance without us nearby for every step. I knew he was in good physical shape, but I was more worried about him being in a crowd. I worried about how he would handle it if he was accidentally bumped. I also worried about what would happen if he wasn't able to finish the race. Sometimes he has an emotional melt down. I was concerned that people wouldn't understand how to help him. I was also worried about him embarrassing himself by crying in public. I probably shouldn't worry about those things, but I can't help it. I just don't want people to laugh or make fun of my son.

Before the half marathon started, my dad said to me what he said before every road race, "Pick a pace that you're comfortable with and stay with it." My strategy was to pace myself because it's a long race. I was not planning on running too fast for all 13.1 miles. I've been running road races for only thirteen months, but now I was about to run the biggest one of them all. I used my free time in the fall to practice running long distances, which allowed me to be ready for it.

After a series of extensive stretching, I was about to start my trek, along with hundreds of runners young and old, experienced and new. I was to run two clockwise loops along the Merrimack River. The race started in the middle of the morning in French Street in downtown. The runners would merge onto Middlesex Street and take a right onto Rourke Bridge. After crossing the bridge, I took a right onto Pawtucket Boulevard and ran right alongside the Merrimack River. Pawtucket Boulevard eventually became VFW Highway once I arrived at the UMass–Lowell North Campus. Then I turned right and crossed Ouelette Bridge toward LeLacheur Park. Then I turned left onto Perkins Street, turned right onto Suffolk Street, turned right onto Father Morissette Boulevard and proceeded to make my second loop of the half-marathon course. After crossing the Ouelette Bridge a second time, I proceeded to enter LeLacheur Park. Just like I did at the Spinners five-mile road race back on Memorial Day weekend, I entered the ballpark from short left field on the warning track and ran along the track in the outfield. After nearly two hours of constant running, I was almost done. I went past the Spinners bull pen and crossed the finish line before the Spinners dugout. I finished the *Sun* half marathon at a time of one hour, fifty-seven minutes, and fifty-nine seconds. I had completed my most arduous road race, the longest of my many road races, and I have certainly done what no one in my family has ever done before or since.

When I look back now, I not only think of it as a great experience, I think of it as my greatest accomplishment in terms of road racing. At the time I was not thinking about winning the race because I knew I that I wasn't good enough to win. With the pace I expected to run, I would've finished in two hours and ten minutes. When it was over, I had exceeded my expectations by finishing in less than two hours. Running

13.1 miles on my own wasn't meant to be easy. I had to get more used to running, work harder than I was used to, and set higher goals along the way. I had to devote a few days a week of running and I had no problem finding the time to run since I was out of work. I learned that I didn't have to be the fastest to run a race. But if you are committed to running and work hard at it, running won't be all that hard. I felt sore from all that running, but it was all worth it in the end.

I was the youngest man among local participants running in the half marathon. I was seventh in my age-group, but to me I finished first in effort, grace, heart, and will. I didn't need talent to run the race. I just needed something to motivate me. My motivation for the *Sun* half marathon was Kids in Disability Sports, and my autism. Throughout the whole race, I wore my blue KIDS Inc. wristband to remind myself of this organization that has enabled me to continue playing sports into adulthood. I did this for the KIDS group, my family, my friends, myself, and for those living with autism and other intellectual disabilities and their parents because I thought it would mean something to them who have had to deal with those things. I believe I did a good job at it, but I was not done there.

Two weeks after running the half marathon, I took part in the Monster Dash Duathlon. A duathlon is a 13.5-mile bicycle ride in between two 5k road races. The start of the event took place at the Lowell Elks on Sunday, October 29, 2006. I almost had no time to ride my bike because I was primarily focused on my running for the half marathon. The only bike I had was a mountain bike and I hardly used it, and of course it wasn't designed for racing. The biking part wasn't the only serious factor in the duathlon, the weather that day called for a high wind warning with gusts of forty miles per hour and perhaps more. The wind was most relentless along the Merrimack River and it was going to make it very difficult for all the participants.

The 2006 Monster Dash Duathlon started on Old Ferry Road outside of the Elks at 10:00 a.m. The 5k part of the duathlon was a clockwise loop beginning on Old Ferry Road, then turning right onto Varnum Avenue toward Lowell General Hospital. Next was another right onto Pawtucket Boulevard where the wind started to pick up. I spent at least a mile on the Boulevard before taking a right onto Old Ferry Road, and into the Elks parking lot where I finished at a time of at least twenty-five minutes.

After the first 5k, I began phase #2 of the duathlon, the most difficult part of it all, the bike ride. After putting my wind jacket, liner, gloves, and helmet on, I was off on my bike. For 13.5 miles, I had to deal with the wind, the hills, and the growing pain in my body. I had never been in a bicycle race before. The bike course started at the Lowell Elks, took a left turn onto Old Ferry Road, and took a right turn onto Pawtucket Boulevard, where the course went through my home of Tyngsboro. Tyngsboro was where the course was most hilly, and they took a toll on me both physically and mentally. I then took a right onto my street, and I was on the verge of quitting because my body was simply spent. Then I encountered a group of people that were rooting for me. The Brownings were there to give me a boost and help me keep going. Then I passed my house where my mom was there to cheer me on. Then I was in Lowell where Dad was near Old Ferry Road to cheer me on. I kept on going toward Lowell General Hospital and took a right onto Pawtucket Boulevard where the wind was howling at my face. The wind was so strong that it slowed me down. Then I turned right onto Old Ferry Road where the Lowell Elks was located. I was on the bike for over an hour. It felt so good to be off the bike but I was not done yet.

When I transitioned from biking to running, my legs were so sore that I couldn't run the way I normally do. I didn't go at full speed so I took it easy so my legs could recover. My whole body was aching, the wind was robbing me of energy, but I knew I had to finish the race. When I crossed the finish line, I did it, my whole ordeal was over. My time was two hours, four minutes, and forty-nine seconds.

I was very nervous for Tyler during this particular race. It was so windy and cold that day. Ron and I decided that we should stand in separate places and call each other when Tyler would pass us. We called our friends and asked them to call us when Tyler passed their house. The fact is: Tyler set his sights on a new accomplishment and he succeeded!

The year 2006 was the year that I golfed in November and December for the first time ever. I went to Whip-Poor-Will in Hudson on the day before Thanksgiving and Green Meadow a week before Christmas. It was one of the warmest months on record that year. On Christmas Eve I ran a half marathon on the treadmill and finished in one hour and fifty-six minutes, a minute and a half faster than before. Mom said to me, "You're in the best shape of your life and you get better every day."

In 2006, I was not only a state golf champion for the Special Olympics. I not only took part in a half marathon and a duathlon, I went to college for the first time that year and earned *As* in Fundamentals of Mathematics and Algebra I. I had my name in the *Lowell Sun* newspaper twice. The year 2006 was when I faced serious challenges head-on and took giant steps forward as I devoted myself to making my family proud, and I did a very good job with everything I did. If not for the support of my family, friends, and relatives, none of this would be possible. I thanked them and God for helping me get through the year and letting me have a great year. But I was just getting started. If 2006 was any indication of things to come, 2007 can be described as . . .

2007: "Something Else"

MORE THAN A YEAR AND a half since I graduated, I returned to Cotting School in Lexington to play some basketball and reunite with some of my teammates and classmates. The basketball court had undergone some changes while I was away. New seats were added to accommodate more fans, new lights were installed to brighten the gymnasium, and poster size pictures of Cotting School players were put high up on the walls around the court. I played two games for the alumni, one in January and one in February. The alumni lost the first game but we went on to win the second game. Before my second game with the Alumni, I got to see David N., my former sidekick and now rival.

In March I went back to the Cotting School a third time to play in the annual Cotting School basketball tournament and jamboree. I didn't think I was going to go at first because I caught a cold and it left me feeling like crap. But at the last minute I decided to go anyway. My handpicked team did not do so well, and of course I did not play all that much because of my cold and so that everybody on my team got a chance to play. However, I got to see some old friends and teachers once again. I only stayed for the second game, the pizza lunch, and the jamboree, but I had a good time in spite of my cold.

I went back to Middlesex Community College for the spring 2007 semester. This time I took a Math Connections course at the Bedford Campus, which was a little farther from the Lowell Campus. Math Connections involved solving problems on a computer and doing spreadsheets on Microsoft Excel. In those spreadsheets I had to punch in certain equations, formulas and data, and make different types of graphs to describe the data. I wasn't alone in that class, there was a friend of Mom and Dad who was taking this class and was also there to take me home when my parents were not available. He made me feel very comfortable in that class. Once I did a PowerPoint presentation on Gordie Howe and I backed up my presentation with data and graphs. I got an A minus in that class when the semester was over.

But early in 2007, the one thing that I was looking forward to the most was golf. I could not stop thinking about golf since winning the gold medal at the August Games in Amherst. I set out to work on my putting during the offseason. So I found that putting machine with the long green carpet attached to it that I got for Christmas back in 1996 and took it up to my room to work on my putting. It was then that I decided to switch to my backhand grip and in order to get the feel of it I would practice it one hundred times a day for several days. I have not changed my putting grip since then.

The beauty of some of Tyler's challenges is the fact that once he puts his mind to something, he is willing to do the work to accomplish that goal. He has such a strong work ethic. He puts in the hours necessary to achieve his goal.

Just a couple of weeks after the August Games, a strange thing happened to my driver while I was hitting some balls into the woods from my backyard. For the second time in exactly fourteen months, my driver head snapped from the shaft as I was about to hit the ball. I did it again, this time I broke my $50 driver that I got at Play It Again Sports. Once again I needed a new driver but I had to play out the rest of 2006 without a driver. Dad told me, "You might get a new driver for Christmas. You'll never know." Then when my twentieth Christmas came in 2006, my prayers were answered. I got a new Nike Sasquatch Driver from Saint Nicholas himself, just the one I wanted. The label on the head cover said, "To Tyler, from Santa." In case Santa Claus existed, I said to him while looking up at the ceiling, "You're beautiful, man."

Ron and I could never tell if Tyler believed in Santa Claus or not. When he was very young, we went through the normal routine of taking our children up to the mall to have their picture taken with Santa. Tyler usually cried when we went to the mall. It was way too overstimulating for him. Never mind the fact that we would plop him on the lap of a complete stranger! Many times when Christmas or a birthday would come around, Tyler would usually leave the room until the noise settled down. He didn't really like the change caused by the decorations either. He liked things to stay the same. At some point, probably when he was thirteen or fourteen years old, he let us know that he believed in Santa Claus. I guess we figured, "Better late than never!"

When the Lowell General Hospital golf season finally arrived in May of 2007, I was off my game. I could not hit the ball straight, I could not hit it far, and I couldn't make good contact. I found myself shanking the ball badly left and it would plague me once in a while during 2007. I would later figure out that I was hitting the ball off the heel of my club and I was positioning my hands ahead of the ball therefore causing my ball to go way left. I had not played since December, so I was coming back pretty rusty. In the first week of the LGH golf season, I shot 50 in nine holes, although I did finish strong with three pars and two bogies on the last five holes.

Then the very next week, I had finally returned to my form from the 2006 SOMA tournament. After beginning the round with par-bogey-bogey, I stepped up to the most difficult hole on the course, the 511-yard par-5, fourth hole. I have played at Tyngsboro Country Club for almost a decade and I can only remember making par on that hole three times, twice last year up until that round. For the first time ever, I was flirting with birdie on the #1 stroke hole on the course. My first two shots were very good, a 3-wood off the tee and a 5-wood to get to within seventy-five yards of the green. I came very close to trouble as my third shot just dodged the water near the green. Then for my birdie try, I used my sand wedge to chip to the green. The ball was headed right for the pin but it hit the pin and stayed out of the hole. It was actually my best shot of that day, which led to a hard-earned par. Two pars and three bogies later, I would finish ten strokes better than before, with a score of 40. For the first time ever at Tyngsboro Country Club, I had a nine-hole round without a double bogey or worse. I had also set a record for most consecutive holes of bogey or better at fourteen holes, the streak would later end at 16. Throughout the 2007 LGH golf season, my scores would consistently hover around 45 in nine holes. I would shoot below 45 at Tyngsboro nine times in 2007, while shooting a 40 three times.

To this day, Tyler continues to save every score card from every round of golf that he plays. On more than one occasion, I have seen him looking at his old score cards and analyzing them.

On Memorial Day weekend in 2007, I ran in my second Lowell Spinners five-mile road race at LeLacheur Park. This time I was going to be better than last year because my body was more race-ready. I've done a lot of running on the treadmill over the winter, so I was poised for a better run the second time around. The course was the same as last year. Last year the whole family raced, Mom, Dad, and I. This time around I was the only one running.

I must admit, I started off pretty fast, doing 7:50 after the first mile. For the middle three miles of the race, I was running 8:10 miles. At the four-mile mark, the time was 32:20. Before the race, I told my dad that I wasn't going to think about breaking forty minutes in a five-miler until next year. If I was going to break forty now, I was going to have to run the last mile in faster than seven minutes and forty seconds. I started to run a little faster than I would normally run. Once I entered the ballpark, when that Ram Jam song was playing over the loud speaker, I had to give my all. While I was on the warning track, I looked at my wristwatch, and it said thirty-nine-something. I actually had a shot at running in less than forty minutes. My body may not have let me but I tried my hardest to finish strong. As I crossed the finish line, the clock said 39:59. According to my watch, my time was a few seconds shy of forty. I had broken forty!

I may not have finished in the top three of my new age-group, but I was less than six minutes faster than last year. I set a new personal best in a five-mile run. In a field of 140 runners, I finished in forty-fourth place overall. I was both emotionally and physically exhausted that day. I saw my dad in the front row near the Spinners dugout, and he told me, "You broke forty! You said you weren't going to break forty." When I read the race results in the newspaper, it said I finished in a time of exactly 40:00. I still say that I finished in less than forty minutes.

Tyler loves to set goals for himself and shatter his records. He is so competitive in all aspects of his life.

In the summer of 2007 Dad and I went to Nashawtuc Country Club in Concord, Massachusetts. The Bank of America Championship was held there and professional golfers from the Champions Tour (formerly the Senior PGA Tour) were making their only stop in the state of Massachusetts this season. An acquaintance of Dad's bought us passes that were only good for the pro-am part of the tournament on Thursday, June 21, 2007. We checked out the whole golf course, the hospitality tents, and the many golfers that were there at historic Concord, the town where I was born. This was my first time going to a real professional golf tournament, and it certainly was a thrill. The golf course was breathtaking but the tournament atmosphere there was truly *something else*. The greens at Nashawtuc were pretty fast and the grounds were nicely kept. Dad and I got hats and one of those sharpie pens in case we asked for some autographs. We did see some pros and other celebrities and former athletes out there playing in foursomes. One of the well-known pros or Champions Tour fixtures that we saw was Jim Thorpe. We also saw former Washington Redskins quarterback Joe Theismann make par on one of the holes at Nashawtuc. We walked through every hole on the course but one that day. Two words best described that summer day with Dad at the Bank of America Championship and would best describe the summer and eventually the year, and those two words were "something else."

Tyler loves going to sporting events. Golf events are probably one of his favorite types of venues to go to. He knows the history and background of the venues as well as the athletes.

During the first half of the summer, I went to the Bedford Campus of Middlesex Community College to take Algebra II. For nearly two months, I worked tremendously hard on it. There were times when I couldn't get some problems right, but I still managed to gut it out. I scored a 91 on my preliminary exam, but on the midterm I scored a 95. For my final exam, I looked over what I've learned, did my homework tests on the computer, went over my notes, and did some serious studying. Not only did I try to get through my final, I was pursuing perfection. I was given sixty questions for this final test, just as I was given in the midterm. I looked at the questions carefully, answered them all and checked them in case I made any mistakes. It took me just two hours to do the whole test. As soon as I was finished, I passed in the exam to my professor. When I got my test back, I learned that I got a 95 on my final, three wrong out of sixty questions. I got an A for the entire course. All that hard work and commitment on this course had paid off.

Tyler does need extra time to take his exams. That is the only accommodation he receives at college. He spends several hours each day studying for each course. He puts so much pressure on himself to do well in school and in sports. He uses the same skills for academics that he does for sports . . . study, study, study, practice, practice, practice. We could all take a lesson on perseverance from Tyler.

During Christmastime in 2006, Richard Reault Sr., father of my dad's friend Rick Reault, came up with the idea of having a scramble golf tournament in honor of me. So Mr. Reault brought in some sponsors, printed out some flyers, and made my tournament a reality. On Saturday, August 4, 2007, the inaugural Tyler Lagasse Scramble Golf Outing took place at Townsend Ridge Country Club. It was one of those days where it was *something else*. Frankly, I described this day as the most special day of my life to date. This tournament and the game of golf meant so much to me. All of the proceeds of this tournament went to Special Olympics Massachusetts.

On the day of my tournament, I woke up at 5:00 a.m. so that I could have time to get ready and get to the golf course by 6:30. Once my family got to Townsend, I shook hands with Mr. Reault, the creator of this event, and thanked him for getting all of this off the ground. I found some time to loosen up, practice putting, and get some swings in at the driving range. There was an 8:00 shotgun start where every golfer in each foursome or team tees off at their own holes at the same time. My foursome was a threesome because one of the golfers did not show up. Dad, Rick Reault, and I teed off on the first hole, while fourteen other foursomes, mostly friends, teed off from their respective holes.

After golf, there was lunch, a silent auction, and prize giveaways inside the clubhouse. I gave a speech to the attendees out of what I wrote in my journal from last year. I picked the raffle tickets out of a bag for the prize giveaways. In the silent auction I won myself some autographed pictures of three Boston Red Sox, one Jon Lester, one Kevin Youkilis, and two Dustin Pedroias. I bought a hat, polo, and a short-sleeved rain jacket with the certificates that I was given. I also got a free round of golf at Townsend Ridge. I had a blast at Townsend Ridge and I will never forget it.

This was the first time that Tyler had given a speech during a golf tournament. Basically, he just read from his journal entry about his experience during the Special Olympics August Tournament where he won his gold medal in golfing. As I looked around the room, I saw grown men brought to tears as they listened to the joy in Tyler's voice as he described his experience. It was at that point, I realized how Tyler could have real connections with people. He has such a way with words. He uses such descriptive terms to share his experiences with his audience. A gentleman named Nick from Special Olympics was with us this day and after Tyler's speech, he asked us if Tyler would be interested in becoming a global messenger for Special Olympics. Global messengers are asked to make appearances and share their experiences about participating in the Special Olympics with people in the community. That is actually how Tyler's speaking career began.

One week after my tournament, I went back to Amherst to take part in my second SOMA August Games. While my mom and Memere were headed to Seabrook Beach, New Hampshire, to start their annual August vacation, Dad and I spent the weekend of the tournament at a Hampton Inn in nearby Hadley. Dad and I did not do a practice round at Cherry Hill like we did last year. We did find a nearby driving range not far from our hotel so that I could get some swings in before each round. I just hoped that I could correct some flaws at the range and at the same time enter the tournament looking sharp with all this practice.

At exactly 11:00 a.m. on Saturday, August 11, the 2007 SOMA golf tournament officially began. I started the first round on the fourth hole, the longest par-4 on the course. I used my Nike Sasquatch driver off the tee and hit a rare hook to the right and into the fifth fairway. Two shots later, I was a chip shot over the sand trap away from a chance at par. My third shot just hit the lip of the bunker and I would later end up with a bogey after a "nice out" from the sand.

On hole #5, I hit my 3-wood to the right but my ball was still playable. Two shots after that, I was on the fringe with a chance at birdie. I putted my ball just short of the hole and tapped in for par. On the par-4, sixth, I hit a nice drive with my 3-wood. Last year on that same hole I ended up with an 8 after such a good drive. This year I ended up with bogey after blowing a chance at a par and birdie. Then I was on the behemoth of the course, the par-5, seventh hole from hell. I teed off with the Sasquatch and went right and at a tree. I did recover with my 3-iron but two shots later, trying to get on from 140 yards out using a 7-iron and with a ravine separating my ball from the green. I thinned my ball into the drink. As a result, I got on the green in 7 and 3-putted for a score of 10.

On the par-3, eighth hole after a mediocre pitching wedge from the tee, I hit a nice chip shot on the green and salvaged a par. On the par-3, ninth, I saved par again, this time I had to drain a putt from ten feet. On the next two holes, I was hitting really nice drives—driver on the first hole and 3-wood on the second—but each hole ended with a three-putt. I made a 5 on the shortened par-5 first and a 6 on the par-4 second. Finally, on the third hole a short but elevated par-3, I hit my second shot to within five feet of the hole for a chance at par. I missed par and then I missed bogey and once again had to three-putt. The last three holes were three putts as I finished the front nine with a score of 46. I slammed my putter on the ground outside the green in disgust after my putter failed me. Instead of three promising holes to finish the front nine, I had three lousy holes.

After a lunch break, I began the back nine of the first round on the second hole hoping that I would fare better. I hit two magnificent shots to the green, and before I knew it I was a five-foot putt away from a birdie. I made that putt for what would be my only birdie of the day. In fact, it was my best hole of the day to that point. After saving par on the par-3 second that I made a double bogey on, I popped up my tee shot with the Sasquatch on #4. Three shots later I hit my putt for par from the fringe on the back end of the green too soft and ended up with a triple-bogey 7. On hole #5, after a tee shot to the right side, I duffed my second shot and would later make bogey. On the sixth hole, I sliced my tee shot left, but the ball hit a tree and bounced back into play. But I had trouble getting on the green and left the sixth shooting a double bogey 6.

On the evil seventh hole, I hit my worst tee shot of the day by topping the ball and seeing my ball go down the hill one hundred yards. I used a 3-wood and a 7-iron on my second and third shots, which set up my fourth shot over the evil ravine. I took out my 9-iron, took some practice swings in and then I hit it. The ball's trajectory was low but somehow I managed to get over the ravine. That set up my fifth shot, from the rough going uphill, thirty yards from the green. When I hit that ball, I knew it was a good shot. I thought that ball was going in the hole but it hit the flag and bounced away from the hole. It would have been the most miraculous par yet if I put a little less mustard on it, but I was glad enough to take a bogey.

After a bogey on 8, I inexplicably tried to putt my way on the green from the fairway of the par-3 ninth hole. The end result would be a two-putt bogey. Then on the last hole of the first round, the shortened par-5 first hole, I sliced my tee shot left but managed to stay in play. My next shot got me on the fringe, forty feet from the hole. I would later make a birdie 4 on the last hole to finish the back nine with a score of 42. My total score for the first round was an 88, one stroke better than last year's first round. I had a very comfortable lead heading into the second round as my opponent Keith Peabody had a score of 102.

Day 2 of the tournament was Sunday, August 12. My goal for this tournament was to break 40 in nine holes and 85 in eighteen holes. Right off the bat, it looked as if I was about to do so when I slapped a 250-yard bomb right down the middle of the fairway in the "hole from hell" with the Sasquatch driver. Two shots later, I was 150 from the green with water in between. But just like that, I hit the ball with the 7-iron too low, too thin, and into the drink. In the end I finished the hole with a 9.

Then just when I thought it could not get worse, on the tee at the par-3 eighth hole, I hit the ball off the hosel of the club and saw it go left and into the woods. I teed up another ball and I shanked it to the left again. It was the lowest I've ever felt that day. I was lucky to find my first tee shot on a pile of rocks and stones and took a drop from behind the pile. My third shot went over the green and near the main road. I made a nice chip toward the hole and finished with a 6. In my first two holes, I was not playing the way that I wanted, and I wasn't all that focused out there. I knew I was a good golfer and it was no fluke that I played well there last year but this year in Amherst I doubted myself. However I knew I had to move on because I had sixteen holes left to go that day.

On my third hole, the par-3 ninth, I finally had my first good hole as my tee shot with a pitching wedge from 117 yards landed five feet from the hole. I had a great chance at birdie, but I settled for a par instead. I was glad enough to take it because I did not remotely have any chance at par on my first two holes. On the first hole, after a fine drive, my approach shot to the green came up short, and I made two putts for a par-5. After two awful holes, I bounced back with two good holes, both pars.

Then I was back to my inconsistent ways on the next two holes. I pulled my tee shot into the woods on the right on #2. I wouldn't recover as I ended up with a triple-bogey 7. After a double bogey on the par-3, third, I regained my form with pars on #4, the longest par-4 on the course, and on #5. On the last hole of the front nine, the sixth hole, I pulled my tee shot to the right. My short game was not there to save me as I scored a 6 on the sixth hole and finished the front nine with a score of 49. The front nine for me was a disappointment to say the least because I knew I could do better than that.

During the break between rounds, my dad and I had a talk. He had a reason to believe that I was putting too much pressure on myself. Dad and I were both too busy to play eighteen holes of golf together in 2007, which contributed to my rough outing. I told Dad about my goal of breaking 40 in nine holes and 85 in eighteen holes, and right now I would have to shoot a 36 to do so. But with the way I was playing, I did not see how that was possible. Keith had shot a 46 and cut my lead to eleven strokes. For the last nine holes, I decided to stop worrying about the score and have some fun.

My back nine began on the first hole. I hit an embarrassing pop-up off the tee and would later bogey the hole after making three putts. On #2, I found the woods to the right. Two shots after getting out of the woods, I thought I made my best chip of the day. My chip started right then it went left and then it stopped just eighteen inches from the hole. I ended this hole and the next two making bogey. I would make what would be my last par of the tournament on the par-4 fifth hole.

On the sixth hole, I hit a good 3-wood off the tee. Then my poor short game cost me as I would end up with a dismal double bogey 6. Then on the hellish seventh hole, I was 125 yards away from the center of the green on my third shot. I took to studying that shot harder than any shot that weekend. After taking some swings, I got myself set and let her fly. From that moment on, it looked like the shot of the year. My ball landed on the fringe, just short of the green. After my chip shot went by the hole, I had a twenty-five-foot putt for par going right to left. At first it looked to go in but it stopped an inch short and I made bogey. The last two holes were par-3 holes and each one of them ended in disappointing bogeys. My score for the last nine was 44, and my score for the second round was 93. I was not satisfied with the outcome, but for the second straight summer I won the gold medal in golf at the August Games.

After that tournament, I made a commitment to improve my game. The real Tyler Lagasse was going to be more improved, more consistent, and more experienced when I return to Amherst in 2008. There was not going to be a repeat of the disappointing showing in 2007. I was sure to come back more ready and more prepared. I was going to break 40 in nine holes and 85 in eighteen holes. And one more thing, I was going to keep improving in the near future.

I went right over to Seabrook to meet up with my mom and Memere as soon as the tournament was over. This was my fifth straight year going to that beach in New Hampshire with my family. Every day was a beach day as I would find time to tan, run, and build stadiums out of sand. Outside of that, I would go out to eat at the many nearby restaurants, visit Playland Arcade on Hampton Beach to play games and win some prizes such as this Tedy Bruschi figurine and three miniature wooden sculptures of sea captains. I bought this five-hundred-piece jigsaw puzzle of a fictionalized Wrigley Field at Galley Hatch in Hampton. I tried out my new bicycle around the neighborhood of Seabrook Beach. Inside the beach house, I would play this Parcheesi-like game called Tock, where you use playing cards to move your pieces instead of dice. Normally every summer since 2002 my family would watch *On Golden Pond*, but instead we watched *Dr. Strangelove*, my personal all-time favorite comedy. Overall, I had a very nice week at the beach with my mom, my dad, and Memere.

After leaving Seabrook for good, Dad and I had to go to Providence, Rhode Island to pick up my brother Clint and his new girlfriend at T. F. Green Airport. I had never been to Providence nor had I been to the state of Rhode Island before. Vermont is now the only New England state that I have yet to visit. Clint had just finished his vacation in Florida at the time. On Friday night when he was supposed to land in Providence, inclement weather forced his flight to land in Kennedy Airport in New York City. They did get a flight to T. F. Green the next morning and we picked them up at noon time.

On the way home there was construction causing serious traffic in the downtown area. I had to go to a men's room really bad that moment. There was a rest stop off of I-95 in Mansfield, Massachusetts. Once the green Chevy stopped I got out of there as fast as I could. And then the next thing I know as I was about to sprint across the street, some nut job in a silver sedan was zooming to my right. I managed to back out of the way in time before that car could hit me. I bet that car was doing 40 mph and the driver was not paying the slightest attention to the road. I almost didn't see it coming until that split second where that car was destined to end my life. That car kept on going down the road, and I yelled, "Stupid!" to that silver sedan. I was lucky not to wet my pants when that happened. I was able to go inside the men's room and do my business.

As I was going in the urinal, a gentleman behind me said, "You must have had some scare. Are you all right?"

I said in a cool tone, "I'm fine."

This is one of the few moments in my life that I won't forget. I almost died that day on August 18, 2007. I'm forever grateful that I'm alive, and I had the right mind to look out while I needed to be relieved. My life was very important back then because I wouldn't be the man I am today and I wouldn't be writing this story. And I'm far from finished because there is much more to my story.

To this day, Tyler sometimes has a hard time predicting cause and effect. We've all been in the same situation before. The difference is we expect traffic to be coming and going. Tyler just focuses on his needs and doesn't pay attention to his surroundings. He is very childlike in those situations. It still is a concern for Ron and me. He looks so strange as he is "sprinting" across a parking lot trying to get to the restroom. For that reason, we often ask him if he needs to find a restroom, so that we can begin the process of finding a rest area along the way.

A couple of days after coming home from vacation, I resumed playing golf with Dad in the LGH Golf League. I played two nine-hole rounds at Tyngsboro Country Club and ended the month of August on high note by shooting scores of 43 and 42. On Labor Day Dad and I played our only eighteen-hole round together that year at the Jungle Course of Green Meadow where I shot a 93. Two days after that we played nine holes at Whip-Poor-Will, another course in nearby Hudson. My biggest highlight came on the 280-yard, par-4, seventh hole where I barely overshot the green. I had a shot at eagle but came up short. My birdie putt was hot as the ball jumped over the hole and continued down the slope. I had this uphill ten-footer for par, and I was able to save it for my only par in the round where I shot a 48.

On the last day of the LGH Golf League, I began the round with two big par saves on holes 1 and 2. On #3, the long par-3, I hit a good tee shot with my 3-wood to just a few feet from the green. My second shot got me to within a dozen and a half inches of the hole but once I tried to tap my ball in, I missed the hole to the right. I must have tried to rush myself to complete the hole. That muffed putt would later make a big difference later on. My worst hole came on the wicked fourth hole, the most difficult hole on the course, as I ended up with a triple-bogey 8. After that I would make a double-bogey 5 on the par-3 fifth.

I would finally turn the corner on the par-5 sixth as I hit my tee shot toward the blue 150-yard post. I used my 8-iron to attempt to get on this par-5 hole in two shots. I did just that as my ball landed on the front end of the green and later make birdie on this hole. On hole #7, I played it safe with a 5-wood like I did all season long, hit my pitching wedge to the green, and two-putted for a par. On #8, I hit a nice 3-wood, chipped on, and two-putted for par again. On the last hole, I went a little left and short of the green and the bunker. I did hit a nice chip on the green to get to within three feet of the hole and make my fifth par of the day to card a 40. Now this was definitely the type of round where I should have easily broken 40. That missed par chance on #3 most likely cost me my chance at breaking 40. It was my third round of 40 this year, but this was the best golf I played all year so far.

I did not take any courses for the fall 2007 semester at Middlesex Community College. In late September my mom took me to this medical building adjacent to Saints Medical Center in Lowell to have my wisdom teeth removed, all four of them. When you're about to enter adulthood, this is the best time to have your wisdom teeth removed. I was almost twenty-one when I had them removed. The last time I visited that building, I had an abscessed tooth removed when I was eight. Back then I had a mask put over me and I tried to fight my way out but they told me to breathe and then I blacked out. While I was under, they pulled the tooth out. Then as I woke up, I threw up. It was one of the most unpleasant moments of my life. For a couple of hours I felt really dizzy and nauseous, but after I felt better.

Thirteen years later, I was back at this building. Before my appointment I visited the office and saw a tape of the procedure and learned of the risks of not having the procedure. I was in the low-risk stage, which meant that this was the right time for me to have this done now rather than later. On the day of my appointment, I spoke with the nurse and signed a consent form. I was hooked up to machines to tell what my heart rate and pulse were. I was not going to have a mask put over my face. Instead I was injected with a fluid through my left arm and then I was told to go to sleep during the operation. I started to lose feeling in the lower half of my face and then I dozed off just like that, not remembering a thing during the procedure. The operation lasted just thirty minutes. Then at one point my nurse told me to wake up.

I got out of the chair with gauze in both sides of my mouth. At least I did not vomit at all. I was woozy and dizzy and my face was so numb that I couldn't move my lips, couldn't feel my chin, and couldn't feel my tongue.

When I tried to have my first meal, it was as though my lips were the size of a baseball. Every time I removed the gauze out of my mouth, there was lots of blood and then some. I spent the evening after the procedure holding an ice bag on one side of my face and then the other to bring the swelling down. I did not have 100 percent feeling in my face until about nine at night. For a whole week, I took painkillers to help myself fully recover until my whole mouth was back to normal.

Tyler is remarkable compliant when it comes to any medical challenges. He doesn't complain and he follows the instructions from the doctor precisely. Therefore, he is a wonderful patient and his recovery time is quick.

The Golf-a-thon and the
New England Invitational

On Tuesday, October 4, 2007, my dad and I went to this thirty-six-hole golf course in this quiet town just twenty-something miles west of Boston called Stow Acres Country Club. This all-day golfing event known as the inaugural Special Olympics Golf-a-thon was taking place there and I was one of two Special Olympic golfing guests there. From 9:00 a.m. to 3:00 p.m., I would have my picture taken with a foursome, tee off from the sixteenth tee of the North Course and the rest would tee off from there and continue to golf all day. As many as ten foursomes representing their own businesses sponsoring the golf-a-thon were at Stow Acres that day. I believe three foursomes had played as many as five rounds of scramble golf that day. That's an astonishing ninety holes of golf. The rest of the foursomes must have played two or three rounds.

I was on the sixteenth hole all day long and I played the same hole with different foursomes coming by. The sixteenth is a pretty long par-3 hole, 170 yards to the center of the green. I remember my first shot of the day. I used a 6-iron off the tee and my ball stopped thirty feet from the hole. Then I made the next shot for birdie, on my first ever (unofficial) hole at Stow Acres. Then on my second try, I made birdie again. Unfortunately, I made those two birdies before the first foursome arrived.

When I was teeing off with the foursomes around, I did not reach the green with my 6-iron, and I could not reach the green with my 5-iron either. It must have been the wind, maybe it was the slices that robbed me of my distance, maybe it was just jitters from meeting new people and that I was trying too hard to impress them. Still, I'm sure that they enjoyed being with me and seeing what I could do on the course. I did my best to have as much fun as possible out there because it was the day where I was going to do nothing but golf. When there were no foursomes in sight, I entertained those that were around by bouncing the ball off my wedge or practicing my tee shots with my dad around to shag them. One time I teed off from the back tees with my 5-wood, 190 yards out. I took my usual stance, gripped it and ripped it. Then I noticed that my ball was fifteen to twenty feet from the cup. I want to remember this shot for a long time.

My mom came to the golf course from her job at the Greater Lowell Voke by the time I was finished shooting off the sixteenth tee. Mom, Dad, and I went to the clubhouse for a while before Mom wanted to see Dad and I play a little golf of our own. Stow Acres is made up of two eighteen-hole courses, the North Course and the South Course. Dad and I played the back nine of the South Course late in the afternoon. I shot a 47 with the highlight coming from the par-4 twelfth hole where I made my lone birdie by hitting a wicked good driver off the tee, followed by an amazing pitching wedge to the green that set up the four-foot putt for birdie.

When the sun came down, I went to the banquet hall adjacent to the clubhouse and pro shop. This was the time of day where I felt like a celebrity. Before I knew it, I was signing autographs, five of them to be exact—to some golfers I played with that day. One of the pictures I signed was to be auctioned off on eBay. After that, Special Olympics Massachusetts president Robert Johnson gave a speech on how Special Olympics have come a long way since the organization's beginning. I met President Johnson for the first time that night. Then I came up to the podium to make a speech myself. I expressed my thanks to Special Olympics and described how it has had its effect on me. I was given this humongous ovation after making what was then my best speech of the year so far.

After my speech, a comedian did his skit composed of abbreviations and text messaging terms such as FBI, CIA, OMG, CBS, ABC, you know stuff like that. He gave an interesting performance for the audience that was almost fully consisting of golfers. After the comedic performance came a live auction. By the time the golf-a-thon was officially over, I made out with $300 worth of Stow Acres gift cards. The first annual golf-a-thon was a hands-down success, in my opinion it was better than my tournament at Townsend Ridge in August. I had a blast that early October day in Stow Acres. It's a nice place to golf, and it's one of the ten best public courses in Massachusetts.

Tyler was quite impressive that evening at Stow Acres Country Club. All the players were quite generous with their donations to Special Olympics and, best of all, made connections with Tyler by having conversations and including him in their conversations. It has been a wonderful relationship for Tyler.

On Sunday, October 7, 2007, I played in first ever round of golf outside of Massachusetts and New Hampshire. I accepted an invitation to play in the New England Invitational at this forty-five-hole course west of Hartford. Tunxis Plantation, as it was called, had three different courses, two eighteen-hole courses (White and Green), and one nine-hole course (called Red). The Special Olympic competitors played on the Green Course that day. I was to play eighteen holes while my playing partners consisting of two teams of two, an athlete and a partner, would play alternate shot.

Two months had passed since I won my second straight gold medal at Cherry Hill at the state games. Even though I won the gold medal, I still did not feel all that satisfied with my performance there. Coming into Connecticut, I had little to expect. Initially, I had just wanted to feel glad to be there, and represent the state of Massachusetts proudly. However by the end of the day, I would have something to be most proud of.

I wore my yellow polo for good luck that day as I left with Mom and Dad for Farmington in the morning. It had been more than ten years since I visited the state of Connecticut, and that was when my family stayed at a hotel in Danbury before heading to Maryland for my cousin's wedding. I helped my parents get to our destination, just like old times when we would take long trips. We passed through the great city of Hartford on our way to the site of the New England Invitational. The Tunxis Plantation Country Club was such a huge place, such a nice place to golf. It was just shy of midday by the time we got there. The clubhouse was elegantly constructed like an old church or castle with old stones on the exterior, just like Mount Hood in Melrose. As soon as I took out my clubs, I went to the course range to squeeze in some practicing. I needed to get sharp just before the tournament began.

As was the case for prior Special Olympic golf tournaments, my starting hole did not take place on the first hole. My first hole of the tournament was the par-4, third hole. My first shot of the day was a 3-wood off the tee and I hit it straight. I made the green in two shots and two-putted for a par to begin my first ever round of golf in Connecticut. A par on my first ever hole in Connecticut! Can you believe it? Then after that I ran into a long string of adversity starting on the par-4, fourth hole, a dogleg left. I hooked my tee shot with my Sasquatch and lost my ball. I took my provisional from the tee, using a 3-wood this time, and later made a double-bogey 6. If I played a little smarter than to use a driver, I would have made par right there. Instead it was the first of three straight double-bogies, the second was on the par-3, fifth and the third was on the lengthy par-4, sixth.

After a bogey on #7, which put me at seven strokes over par just five holes in to the invitational, I was on the par-3, eighth as I teed off with a 6-iron. My ball landed on the fringe to the right of the green. Two shots later I made my first par since my first hole. On the ninth hole, I hit my tee shot with the Sasquatch to the left side of the fairway. After hitting the green in my second shot, I two putted for another par. On #10, I used my driver off the tee again and hit a brilliant drive that landed in the fairway. My second shot found the rough, but thanks to my chipping practice in my big backyard at home, I chipped on to get close to the hole and made a crucial putt to save par. After bogey on #11, I finished the front nine with a score of 42.

I stepped into the par-3, twelfth hole to begin the back nine. My shot to the green was short, but my second shot rolled to within two feet of the hole. I was able to make my third par save of the day, my fifth par overall. The thirteenth hole was the first of four straight par-4 holes. My third shot went by the hole and I was left with a rather difficult putt for par. To be honest, this was the kind of putt that I did not think I would make. I tried to stay collected, keep my poise, and pictured that ball go in the hole. And the ball did go in as I saved par for the fourth time. The fourteenth was my last bad hole of the day. My tee shot struck a tree forcing my ball to a spot where I could not get a clear shot to the green. After laying up to get a good shot to the green, I sliced my third shot to the left barely missing the water and into the rough. In the end I finished #14 with a double-bogey 6, my last hole of double bogey or worse that day.

On the fifteenth hole, I hit my drive more to the right than I wanted and wound up under tree branches. Using my 5-iron I was able to stay low and get my ball to park itself shy of the green. Then I made a near perfect chip from the rough to get to no more than thirty inches from the cup and made my fifth one-putt par of the day. It was a blue-collar par. Most golfers, whether they are pros or amateurs, diehards or casual, would think the same way too. I had seven pars so far, but I had five holes to go.

My best hole to me came on the par-4, sixteenth hole. My tee shot from "sweet #16" was a monster—NO! It was a Sasquatch! My second shot was from the right side of the fairway, 150 yards to the center of the green. I used an 8-iron and hit it to the center of the green. I ended up two putting for my eighth par, on the second most difficult stroke hole of the Green Course.

The seventeenth was my first par-5 hole of the invitational. I sliced my tee shot with the Sasquatch and found a fairway bunker on the left side. Then I used a 5-wood to muscle the ball out of the sand and hooked it into some trees to the right of the fairway. On my third shot, I used a 5-iron to try and stay under the trees like I did on #15, but I hit it too high and hit one tree branch and hit another, but somehow that ball found the fairway. I was able to chip on to the green for a chance at par. Unlike all the par saves I executed that day, I missed that par putt on #17 and had to settle for bogey. On hole #18, a par-3, I hit a fade to the left off the tee with a 5-wood. I was ninety feet from the pin where I attempted my second shot on #18. It had to be the best shot of the day. I played my ball perfectly and saw the ball stop within two feet of the hole. I made my ninth par of the day after the tap-in. After a restroom break I resumed my round at the first hole. I would only get on the green in three shots and make a bogey 5.

The last hole of my memorable New England Invitational was the longest and most difficult stroke hole on the course, the 511-yard second hole. Off the tee, I let out a big bang with the Sasquatch. It was my best drive of the day—a high, straight, and long 250-yard drive to the right of the fairway. From there I used a 3-wood to get to the left side of the fairway, 100 yards from the center of the green. My third shot went left of my desired target but it made the green. I was thirty feet away from making my first birdie, but I missed four feet to the right. Now all I had to do was make this putt and I would have a total of ten pars. Even if

I didn't make it, I would still set a new personal best at eighteen holes of golf. I took a lot of time, took some swings, took my stance, hit the ball and the putt was good.

As soon as I looked at my scorecard, I found out that I just shot an *82!* The scorecard also said that I shot a 39 on the back nine of the Green Course. So I had set at least three milestones:

1) I had shot under 40 in nine holes.
2) I had shot under 85 in eighteen holes.
3) I had made more pars (10) than bogies (4) and double bogies (4) combined.

I did all that in a golf course I never played on and in a state where I never played golf before. Setting my first two milestones was one thing, doing them on a course I never been to and doing it in Connecticut was my theme of 2007: "Something else!"

Before I attempted my third shot on my last hole, one of the golfers that played with me asked for my autograph. I was treated like a celebrity again. With that performance, I earned a gold medal, my fourteenth Special Olympic medal overall. So far it was the best golf I've ever played in my twenty-plus-year life. Today, I think of my performance in Connecticut in 2007 as a "second chance," because I did poorly in Amherst two months earlier. I believe the good Lord was with me that day because he felt that I deserved better than what I got at the August Games and believed something very special was there for me in store. What I got in Connecticut was a second chance, a performance I will never forget.

The day after my breakthrough performance in Connecticut was Columbus Day, and on that day, a sportswriter from the *Lowell Sun* named Lynn Worthy came over my house to write an article on me. I have never been interviewed by anyone from a local newspaper before. Back in the fall of 2001, my brother Clint was interviewed by the *Sun* and they did an article of him and his soccer skills. I myself was also mentioned in that article, so back then it was a huge thrill for me to even have my name in a newspaper. I not only explained about my record breaking performance, I talked about my life and how much sports mean to me. Lynn also asked questions to Mom and Dad. We talked for at least an hour and a half. I fondly remember him asking me, "Why do sports mean so much to you?" I kind of froze while I was trying to think about it. I don't know what I said after that, but what I *should* have said was "Without sports, my life would not be complete. Without sports, I would be just like most people with autism—lost, trapped, and confined to their thoughts and disabilities, cut off from the real world and not being able to prove themselves. Without sports, I would not be having this interview with you." After the interview was over, Lynn said that the up and coming article would be ready soon. However back in October of 2007, the Red Sox had already advanced to the American League Championship Series and the Patriots were in the middle of putting together a 16–0 regular season. I didn't expect to find myself the paper right away, but it was going to come in a way I could not imagine.

Two days after the interview, I put on the exact same clothes that I wore at the invitational in Connecticut and prepared myself for a photo shoot in my backyard. A photographer from the *Lowell Sun* came over in the afternoon to take pictures of me with my Nike Sasquatch driver. I also wore the gold medal that I won in Connecticut. The photographer loved my poses for the camera. I was kind of nervous, since I have never been photographed for a newspaper, which seems understandable. However, I handled it very well and did a good job during my photo shoot.

On Monday, October 22, I picked up the *Lowell Sun* newspaper and saw pictures of the Boston Red Sox winning the pennant on the front page. Then I looked on the other side of the folded front page and I see this picture of me in my yellow polo holding my driver toward the camera. My article was on the front page along with the Red Sox winning the pennant! The next thing I did was call my dad on his cell phone and told him that my article had made the paper at last. Afterward, I was being flooded with phone calls, gifts, pictures of me golfing, four tickets to a UMass–Lowell hockey game, and letters congratulating me on a great golf match. It was like my high school graduation all over again.

Three days after I was in the paper, my dad and I had to go to Boston. We went to the Bank of America building for this Disability Awareness Day. Between 11:00 a.m. and 2:00 p.m., which was lunch period at the time for the workers there, I sat next to a pair of Special

Olympic athletes from Massachusetts, Michael Findlay and Colin Davidson. All we did was speak of our accomplishments to some people passing by the Special Olympics desk. We all gave out information and business cards from Special Olympics to the employees of Bank of America. We also got them to sign up to be volunteers for up and coming Special Olympics events such as the Jolly Jaunt, which was coming up in December. The Jolly Jaunt is both a road race and walk that takes place in several locations across Massachusetts and all the proceeds go to Special Olympics.

The next day was the annual Kids in Disability Sports banquet at Lenzi's in nearby Dracut. There was a slide show of the athletes performing in their sports and attending the dances and outings. On the way inside the place, there was a poster with pictures of me golfing, a speech written by me, and my article from the previous Monday issue of the *Lowell Sun*. The top of the poster read, "TYLER IS MY NAME, GOLF IS MY GAME." The bottom read, "GOLD MEDAL WINNER." Like all the people that participated with KIDS Inc., I was given a trophy.

The special guest of the banquet was a young man from the greater Boston city of Everett who has cerebral palsy. His name was Sean Cronk and he was the guest speaker for the night. There was an article written about him by *Sports Illustrated*'s Rick Reilly. Cronk actually was on the varsity high school basketball team in his town. He was probably this year's version of Jason McElwain, the kid with a disability who comes off the bench and helps his team to victory. Cronk had made two free throws by putting the ball over his head and throwing it into the hoop to help his team win the Boston City high school basketball title. I shook hands with him after receiving my participation trophy and had pictures taken alongside him.

Tyler had a remarkable golf season that year, but more importantly, he grew as a person, too. He became more confident, mature and congenial. Those are three words not generally used when describing a person living with autism. Sports have been such a catalyst for much of Tyler's growth and development.

Jaret

I GREW UP ADMIRING LOTS of athletes back in the day. The first one I remember admiring was the great basketball legend Larry Bird. I was lucky to see him play in his last year with the Boston Celtics and the Dream Team in 1992. I also grew up watching Roger Clemens play when he was with the Red Sox. I got to see him pitch in two games— one was my first baseball game at Fenway Park in 1993 and the other was down in Baltimore's Camden Yards in 1996. He lost both those games unfortunately. When Bird and Roger were on their game, they were the best in their professions.

But between 1995 and 2002, the one person I looked up to was Jaret Foley. I needed a friend and something like another big brother to look out for me. Luckily for me, I found Jaret. I remember during the summer of 1995 going with my older brother Clint to see his friend and youth soccer teammate Todd Foley. Then this big guy who happens to be Todd's older brother shows up and the rest is history. I told my mom about Jaret and said that I liked the guy. My mom knew the Foley's through soccer and baseball. Jaret's mom, Donna, coached my brother and Todd in soccer and figured that it was a good idea to have Jaret babysit me.

Before Jaret came along, my dad's Cousin Shirley Noval would babysit me. She was around the same age as my dad, a little older. She did all she could to get me into her interests such as listening to this dinosaur record but I refused. Maybe I just wasn't ready for it because it was not that I didn't want to hear it. Eventually we got along just fine. Then she got sick and died of cancer back in 1996. I just did not know her all that well. After she had died, I heard that she was into '60s music. Shirley left some of her CDs, which also included a collection of nearly every Beatles CD for my dad. I later got to listen to them as I got older. Today whenever I feel down on myself, I honor her memory by listening to whatever she listened to.

What started out as a brief first visit eventually turned into a life-changing friendship. For four years when Jaret went to Tyngsboro High School, he was my babysitter. Sometimes he would bring Todd over and it would be the four of us at my house, Jaret, Todd, Clint, and me. Jaret and I grew closer the more we saw each other. He would take me out for ice cream, take me to a movie, play some football and Wiffle ball with me in my backyard, and swim in my pool. Those were the days, man.

By the time I got my first set of clubs, he would take me in his 1983 red Honda Prelude to Mount Pleasant Golf Club, in the nearby city of Lowell. It was a private golf course, and only members can play there. It is one of three golf courses in and around Lowell where the Cities golf tournament is played. It was a beautiful looking nine-hole course, and more challenging than that of Tyngsboro Country Club. This was the place where I learned golf etiquette. For guests who wished to play there with members, it was difficult to get a tee time there. This course had this dress code where every golfer must wear shirts with collars. Jaret's mom, Donna, let me wear one of Jaret's old collared shirts so that I can play.

Golf is different than most other sports I've ever played before it. Jaret taught me many things about golf that I didn't know before. When you are on the course, even when you are not playing, you have to be quiet when golfers are about to hit the ball. You are responsible for every shot that you attempt and you must keep track of your score, of course I had little to no problems with keeping track of my score since I was good with numbers and all. When there is a group of golfers in front of you, you do not shoot until they are out of the way from your desired target area. Sure enough I was able to understand the rules of golf etiquette. I remember one time on a rain soaked day at Mount Pleasant, Jaret and I got to golf with then-Massachusetts attorney general Tom Reilly.

Just like Mom and Dad with other sports that I played, Jaret also taught me the values of good sportsmanship on the golf course. He said that you could throw your clubs and swear all you want, but that was not going to make you a better golfer or improve your score. He also stressed that I shouldn't be throwing my clubs or cursing after every bad shot. More often than not I was making bad shots, and that was mostly because I was just new to this sport. However Jaret and I each saw the potential in me, and boy, did his advice pay off. Not only did Jaret teach me a lot about golf, he taught me a lot about life. Ten years later and after two Special Olympic gold medals in the state games plus the performance at Connecticut, I owe it all to Jaret.

Jaret Foley was the cocaptain of the Tyngsboro Tigers Football Team. He played linebacker on defense, and on offense he was a tight end. Most of the time he was on defense and he did the best he could. In 1998, his senior season, the Tigers were poised for a state super bowl appearance and I followed them religiously that year. I kept track of every game from the beginning by writing scoring plays and final results in my notebook and cut out some newspaper articles from the *Lowell Sun* of those games. After beating their crosstown rivals Greater Lowell on Halloween, they were undefeated at 7–0.

After that game against the Voke, I got to wear Jaret's red #48 football jersey and went trick-or-treating in it. Not only did he lend me his jersey, he lent me his pants, his shoulder pads, even his helmet! The uniform may have been big but I was able to walk the whole neighborhood in it. I went with my friend Michael Reault who also wore a Tyngsboro High Football jersey that night. It was the best Halloween ever for me.

The next game was arguably the biggest game of the season. The undefeated Tigers played at home against the undefeated Reggies of Greater Lawrence on Saturday, November 7, 1998. The winner of that game was automatically going to the Division 5 Super Bowl. The Tigers made their only Super Bowl appearance before in 1994 and won it easily. The one against Greater Lawrence was one of the greatest games ever played by Tyngsboro. It was close from beginning to end. Tyngsboro led the Reggies 10–0 at the half, fell behind 12–10, and later retook the lead 18–12. Then it was tied at 18 apiece. Finally, on the last play of the game, the Reggies won with a fifteen-yard touchdown run. Oh my god, we lost!

I was right behind the end zone when the winning touchdown was scored. I took that loss very hard, like I always did as a kid. Jaret took that loss very hard since it was his best and last chance of ever going to a Super Bowl. I punched and kicked the padding on the goal post in sheer frustration. My parents did not take me to the game as they went to see Clint play soccer for Greater Lowell. I was very inconsolable that day. I did not get a chance to speak to Jaret for a couple of weeks after that game.

Somehow we got together and moved on with our lives. Through good times and bad times, through thick and thin, we were still best friends. When Christmas came in 1998, I was given a poster from the Tyngsboro Football Team that said, "TIGERS 98" with a picture of the team running onto the field. Below the picture were autographs signed by nineteen members of the football team, plus four stat girls. Of course Jaret who was the one behind this gift wrote, "*To our diehard fan, thanks for all the support pal, #48 Jaret Foley.*"

In 1999, Jaret graduated from Tyngsboro High School and would attend Westfield State College all the way in the Berkshires. It was tough for me because he was going to be so far away as I was moving on to Gifford. But we were both moving on to the next chapter of our lives at the same time. We spent a good portion of the summer together. We both found the time to golf several times at Mount Pleasant here and there. During that summer when I was playing baseball for my all-star team, I got hit by a pitch in the back of my leg. Two days after that, Jaret took me and Clint to a driving range up in Hudson, New Hampshire. I was teeing up my ball when Clint to the left of me shanked his ball, and it ricocheted off the white wooden plank separating me and Clint and clocked me on the top of my head. The driving range in Hudson was the one where you shoot off the grass, and there was no fencing to separate the golfers. The pain was worse than getting hit in the leg with a pitch. Jaret was quick to tend for me. I did not need stitches, but I would have a little headache and a big lump on the top of my head. I was able to play in my baseball game later that day.

We did spend a few more summers together from 2000 to 2002 to play a little more golf. I would go to just two of his games, one in UMass–Boston in 2000, and the other in Fitchburg State in 2002. After that game in Fitchburg, we never spoke to each other for a while. We began to be too busy building our lives. He was working on his degree and making new friends of his own at Westfield, I was at Cotting making new friends of my own and earning high ranks there. The time away from each other turned out to be good for us.

One day while I was running down Sequoia Drive, I finally met up with Jaret Foley. He was in the middle of doing his side job on the street that I was running on. I talked to him about whatever I could about myself and what has happened to me since I last saw him. I told him I was training for the half marathon. He said that he was trying to make it as an officer in the House of Corrections in Billerica, Massachusetts. That day he was just doing his side job. The odds of us meeting each other at the time were obviously long indeed. If I had not taken up running and continued it or if Jaret was still doing his regular job, I might not have reunited with him at all. It felt so good to see Jaret again. It was as if a giant psychological weight was lifted off my shoulders. Seeing Jaret again probably gave a lot more energy to finish my run because I was running a lot that day.

As I was trying to find myself through running, I found Jaret. Maybe it was a kind of magic that put us together again. He was working at his side job trying to support himself. I was training myself for the half marathon in Lowell. Just to see him again brought me so much inspiration to work harder at my training and my life. Then we moved on once again so that we could continue our daily lives and building processes. It would be another year before we got to see each other again.

Then I get this call from Jaret on the week I was in the paper in 2007. It was obvious and apparent that he was excited over the phone. Then he asked me if I wanted to golf at Mount Pleasant with him on Halloween. I told him, "I would be honored and delighted." I had not played a single round of golf at Mount Pleasant since 2002. I was more than glad to hear from Jaret again and I was more than looking forward to going back to Mount Pleasant again.

On the day of Halloween in 2007, I got to spend a day with Jaret Foley. I was practicing my swings out in the front yard waiting for Jaret to come. He pulled up in his Jeep, and after he got out, I said to him, "You're not as big as I last remember you." Of course he was the same old Jaret. I gave him a big old hug as sign of feeling so glad to see him.

And so we went to Mount Pleasant, the place where the City Tournament takes place every June. The place had recently gone though some changes since my last visit in 2002. The dining room and the functioning room above it had undergone serious renovations. Outside of the dining room, there was a patio with tables and chairs, something I didn't recognize before. As for the nine-hole course, not much had changed. Each of the first three holes was a par-4. The fourth was a par-5 that was reachable by some in two shots. The fifth was a short par-4 that was reachable off the tee but with trees guarding the green. The sixth and seventh holes were the only par-3 holes on the course. The seventh was wicked downhill toward a green that was in the shape of a bear. The par-5 eighth was the longest hole on the course. The ninth and final hole was a dogleg par-4 bending to the left.

We played eighteen holes that Halloween day. Jaret shot a 74, two strokes over par, still showing that he still has it. I had a pair of 46s to finish with a score of 92. I did have some glimpses of greatness as I outdrove Jaret on nearly a couple of occasions. This day would not be defined by our scores as he was there to witness the differences between the Tyler of the late '90s to the Tyler of 2007. He noticed how much I've progressed and how much I've matured since our last golf round together. Jaret was really impressed with my demeanor that day. He said that I no longer get upset over a bad shot for more than one hole because it would wreck my game.

During our round, we talked about what we've done since we last got together in 2002. So many things have happened to Jaret and me over the course of a half decade. I told him that the football game that Tyngsboro lost to Greater Lawrence was not the worst day of my life. It was April 19, 2004, when the Boston Bruins lost their first round playoff series to the Montreal Canadiens of all teams after leading 3 games to 1. But that worst day would be trumped by the one in Super Bowl XLII in February 2008 where the Patriots quest for perfection came to a tragic end. After finishing college, he got a job as a corrections officer at a state prison in Billerica. He would also meet his wife and I would meet her a year later. Anyway it was so much fun being with Jaret again, it was like old times all over again.

Jaret has continued to be a huge influence in Tyler's life. This was the first "real connection" that Tyler had made. The truth is Tyler worships Jaret! He is a gentle giant in my eyes. He understands Tyler's challenges and brings out the best in Tyler. He looks past Tyler's autism. In short, he believes in Tyler.

Dressing up as Jaret Foley on Halloween night, 1998. If the term "man-crush" existed back then, then that would be taking it to another level.

After Jaret's Basketball game during Christmas Break 1998-99.

Jaret may have left to go to Westfield State College but we were
never apart. Those two pictures were taken after each of Jaret's
football games. At UMass-Boston in 2000.

At Fitchburg State in 2002. I must have grown at least six inches between those two pictures that were taken.

The Red, White, and Bid

TWO DAYS AFTER MY OFFICIAL reunion with Jaret, I went with Mom and Dad to downtown Boston. We visited the Omni Parker House for a Special Olympics fundraiser called the Red, White, and Bid, which was a wine tasting and silent auction. The event took place on the top floor of the building. I bid on Red Sox tickets and a trip to Foxwoods but didn't win them. I met a lot of people there, had some food, and enjoyed some jazz music. However the most intriguing moment came when I was brought over to speak to a crowd. Before I get to my speech, let me tell you how I got there.

It started with my 2005 graduation speech that you just read. But two years later, in September of 2007, my dad and I went to Danvers where the headquarters of Special Olympics Massachusetts was at the time. From that point on, I became a member of the Special Olympics Global Messenger Program. Its primary mission is to spread awareness and support for Special Olympics. Generally, global messengers are Special Olympic athletes who talk about their experiences and how this organization has changed their lives, in front of audiences big and small.

At the Omni Parker House that night, I talked about how I got into the Special Olympics, thanked the people of this organization who have made me feel like a part of their family, and talked about my most favorite moments as a Special Olympian—such as meeting Tommy Heinsohn and shooting an 82 in Connecticut. I wore my golfing gold medals at the Omni Parker House as proof of what I have accomplished recently for Special Olympics and told them that "even though I have autism, I can accomplish big things." The most touching moment of my speech came when I talked about going to CTDS and that I wanted to be a normal individual but not everybody in this world is normal. After saying that "some people are extraordinary, and I am one of the extraordinary people," the crowd erupted in applause.

That speech would mark the beginning of a long and successful career of public speaking. That night, the crowd on the fourteenth floor of the Omni Parker House was buzzing over me. My family and some people there later said that I was the closer of speeches for this event, the same way Jonathan Papelbon is for the Boston Red Sox. My speech just lasted a few minutes. I really touched everyone in the crowd of a hundred with my words. That must have been the loudest several seconds of the night after saying it. Later in the night, Nick Savarese had me come over. Nick's dad had won himself an autographed jersey signed by Rodney Harrison of the Patriots. And when he offered me the jersey, I said, "Whoa!" That was not just unbelievable of Nick's dad, it was something else, and so the theme continues. In a year full of big moments for me, this was the latest but not the last.

On November 17, 2007, I officially became an adult as I turned twenty-one years old on a Saturday. For my birthday, Mom and Dad gave me a big map of Eastern Massachusetts and a nostalgic booklet of 1986, the year I was born. My brother got me scratch tickets, a blue hooded Red Sox jacket, and pictures from when he was in the 2007 Red Sox World Series victory parade in Boston. Memere got me a long-sleeved half-zip shirt for golfing and a 2007 Red Sox World Series outfit with a shirt that could be both long-sleeved and short-sleeved. I also got this orange running jacket from the 2007 Boston Marathon from one of my mother's friends, and my uncle Craig came over in the middle of the day to give me a big bag. Inside it was a tool belt and this bottle of Guinness Extra Stout since I was now 21, and a card with twenty-one reasons to make me feel special.

When it started to become dark, I felt like going out to dinner at Homestead Restaurant up in Londonderry, New Hampshire. My whole family came up with me plus Memere. After we finished ordering our food, the power went out inside the restaurant. Without power, there was no way that we were going to have our food served. I was hoping that this was just a short-term outage but it stayed dark for a while. I did have my buffalo shrimp but with the power still out, my family decided to leave here at six and go to Owen and Ollie's, a converted mill in Dracut that became a restaurant.

After we made our orders, Clint talked me into playing Keno. I did not want to play it but I did play anyway. Every booth had a TV and one of the channels was a Keno channel. My brother paid for my Keno drawings, and I chose the following numbers: 4 for Bobby Orr, 9 for Ted Williams, 17 for the day in November when I was born, 21 for the age that I turned, and 48 for Jaret Foley's football number. I made a mark next to bonus so that I could have a chance at winning more money. I played five games of Keno, $2 a game with the bonus doubling the amount to $4. If at least three of my numbers matched the ones on the screen, that meant I won some money. After I turned in my ticket, I learned that I won $172. It was the best part of my birthday that night winning $172 in Keno after leaving a restaurant that just lost power. Now that was *something else*.

After dinner, we dropped off Memere. It was seven, and the Lowell Devils hockey game had just started. We arrived at the Tsongas Arena with two minutes left in the first period. Lowell was playing the Hartford Wolf Pack that night. The Devils were down 2–0 after two periods but came back to tie it up in the third period. Then with only minutes left, Hartford would score and would win 3–2. It was a very entertaining game and I had a good there even though I arrived late and my team lost. I had a great twenty-first birthday, but since it was on a Saturday, this birthday was something to remember.

One week later I went back to the Tsongas with to see the UMass–Lowell River Hawks play hockey against Merrimack College. Remember I got those tickets just after my article in the *Sun* came out? They were given to me by a man named Mike Kuenzler, who is the head of All Sports Promotions and owns a clothing store called Heroes. Well I had another great time there as I saw a River Hawk complete his first hat trick, and got a ticket that was good for two free tickets to another UMass–Lowell game in December against Bentley College from a flying blimp. Imagine that! The final Score for the River Hawks game was UML 6, Merrimack 2.

The last month of 2007 was downright memorable. On the first day of December, a Saturday, I went with Mom and Dad to Boston to participate in a Jolly Jaunt, a 5K road race/walk benefiting Special Olympics Massachusetts. It takes place in several places in Massachusetts, including Boston. The weather was bright and sunny but it was also cold and windy that day. We arrived in the city just a couple of hours before the race began. I did a few minutes' worth of stretching, and walking and jogging around before the race began at ten in the morning. I did not expect to win or set personal bests because I knew I was doing it for a cause, for myself, for my teammates, and for the Special Olympians.

The course started on Charles Street next to Boston Common and took a left turn onto Beacon Street. I actually ran past the world-famous bar Cheers to my right while running on Beacon Street. Next, I went left onto Arlington Street followed by a right onto Commonwealth Avenue where I passed the John Hancock and Prudential Towers. I ran into the Mass Ave. Tunnel and turned around at the Charlesgate Overpass. I was facing the wind in the first half of the race, but afterward I was running with the wind behind me the rest of the way while listening to Styx on my MP3. Once the Boston Common was in sight, I was almost done. I took the right onto Arlington Street followed by a left onto Boylston Street. Once I crossed the finish line, my watch read 24:15. I pumped my fist into the air and had enough energy to hop. As soon as I found Mom and Dad, I hugged them. The most important thing for me that day was for one day in Boston, I ran a race for what I felt was a cause for an organization that has helped me succeed and become the person that I am today.

On December 14, 2007, I came up with a brilliant idea for myself. I realized how far I've gone in my short life and I have been keeping track of it in two journals since 2005. This idea was going to be big and it seemed like a good idea at the time. I was going to write a book, an autobiography of me, my autism, my accomplishments, and my struggles to attain them. Originally I wanted my book to be about my life in the years between 2000 and 2009, since there was going to be two more years left in this decade at the time of the idea for my book. I decided that it was time for me to take a look back at my life to see how far I've come.

So I took out a yellow notepad and started a rough draft. Before I knew it I had three notepads all filled up. I had a few ideas for a title. My mom suggested that my book be titled *He's His Own Best Friend (and His Own Worst Enemy)*. It seemed to my mother that I was my own best friend and at the same times my own worst enemy. It was a good title for my book but I just was not wild about that idea. I came up with *My*

Decade of Character: 2000–2009, because of the character I expressed all decade long. Then there was *The Making of Tyler Lagasse*, because I went from being a reticent and precocious child to the man I am today. Finally, just a couple of years after I started my rough draft, I came up with a great idea for a title. I decided to name it after one question an old friend would ask me almost every morning at the Cotting School library: *"What do you say, Mr. La-ga-say?"*

The person who asked me that question was none other than Mr. John Navaroli, the custodian who would come by my classroom to lecture at least once a year. I've had some magnificent educators at Cotting, but none that moved me more than John. Thanks to him, after listening to his music from a different angle and reading the lyrics to those songs that he played to describe his topics, I enjoy music from the '60s more than I had ever expected. I cannot thank him enough.

Just two days before 2008 began. I had one last taste of the limelight in 2007. The Sunday edition of the *Lowell Sun* did this piece about the twenty-five most fascinating people in Greater Lowell in 2007. They put out the pictures of those people on the front page, on the day after the Patriots completed their undefeated regular season! There were a few names that I was familiar with such as Lowell's best professional boxer Micky Ward, Massachusetts congresswoman Niki Tsongas, and one other fascinating person from the area, *Tyler Lagasse!*

I had made the paper again! On the same page with an historic moment in Boston sports again! There was no longer any doubt about it. This year was officially *something else* for me. Before I was in the *Lowell Sun* for the second time, my picture from this year's Red, White, and Bid made the Special Olympics newsletter called the *Spotlight*. My speech at this event also made the *Spotlight*.

It was 2007, the year when the Red Sox won the World Series again, the year when Ray Allen and Kevin Garnett joined the Celtics, the year the Patriots pulled off a 16–0 regular season, and the year when the Bruins began their return to relevance and winning hockey. These events and my accomplishments in 2007 could not have been timed more perfectly. Could you believe that I could go from shooting a 50 in nine holes on the same golf course that I play every Monday afternoon with Dad in the month of May to playing my best round so far at a course I never went to? Who would have thought early in the year that my face would be in a newspaper, not once but twice? And to be named one of the twenty-five most fascinating people in the area I live in by a newspaper that I read almost every day is a complete honor. I also had a golf tournament named after me, a golf tournament!

There was a time in between when I could not have a conversation without repeating what the person had just asked me or said to me. There was a time when I could not pull my own baby teeth out. There was a time when I was resistant to change around me, even the slightest trace of change. There was a time when I could not last a whole day without my mother. There was a time when I felt so selfish and so greedy, and thinking about myself so much that I did not care about other people's feelings. There was even a time when I couldn't go through a whole day without crying or whining.

My journey to adulthood was finally complete. It was along the lines of chaotic to say the least but above all that journey ended very well for me. I was now twenty-one years old, a grown man with more responsibilities and more privileges than I had since childhood. I had just started going to college and had done so well after taking four courses. I had more than my share of great moments with Special Olympics and was only going to get better now that I was with the Global Messenger Program, where I was making speeches about how Special Olympics has changed my life for the better. I had done so much in the two and a half years since graduating Cotting. Back when I made the speech at graduation, I said that my future was as bright as it can be. At the time, I never thought about making speeches on a regular basis or winning state golf titles for Special Olympics. I didn't think for one moment that it would be this bright, this early. It's strange to understand that your life does not always turn out the way you dream it. But in my case, it has turned out all right. Sometimes the best things in life are the ones you don't expect.

One of the biggest misconceptions about people living with autism is that they don't make "connections" or have empathy or emotions. I hope that the one thing this book accomplishes is to abolish that misconception!

2008: "Anything Is Possible!"

IN 2007, THE PLANETS COULD not have been better aligned. I'm not sure if I could have asked for more. I was one lucky young man in a year that was definitely *something else*. Just hours before the year ended, I wrote in my journal, "May 2008 be a year full of peace, promise, and harmony, and not of incident, controversy, and deceit." If 2007 was "something else," 2008 would be the year in which "anything is possible."

In January, Mom, Dad, and I had to attend a biennial Special Olympics Global Messenger summit at the Sheraton Hotel in Danvers and we were going to stay there overnight. After having a bite to eat, we went into another room for a kind of icebreaker or introduction where we got to meet more people and learned about what to expect of tomorrow. Next, we all went back to the ballroom to play this *Family Feud* composite game called Fabulous Feud. The next day, I prepared myself for the speeches I was about to make along with the other global messengers in training, which were divided into three groups: beginner, refresher, and advanced. I was with the advanced group. I went to the beginner group to play this break the ice game where I ripped a piece of toilet paper every time I spoke a sentence. After a break, I moved on to session two where we talked about where and why we are talking about Special Olympics. Then during session three, I gave of the Special Olympic athletes an interview so that I can introduce that athlete during the presentation. I practiced my introduction a few times. Then during the presentation I made a brief speech. I introduced myself, and mentioned the athlete I interviewed early in the day. I said some good things about him while looking at the crowd of a hundred without looking at my notes. I did not notice until after I was done speaking, but I screwed up the name of the person I was introducing. It was a very busy weekend for me and my family because on the day after the conference, I played basketball in the Martin Luther King Jr. Tournament at Milton Academy with the Kids in Disability Sports group.

Late in January, I went back to Middlesex Community College in Lowell to take this Monday evening Microcomputer Applications course. This course had to do with learning the basics and specifics of Microsoft Office 2007, which included spreadsheets, PowerPoint presentations, and Word documents. It was generally about learning how to use Microsoft Word, Excel, and PowerPoint to the best of your ability. My teacher for that class was an acquaintance of my mother, named Charlene Ryan. She helped me feel really comfortable in my four months of this course. I remember doing word documents, spreadsheets, and PowerPoint when I was in Cotting School. Microcomputer Applications was a quite a challenge, but I was able to figure it out and in the end I would get an A.

Early in March of 2008, I learned that I had some big news. On one afternoon in March, Mom took me to the Massachusetts Registry of Deeds in Lowell for an important job interview. I went inside the building alone without my mother, who had to do some business. The building I went into was very old-fashioned from the outside. Inside the building housed the courthouse and the registry. I was to meet with the head registrar, Mr. Richard Howe in his office accompanied by his assistant Tony Accardi. Another person who arrived during the interview was Frank Heslin from the Career Center in Lowell.

Mr. Howe and I had a pleasant talk for a while as we got to know each other. He seemed like a nice person to be with. I talked to him about myself while trying to be as professional as possible. I told him what I was capable of doing and he then told me about the specifics of the job. He said that the job involves using a computer in an office and scanning documents with a scanner. He pointed out that the town hall in nearby Westford was in need of repairs and they cleared out their records and sent them to the registry in Lowell so that they can be scanned into the Westford home page. My supervisor Tony Accardi would be there to teach me how to use the computer and scanner until I could do the job all by myself. My job was provided by the Career

Center in Lowell so I was going to be paid by the city of Lowell. I just had to fill in my time sheet just so that I could get paid. By the time the interview was over, I learned that I got the job and told them that I could work right away. I worked Mondays, Tuesdays, and Thursdays, five hours a day from 8:30 a.m. to 1:30 p.m. I was going to share an office with two other workers, one of them had autism. My first day of work at the registry was Monday, March 10, 2008.

I got a new part-time job at last, but getting there was going to be another obstacle. A couple of days before my first day at the registry, my dad and I rode a city bus from Greater Lowell Tech (my mother's job site) to the Gallagher Terminal in Downtown Lowell. After getting off at the terminal, Dad and I took a walk from there to the registry, which lasted about ten minutes. Then as Dad went in the car with Mom, I rode the bus all by myself from the terminal to the Voke. Three times a week from March until the middle of June, my working routine consisted of getting up at six in the morning, followed by getting dressed, eating breakfast, and brushing my teeth. Then before seven, my dad would drive me to the Voke, and I would stay in Mom's classroom for a little while until my bus arrived at seven twenty-five. Normally I would be the first one to get picked up. My bus would later make a stop at Lowell General Hospital. I would then go through the UMass–Lowell North Campus down the VFW Highway, cross the Aiken Street Bridge, and go by LeLacheur Park on the right. Then it's through the Acre section of the city until the bus reached the downtown area. After several stops, the bus would crowd up, mostly with students heading to Lowell High School. Then the bus would go down Dutton Street, which then becomes Thorndike Street. Traffic in the city plus several stops would cause the bus to arrive at exactly eight, a little later than its scheduled time. After getting off the bus, I would buy myself a *Boston Herald* and walk from the terminal to the registry, crossing two main streets to get there.

As for my job, it consisted of scanning documents. One by one or several at a time, I would put some documents in a scanner, make some mouse clicks and see my papers go through the scanner. The images would then pop up on the computer. My first week of work was just about learning how to use the scanner. I started out with various sheets of paper before using the sheets and documents from the town of Westford. By the time March came to a close, I started to get very good at scanning documents and got lots of work done. I was scanning years upon years of board of selectmen minutes dating back to the World War II era. After a while it kind of got boring, but I knew that my job was worth something, $8 an hour to be exact. But most importantly I was doing it for the town of Westford. From then on I grew to be a well-liked and respected worker at the Registry of Deeds. I was able to make a lot of friends there and a few others at the registry. I got along with my coworkers and supervisors great.

After work, I would take the ten-minute walk back to the terminal. I would wait there for a few minutes until my bus to the Voke arrived. The outbound bus was not as crowded as the one in the morning. I would take the same bus route to the Voke and be the last one to get dropped off between two and two fifteen. Finally, I would walk from the bus stop to the school parking lot and wait for Mom near her car. Either that or I would come inside the school and wait for her in her classroom. Mom would then drive me home. Generally that was my work routine.

The 2008 Let Me Be Brave Gala

In March of 2008, I was working on an ambitious speech with Mom for the 2008 Special Olympics Massachusetts Hall of Fame induction ceremony. It was also known as the Let Me Be Brave Gala, named after the first verse of the Special Olympics athlete's oath. The event would take place inside the Gordon Indoor Track Center at Harvard University on the evening of Saturday, April 5, 2008. However this ceremony coincided with the fortieth anniversary of the founding of Special Olympics. The founder and matriarch of Special Olympics, Eunice Kennedy Shriver, was to be honored that night.

One week before the ceremony, I went with my parents to Harvard. Before I went inside the track center to practice my speech, I saw Harvard Stadium, the big original coliseum-like structure that served as the home to both Harvard Crimson football, Boston Cannons lacrosse, and for one season in 1970 the home field of the Boston Patriots. One unique thing about the track was that the corners of the track were slanted or tilted toward the inside, possibly to increase the runners' momentum going down the corner. However, for the gala, the track was definitely not used for running except for a couple of people carrying the Flame of Hope as the hundreds of guests came to Harvard for this biennial event on the first Saturday of April. One week before the ceremony, I wrote in my journal, "After I'm done speaking, I'll be the man of the hour. This will be the speech of the year, and everybody is going to like the way I speak, and Special Olympics is going to benefit from it."

I came up with a few ideas for my most important speech yet. One of my ideas involved character because Mr. Navaroli's views on character permeated me, so I wrote a single paragraph about character. Then one night, not long before the gala, as I was about to go to bed, I had a word that just popped into my head *limit*. Instead of just sleeping on it until the next day, I decided to take some notes on it. I looked it up in my dictionary to see the definition of it and then I set out to tackle the meaning of limit by putting that in my speech.

After the rehearsal, I was asked to make some edits to shorten the length of it. My mother took away a couple of paragraphs and got rid of a few somewhat meaningless things in my speech here and there. Mom not only wanted me to be so sharp for the gala that I got nearly all the words right. She wanted me to look up and speak at the same time as soon as I had at least most of the words memorized by heart. This speech was going to be filmed so I had to practice looking up while I spoke, and I wanted to make sure that I didn't look silly on the podium at the gala. Mom also wanted me to practice speaking loud and clear and slow so that the audience would understand what I was saying. I worked really hard on that speech as any other that I made before or since.

The Let Me Be Brave Fortieth Anniversary Gala was a formal/black-tie event. Before the gala, my dad had to take me to a local Men's Warehouse to get me fitted into a tuxedo. I found one in my size with a black vest and a black neck tie that was already tied. I not only had to sound good at Harvard, I also had to look good as well. And boy was I going to look and sound good. I wore my gold medal that I won when I shot the 82 at the New England Invitational in Connecticut last October. That gold medal made my suit look even better because it completed the outfit.

I can best describe the gala by using just one word: "SPECIAL." It was special because it was the most special moment in Special Olympics history to date, and my most special moment since competing in my first Special Olympics event five years before. Sadly, the Eunice Kennedy Shriver could not make it. I wished that she were there that night to hear what I had to say, and to witness the progress of Special Olympics, the organization that she was responsible for starting thanks to her sister Rose and turning it into the largest amateur athletic program in the world. I wished that I could meet her. That would have made my night something more. Her son Tim Shriver, the chairman of Special Olympics was there in her place and was going to speak on her behalf.

My mom, my dad, and I arrived at Harvard in the middle of the afternoon. Before the gala started, I went outside in the windy and cool but clear weather with Mom and Dad to have pictures taken of me standing in front of several Harvard Campus buildings in the background. My personal favorite picture from the gala was the one of me with Harvard Stadium in the background. Inside the Gordon Indoor Track Center, there were some very tasty appetizers being served. One time I had a brief interview with a fellow Special Olympics athlete. I was a little flattered being interviewed because I did not prepare myself for it. I had a difficult time trying to come up with the right words to describe my Special Olympics experience, but I handled it very well. After meeting with Marge and Keith Peabody for a while, I went to my table to meet up with my parents.

In the beginning of the ceremony, two global messengers, both of them Special Olympic athletes came to their podiums, Melissa Reilly on the right, followed by Marc Segerman on the left. Not long after they were done speaking, another Special Olympic athlete named Michael Jaxtimer-Barry ran along the track with Lieutenant Rich Tavares of the Bourne Police Department. While they were running, they both held the Special Olympics torch, called the Flame of Hope, together. After they made their lap around the track, Michael recited the athlete's oath: "Let me win, but if I cannot win, let me be brave in the attempt." After that, the national anthem was sung by Special Olympics athlete Celeste Wheelock, who was from the Berkshires area in Western Massachusetts and who had excelled at Nordic skiing. Next, an invocation was later given by Bishop John Boles.

Then Robert Johnson, the president of Special Olympics Massachusetts, came onstage. Johnson said some things about Mrs. Shriver and how far Special Olympics has gone since the first games took place in Chicago in 1968. He spoke about how this organization originated from what was known as Camp Shriver back in 1962 when Eunice invited many boys and girls with intellectual disabilities to a place in Maryland. After Johnson was done, a video tribute of Mrs. Shriver was shown on two big screens for the audience. In the opening, Nelson Mandela, the person who helped liberate South Africa from apartheid, described Mrs. Shriver as a "pioneer who literally changed the way persons with disabilities are treated and viewed, not only in the United States, but in Africa and around the world." There were also pictures and images of Special Olympic athletes competing in their sports and winning medals. There were images of Eunice being with the athletes wishing them good luck. I saw Eunice literally get involved in their activities as well as their events in that video. They also showed footage of the first ever Special Olympic Games that took place in Chicago in 1968. Eunice's brother Ted Kennedy and her daughter Maria Shriver commented on how hard Eunice worked to improve the quality of life for not just her sister Rosemary, but the many people afflicted with disabilities all over the United States and planet earth. Not only did the Special Olympic athletes learn a lot from Eunice, she also learned a lot from them as well. I was amazed to see how far this organization has come since its birth. It started with one group and has since spread all over the globe.

After the video tribute was over, Robert Johnson introduced us to Tim Shriver. Tim said that Eunice was frustrated that she couldn't be there. He spoke for a while about his mother and how she touched the lives of the thousands upon thousands of people around the world. He then talked about the Special Olympics Healthy Athletes screening program that took place in West Africa. He told the crowd an inspiring story of five people from Africa that had surgery performed by volunteer doctors from the Healthy Athletes screening program just days after learning they were legally blind.

After that, Michael Jaxtimer-Barry's mom, Joanie, and Peter Meade, both the cochairpersons of the gala, came to speak. Then they both formally announced each inductee and group of inductees of the Special Olympics Massachusetts Hall of Fame Class of 2008. Three athletes, three coaches, two families in which at least one member of each family was a Special Olympic athlete, were among the inductees, as well as several volunteers and donors of Special Olympics. The athletes that were inducted were Denise Carriere who came to Lowell to play basketball against the KIDS group and had joined the Special Olympics Massachusetts Board of Directors and the Global Messenger Program in 2006. The second athlete to be inducted that night was a gentleman named Jody Furer, who had been participating with Special Olympics as far back as the early 1970s. The third athlete to join the Hall was Jessie MacDonald who could dead lift 300 pounds, 285 pounds in the squats, and could bench press 150 in weightlifting. She went on to win four gold medals in the Special Olympics World Games in 2006.

The three coaches that were inducted were Karen Bernardo of the Wellesley Stars Swimming Team, John Odom of the Whitman-Hanson area, and Pat White of the Red Raiders Ski Team based in Massachusetts's Berkshire Mountains. Two Special Olympic families were inducted into the hall that night: the Adler family, in which Michelle Adler was a SOMA Hall of Fame inductee back in 2004, and the Desmarais family. Finally two volunteers became inductees, Mr. Art Goyette from Southeastern Massachusetts, and the good people of Governor's Academy (formerly Governor Dummer) located in Byfield in the North Shore area of Massachusetts. Governor's Academy is a private prep school that hosts the annual SOMA soccer tournament. Their hard work and devotion had earned them a place in the Special Olympics Massachusetts Hall of Fame.

After a brief dinner break, the Special Olympics Massachusetts chairman Geoffrey Nothnagle came up to his podium. As I started walking toward the stage with my speech book, Mr. Nothnagle recognized the friends and donors of Special Olympics and the Let Me Be Brave Gala. He recognized and thanked the Olympic presenting partners, Bank of New York Mellon and the Walmart Foundation. He also thanked the MVP partners, the all-star partners, and the many varsity players and team players that made this organization and this event possible. Then as Mr. Nothnagle was about to introduce me, I was given the cue to walk to my podium. I was about to make the biggest speech since my graduation from Cotting School on 2005.

Before I opened up my speech book, I wasn't really sure if the crowd was going to like my speech. I worked so hard at it, but I wasn't going to know how well my speech was until I was done. Some of you that have heard of me and saw my speech may have a clear idea of who I am. But for those of you that don't know me, well this is your golden opportunity to look at the words written by a person living with autism. This is your chance to see that my life and the lives of those with disabilities are fuller than you think. The words that you are about to read make up a brief story about my life, my world, and the lives and worlds of the Special Olympians themselves in my point of view . . . Here are the words that I spoke that evening . . .

Forty years ago, it began as a dream. Today it is now a reality. A dream come true for the thousands of athletes as well as the millions of people who have been affected by the hard work and commitment to excellence of a very special woman named Eunice Kennedy Shriver. It is through her powerful energy that athletes such as me are able to be rewarded and recognized for being the best we can be, no matter who we are, how we look, and what we can do to participate. Each event celebrates the ways that we are similar to people without disabilities. In the real world we are seen and judged by our differences and challenges. On the playing field, we are seen as champions. We are our own special club. Together, WE are the Special Olympics.

Good evening, my name is Tyler Lagasse, two time state golf champion from the state of Massachusetts. It has been a privilege being a part of the Special Olympics for the past five years. It has meant a lot to me. It has been a life altering experience. I have been able to touch so many lives, make new friends, and yes, go out and try hard to be the best I can be.

Webster's Dictionary defines the word limit *as the point beyond which something may not or cannot proceed, a boundary. In the mythical dictionary of Special Olympics, there is no such thing as the word* limits. *It does not exist. We do not believe in limits here. The fact remains that there may be a limit to our abilities, but there is* NO LIMIT *to our desire to perform, our desire to have fun, our desire to play sports. There is a place for those of us that are either physically or intellectually limited where we can express our love of athletic competition. We can thank Mrs. Shriver for that.*

In 2003, I participated in the Special Olympics State Basketball Tournament and won a gold medal in the State Qualifier and another gold medal for winning the State Championship. I have now won a total of fourteen Special Olympic medals, including ten gold medals. In October of 2007, I competed in the New England Invitational Golf Tournament in Farmington, Connecticut, and played the game of my life! I shot my lowest eighteen-hole round EVER with a final score of 82. For that performance, I received another gold medal. And I am wearing this gold medal to prove it. That just goes to show you that even though I have autism, I can accomplish big things.

I remember fifteen years ago, when my parents found a special school in Lexington, Massachusetts, called the Community Therapeutic Day School—CTDS for short. To be perfectly honest, I did not like going there. I wanted to be normal, like everybody else. But in reality, it doesn't work that way. Not everybody is normal. Some people are extraordinary, and I am one of the extraordinary people. Mom and Dad saw in me what I couldn't see. That is to say, I am something special. In retrospect, CTDS as well as

Special Olympics have helped me become a better human being. Special Olympics really taught me a lot about life, discipline, fair play, desire, how to set goals and to do whatever it takes no matter what.

What is character? An old friend (actually, he was the custodian at one of my schools) once told me, "Character isn't everything, but it is the only thing that matters in an uncertain world." Special Olympics has taught me a lot about character. My fellow athletes in my opinion have demonstrated more heart and character than any professional athlete. Special Olympics has given me the self-esteem in order for me to mature as an individual. I have the ability to overcome by figuring out how to get out of trouble thanks to Special Olympics. I would never be able to continue playing the sports that I love if it were not for Special Olympics. I wouldn't be on this podium now if it were not for the existence of Special Olympics and with the help of loving and caring parents.

For all you athletes, listen up. Special Olympics has done a lot for me and I am sure it has done the same for you. You are all special. You are special because you never stop trying. You never give up. You have this thing inside you called "the fire" inside you. And thanks to this fire, you have what it takes to be Champions. I am very proud of you for being here for this special occasion. Your hard work has earned you a place in the Hall of Fame. There is one and only one word to describe all of you that are being inducted. And that word is simply stated: Special.

Special Olympics has paved the way for a brighter future for not only me, but for everyone who has ever participated in or volunteered for Special Olympics. Only the sky is the limit for me, thanks to Special Olympics and the generosity and vision of people like you.

Like the late John Lennon once said at the end of his song titled "Imagine,"
"You may say I am dreamer
but I'm not the only one
I hope someday you'll join us
and the world will live as one."
Just like you people, I, too, am a dreamer. I believe that through the hard work and dedication to your passion, great things can be accomplished and barriers can be overcome.

Throughout my speech, I felt like the president of the United States giving out the State of the Union address. I hoped that my speech was going to be great, but I did not expect anything like this. I had at least fourteen applauses during my speech. Those applauses may have doubled the length of my speech. I admit I was kind of nervous speaking to a crowd of this magnitude. In the beginning, I kind of screwed up the word *today* by saying, "Tahh-daaayy," since I was not yet comfortable. As my speech went on and as they were applauding me more and more, I started to feel better. The reason I stopped for the applauses was that I wanted everyone to hear me speak and I also wanted to hear myself speak. I could hardly hear myself speak when they were applauding.

The one part that got the whole crowd to its feet was the one where I explained my experience at CTDS by saying that not everybody is normal but that some are extraordinary. I used that part in the Red, White, and Bid months ago. I used those same words at the gala and got the longest and loudest ovation by anyone who came behind the podium. I myself clapped in celebration of what I had just created. I'm sure that a lot of people in Harvard were moved and stunned that night. What I did that night was something that you just don't see or hear every day. Sometimes you have to remind yourself that this is a precious world we live in, and that you need to find inspiration. That's what my speech was all about, to inspire everyone in this room and not take for granted in what we do or how we live. It's a fact that there are uniquely gifted people in this world and that some are not recognized for their skill and character but shied away and shunned for their disability. Before Special Olympics, nobody thought something could be done to help those with physical and intellectual disabilities. Nearly all of them had to be confined to institutions and had to live there for life. Then Eunice and Rosemary came and they set out to change the world along with millions of lives. Although Rosemary never recovered from her problems, Eunice spent more than the last half of her life making Special Olympics a completely legitimate organization with events taking place every day in every continent around the world. I'm sorry for getting off topic for the moment, but I wanted to explain in detail why we should not ignore some people that are disabled yet talented and most importantly, special.

Anyway back to the gala, after I was done speaking, I introduced the auctioneer Charles Bailey-Gates to the stage. He said that this was going to be one tough act to follow. One of the items that were auctioned off to benefit Special Olympics was tickets to the 2008 Deutsche Bank

Championship at the TPC Boston Course in Norton, Massachusetts, on Labor Day weekend. Other items included Red Sox tickets, Patriots tickets plus a Tom Brady autographed jersey, courtside tickets to a Celtics game for next season, Bruins playoff tickets against the Montreal Canadiens, and the WEEI Producer of the Day on the WEEI 850 AM radio's morning show. The last items being auctioned off were a Boston Bruins jersey signed by the entire team and a hockey stick and I got to hold up the frame covering the jersey. Finally, I stayed onstage for this athletes appeal thing where some of them in the crowd wished to donate a certain amount of money to Special Olympics. Most of them in the audience pledged hundreds of dollars. Some of them pledged thousands. I helped out Mr. Bailey-Gates pick out who in the crowd was pledging. There were a lot of hands that were raised so it took more than one person to accept a pledge. It was obviously a great thrill to be on the stage in front of a thousand people on that brisk April night.

After the auction, two more people were honored for their contributions to Special Olympics: Margaret McKenna, president of the Walmart Foundation, and Jim Brett, president and CEO of New England Council and a former state representative. Joanie Jaxtimer came back to the podium to introduce her friend Margaret McKenna. Jaxtimer said a few words about McKenna's contributions and how big a role she has played for this organization. For that, she deserved special recognition that night.

Before I get to the next person who was honored that night in Harvard, I want to talk about 1968, the year when Special Olympics was born. Shortly before I left for the gala, I saw this special hosted by Tom Brokaw on the History Channel that had to do with the year 1968. I got a firsthand look at what America and the world looked like that year. There was a dreadful war that took place in Vietnam and it only got out of hand for the people fighting there and those back home. Martin Luther King Jr. was assassinated that year, as was Eunice's brother, Robert F. Kennedy who was in the middle of a pursuit to the Presidency. Riots were breaking out and many American cities were burning to the ground. It seemed as if the country was tearing itself apart from the inside out in 1968.

However in the midst of all this hatred and hardship, this agony and suffering, this pain and frustration, Eunice Kennedy Shriver brought forth the Special Olympics when nearly all of them around her didn't listen. It's hard to believe that Eunice can create something like the Special Olympics while all of this was happening in 1968, while the third brother in her family unexpectedly died. After all these losses, Eunice gave hope and strength and dignity to those who did not think it would be possible at the time. Forty years later, I was the witness of a very special moment in history, a celebration of a program's fortieth birthday. When it was launched, not many people thought it would last as long as forty years.

Jim Brett was the second honoree after Margaret McKenna. Before Jim Brett made the podium, Peter Meade gave a stirring oratory about the year 1968 and gave a trembling description of how turbulent the year was and how, in a year of crisis, Eunice started this organization that has reached out to the 2.5 million athletes in 180 countries all over the world. Meade also described a meeting a long time ago with Senator Edward "Ted" Kennedy. Meade brought along his friend Dan Hickey who had Down's syndrome and Dan's brother Jim who was a priest. Dan and Jim's parents came to the states from Ireland when work was hard to find in their homeland. The Hickey's came to Senator Kennedy to thank him and his family for bringing them dignity through the Special Olympics. That meeting was such an emotional moment that Jim Hickey and Ted Kennedy both cried.

Then Meade describes this conversation with Kennedy about the start of Special Olympics. After Ted was first told that the program was being launched, Ted said to Meade, "It's never gonna work."

Meade replied, "If you were doing it, it wouldn't work. If I were doing it, it wouldn't work. But because Eunice is doing it, it damn well is gonna work . . . and here we are forty years later." Meade said this after describing how far Special Olympics has gone. After his piece he introduced Jim Brett to the audience. Jim Brett was and still is a bona fide advocate for persons with intellectual disabilities. He had spent around sixteen years with the state congress, but he has been rewarded numerous times for his work toward helping the welfare and the quality of life of those that are afflicted with disabilities.

I admit, besides my speech, Jim Brett's piece was the one that moved me the most. His wasn't has long and did not get as much applauses as mine, but it had no shortage of purpose. After giving out his thanks, he said that "receiving an award the same night as Eunice Shriver is like going to the gym with Arnold Schwarzenegger." Brett described Eunice as a "champion of champions" and "the true and steadfast champion of those thousands of champions here and around the world."

The most stirring things that he said in his speech were a pair of quotes that was used by one Ralph Waldo Emerson. The first one was "to be yourself in a world that is constantly trying to make you something else is the greatest accomplishment." He then said, "Who does that describe if not the Special Olympic athletes?" I believed in what he said because being yourself is better than being someone you're not. It's worth it to be you just as it's worthless not to be you. The other quote that Jim Brett took from Emerson had to do with resiliency or the ability to bounce back from adversity. Emerson stated, "Our greatest glory is not in never failing, but in rising up every time we fail." Brett then said that Emerson's quote reminds him of a Japanese proverb: "Fall seven times. Stand up eight times." He described the Special Olympians at the gala and everywhere as "stubbornly optimistic." I thought Jim Brett's speech was contagious in a good way. It inspired me very much just as my speech inspired the hundreds at the gala very much.

After Jim Brett was done, SOMA president Robert Johnson came onstage to announce that the Yawkey Foundation II made a donation to Special Olympics Massachusetts. As a result, the new headquarters for Special Olympics Massachusetts was going to be named after the foundation. The SOMA Hall of Fame was unveiled after the name of the building was announced. Somewhere inside the track center was a model of what the new headquarters was going to look like. The building would open its doors in the fall of 2009. After Johnson was done, Jim Healey, the president of the Yawkey Foundation II, came up to do a brief speech. He said that if the original donors Tom and Jean Yawkey were alive today, they would be "thrilled and very proud of this partnership" with Special Olympics. Tom and Jean Yawkey were longtime owners of the Boston Red Sox and Fenway Park for nearly seventy years. Healey also stated that there was going to be a big celebration at the new building once it is finished. In the fall of 2009 there was going to be one.

The Let Me Be Brave Fortieth Anniversary Gala concluded with Special Olympics athlete Heather Gardiner doing a sweet version of Josh Groban's "You Raise Me Up." After the gala had officially ended, I was flooded with remarks and compliments from people I have never ever met before. Tim Shriver loved my speech so much that my mother gave him a copy. I had a picture taken with him and this picture of me with Mr. Tim Shriver to this day is on the back of my speech book. Niki Tsongas, the recently elected congresswoman from Lowell, was in attendance that night and I shook her hand too. I got to meet up with Jim Brett and told him that his speech was the best. He himself liked my speech, which was understandable because I had the loudest ovation of the night. I must have shook hands with about ten to fifteen people whom I never met. There were some people saying to me that my speech was a "gold medal performance" and "an 11 on a scale of 1 to 10." I was more than glad to be at Harvard, and I didn't care much about how late I was going to stay there. I must have stayed at Harvard for a whole hour after the event officially ended. I completely stole the show with that epic speech. Months after the gala, my speech would make its way onto the World Wide Web.

It was an amazing night to be associated with Special Olympics, it was an amazing night to be at Harvard, and it was an amazing night to be me. I owe it all to Eunice Kennedy Shriver for making it all possible. She was the one that brought the group of the once seemingly incapable from the ashes to Camp Shriver in 1962 and turned it into a dynamic enterprise spanning the globe. I still wished that she were there to witness the result of the progress of her vision. I was the example of that progress.

I must admit, I had no idea how profound that evening would turn out! Tyler delivered that speech with such poise. His words brought the crowd from tears to laughter in one speech. He made us all pause and reflect on the gift of life, regardless of limitations and challenges. In short, he made us believe that through hard work, anything is possible.

Besides work and college, the whole season of spring was great. In April, I started the track and field season with the Team Micky racing team. After several Saturday practices at Notre Dame Academy in Tyngsboro, my team made their trip to Milton Academy for the Special Olympics North Sectionals of Track and Field. Fifteen athletes including myself represented Team Micky on May 18. A few people from Cotting School and CTDS competed in the games that day. I competed in three events that day. My first event was the one-hundred-meter dash. I finished the event in exactly 12.7 seconds and would earn a gold medal. After a long break for lunch, I took part in the four-hundred-meter dash. I started off the run slow while two runners sped by me. The first thought that went through my mind was *I'm not going to finish first or second*. At the halfway point, I picked it up a notch and I was able to get into second position. Then on the final straightaway I had a chance to win the race. The runner that started hot and was in first place eventually tired out. I kept on going and never looked back as I finished the four hundred in 1:10 and won a second gold medal. The last event was the 4 x 100 relay. Four teams ran the relay and three of them represented Team Micky. My last event was not much of a contest as my team finished in first. All three Team Micky foursomes finished the relay 1–2–3. The three teams had pictures taken and then the entire team and all the coaches posed for the full team pictures. I won three gold medals that day. It would be the last time that I would compete in Track and Field events for Special Olympics.

My 2008 Lowell General Hospital golf season began on May 5 when Dad and I played nine holes at Tyngsboro Country Club. Understandably, I got off to a sluggish start on account of the usual long layoff between golf rounds and shot a 47. Two weeks later, Dad and I returned to Tyngsboro where I began the round with three straight pars. I got to within fifteen feet of the hole from the tee with the 3-wood on the long par-3 third hole. I almost never make par on the third hole. This time I did. Then I returned to earth with a missed opportunity for a fourth straight par on #4, followed by a double bogey on the par-3, fifth. I did get back on track to make another three straight pars on 6, 7, and 8. I had a good chance at breaking 40 at Tyngsboro for the first time ever as I was currently at three strokes over par heading into the par-3, ninth. All I needed to do was to make bogey or less on this hole. It was then that I learned that breaking 40 was not going to be easy. The wind was a factor that day and I missed the green to the left. Luckily I was still in play and was able to get on the green but I missed my putts for par and for bogey and had to settle for a nine-hole score of 40. Instead of finishing out strong, I ended that day with a whimper, which was the last thing I wanted to do.

On Memorial Day Monday, Dad and I went back to Tyngsboro, this time Gary Browning and his son Cody came along with us. This round was not going to count against my score with the golf league since they don't play on Memorial Day. On the first hole, with my third shot from the rough on the left side of the green, I chipped on to get to within a few feet of the hole and saved par. On the second hole, I launched my best tee shot from that hole to date only to three-putt for bogey. On the third hole, I shot my 3-wood to the right of the green. Then I made this pretty good chip to get to allow myself to make my second par save of the day. This was my third straight par in a row on this long par-3 hole. With a little help from the wind at my back, I hit my best 3-wood of the day down the fairway of the fourth hole. But in the end I had to double bogey the hole. On the fifth hole, I finally found a way to get on the green and two-putt for par. On hole #6, I hit a fade off the tee to the left with the driver. On my second shot, I hit a great 7-iron from a downhill lie and made the fringe in front of the green. Once again, just like last week, I had to par the hole. On the seventh hole, after a decent 6-iron off the tee, my second shot with a sand wedge hit a rope in front of the green stopping the ball from getting on and I would later make bogey. The eighth hole is best remembered as the one where Cody Browning hit his third shot to the green and snapped his club at the handle. He did make his par, so did his dad, and so did I.

On hole #9, after hitting a horrible tee shot that went badly short of the green, I went out and made the best chip of the year so far and got my ball to stop within five feet of the hole. I had this left to right putt for an improbable par while Pawtucket Boulevard across from the eighth and ninth holes was filled with people on account of the upcoming parade. No way did I let the crowd distract me as I nailed that clutch putt securing me a score of 39. After more than ten years of playing at the course located just two minutes from my home, I finally got this monkey off my back. It was my first ever time breaking 40 in nine holes at Tyngsboro. It was sweet because I was playing with two other people, and I came so close many times, recently last week. However, it would be the only time in which I was able to break 40 at my home course in 2008.

Golf is the one sport that Tyler can play with anyone and feel just like anyone else. On the golf course, Tyler fits in.

On May 31, 2008, KIDS president Fred Wilkie invited me and my dad to play in a modified scramble golf tournament at Long Meadow Golf Club, a private course located on the Lowell-Tewksbury border. Fred Wilkie was a member there and it was kind of him to invite me and my dad to play that day. I only remember going there once back in the summer of 1998 to see Jaret Foley participate in the Junior Cities. The place was different and much nicer ten years after my first visit.

Dad and I played on the same foursome as Fred and Andrew Dozibrin, who is an athlete with the KIDS group. Andrew also plays regularly at Long Meadow since his dad is a member there. Even though we were on the same team, Andrew looked better at golf than I was.

It was a beautiful nine-hole course, but it was also challenging as well. The first hole was a par-4 that was over three hundred yards long, which seemed easy to me. The second hole was a short par-3 with bunkers surrounding the green. The elevated tee box made the hole shorter. The third hole was a fairly long par-4 that was a dogleg to the right. Hole #4 was another long par-4 with a mound in the shape of a bar a hundred yards in front of the green. The fifth hole was an uphill par-3 that played longer than the 180 yards listed on the scorecard. Hole #6 was a three-hundred-yard par-4 hole, which was a dogleg right. The seventh and eighth holes were par-5s. The seventh was a dogleg right, while the eighth was straightaway up until you encounter some water guarding the green. The eighth was the most difficult stroke hole on the course. Finally, the ninth is a par-4 that is slightly downhill. Overall, the course is a par-36 and the greens are pretty fast.

We played eighteen holes in the tournament that day, and I looked like a lost golfer. I didn't get my game together all day even though it was my first appearance at Long Meadow. One time during the tournament it started to monsoon for a while. Eventually the rain would stop but my problems wouldn't. I did not make a par until the fifteenth hole, the sixth hole of the course. I didn't have as much fun as I hoped I would. I admit to being a bad sport out there, especially after I hit one of my balls in the water on #8 as I tried to get on the green. I must have tried to do too much in terms of trying to hit long drives or good approach shots or hitting clutch shots. The way I played or tried to play, I couldn't break 100. Nothing was clicking for me. It just wasn't my day, but I took it like a man since it was my first time golfing at Long Meadow.

One time during the tournament, Fred Wilkie had a reason to believe why I was not hitting the ball well that day. Fred thought that I was over swinging too much. He told me that "less is more," which meant that if you swing too hard, you're sacrificing a lot of accuracy and that your shots are more likely not to go straight. He also said that if you take a little off your swing, you'll make more contact and your ball will go straight and perhaps longer than you think. I learned that you don't have to hit the ball too hard in order to get distance. Sometimes you've got to let the club do the work for you. "Less is more" is a motto that I would go by for the rest of the 2008 golf season, and many seasons that followed.

Like many golfers, Tyler takes the game of golf too serious sometimes. We often have to remind him that he is not on the PGA tour! I believe it is so good for Tyler when someone else beats his score. He is a good golfer. However, he is not the "best" golfer around. His approach to golf is much like his approach to life . . . anything less than your best effort is unacceptable. Golf has taught him many valuable lessons, such as patience, resilience, manners and how to be humble.

Less than a week later on June 6, Dad and I went to Green Meadow in Hudson, New Hampshire, to participate in the first annual Team Micky Ward Charities Golf Outing. The tournament was a best-ball scramble format, and Dad and I were teamed up with John Busby and Bill Sullivan, fathers of participants of the KIDS group. Two other KIDS Inc. associates were at Green Meadow that day, Fred Wilkie and Bob Majeau, whose son played basketball for KIDS Inc. WCVB-TV Channel 5's Bob Halloran was there and I got to meet him. Rick Dupuis and his associate Mark Bastien were also at the course.

There was a down pour on the drive to Green Meadow but as Dad and I got there it eased to a drizzle. The shotgun start originally scheduled for 7:30 a.m. was postponed until 9:00 due to the rain. The tournament was played on the more difficult Jungle Course. Our first hole was the par-4, fifteenth hole. After finishing up our first hole, it started raining again and it went down in torrents. I did what I could to stay dry. The weather played a big role in my golf that day. My once waterproof fleece became saturated around the shoulders and my pants got pretty much soaked. Eventually play resumed and as I was trying to keep my clubs dry under my umbrella, my team birdied the hole. We would make par on the seventeenth and bogey the eighteenth hole. Before we arrived at the first hole, we all went to the putting green to make fifteen-foot putts to qualify for the $10,000 putting contest. I was the only one in my foursome to qualify for the contest, which would take place after all the golfers had finished playing all eighteen holes. That is as long as it didn't rain for the rest of the day.

I was not able to get my tee shots figured out until I reached the par-5, third hole. My shot was exactly 291 yards with the Sasquatch. But in the end we could settle for par. On four of the next five holes, I was responsible for setting up the approach shots thanks to my tee shots. I helped my team make birdie on the sixth and ninth holes. Our score for the first nine holes of the Jungle Course was a 34, two strokes under par.

After making a par on the tenth hole, we went to the eleventh hole, which was an uphill par-3. Every par-3 hole had a "closest to the pin" contest. Micky Ward was on the eleventh hole, and he had each of us wear a boxing glove while we swung our clubs. I could not grip my club properly with a boxing glove on my left hand. I still managed to hit my ball with it but I could not reach the green. Only two of us made the green with the boxing glove on and we made a par on that hole.

We then managed to make another par on #12 (the hole in which the fairway bent ninety degrees to the left), and on the thirteenth hole (the longest and most difficult hole on the course measured at exactly 538 yards long), we wound up making bogey. My best tee shot of the day was saved for last—the par-4 fourteenth—as I was the only one on the team to find the fairway. I even helped my team get to the green and we wrapped up the tournament with a par. Our score for the back nine holes was 37, making out the total for the tournament a one-stroke-under-par 71. The winning team shot an 11-under-par 61.

After the tournament, I competed in the putting contest for a chance to win $10,000. I was the first competitor to attempt a putt and came up very short. Later on all the golfers gathered around for the awards and the auction. After that, I got to make a speech about Micky Ward, the man who made this tournament and my running team possible. I explained how Micky Ward came from humble beginnings to be a successful boxer and a contributor to those living in Lowell and elsewhere that are less fortunate. I personally talked about myself and how Micky Ward has played a part in me and over a dozen others winning many Special Olympic medals in the track and field events at Milton Academy a month earlier. My speech touched just about everybody there. Rick Dupuis and Fred Wilkie had never seen me speak to an audience before. They later told me that I had done a great job. Micky Ward gave me a big hug and then got to say a few words of his own to the crowd. I heard a lot of positive things that were said about me that day. The more I spoke to a crowd, big or small, the more I felt like a man. Every day, the year 2008 was becoming more and more special.

The Odyssey

Most dictionaries define the word *odyssey* as a long wandering and eventful journey. I called this next chapter "The Odyssey," which took place during the period between Tuesday, June 24, and Saturday, July 5, because it felt like I was going on this magical trip away from reality. They were the kinds of days that most people do not even dream about. For many summer days, I was living in some kind of magical trance. It was a true adventure, the Babe Ruth of vacations. Simply put, it was an odyssey because it felt like I was traveling into an assortment of worlds. This period of the summer of 2008 was one of the most memorable moments of my life.

It started on June 24 when I was invited by the Kids in Disability Sports organization to participate in a scramble golf tournament down in Plymouth, Massachusetts. I was to be with a foursome consisting of me, attorney and KIDS Inc. honorary board member Rick Lalime, KIDS president Fred Wilkie, and Danny Newell. Rick Lalime picked me up in the morning and after we stopped at his house in Lowell for a while, we drove all the way down to Plymouth. The name of the golf course that we went to was Pinehills Golf Club. It was a top notch place, one of *the* best in Massachusetts. The event that took place at the Pinehills was the ninth annual Doug Flutie Jr. Celebrity Golf Classic.

Rick and I were able to find the place all right and were able to find Fred Wilkie and Danny Newell as well. The place was beyond fabulous, the clubhouse building was huge, the pro shop looked nice, the bar and restaurant was jam packed, and there was this function room where the after-golf party was to take place. A lot of famous people were at the golf tournament, mostly former athletes who played their sports in the

Boston area and the whole country. I was thinking to myself, *Oh my god! I used to see these guys on TV when I was a kid.*

Before I went inside the clubhouse, I got to meet Doug Flutie who was hosting the tournament. Doug and I had pretty much the same height. It was amazing that he even became a football player at all, and yet he had such a remarkable football career in the USFL, Canada, and the Buffalo Bills. He was totally undersized but his scrambling skills, strong arm, and his competitive will made up for it. But he is best known for one big play in 1984 when his Boston College Eagles played the defending national champions, the Hurricanes of the University of Miami at the historic Orange Bowl. On the last play of the game, Flutie launches a Hail Mary touchdown pass to his teammate Gerard Phelan to win the game. He went on to win the Heisman trophy not long after that famous pass.

Besides his football career, the most intriguing thing about Doug was that his son Dougie had autism. After the diagnosis, Flutie set out to spread awareness of autism and formed the Doug Flutie Jr. Foundation, also known as Dougie's Team. That's what this golf tournament was about, it was for his son and it was for his foundation to combat this dreadful nightmare called autism.

It makes me so sad that Tyler relates the word dreadful to the word autism. Most of the time, he presents himself as an upbeat kind of person. Obviously, he doesn't see autism as a strength at all.

Just before the tournament was supposed to begin, I went to use the driving range to hit a bucket of balls. I was a wreck out there. I could not hit the ball straight and far like I wanted to. My shots were just so ugly, that it looked as if my ball moved like a car with a stalled engine. I didn't know how I was going to play that day. It turned out that I didn't have to because in the middle of my practice, I heard from a tournament official that there was lightning in the area. By twelve, the scheduled start time for us to golf, it started to rain. By one, the rain turned into a downpour. By two, the whole outdoors was all wet and still the rain only got worse to the point where golfing was out of the question. One thing that I forgot to do before going inside the clubhouse was to change back into my regular shoes. Consequently, I left my shoes out there in the golf cart to get waterlogged along with my golf clubs. Of course, I did not know that it was supposed to rain this hard for this long.

Instead of golfing, Rick, Fred, Danny, and I visited the function hall. There Rick took me around to meet with many famous people, some of them who were once great athletes. The following people that were present at the tournament were (to name a few): Bob Montgomery, Red Sox backup catcher during the 1970s and later Red Sox color commentator; Andy Brickley, former Boston Bruin and current colorman for Bruins broadcasts; Franconia, New Hampshire, native Bode Miller, the Olympic alpine skier; Bob Neumeier, formerly the sports reporter for WBZ-TV in Boston; and Jayme Parker, reporter for the New England Sports Network (NESN). I did not meet these people, but I did meet the following that were at the tournament in Plymouth.

Before the rain started, Rick Lalime introduced me to his close friend who once managed the Lowell Spinners Baseball Team for a while. His name was Dick Bernardino. Then as the rain was beginning to wipe away the golf tournament, I got to meet two sportscasters, Steve Burton from WBZ-TV, and Mike Dowling from WCVB-TV. I also got to meet former Penn State running back Omar Easy. Then I met a couple of former Boston Celtics from the '70s and '80s, Jo Jo White, and M. L. Carr. Jo Jo White told me that it was his idea to have the Celtics draft Paul Pierce out of the University of Kansas in 1998 because White himself played for the Jayhawks in his college basketball days. I also got to meet an accomplished local amateur golfer named Ben Spitz. He was a left-handed golfer like me and had won a mid-amateur golf title so far. This was ridiculous. I had never seen anything like it. I had never seen so many local and regional celebrities in one room, up close in my entire life. But it only gets better.

The one person who I met that stood out above all the rest was ESPN's Chris Berman, the Boomer, the Swami, the big guy. He was the master of the ceremonies on that rainy day. That guy really was a giant just standing up next to him. As a young boy I would watch him on NFL Primetime any chance I got. He made every sporting event worth watching. I had my picture taken between Berman and Doug Flutie. I even gave him some golf pointers even though I felt that his game wasn't all that bad. I told him some stuff about myself including my 82 that I shot at Connecticut. I told him that I was attending Middlesex Community College and that I lived in Tyngsboro.

As soon as all of the participants were inside the big room, Chris Berman came to the podium, said a few words, and then handed the microphone to Doug Flutie. Doug told his version of the story about his final NFL game with the Patriots, which took place on New Year's Day 2006, against the Miami Dolphins. After the Patriots scored a touchdown, they appeared to be going for the 2-point conversion and Flutie came onto the field at Gillette Stadium. Flutie was in the shotgun formation, took the snap and did something that had not been done in the NFL for nearly sixty-five years. He successfully attempted a drop kick through the uprights for the extra point. Who drop kicks in football anymore?

After Flutie's speech, there was this auction and an official announcement that the tournament was cancelled. As consolation for not playing golf, I received a certificate for a free round of golf at Pinehills. The best part about that certificate was that there was no expiration date so I could use it at any time. Even though the golf part was all washed out, I had an unbelievable time at Pinehills. Mother Nature could not prevent me from meeting several people of large importance and having pictures taken with some of them. However, the Pinehills was only the beginning of my odyssey.

Almost a year before it happened, Mom and Dad plus Uncle Bob and Aunty Beth Lavoie were planning a trip to the state of *Arizona*, in the summertime! Uncle Bob had a relative who lived in the town of Gilbert, located southeast of Phoenix and were allowed to spend some time at their home in the summer of 2008. We were also going to some other places in Arizona. Originally we were going to visit the Grand Canyon and then we were going to visit the Hoover Dam and Las Vegas for a couple of nights. For at least a year, I saved up my money just as my parents and relatives did for our trip to the Grand Canyon State.

On the afternoon of Wednesday, June 25, 2008, Mom, Dad, and I packed our bags and drove up to Manchester-Boston Airport to meet up with Beth and Bob. We were supposed to be off the ground by three, but due to mechanical problems with the plane, we didn't leave until after four thirty. It was the longest flight of my life as I was on the plane for at least five hours. It was seven, Phoenix time, when we arrived at the Valley of the Sun. I thought it was eight since Phoenix, Arizona, was in the Mountain Time Zone, but I later learned that there was no daylight savings time in Arizona. After we went downstairs to get our luggage, we exited the airport and went outside to get on a bus headed for the rental car place. My first Arizona heat experience was as if some giant beast threw a left jab at my whole body knocking me to the ground, although I did not actually fall to the ground. Just being outside was like walking into an oven, and the day was waning at the time. The heat over there was much different from the heat I experienced in New England. They call it a dry heat.

We got around the city and the state in a silver Dodge Durango that we rented not far from the airport. Once we got onto the freeways, it was beautiful. Who would've imagined a large city situated in the middle of a desert? Another unique thing about the city highways was that its overpasses were decorated with some kind of Native American art, something I've never even seen or dreamed of before. I absolutely wished the highway overpasses of Massachusetts and New Hampshire looked this attractive. Well, the Arizona highways and overpasses were brand-new and had just been recently built. I believed that Arizona is the most artistic state in America. It is also the last of the lower forty-eight continental states to enter the union in the year 1912.

We had a difficult time finding the house once we got to Gilbert. It was located in a densely populated residential zone in the shape of a square called Vintage Ranch. It was like a maze of the same houses, all of them looked as though they were finished recently. More than half the population of Arizona lives within a forty-mile radius of Phoenix. Eventually we were able to find the house.

Two aspiring NFL players were living there while we stayed. One of them was Pete Clifford, who actually came from Salem, New Hampshire, and played on the offensive line for Michigan State. The other was Chris Harrington who played linebacker for Texas A&M. Both were trying out for the Arizona Cardinals for the 2008 season. Several months later, the Cardinals would end up going to the Super Bowl. But unfortunately, they would not be on the team that made it.

After we all unpacked our bags, we decided to go out to eat at a nearby Chili's at ten at night. It was after midnight back home in Tyngsboro. My body did not have the energy to eat steak fajitas. One time I nearly dozed off while waiting for our food to come. I was pretty exhausted from the plane trip to Phoenix. It obviously took all of us some time to get used to living in an atmosphere like Phoenix. Just think, one day I was having a photo taken with Doug Flutie and Chris Berman, and the next day I was in Arizona in the dead of summer. It was one of the most surreal two days I have ever lived so far. But for the next ten days, I was going to be taken in by Arizona's charm, learning new things, experiencing new extremes, and discovering the new meaning of amazing.

We try to give Tyler new experiences as often as possible. Vacationing is always a challenge due to Tyler's sensory overload issues. He is so much better at making adjustments since he graduated high school. He likes to keep on a schedule and we did our best to accommodate him on that issue.

My first full day of the trip was spent trying to adjust to my new surroundings. But my adjustment would later turn into an adventure. I joined my family in the inground swimming pool in the morning. We never swim in our pool in the morning, so this was definitely something new for all of us. The water temperature was the same as bathwater outside since Arizona is typically one hot state. After that we went out for a little breakfast at Denny's, located at the same plaza we went to last night for our late dinner. Then we went to a nearby Target to get some groceries to last us the entire vacation.

After coming back to our place that day, we got ourselves ready for our first big trip across Arizona. The place that all five of us were headed to (Beth, Bob, Mom, Dad, and me) were the Kartchner Caverns, located some forty-five minutes southeast of Tucson. Bob was driving and I was in the front passenger seat. The first half of the drive was nice, nothing but sunshine and desert until we reached Tucson. Then as we were about to come up on the city, we all noticed something strange. There were dark clouds right in front of us. At first I thought Arizona was a place where there is sunshine almost every day. I heard that it only rains in the state one month out of the whole calendar year. And when it does, it comes down hard. Not long after we passed Tucson, the skies were getting darker, and all of sudden it started to rain, thirty miles from our destination.

The rain on our way to the caverns was even worse than in Plymouth two days earlier. It was coming down so hard and so fast and it was so loud that we could not hear each other speak. The lightning from the storm appeared to be wicked dangerous. For a moment there, I thought we were either going to get struck by lightning or drown or get swept away in this rainwater, which was rising so rapidly. I thought that I was about to die, and I was not nearly ready to die because I was so young and I got my whole life ahead of me. I even told Bob to turn around, but he still kept driving through this unexpected thunderstorm. Eventually the storm weakened into a shower and then a drizzle.

Tyler was certainly afraid of the monsoon-like rain. He has never liked rain, and it was raining so hard! We tried to talk him through it. I was glad that he didn't cry or "check out" like he has in the past. I was so proud of him.

We did make it to Kartchner Caverns safe and sound. I had my tank top shirt with gym shorts on believing it was going to be hot. But it was actually cool and breezy, possibly on account of the storm. I felt chilly throughout the visit. The first thing we did was go inside the main building. Then we went into a theater to see a show about the caverns. I saw more details on how the caverns were formed at this exhibit. At exactly three, we all joined the tour group to see the caverns up close.

I got to see what was inside the cave firsthand with my family. Dad got to the entrance but didn't join the tour group to see the caves because he has this thing with closed spaces. There were three rooms in the caverns, the Rotunda Room, the Throne Room, and the Big Room. The Big Room was not open at this time of year, so we visited the Rotunda and the Throne only. We were only allowed to touch the railings because if we touch the caverns they would suffer from long-term damage.

Inside the Rotunda Room, there were things that took millions of years to turn into what they look like today. There were some soda straw shapes that were dripping from the ceiling of the cave called stalactites. They were so fragile and grew so slowly that it became important to the caverns' dignity, and they still grow to this day as long as nothing ever happens to them. I saw a bunch of things inside that looked like icicles and wax but were not such. There were also things that looked like bacon sticking out of the walls and the ceiling. We saw some footprints in this vast valley of mud that were made by the men who first discovered it.

After that was the grand finale, the Throne Room. Inside the Throne Room was the longest soda straw stalactite in the United States, and one of the ten largest in the world. For security reasons the group was not allowed to see it. But we were allowed to see Kubla Khan, the tallest and most massive column the state of Arizona has to offer. The tour guide put on a show for us to see the gigantic room with the music in the background to help describe this room. Kubla Khan looks like a monster of some kind standing exactly fifty-eight feet tall, and it was made by nature. This place was ridiculously miraculous. At the end of our visit, we checked the gift shop out for a while, and I got myself some neat things—a hat, three collectible golf balls, and a bag of rocks. The Caverns was quite an interesting place. The trip there made that day an adventure thanks to the storm. I admit that I was a little scared during this freak rainstorm. The most important thing was that I survived and enjoyed the visit to Kartchner Caverns.

Day 4 of the odyssey was on Friday, June 27 as Mom, Dad, and I took a trip of our own to a place just north of Phoenix where an old friend of ours lives, while Beth and Bob stayed put in Gilbert. On the afternoon of that day, we took an hour-long drive all the way up to a place between the towns of Carefree and Cave Creek. That house was situated in a desert setting as opposed to the house in Gilbert where it was surrounded in a suburban atmosphere. As soon as we got to the place, there was a group of people waving at us. It was Mark Yates, and his wife and children.

Mark Yates is a longtime friend of my dad. Before Mark moved his family and his dental practice all the way to Arizona, he used to live near Lake Winnisquam in Meredith, New Hampshire, and I would pay a visit there with my family as a child. I really enjoyed visiting the Lakes Region, and going to Mark's place in the area made our trip there all the more merrier, whether it was sledding on the hilly backyard in the winter or boating on the lake in the summer. One time Mark took me on a snowmobile ride along Lake Winnisquam and I feared for my life as he was flooring it down the snow packed lake.

Their new place in the desert was wicked nice. The backyard had an inground pool, a basketball hoop, and a small area that had this artificial grass called FieldTurf. There was this roofed patio with a bar, a fridge, and an HDTV set. Like the house in Gilbert, Mark's house as many other houses in Arizona has no basement or cellar for whatever reason. Dad and I threw a Nerf football for a while and then we went inside and Mark let us watch golf, tennis, Diamondbacks baseball, and a White Sox–Cubs ballgame. I read some of Mark's books such as a century of pictures by Life Magazine, and a book about the events of September 11, 2001. I also did this puzzle phenomenon called Sudoku for a while.

After we had dinner at Mark's place, we drove to a bull riding contest in the town of Carefree. I did not like it there because the smell of cigarette smoke bothered me, and I could not see all the action on account of the crowd. After that we went back to Mark's to swim in his pool at night. Like the pool back in Gilbert, the water at Mark's was bathwater. Everybody came to the pool, me with my parents and Mark and his family. Finally I wrapped up the day by sleeping on my AeroBed.

The next morning I went outside for a tan, then a swim, then another tan, and then another swim. It's amazing how quickly you can dry out and warm up after getting out of a pool in AZ (the initials for Arizona). Mark picked one heck of a place to live. I'm sure that it's the ideal winter place for us if my family wishes to avoid the New England snow. To me it's a great place to play golf in the winter.

Later in the day, I went out to lunch at this Mexican place called El Encantado's. Our seats were right next to this pond filled with ducks and turtles. I ate this fajita taco salad with grilled chicken. This salad had lettuce, red cabbage, onions, cheese, and chicken in a taco shell bowl with guacamole and sour cream on the side. After our lunch, we went to Frontier Town to check out their shops. Inside one shop, I bought this license plate of the Arizona state flag, a golf ball and a U.S. Marshals badge. We visited a few other shops where they sold necklaces, pottery, cheap jewelry, mostly stuff made in Arizona and the American Southwest. The last store I went to was a place where they sold Life is Good merchandise. I bought a shirt with the company mascot with a golf club in his hand and the name brand below the golfer. I also got a burnt orange baseball cap that read, "Red Dirt Arizona," on the front. After shopping for a while, we went to this sports bar called Gallagher's. The place had a lot of TV's with almost every sports channel imaginable broadcasted in high definition. We only came here for a drink as I had myself a root beer. Then after a brief visit to the supermarket, we went back to Mark's. Finally, it was time for us to go to Beth and Bob. We said our goodbyes and drove out into the sunset, although it was already dark by the time we left.

After an off day Sunday, we embarked on the biggest part of the trip since coming to Arizona. Mom, Dad, Beth, Bob, and I packed up and drove off in the Durango early on the morning of Monday, June 30. We were going from the comforts of our suburban vacation home to the true frontiers of Northern Arizona. After stopping for breakfast at a Denny's, we continued our journey northward. Our first stop was a tiny cozy town called Sedona. We came upon a visitor center off Interstate 17, ten minutes south of the town. I used a $10 bill that Denise Borghi gave me to buy four Native American style woven coasters, a book about Arizona, and a handkerchief with a little map of Arizona on it. I even got a free DVD called *So, Why Are the Rocks Red?* with my purchases.

The first thing I said when I first saw the redness of the rocky hills and mountains was "Oh, man!" It wasn't until we got off at the exit leading to Sedona where I really got to see the true color of the Arizona landscape. There are not many places like that on earth I'll tell you that. The gods must have taken it to the limit to create all these colorful places and sculpt all these distinctive hills. This terrain and color is as close to perfect as it can get while visiting Sedona.

The state of Arizona should be proud of their mountains, plant life, and wildlife. They are too beautiful not to be enjoyed and too sacred to be used for development. This landscape around these parts is second to none. It should be, no, it must be enjoyed by everyone for generations to come. I can hardly imagine how they felt when they first set foot there. The colors represent the character of the whole state of Arizona because those well-made places, the redness of the hills, the distinctiveness of the plants are Arizona.

After taking some pictures of ourselves with the red mountains in the background at the visitor center, we went to this church a few miles up the road. Sedona had a lot of churches but the one that we went to was designed by the great architect Frank Lloyd Wright. It was called the Church of the Holy Cross. I took some pictures of the writing, which explains the reason for building this place. Also at the church, I saw some visitors toss coins on the rocks at the bottom of the church to make a wish of some kind. Sometimes the coins would roll down the rocky hill and eventually end up onto the parking lots at the bottom of the church. As long as you are in Sedona, I don't think that you are allowed to pick up loose change. The people who first came to this place must have thought that this was the best place for them to practice their faith. That would possibly explain why there are so many churches in this one area south of Sedona.

After visiting the church we went into town. We found a Mexican restaurant where I ordered a chicken burrito but ended up getting a pulled pork burrito by mistake. A few minutes later I was given what I asked for. After lunch we went to an overlook to get a good view of the town of Sedona and the scenery surrounding it. From the overlook you can see that the redness of the hills was so pervasive, the top half of Sedona was all red from right to left. At the bottom was West Sedona, all houses and small buildings. You have got to be there and see it to believe the colors and artistry of Sedona.

We then drove through the uptown section of Sedona and into the forest for the first time on vacation. First, we were at five thousand feet in elevation heading toward Oak Creek Canyon. Then we were at six thousand feet, then seven thousand feet. I've never been this high up on land before. When you're going north on Route 89A between Sedona and Interstate 17, it feels like you're traveling up Interstate 93 between the Flume Gorge and Franconia up in New Hampshire. It was a huge forest with more pine trees than I had ever seen during the vacation. The temperature got twenty degrees cooler as we got higher in elevation deep into the Coconino National Forest in the area of Cave Creek Canyon.

I had to use the restroom as soon as we found another rest area. We stopped at this place in the forest and after I was finished with my business, I checked out these Native American arts and crafts fair to see what they were selling. I bought only two things there, the first was a dream catcher otherwise known as the "last legend" because the Indian said that it was the last legend on the table. The last was a necklace in which the man said it keeps away evil spirits once you wear it. From Sedona to Flagstaff, there are many tall pine trees. We made our way back to I-17 before the highway ended at Flagstaff. From there we went west on I-40 toward Las Vegas and California. On I-40 heading west, the forest gradually turns into farmland and flat green space with mountains in the background. I had no idea how much farmland Northern Arizona had.

Fifty miles from our next destination, *the Grand Canyon*, we took a right onto Route 64 northbound near the town of Williams and this area is as rural as you can get. On this fifty-mile stretch of road, there are only a handful of buildings. The ones that stand out are the Planes of Fame Air Museum at Grand Canyon Valle Airport, the Flintstone's Campground with a big sign of Fred Flintstone welcoming visitors to the place, and a Chevron gas station that was charging $4.50 for a gallon of gas. Uncle Bob filled exactly 15.121 gallons for a total of $68.03. It was certainly the most outrageous price for gas I have ever seen at the time.

By the time we got near our destination, it looked like every American small town, only there were a bunch of automobiles clogging up traffic. After we checked in to the Best Western Hotel in town, we made the drive up to see the best creation I've ever seen made by Mother Nature. The first thing I said as we entered the area was "Oh my word! Look to the right." The Grand Canyon looked best when the sun was shining right on it. Monday afternoon, when the sun was to the west, only the east side of the Grand Canyon would stand out the best.

I couldn't believe how many people go to this place. You could not believe it either. This is a world-famous place all right. I was slightly overwhelmed by how many languages were spoken at this place in Northern Arizona. People from all walks of life come to see this massively cut out area. They go there because there is no other place like it in America, not even on earth.

The Grand Canyon was perfect in every way. There were colors from one end of the canyon to the other. There was red, there was yellow, there was green, and there was blue. This place looked as if it could go on forever, but its actual dimensions are 277 miles long, 10 miles wide, and 1 mile deep. We only went to see the Grand Canyon from the South Rim that evening. God had to have painted that place too darn good. The depth of the Grand Canyon is so big and it's such a long way down that I kind of got a little dizzy looking down. Only one word best describes this place, and this word is *grand*.

After our taste of immortality, we had some dinner at a place called Yippie-I-O's. I thought the Canyon was overwhelming until I entered that restaurant. There were people from as far away as Europe and Asia coming there in this one building. They all wanted to get a taste of America. There was this waiter who came over to carry all five plates after we finished eating. We then went to our hotel to call it a night. That hotel had a swimming pool, an arcade, even a bowling alley. I only visited there for just a few minutes before hitting the sack.

The next day, we returned to this gigantic colossus of America one final time. This time we went more to the west than yesterday. The first view of day 2 was when we saw a building with a green colored roof and a few more buildings with red colored roofs not far from it at the bottom of the Canyon. We also visited a merchandise store or curio called Verkamp's. We went to the Hopi House and the El Tovar Hotel. We then took a bus from Bright Angel Trailhead to a trail leading to the Trailview Overlook. Just when I thought I saw enough, I kept seeing new parts of Grand Canyon. Then we all took a bus to Maricopa Point. From there, it probably had to be the best view of all. This place was better than anything I've ever dreamed of. The second time visiting the Grand Canyon was better than the first time because the sun was shining on more areas of the Canyon. This place is so big, you can go to a different spot every day for one year and still not see the whole thing.

Next, we all took the bus back to the Bright Angel area where Dad and I then walked through the trailhead while Mom, Beth, and Bob checked out the Bright Angel Lodge. The trail that I walked on led to the bottom of the Canyon. It would take some people four to five hours to get to the bottom and twice as long if they want to go back. Dad and I walked the trail for only a few minutes. Once we got back, we had to find Mom, Beth, and Bob, which we managed to do. After getting together, we went to a porch at the El Tovar Hotel where we met this middle-aged couple from Philadelphia.

Afterward we went inside Verkamp's to shop for some Grand Canyon memorabilia and mementos. Mom got Clint a T-shirt so that Clint could get something from our trip. I bought myself a 2009 calendar, a collared shirt and T-shirt all saying Grand Canyon on it, and five arrowheads each with different colors. Mom really enjoyed sharing the moment with me. I had a time to remember and nothing can take it away.

Like I said, there is no other place in America like the Grand Canyon. You can think of certain American attractions and points of interest such as the Statue of Liberty, Mount Rushmore, the Golden Gate Bridge, the Arch in St. Louis, the White House, and even Fenway Park. All of these places were built by man, but Grand Canyon was created by nature. It sets itself apart from most monuments, buildings, and sculptures because it is a natural wonder similar to Niagara Falls and Mount Rainier. But only the Grand Canyon has the spectacle, aura, size, artwork, or character that it offers. It is hands down the most sacred place in America.

I did mention that there was talk about going to the Hoover Dam and Las Vegas after visiting the Grand Canyon. Then we figured that going there was a waste of time so we decided to skip it altogether and visit Sedona instead. After saying goodbye to the Grand Canyon, we drove through Flagstaff to see how it was but we decided to continue to

Interstate 17 toward Sedona. We got a couple of rooms at a La Quinta Inn on the south side of town. After checking in, we ate at a place called Stakes and Sticks, and I got to play some billiards with Dad and checked out some pictures of a couple of great golfers before they were pros. There was one of Annika Sorenstam when she went to college at the University of Arizona, and one of Phil Mickelson when he was in Arizona State. Of course there were other framed pictures of athletes inside the billiard room. Afterward we went to Uptown Sedona to find a diner so we can eat breakfast the next morning. Then we browsed around some shops and ended the day by going back to the inn.

After spending the night at La Quinta, we had our breakfast at Uptown Sedona. I had a Denver omelet that tasted better than the omelets that I had at Denny's earlier in the vacation. Then we went to a nearby shop where I purchased a rattlesnake skin decorated golf ball, a golf ball marker, and a little red rock known as Sedona Real Estate. Then we returned to our hotel, got our things, and drove all the way back to the sweltering dry heat of Phoenix. Our three day expedition was over. We left for the Valley of the Sun with fond memories of the Grand Canyon and the colors and the true beauty of Arizona. I was in awe of what I saw, heard and smelled up there. Exactly one week had passed since I landed in Phoenix with my parents and relatives with not a hint of an idea of what we were going to expect. Seven days into our visit to Arizona, I thought that I had seen it all.

Then on Thursday, July 3, my odyssey took a strange turn. On that afternoon, Mom, Dad, Beth, Bob, and I went to a baseball game. The Arizona Diamondbacks were playing host to the Milwaukee Brewers at Chase Field in Downtown Phoenix. The D-backs ballpark was the third Major League ballpark I had ever visited after Fenway Park and Camden Yards. Unlike Fenway Park in Boston, it was easier to find a parking spot at Chase Field since there is a big parking garage located within walking distance of the park and costs just $10 there. Chase Field (formerly known as Bank One Ballpark) was the place where the Diamondbacks beat the New York Yankees in a seven game World Series classic in 2001. It is the first baseball park in America to have a retractable roof that can open and close anytime. The roof usually stays closed on account of the heat and is at least twenty degrees cooler with the roof closed. Chase field is also known for its swimming pool and hot tub located behind the wall at right center field.

We sat in the second to last row along the third base side. The place was spacious, the seats were big and comfortable despite having no padding on them, and each seat was positioned directly to the field. The ballgame atmosphere in Phoenix is not the same compared to that of Fenway Park. In Phoenix, there seemed to be hardly anyone there. According to the attendance figures, only 23,842 people showed up that day, but it seemed a lot less than that since the ballpark is so big that it could hold twice as many people than there were at the game I went to.

The last full day of vacation was spent at the place in Gilbert on the Fourth of July. I have never spent the fourth away from New England before. It was the most boring day of vacation. All we did was rest, swim, and hang around for a change. None of us had any energy left, and all we could do was spend our country's birthday recharging our batteries for the trip back home very early next morning.

At approximately 4:00 a.m., we all gathered our things and got ready to say goodbye to the city of Phoenix and the great state of Arizona. We had to leave in the dark so that we could make the 6:00 a.m. flight to New Hampshire. I was going to miss this place a whole lot because I won't be coming back there for a long time. All I could do is take a bunch of memories from my visit and look back and say that it was the best experience any person could ever have. No person can script what I went through those past many days. That vacation made it the best summer of my life so far and gave me a new lease on life and told me that the world is both a small place and a giant place after all.

When I came back to my home in New England, the weather there was cooler and more comfortable just like home. The airport in Manchester looked the same but it seemed different than when I left there for Phoenix in the first place. Nevertheless, it felt great to be back to my home in Tyngsboro, Massachusetts. I returned home a different person than before I. I was a bit smarter, wiser, older, but more importantly, a lot more inspired from those twelve days.

Tyler is a terrific travel companion. He loves history and researches the places we go. He is great at reading maps, so we don't get lost often. When he does have downtime, he usually writes in his journal. All in all, he is pretty relaxed when we go somewhere new. He has grown and matured so much over the years. I don't worry nearly as much as I used to about going to new places. As long as he is given a fair amount of warning that we are heading somewhere new, he usually makes a pretty good transition and ends up having a positive experience.

The 2008 Special Olympics Massachusetts August Games were a month away, and I had only gone to Tyngsboro Country Club six times in 2008. I had not played a round of golf in three weeks, and I did not golf at all during the trip to Arizona. As soon as I got back to Tyngsboro, I went right back to work on my game. On Monday, July 7 Dad and I resumed our golf league season and played in the Red, White, and Blue Tournament, it means we played three times off the red tees, three off the whites, and three off the blues.

One week after the Red, White, and Blue, I paid my third visit to Mount Hood Country Club in Melrose for the assessment round of golf for Special Olympics Massachusetts. I came back to Melrose hoping to fare better than the 96 I shot last year. Once again I was paired up with Keith Peabody. I started off quite promising by making a ten-foot putt for par. Then for the rest of the front nine, I was in a prolonged slump, which included a 9 on the par-5, fourth hole, and a 6 on the par-3, seventh hole. When it was over, I ended up shooting a front-nine 50. It was embarrassing to me because I expected to do better than last year.

After a long break, I began the back nine pretty much the same old slumping golfer with a double bogey on the par-3, tenth hole. After a bogey on #11, I popped up my tee shot and the ball landed in a muddy grassy area left of the fairway. The ball didn't just land. It got buried. I still felt that I could hit my second shot. I used a sand wedge to at least try and get the ball up in the air. After I completed my swing, the ball came out floating and moving around like a knuckleball. It did stay in play but wasn't much closer to the green. I did get on in three shots, but I two-putted for bogey.

Then I finally found my groove on #13 as I made par. After a par on the fourteenth hole, I did something that was almost bad. As the group in front of us was about to leave the green on the par-3, fifteenth hole, I teed off a little too prematurely, rather than wait until they were out of sight. I hit the ball anyway, and it went left of the green, right where the golf carts were! Nobody got hurt but the ball hit the roof of one of the moving carts. It bounced into the woods left of the green. I admit that I was careless and I was not paying attention to what was happening. I did bogey the hole. After a par on the sixteenth, I would make bogey and double bogey on the last two holes. My back nine score was 42, and for all eighteen holes, I had a 92. I was four strokes improved from last year. But for some reason, I knew I could do better and I knew I needed to work harder on my game. I knew what I was capable of. One day after the assessment round, I went to Tyngsboro Country Club with my dad and shot a 41.

On Saturday, July 26, Dad and I were invited to play at United States Specialty Sports Association scramble golf tournament at Wayland Country Club. Dad and I joined a pair of gentlemen named Ryan Vigue and Klete Squires, the latter who worked for Special Olympics Massachusetts. Rain had cancelled golf at Tyngsboro the previous Monday and I had hardly practiced. I came to Wayland just trying to do the best I can. It was good practice for me because the August Games was already two weeks away. For half the tournament, I couldn't hit the ball straight and far and I was still inconsistent. In spite of my struggles, our team looked great overall. Our score after nine holes was a 31, three under par.

After a par to begin the back nine, Klete's second shot got us to within a couple of feet of the hole on the par-4, eleventh. I made the birdie to put us at -4. Then on the par-5, twelfth hole, and I hit a brilliant drive down the left side of the fairway with my Sasquatch. That drive enabled us to set up our fifth birdie of the afternoon. Then for the next five holes, we would only make par. The sixteenth was the longest drive hole, and I hit the farthest drive while staying on the fairway. I would go on to win the Longest Drive Award from that hole. The eighteenth was a five-hundred-yard par-5. After topping my tee shot, I used my only mulligan and bombed the next shot about 250 yards down the fairway. Two team shots later we were forty yards from the center of the green, almost chipping distance. My chip was closest to the pin out of all my teammates. We each had a chance to make birdie from eight feet out. I went first and missed, Dad went next and missed, and then Ryan came up and missed. Now it was all up to Klete Squires to give us our sixth birdie of the tournament. He made it. His birdie putt put us at -6, for a final team score of 64, good enough for second place in the tournament.

Later on at the awards ceremony, Ryan, Klete, Dad, and I each received a trophy for our second place finish. I was given a small golf sculpture for winning the longest drive contest. Later on there was a raffle in which I won $75 and Dad won a box of twelve golf balls. I was supposed to make a speech after the awards and prizes were given away, but I didn't get that chance. I had a great time playing golf with Ryan and Klete, they were nice guys.

Vesper

ALL MY LIFE, I HAVE lived close to two golf courses. One of them was the place I go to regularly, which is Tyngsboro Country Club, and the other is the one where until I was twenty-one years old, I never even set foot in. That golf course is called Vesper Country Club. Vesper is a private course, like Mount Pleasant and Long Meadow are private courses, but unlike those two, it is an eighteen-hole course with half of the holes and the main clubhouse situated on Tyngs Island on the Merrimack River. It is also a very difficult course not only to play but to join as well. It's one of three courses where the Cities take place every summer.

Back on June 24 the day I went to Plymouth with Rick Lalime, I talked about Vesper and how I would pass it every time I went to school or work but never visited there to play just one round of golf. Later in the evening before I left for Arizona, I get a phone call from Rick Lalime and he said that we were going golfing at Vesper this summer. I felt flattered just to hear the news, how could I say no to that? He said that he would set up a tee time in July and I accepted it. But we went on the first day of August, a Friday.

Every time I ride by the golf course, I would only see a few holes. But once I crossed the bridge onto Tyngs Island, the golf course was an entirely different place. The road leading into the clubhouse crossed the first hole at Vesper. This place was unique in its own right. It's hard to believe that a golf course can be situated on an island along the Merrimack River in Tyngsboro. This place was established in the year 1875. Vesper is one of the most exclusive golf courses in Massachusetts, if not New England.

Rick Lalime and I arrived at Vesper just shy of noon. We did not play right away because we had to wait for the gentleman who invited us to play for the day. The man who was joining us was one of Rick's colleagues and a member of Vesper named George Malliaros from Dracut and his eleven-year-old son with him. Between being here and teeing off, I practiced my putts on the putting green, and even did some chipping on their chipping area. I practiced my drives into a screen near the first tee and later checked out their clubhouse.

We teed off a little after one thirty. The first hole was a short par-4, the shortest on the course at 281 yards from the regular men's tees. My first ever tee shot at Vesper was low and a bit to the right. George said that it was a "good" miss because the fairways are fast and the ball was going to keep on rolling. But I could only shoot as good as an 8 because I had a difficult time getting my ball on the green.

The second hole was a 411-yard par-4. I sliced my tee shot, pitched out under a tree, and made the green in four shots to 3-putt for a 7. The third hole was another par-4 as I again went left off the tee, which forced me to just get back onto the fairway. From eighty yards out, I hit a good sand wedge and got the ball to land within ten feet of the flag. I had my first shot at par. I remember reading that putt going right to left perfectly and got the ball to sink into the hole. I knew right then that I had to be at my best to make par on any hole in this course.

After double bogey on that par-3 fourth hole where you had to shoot over the river to get on the green, I hit three well executed shots on the par-5 fifth hole to get near the green only to make bogey in the end. After a bogey on the par-4 sixth, I made double bogey on the longest hole of the course, the 544-yard seventh hole. The strangest part of the round happened on the eighth hole. Rick Lalime hit a low line drive that ricocheted off a tee box marker, took a left turn and hit a tree, and somehow found its way back into play. The ball literally made this number 4 in front of us. I've never seen anything like it on a golf course before. I got down the 377-yard par-4 hole with my driver. Then I went past the green with my 3-wood to stay below some branches while trying to get on. After getting on in my third shot, I almost made a par putt from five feet.

On the ninth hole, a two-hundred-yard par-3, I used my 3-wood to get myself on the right side of the green. For my birdie putt from fifty feet out, I got to within a couple of feet of the hole and finished the back nine with a par. My score for the first nine holes was 50. Not too bad for my first time at a very difficult course. After wrapping up the front nine, we entered this snack shop. One unique thing about Vesper is that the ninth hole does not return to the clubhouse like all the courses that I've been to.

The tenth hole would turn out to be my best hole of the day. It was a par-4 hole that was a dogleg to the left and I played my slice from the tee with my driver perfectly. I was from 120 yards to the center of the green and I used a pitching wedge from there. The moment I hit my second shot, I had a sense that my Titleist Pro V1 was headed right for the flag. Rick and George liked what they saw, a good sign. When I came to the green, I was in sheer amazement. My ball was eighteen inches away from the hole, and I made the easy tap-in for birdie. I did not expect to make birdie in my first ever appearance at Vesper, and I thought it would take more times to play it until I got one. To make birdie on the tenth hole at Vesper the first time around is a momentous accomplishment. Nothing can take it away, that's for sure.

I was not done there. On the eleventh hole, a par-5 that was a dogleg left, I hit two good shots, a driver off the tee and a 3-wood from the fairway. My third shot got me on the green, but my putt for birdie was fifty feet long and uphill, and so I had to hit it firm. The flag was in when I attempted my putt and the ball was hit firm and it hit the flag. The ball settled a couple of feet away from the hole and I tapped in for par. I was on an unexpected roll with par-birdie-par on holes 9 through 11.

Then on the 406-yard par-4 twelfth, I stumbled back to earth and I made double-bogey on it. I made double-bogey again on the par-4 thirteenth hole. On the par-3 fourteenth hole where I had to clear the river to get on the green, I had some trouble getting on. I ended up putting for bogey from the fringe and missed the hole. Since we were there to have fun, Rick let me score a bogey on that hole.

I would get it together again on the longest par-4 hole on the course, the 429-yard fifteenth hole. I got on the green in three shots and saved par. This was how I played in the New England Invitational in Connecticut last October—scramble golf. Most of the pars I made on a par-4 there, I would normally get on in three shots and make par in the end. On the sixteenth hole, another four-hundred-yard par-4, I did it again—on in three, one putt for par. It would be my last par of the day as I would make double-bogey on the par-3 seventeenth, and a bogey on the par-5 eighteenth hole.

My score for the back nine was a not-too-shabby yet impressive 44. My score for all eighteen holes was 94. Rick said, "No s——," after I told him my score. I felt I did pretty good all day and since it was my first ever round at Vesper, 94 was a decent score. What was more astonishing about my first round there was that I never lost my ball into the woods or the water all day. I owe it all to Rick Lalime and George Malliaros for making all this possible. It was more than a special time, it was a long time coming, and it was worth the wait in the end.

The next day, I golfed again, this time in the second annual Tyler Lagasse Scramble Golf Outing at Townsend Ridge. I woke up really early so that I could arrive at the golf course at 6:45 a.m. After practicing my swings and putts for a while, I got to tee off at 8:00 sharp with my team consisting of me, my dad, Rick Reault, and Gary Browning. On the first hole, a straightaway par-4, Rick Reault hit the best tee shot, and then I made the best shot to the green, fifteen feet to the hole. I putted first for my team. It was a downhill putt but I still managed to make the putt for birdie. We were off to a great start, but the best was yet to come.

On the second hole, another straightaway but narrower par-4 hole, we got on the green in two shots once again. This time we were forty feet from the hole. I went first once again, read my putt going right to left. I was hoping to get it close enough so that we had a great chance at a par. Then I attempted the putt, and after I followed through, I looked at my ball and I soon turned out to be right about where my putt was breaking. Then all of sudden, that ball was headed right for the hole! The putt was good, I dropped my putter in disbelief as Dad, Rick, and Gary made some noise behind me. It was the putt of the year so far. Nobody helped me out with the putting line because I putted first. Already we were two strokes under par after just two holes of my tournament.

After a par on the par-3 third hole, we encountered the most difficult hole on the course, an uphill 383-yard, par-4 fourth hole. With a little help from the momentum from my birdies on 1 and 2, we not only conquered the hole, we made birdie on it. On the par-5 fifth, I hit my best driver of the day so far, a 280-yard drive that outdistanced each of my teammates. We later birdied that hole to go four under par after just five holes. It was the best start that we could all hope for, but we would never make birdie on the rest of the front nine after that. We would par every hole besides the bogey on the par-3 seventh hole to shoot a back nine score of 32, three strokes under par in the first half of our tournament.

On the tenth hole, I helped get to the green closer than each of my teammates. However our birdie drought continued as we two-putted for par. On the eleventh hole, the second most difficult hole of the course, Rick hit a good drive, Dad got us on the green, and Gary made the birdie putt to get us right back at 4 under par. After making par on the twelfth, we got on the green in two on #13 and made a hard earned birdie that put us at -5. After a par on #14, I got my team closer to the hole than anybody on 15. My tee shot landed on the fringe ten feet away from the hole. The magic from the first and second holes carried over to that hole as my birdie putt got us to six under par. On the sixteenth hole, we would make birdie again, our eighth overall, to get to -7. On the par-3, seventeenth, we played the ball I shot from the tee for another chance at birdie. Unlike our magical holes before this one, we had to settle for par.

On the eighteenth and last hole, a 364-yard par-4, as we were waiting for the group ahead of us to move on, Gary Browning regaled us with a story about the time he golfed in Maine. Before he could tee off, someone very famous played through. It was George Herbert Walker Bush, the forty-first president of the United States. Bush was in office at the time Gary played in Maine. According to Gary, he saw President Bush tee off, and his ball wound up hitting many objects imaginable—rocks, trees, anything.

When it was time for us to tee off, I drove my ball into the water in front of the green. I did retrieve my ball and found another in the water. We played the ball that was closest to the green. After all of us hit our shots, I used the last of my few mulligans to try to get my ball closer than any one of us. The closest we could get to the hole was thirty feet. Me, Dad, and Gary missed our putts. With no mulligans left, it was up to Rick Reault, the son of the gentleman who put together this tournament for me once again. This was possibly the most difficult and most important putt of the day. Rick didn't feel much pressure because we were generally playing for fun. Once Rick's putter hit the ball, I had a feeling that that ball was going in. Just like in Super Bowl XXXVIII, Gary said it was as good as Adam Vinatieri was about to make the game-winning kick. And what do you know? That ball went *in the hole!*

Rick's birdie putt on the eighteenth hole put us at eight strokes under par for a score of 62. We had made five birdies on the back nine and four out of the last six holes for a total of nine birdies in eighteen holes. That is half the course. Our fast start, strong finish, and my big birdie putts were the reason why our score was what it was. It was our best performance as a team in any scramble golf tournament. Fifteen foursomes participated in the second annual Tyler Lagasse Scramble Golf Outing at Townsend Ridge, and my foursome finished in eighth place.

After the tournament, we made our way to the big room on the second floor of the clubhouse. At the silent auction, I spent $230 on a big frame called Celtic Pride. It was big enough to fit five pictures in it. Two of the pictures were of the old Big Three, with Larry Bird, Kevin McHale, and Robert Parish. Two more pictures featured the new Big Three of Paul Pierce, Ray Allen, and Kevin Garnett. The last one was a big team photo of the Boston Celtics when they won their elusive seventeenth NBA title. There was also this gold plate below the team photo with autographs of the entire team.

During the awards ceremonies, a disk from my speech at the Let Me Be Brave Gala in Harvard was played to the crowd. After that, I made a new four page long speech. Some participants that came to Townsend Ridge included Jaret Foley and his family. There was Rick Dupuis, the manager Gold's Gym in Chelmsford and the head of the Team Micky racing team. Micky Ward was also there and a host of others that came to Townsend for the day. Lunch was served and there were raffle prizes that I helped give away. I won $100 worth of Townsend Ridge gift certificates, and got a $50 one from the long drive competition winner there. I autographed his Patriots hat in exchange. The second golf tournament to be named after me was a success, if not better than last year. Once again, I can thank Mr. Richard Reault Sr. for it. A week after the tournament in Townsend Ridge, I went to Amherst for the third straight year to take care of some business.

Unfinished Business:
The 2008 SOMA Golf Tournament

ONE YEAR AGO IN AMHERST, I repeated as the Massachusetts state golf champion for Special Olympics. But I was not happy with the way I played in 2007. My scores of 88 and 93 were not up to my satisfaction. I believed that I could do a lot better and I was poised to improve on what I did in 2007. So the 2008 tournament in Amherst was all about unfinished business. The "real" Tyler Lagasse was going to show up this time.

Before I went to Vesper, I golfed in the golf league in Tyngsboro on July 28 with Dad. I had not golfed in two weeks on account of the weather. I shot my worst round of the year as I ended up losing to my dad that afternoon by four strokes. I shot a 48, and Dad shot a 44. Then I went to Vesper and then I had my tournament, and then some things started to click for me. In my last LGH golf round before the state tournament, I made five pars including four in a row from holes 5 through 8. I would shoot a 42 as would my dad. He missed a par putt on the last hole for a chance to beat me again. After a slow start to the season, Dad got hot as he broke 45 four out of the last five times, his lowest score was 41, and that was on the week before the trip to Arizona.

It was the eighth day of the eighth month of the eighth year of the "new millennium" as Dad and I arrived in the Amherst area on the afternoon before the August Games. We stayed at a Courtyard by Marriott this time. After checking in, we went to Amherst center to have dinner and later on in the evening we went to the UMass–Amherst Campus. The Opening Ceremonies took place at the Mullins Center, the home of UMass Basketball and Hockey. The Opening Ceremonies of the 2008 Summer Olympics in China were also happening that night. The last time I went to the Mullins Center was for a UMass basketball game in 1999. A performance by Pittsfield's Youth Alive took place, followed by an introduction of Massachusetts law enforcement officials featuring an entrance of a motorcycle, two cars, and a SWAT truck. Finally the torch was lit and the August Games was officially declared open.

The first of two rounds at Cherry Hill Golf Course began on the fifth hole after 10:30 a.m., where I was once again paired up with Keith Peabody. My first shot of the tournament from the short par-4 hole was a wicked good 3-wood down the left side of the fairway. My second shot found the left bunker in front of the green. Although I did get out of the sand, I had to two-putt for bogey to begin the day. On the sixth hole, another short par-4, I hit a decent 3-wood off the tee down the left side of the fairway, which led to my first par of the 2008 state tournament. Now and inevitably, I was on the hole from hell, the par-5 seventh hole. My first two shots from there were not all bad, but third shot was in the rough and on a bad lie, and I laid up. I got over the water on my fourth shot but would end up with a double bogey.

After back-to-back bogies on the eighth and ninth holes, both par-3s, I would start to find a groove. I hit a beautiful driver off the shortened par-5 first hole. I made the green on my second shot and two-putted for a birdie 4. On the second hole, I went right toward some trees but stayed in play. My second shot went past the green two shots later I sank a crucial five-foot putt to save par. On the par-3 third, after coming up short of the green, I took out my sand wedge—the one club that I practice with most in the backyard—and hit a flop shot high in the air and got it to land within a foot of the pin where I would make an easy tap-in par. On the last front ninth hole, the long par-4 sixth hole, I lost my ball in the woods to the left, resulting in a double bogey 6. In spite of that, I had just shot my lowest nine-hole round at Cherry Hill with a score of 41. My playing partner Keith Peabody shot a 50.

After a lunch break, I resumed the first round on the sixth hole. I started the back nine slow with a bogey on 6, followed by a series of bad shots on #7, which led to a triple-bogey 8, then a 3-putt double bogey on #8, and a bogey on #9. My score for the first four holes of the back nine was +7. It seemed that I was on pace to repeat what happened last year. That's when I decided to make an adjustment.

On the first hole, I switched from a Titleist NXT to the more advanced Titleist Pro V1. The Pro V1 is in my opinion the most effective ball in golf. It is also the most expensive golf ball in the world because it is so good. One time Dad and I went to Dick's Sporting Goods and saw that a twelve-pack of Pro V1s cost $45.99. The pro shop at Cherry Hill was selling a sleeve of three Pro V1 balls for $14. I had eight Pro V1 golf balls in my bag and I didn't have to pay a dime for them because I found some of them in the woods of the golf courses I played this year.

My first two shots on the first hole were subpar to say the least. I did get on the green of the par-5 hole in three shots. I was left with a twenty-foot putt for a 4. The putt was downhill and right to left. I had a good read on that shot, hit it perfectly and saw that ball go in for a birdie. It was the latest of big putts that I had made in 2008. Switching balls was my best decision of the day and I got results right away after that. On the second hole, I hit my 3-wood right, but not as right as earlier. My second shot was disappointing because I went short of the green with a sand wedge. I was on in three shots just like earlier in the day. For the second straight hole, I had to make a big putt, this time it was from twelve feet out for par. Once again, I made the big putt and I only needed one putt to finish a hole. On the third hole, I got more club than before as I went over the green. After a chip onto the green, I missed the putt to save par. On the fourth hole I did bounce back by getting on the green in two shots, setting up a thirty-foot putt for birdie. I almost made the putt of the day as my ball missed the hole by inches. On the last hole of the first round, the fifth hole, I didn't hit my tee shot long but I stayed in play. My second shot found the green, and I was left with a twenty-foot putt for birdie. The greens at Cherry Hill are wicked fast compared to those at Tyngsboro. After taking my time reading the putt, I got into my stance, kept my eye on the ball, let it go, and a few seconds later I watched as my ball rolled all the way to the hole for a birdie.

That birdie gave me a back-nine score of 41. After one round, I matched a familiar number that I shot somewhere down I-91 in Connecticut. *It was 82!* I did not notice that I shot an 82 until after my round was over. I owe it all to my putter and my Pro V1. The *real* Tyler Lagasse showed what he was made of in the first round. I beat my state tournament record from the second round in 2006 by four strokes. After having an equal share of good shots and bad shots, I still shot an 82. But I was far from finished. There were eighteen more holes left for me to play the next day.

On the night before the second and final round, I wrote in my journal that "tomorrow will definitely be one day to remember." I also stated that "I need to play my game, stay focused, move on after a bad hole, take it easy, be a good sport, keep my cool, respect the game, cheer for my other golfers—including Keith—and most importantly, have fun, always!" Like I have said before, my parents have always stressed the importance of good sportsmanship, especially in big tournaments like this one. I also had to get good at golf and in order for that to happen, I had to take the advice of others. In 2008, Fred Wilkie had taught me this "less is more" golf swing strategy. It meant that you don't have to overswing your club to increase your swing power. Just keep it at 85 percent but no more than 100 percent or else your shots will go wild.

It was ten thirty, and I was going to start the front nine with an athlete and a unified partner. My second round began on the elevated par-3 ninth hole. My first hole was nothing special as I made a two-putt bogey. Then on my next hole, I started to put it into gear by hitting a brilliant tee shot with the driver, followed that up with a chip shot that went by the hole, and a two putt for my first birdie of the day. On the second hole after my drive went left, I hit my second shot on the green, ten feet from the hole with another chance at birdie. I read that putt very closely, I've never taken this long to read a single putt before, and I have been doing this all weekend. I studied my feel for the green, practiced swinging my putter until I got the right feel. I took my stroke and watched my Pro V1 roll in. That birdie was my second in a row, but it wouldn't be my last.

After a double bogey on the third hole, the uphill par-3, I recovered nicely on the fourth hole that was extended by forty yards because the tee box was moved back. I hit an exceptional tee shot without the intent of overpowering the ball. Then I hit an even better second shot to the green, a 7-iron from 150 yards with a good bounce to the green. For the third time in the last four holes, I had a shot at birdie. This birdie try was from more than ten feet out. Once again, after a careful observation of my putt, I hit that ball perfectly and into the bottom of the cup. I was playing so well that I didn't even bother checking my score. The scorecard said that I had made birdie on the second and fourth holes. The fifth and sixth holes were pars. On both of the holes, I hit a good tee shot, got on in two shots, and two-putted for par. I teed off with a 3-wood on #5, and I began the sixth using a driver.

Then I found trouble on the seventh, the hole from hell. I sliced my ball into a row of trees on the left side. It took me an additional two shots to get back on the fairway and I later made double bogey. Finally on the last hole of the front nine, the par-3 eighth hole, I teed off twenty yards behind the tee markers from yesterday. I overshot the green but I was able to get on in my next shot. The following was an ending that was very fitting indeed. The youngest of the pair made a fifteen-foot putt to save par. I followed that up by making a fifteen-foot putt for par, the latest in a long line of putts that I made all weekend.

My partners were so impressed by my playing that they called me an animal. After we shook hands, my dad said to me, "You shot a 37." It was the lowest nine-hole round ever for me. I have never played this good before and I had two double bogies. I picked a wicked good time to break records because I was not the same golfer that shot 88 and 93 last year. After I was done with golf that day, I wrote that "those are nine holes that I will remember for a long time." I thought I would remember this day for quite a while because I actually did something I had never done before.

I still had to play nine more holes in the afternoon. If I kept playing like this on the back nine, I had a shot at breaking 80 in eighteen holes for the first time ever. I had to wait more than an hour to golf because it was lunchtime for all the golfers at Cherry Hill. I was paired up with Keith Peabody for the one-thirty tee time on the ninth hole. There was a threat of storms coming by in the afternoon so I kind of rushed myself to stay ahead of the weather. I began the back nine with 4s on the ninth and first holes.

On #2, went back to earth as I found the woods to the right. My rhythm was hindered on account of the long break. I ended up making triple bogey on that hole. I would recover with par saves on the next two holes but that was all I had left for the day. I made bogey on the fifth, double bogey on #6 and #7, and a bogey on the last hole of the tournament. In the end I ended up with a back nine score of 44, the highest for nine holes all weekend. I did not get to break 80 when I had the golden opportunity to do so that Sunday. I did break my two personal bests that Sunday, I shot a 37 on the front nine, and I shot a final round score of 81, eclipsing the two 82s that I shot—the one in Connecticut and the other the day before.

For that performance, I received a third gold medal in the SOMA state golf tournament. The second one was bittersweet because I did not play to my expectations with the scores of 88 and 93. In 2008, the *real* Tyler Lagasse showed up. I was on top of my game, right where I ought to be, right where I belong. It was not even the halfway point in August, and already I was loaded with one of the best days of my life. I simply came to Amherst to do better than last year and I've done it. I've rediscovered the talented golfer in me. My numbers from the tournament went like this. For thirty-six holes over the course of two days, I made seven birdies (four of them came from the first hole), ten pars, and ten bogies. For the third straight year, I had a great time visiting such a wonderful small town nestled in Western Massachusetts.

After the state golf tournament, Dad and I drove all the way to Seabrook, New Hampshire, to catch up with Mom and Memere in our usual-rented beach house. We spent the whole week there watching the Summer Olympic Games and paid visits to the shore when the weather was ideal. It wasn't as much fun as the previous vacations there but the Olympics may have made up for the potential futility of the vacation. We all went out for dinner almost every night to certain nearby restaurants in Hampton. Sometimes in the evening we would play card games such as canasta and tock.

Starting after the trip to Arizona in early July and ending in the middle of August, I worked five days a week at the Registry of Deeds and made some extra money. I took a week off from work to be with my family at Seabrook. My last day of work with the registry in 2008 was on a Wednesday, August 20 to be exact. For five months I worked really hard at getting my job done. The Town of Westford was grateful for my work because they needed someone to put their documents from their dilapidating town hall onto the town's computer database. I did almost everything they could ask me to do and I did it with as much effort as I could.

The Career Center of Lowell gave me a chance to work and the registry hired me to scan all the documents from Westford. When I first worked there, I didn't know much about digital documentation. After a month on the job, I got the hang of this scanning process. I had scanned more than a half century of Board of Selectman minutes, some School Committee minutes, Conservation Committee minutes, Finance Committee minutes, and much, much more. I even made a spreadsheet to keep track of all the work that I have done.

On my last day of work, a lady from Westford stopped by with a gift bag in her hand. She told me that I had done an amazing job for the town of Westford. In that bag were a mug and a card explaining to me what a fantastic job I've done. It wasn't my last day of work ever at the registry, but I did not come back for a while. It did not mean that the Registry of Deeds did not want me back, nor did it mean that the Career Center did not want me to work for the registry again. The people at the registry, Richard Howe, Tony Accardi, and several others liked having me there, and they were going to miss my work ethic over there.

For the rest of the year, I had no real hands-on job. I also did not attend college for the fall semester at Middlesex Community College. My parents tried to enroll me at the last minute but it didn't work out in the end. I spent the rest of August and parts of September putting together a basement bathroom with my dad, and doing some paint jobs around the house. Our house had a new patio installed next to the basement door, another change that was made during the twenty-fifth anniversary of the construction of the Lagasse Family house.

Sometime late in the summer, I accepted an invitation to participate in the 2008 Special Olympics Golf National Invitational at the PGA Golf Club all the way down in Port St. Lucie, Florida, on the first weekend in the month of October. I was going to golf outside New England for the first time ever. My nearly unexpected amount of free time enabled me to practice some golf and for me and Dad to do get out onto the course in September. After the Seabrook vacation, we made four trips to Tyngsboro Country Club and finished up our season with the Lowell General Hospital Golf League. I played at Tyngsboro fifteen times in 2008, and shot a score of 42 or less seven times, compared to six times in the first two years that I have been a part of the golf league. In my last round at Tyngsboro in 2008, I shot a 40. Dad and I also made a couple of trips to Green Meadow up in Hudson to play on the Prairie Course before the invitational.

Also in September, I went with my dad to World Series Park in Saugus for the Harry Agganis Special Olympics Day to make a speech.

I added in the part where I shot the 82 and 81 at the August Games. Just as in the gala in April, I got the longest ovation. Several Olympians were on hand at Saugus. The highest profiled Olympian to attend the event was Massachusetts native Nancy Kerrigan the two-time Olympic medalist at figure skating. She liked my speech and gave me her autograph. A couple of members of the National Judo Team and the U.S. Women's Ice Hockey Team were also on hand and I got the photo of the Women's Hockey Team from the 1998 Winter Olympic Games in Nagano when they won the gold medal.

On the Monday before the NIT, the second annual Special Olympics Golf-a-thon took place at Stow Acres Country Club. There was a cocktail inside the clubhouse on the night before the golfing took place. I made a speech to at least a dozen guests there and explained the word *phenomenon* and made myself clear about character once again. I told them that I was going to Florida to participate in the Special Olympics NIT. There was also this raffle thing and I was given eighty tickets by one gentleman. Those tickets cost $10 each, and I had ninety-nine of them. Most of them were given to me. I couldn't believe it.

The 2008 Golf-a-thon was the same as last year. I was on a par-3 hole, but this time I was on the fifteenth hole of the South Course. Dad would not be with me at the golf course all day because he had to go to work. I stayed with a lady named Heidi for most of the day. So the drill was to wait until a foursome arrived and once they did I would play the hole with them in an effort to be closest to the pin than each of the golfers in the foursome.

Nine foursomes showed up at Stow that day and I could only think of seven that came by the fifteenth. I would tee off last just to make the showdown more dramatic. I was the closest to the pin against each of the first three foursomes that came by. I was beaten by the next two foursomes until the sixth foursome came by. One member of the sixth foursome was James Duncan. The night before, Duncan gave me a Canadian $5 bill. If I got closer to the pin than he did, he would give me another five Canadian dollars. If he was closest then I would have to give that $5 bill back to him. One of his teammates was closer to the hole than me. Meanwhile the distances of our balls to the hole seemed identical. It was close but Mr. Duncan was kind enough to give me his other Canadian $5 to me. After that a gentleman came by to give me a box of nine Titleist Pro V1s with the logo of the company that he was representing in the golf-a-thon.

When there were no foursomes coming, I would practice my swinging, look for some golf balls in the woods on the right or behind the green, and talked to Heidi about how I took up golf. The tee box was all wet from the rainfall on the weekend before the golf-a-thon happened. Heidi and I then drove all the way to the clubhouse for two hot dogs. Then Heidi and I went back out to search the whole course for some foursomes that we might have missed. We found two of them, one on the eleventh hole of the South Course, and one that just finished playing the hole that Heidi and I waited on all morning. The latter foursome was called the Muppets, and on that team was the guy that gave me eighty raffle tickets. All of the foursomes that showed up on the fifteenth tee were not only impressed by my golfing ability, they were more impressed to see that it was a person with autism that had golfing ability.

At four in the afternoon, Mom, Dad, and my brother Clint showed up. Clint, Dad and I played the front nine holes of the South Course. When we were kids, Clint and I would hit a bucket on several occasions. But Clint had not golfed with me and Dad since Memorial Day 2004. There was this one time when I hit my ball in the sand trap on the par-3 third hole. My ball was actually in a puddle inside the trap. I pulled up my pants and pulled down my socks and decided to play the ball from the puddle. I swung at least 100 percent, got a little wet from hitting the water, and somehow got this ball to land on the green. I bogied the hole but that was a great shot. I shot a 44, eight strokes over par. It felt so good to have Clint golf with me and Dad again, I had a great time.

After the sun went down, everybody went to the functioning room for dinner and awards. My mom made a speech about me, and I thought she used very appropriate words about me and how Special Olympics has made a huge impact on me. I was being treated as a celebrity that day, I knew because most of the golfers knew my name. I have never felt more humbled and pumped over all this before, but I behaved like a gentleman. The second golf-a-thon was success on a day when America would start to plunge themselves into the worst economic crisis in the twenty-first century. The 2008 Special Olympics Golf-a-thon would then become a preview to my next big tournament in Florida.

Florida: The 2008 Special Olympics Golf National Invitational

ON THE DAY BEFORE MY second trip to Florida, Dad and I went to the driving range near Green Meadow in Hudson for one more warm up before my next tournament. The weather in New England started to get cooler by the time October came. That day, I was wearing long sleeves and pants, but the next day I was going to wear shorts. I had only been to Florida once in 2005 for the Cotting School senior class trip to Disney World. I was sure to have a much better time in my second trip to Florida.

I woke up at 3:00 a.m. on the morning of Friday, October 3, so that Mom, Dad, and I could get to Manchester-Boston Airport early enough to meet the delegates that were headed down to Florida with us. We arrived in Manchester just before 5:00 a.m. in time to go through security and catch the 6:15 flight to the airport at West Palm Beach with a stop at Philadelphia on the way. It was my second flight of the year and fifth flight overall for me. Our two flights went smoothly as we arrived at the airport at West Palm Beach early in the afternoon. We rented our vehicles and made the one hour trip to Port St. Lucie.

The place that my family stayed in was the Castle Pines Golf Villas, located a couple of minutes from the PGA Golf Club. I had my own bedroom to sleep in as did Mom and Dad and Jennifer Maitland who was a part of the SOMA delegation. As soon as I felt like practicing, Dad and I went to the PGA Learning Center nearby. This place had putting greens, a big driving range, and even practice bunkers with different kinds of colors. I fell right in love with this place as I practiced my putts, worked on my situational shots such as getting out of the sand, and took some swings at the driving range. The PGA Golf Club also had its own range and practice green so that I can warm up and get myself ready before golf. This place felt like golf heaven to me, because Florida is a year-round golf destination.

Later on that Friday night, we went to the PGA Golf Village for a dinner, a meet and greet, and the opening ceremonies. It was amazing to see a whole bunch of Special Olympians from all across the country to come to one place. It was my first taste of national competition, and I took it all in. At the opening ceremonies, I got to hold the Massachusetts sign while leading my team down the walkway on this balmy night. I had not played a single hole of golf in Florida yet, and I was playing the role of team leader in the opening ceremonies. It was a big moment for me in a year crowded with big moments, but I was headed for something bigger the next morning and the days that followed.

Day number 1 of the three daylong Special Olympics Golf National Invitational was beautiful. There were three rounds of eighteen-hole golf, the first round took place on a Saturday, the second on a Sunday, and the third and final round was on a Monday. The PGA Golf Club had three courses, the Ryder Course, the Wannamaker Course, and the Dye Course. The course I was playing was the Ryder Course. My main plan for round 1 was to get familiar with the course and take it easy because it was not a sprint. Just like in prior Special Olympics golf tournaments, it was a shotgun start where every golfer started on different holes at the same time. This was the highest level that I could possibly compete for in Special Olympics, and I was competing on a national level for the first time.

Round 1: I was paired up with a middle-aged Level 5 golfer from the state of Utah named Tony Marino for the opening round. Tony played golf all the way in China not long before the NIT. My first hole for the invitational was the seventh hole, a par-3 that was 123 yards to the center of the green. I got my feet wet as I was about to hit my first ball in the state of Florida. The white tees that I played on were being played closer than they normally would for the event. I started the invitational by making bogey. Then on a three-hundred-yard-long, par-4 eighth hole, Tony lost his ball and looked for ten minutes until he played his next shot between my first and second shots. I made my first par by getting on in two shots and completing two putts. I would make bogey on the next four holes after that.

On the par-5 thirteenth hole, I hit a high pop up with my Sasquatch off the tee that found the bunker closest to the tee. I used a 7-iron to get out of the bunker and hit it beautifully down the fairway. Two shots later I was on the fringe, and after that I got to within three to four feet of the hole where I made my first par since the eighth hole. After a bogey on #14, I hit a brilliant driver down the middle on #15, setting up a two-putt par. The sixteenth hole was the shortest par-3 hole of the course at 108 yards. After hitting the green with my pitching wedge, I three-putted the hole for bogey.

The seventeenth hole was the longest hole on the Ryder Course at only 441 yards from the white tees. I used a driver and 3-wood on my first two shots. My second shot found the bunker, but my third shot would be the shot of the day. From fifty yards out, in the sand, I did something that I did not believe was possible. I used my sand wedge, took a full swing and got the ball out of the sand and in the air. Once the ball touched the green, it stopped two feet from the hole. I had never done anything like that before, making a sand shot from that far and getting the ball to within tap-in distance of the hole. That shot from the sand helped me make a birdie, my first and only one of the first round.

After that brief high from the birdie at #17, I plunged into the worst three holes of the day. On the eighteenth hole, I hit a bad hook to the right and under a bush in the woods. After taking a drop I made double bogey to finish with a score of 42 for holes 10 through 18. On the first hole, I hit a bad slice to the left and out of bounds. I took a provisional, which meant that I re-teed my ball and hit my third shot from the tee box. I ended up with a triple-bogey 7 to finish the hole. The second hole was not much better as I kept getting into trouble by finding another bush on my shot to the green. I ended up with a double bogey 6 on that hole. On the par-4 third hole, I hit a nice chip to the green only to miss an easy par putt.

Then I encountered this par-5 fourth hole that was a dogleg right with water on the right side. The man in the cart told me not to use a driver on this hole, so I used a 3-wood and saw my ball run past the fairway on the left side but stay in play. I did get on the green in three shots and I was able to make two putts for my first par since the fifteenth hole, fourth overall. The fifth hole was a short par-3. I hit a pretty good tee shot to the green but had to make bogey after making three putts on this fiendish green. My last hole was the par-5 sixth hole. I hit a wonderful drive with the Sasquatch, came up shy of the green with a 5-iron, made the green in three shots, and two-putted for a par, a solid finish to my first ever golf round in Florida. My score for the first round of the Special Olympics Golf National Invitational was 87.

I felt pretty good out there considering that it was my first Florida golf experience. There were plenty of shots that I wanted to have back, particularly the ones that got away from me. There was room for improvement now that I have eighteen holes under my belt and thirty-six more to go. After one round, I was in fourth place out of twenty Level 5 golfers in the invitational. I had a great time playing with Tony Marino. We got along great during the competition and he did the best he could.

After the first round of competition was over, Mom, Dad, and I went to the driving range area to watch a trick shot performer named Dennis Walters. He was unlike any golfer I have ever seen. What was unique about Dennis Walters was that he would hit balls while sitting down on his customized golf cart. The reason why he could only do so was when an accident left him paralyzed from below the waist. Two years after his accident, he started taking up golf and he has been practicing golf shots and going around the country to perform his magic while sitting down ever since.

On that overcast but humid Saturday afternoon at the PGA Golf Club, he did not disappoint. He swung with custom made golf clubs to fit his swinging style. One time he used a club that looked like a fishing pole. He even used some clubs with weird looking club heads such as ones in the shape of a cell phone, a gavel, and a doggy bone treat. In fact, he had a dog named Benji who would always be there for Dennis's performances. Sadly, Benji the terrier passed away not too long ago. In honor of his terrier, Dennis hit a shot for him because Benji wanted it so much.

Dennis Walter had no use of his legs whatsoever and yet he can still hit every golf ball straight and long. I've never seen anything like it. He was like a machine on the golf course. The more golf balls I saw him hit, the more choked up I got to the point of crying. I almost broke down at one point but I managed to keep myself collected. I can't help but to say that he was amazing out there.

He said such great things during his performance and gave such great advice to the audience. For instance, he said that if you are not able to realize one dream, then work on another dream instead. That was such great advice because in case things don't work out for me with the golf or college or work, then I'll try to focus on the other things that I am good at, such as art, writing, and drawing. Back then I wanted to play golf because I was good at it. But I wanted to get better at it too because I saw the potential in me, I had built my own track record, I believed that there was a future in me for golf and I also wanted to keep my dream of being a professional golfer alive.

One time during the performance, Dennis Walters used an old-fashioned persimmon club. Then as he made contact with the ball, there was this loud *BANG!* as if a gun were fired. He could hit golf balls off anything from a two-foot-tall tee to a can of Arizona Iced Tea. He hit a ball that was hung from a string, and hit a ball many other different ways. Every time he hit a ball, it was the same result: straight down the middle of the fairway.

That guy was an inspiration that just kept on going. He had to have practiced those shots every day in order for him to stay sharp. If he can get down the fairway without any problems all the while sitting down, I can do better at my game with my own two legs to aid me. I was not only wicked impressed, I was wicked inspired by what I saw that afternoon. That guy was a wonder that performed magic acts out there. It was so fun to see him use one iron with three club heads, another that was a multihanging club, and another that had a rubber shaft and still get the ball down the fairway. It was one heck of a show put on by Mr. Dennis Walters.

Later on in the evening, I went out for dinner at Sam Snead Restaurant inside the Hilton Hotel across the street from the PGA Learning Center. This restaurant looked like a golf club house. There were many pictures of Sam Snead there, a lot of medals from his PGA Tour victories, and many more things golf. Mom and Dad came with me for dinner, as did Nathan S. who competed in Level 3 golf with his playing partner and Father Geoff. Nathan was celebrating his birthday that night. Jenn M. was there as were Level 4 golfer Scott and his mother, June. Our waiter was pretty talkative and seemed very knowledgeable about the food that was served here. I ordered a Caesar salad followed by a filet mignon with mashed potatoes. We spent two and a half hours at Sam Snead's and didn't leave until nine thirty when a couple of us had dessert, and since it was his birthday Nathan had some cake.

Round 2: Coming into this Sunday morning round, I did not expect much out of myself, but I was in for a real surprise when this round came to an end. If there was one thing in my game that I needed to improve, it was my putting. I was not making putts that were makeable on most courses. I wasn't making the clutch putt. I had thirty-six putts in the first round, an average of two putts per hole. I have had more than my share of making long putts, birdie putts, and difficult putts. But the greens that I played on were inconsistent, hard to read, and difficult to make from outside ten feet. Somehow by the time this round was over, I was going to do something surprisingly historic for me.

I had a good recollection of the course, which would suit me well for this round and the last. For the second round, I was paired up with a young Connecticut golfer named Michael Hedrick. We teed off from the par-3 fifth hole to begin the day. My first shot was a pitching wedge off the tee that landed fifteen feet of the hole. But just like yesterday, I was unable to figure out those greens and I would three-putt for bogey. The sixth hole was a 418-yard par-5, and I was able to make the green in two shots. I had a golden opportunity to make birdie there, but I three-putted yet again, this time for a par. On the par-3 seventh hole I made the green from the tee box and two-putted for a second par. On the eighth hole I made the green in two shots and two-putted for my third straight par. Then on the ninth hole, I made the green in two again but unlike the previous hole, I was unable to save par. I three-putted for the third time in this young second round for bogey.

On the par-4 tenth hole, my tee shot found the sand on the fly. Similar to the one on the seventeenth hole yesterday, I was sixty yards from the green, and I used my pitching wedge to not only get out of trouble but on the green where I two-putted for par. The eleventh hole was a tricky hole. It was a par-4 that was straightaway until I noticed the green was to my right. I hit a good tee shot but I had to get over the front bunker that was guarding the green. I was able to get on the green, but once again I three-putted to make bogey on #11. I would never three-putt again for the rest of the day.

The twelfth hole was a great hole as I hit a near-perfect pitching wedge from 114 yards out. Two putts later I finished with my fifth par of the day. On the par-5 thirteenth I sliced my ball left toward one of the many townhouses blanketing the courses of the PGA Golf Club. Luckily for me my ball was still in play, but I could only make bogey on that hole. Then on the fourteenth hole, a par-4 hole that was a dogleg left, I elected to use my Sasquatch driver in the hope of playing my fade so that the ball could drift left and land on the fairway within chipping distance of the hole. Instead, my ball went straight, went over the fairway, over the cart path until it stopped on one of the tee boxes on the fifteenth hole. My ball was still playable with a shot to the green. I did manage to get on the green from there with my sand wedge and make two putts for par. Then on the fifteenth hole, the short par-4, after a drive to the left side of the fairway, I hit my best approach shot of the day if not the invitational. Using a pitching wedge from one hundred yards out, I got the ball to land two feet of the hole setting up a mere tap in for what would be my only birdie of the second round. On #16, I made the green from the tee and two-putted for par. Then on the "monster" of the course, the par-5 seventeenth hole, I used my driver, a new hybrid that I got at the golf-a-thon at Stow Acres but didn't use until this round of the NIT, and a pitching wedge to get on the green, where I two-putted for another par.

Now I was up against the three holes that doomed me in the first round. On the eighteenth hole, I hit a great drive to shrug off any hint of a repeat from yesterday. I followed that up with a 7-iron from 150 yards out and overshot the green. My chip on to the green was too strong, my putt for par was also too strong, and then I finished by having to hole a seemingly long putt to make bogey. It was the longest putt I've ever made all day.

On the first hole of the Ryder Course, my first two shots looked all right even though my second landed on the fringe. Then just like the hole before it, I couldn't get my putter to work right as I was trying to be too aggressive at my chance at birdie. I then tried to be too conservative at my shot at par and came up short of the hole resulting in another bogey. On the second hole, I teed off with my new hybrid club and hit a good shot. Then my second shot found some sand. My third shot was on a downhill lie facing the green but I got out and got my ball to stop two feet of the hole. I was poised for a crucial sand save until I pulled my ball right of the hole costing me that much needed par. After making 6–7–6 on those three holes yesterday, I bounced back with 5s on each of them.

On the third hole, I drove my ball into the sand. I used an 8-iron to get out of the sand. Then from sixty yards out, I hit my sand wedge to near perfection as the ball parked a couple of feet of the hole. This time out, I did not make the same mistake twice as I hit my ball in the hole. It would be my last par of what would be a tumultuous second round. A bogey on the par-5 fourth hole wrapped up the second round. Before I knew it, I had just set a new personal best in eighteen holes. I heard a lady say to me, "You shot a 79." Last year, I met my expectation of breaking 40 in nine holes and 85 in eighteen holes in a course that was foreign to me. This year, I broke 80 in a hot and humid place, in yet another place that was foreign to me. On a day when I missed a whole lot of putts that should have gone in, and on a day when I did not make a single double-bogey or worse that day, I still shot a 79.

I've come a long way from the ten-year-old that started taking up golf at about the same time as Tiger Woods winning his first Masters tournament. It took me more than half my life to achieve this latest milestone. Every year I try to improve on my best scores. In 2006, my lowest eighteen-hole score was an 86 in the August Games. In 2007, I broke that record with the 82 at the New England Invitational in Connecticut. This year I have set my personal best twice, the first coming in August at the second round in Amherst with the 81, and now the 79 at the second round of the Special Olympics Golf National Invitational in Florida. In a year full of highlights, this was the biggest of them all. I'm thankful to have finally broken that barrier, which was number 80, at the tender age of twenty-one. I'm glad to have reached a new peak in my golf playing. But I was not done yet as I still had to play eighteen more holes in what has already become a memorable golf tournament.

Round 3: Once again I was paired up with Connecticut's Michael Hedrick, and again I started on the exact same hole as the day before. I did not want to get caught up in my record. I had to keep my composure, stay focused, and swing my normal swing just like I did all year. The 79 I shot was in the past, and if I was ever going to maintain my momentum or improve on yesterday, I was going to have to stay present. It was the biggest and longest tournament I've ever participated in. I've never golfed this much in so little time before, fifty-four holes in three days.

My first hole of the last round was the par-3 fifth hole. I began the third round with a par there and another on the par-5 sixth hole. Then on the par-3 seventh, I found trouble in the form of a sand trap to the right of the green. I did get out of there, but my mediocre putting caused me to double-bogey the hole. My streak of holes of bogey or better ended at twenty-four holes dating all the way back to the first round.

Round 3 was the sunniest of the three days I spent in Florida, it was also the hottest and most humid of the three. On the eighth hole, the heat and humidity were beginning to get the better of me. Four holes in and not even ten yet, and my whole body was all wet from this tropical humidity. My cotton team polo was getting saturated from the sweat. I bogied the eighth hole and made double bogey on the ninth. After the ninth, I untucked my shirt to get some cool air on my half-waterlogged body as soon as I was granted permission by one of the tournament officials. Right after that, I hit my most well played tee shot of the day on the tenth. I took my Sasquatch and played my fade perfectly on the short par-4 hole while dodging bunkers in the process. My second shot, within chipping distance to the hole, was just as good as my tee shot. I would then make an easy two-foot putt for my last birdie of the invitational.

On the eleventh hole, I used a hybrid off the tee, followed by a pitching wedge to just get over the front bunker and land on the green where I two-putted for par. The twelfth hole was when the flagstick was located on the front part of the green. I went with a 75 percent swing because the pin was positioned very close to the tee box. I saw my ball roll into the sand on the left side from the tee box. Then on the ensuing shot, I got out in style as my ball made its stop a couple of feet away for me to make par.

On the short par-5 thirteenth hole, after a nice drive, I took a gamble from inside two hundred yards out as I tried to use a 6-iron to get to the first cut of grass in front of the green. The gamble didn't pay off as my ball found the sand in front of the green. However I was able to get out of the sand just like I had all tournament long. I finished the hole with a hard-earned par. On #14, the dogleg hole, I sliced my drive with the hybrid and the ball landed on some pine needles near the cart path on the left side of the hole. I did punch out of trouble, chip on the green, and two-putt for a bogey 5. On #15, I drove my ball into the rough, left of the fairway but was able to get on in two shots. I missed a fairly easy birdie putt and had to settle for par. After a restroom break, I resumed my round and made par on the par-3 sixteenth hole.

On the par-5 seventeenth, after a fairly decent driver, my next two shots worked out poorly for me and I ended the hole with a bogey. On the eighteenth, I ripped my driver to the right and two shots later I got free relief when my ball was on a fire ant hill. I hit a great third shot, which led to my eighth and final par of the tournament. After that it was all downhill from there. After a bogey on the first hole, I double bogied holes 2 and 3 and finished the tournament with a bogey on the par-5 fourth hole after rimming out what would have been a miraculous putt for par. For the last round, my score for holes 1 through 9 was a 47, and for holes 10 through 18, I shot a 37, which gave me a combined eighteen-hole total of 84.

For the whole tournament, I had three birdies, twenty-one pars, twenty-one bogeys, eight double bogeys, and one triple bogey. My total score for the three-round national invitational was 250, the lowest score in my division, and second overall in Level 5 by just a mere two strokes. I was a little disappointed that I did not get the lowest score of the tournament in Florida, but I still felt a sense of accomplishment. I knew that I had shot a 79 in the second round and nothing could take that away. It was my first golf tournament outside of New England and it was my first time golfing in the Sunshine State. I loved it down there, the course was immaculate, the people down there were real nice, the volunteers did a phenomenal job, and I enjoyed every second of playing with Tony M. and Michael H. I felt like a really special person during those four days in Florida. I made a brilliant first impression playing on a national stage early in October of 2008. I was a twenty-one-year-old who now had experience playing golf on a national stage.

For Mom and Dad, it was their first ever visit to the state of Florida. I thank them for being there for me during one of my most historic moments to date. Mom got her first real taste of golf by playing the role of my caddy at the invitational. She was there to help keep me in line and she wanted me to have some fun out there and enjoy the moment. I thank God for letting the weather cooperate so that I could play all fifty-four holes of the tournament, for letting me break another one of my personal bests in a place where I never played before the NIT, and for letting me realize my full potential.

I didn't stay for the medal ceremonies because we had to drive to the airport at West Palm Beach to catch our flight home. There was a little delay to our flight but we arrived in Manchester just in time to see the Red Sox beat the Angels to win the division series. Three days before my twenty-second birthday, I got my Special Olympics Golf National Invitational medal in the mail. The NIT was the last golf that I played in 2008. This was my last tournament using the clubs that I had played with for six years. I was going to get a custom set of clubs for next year with the gift cards that I got at the golf-a-thon. What a way to end a golf season.

Weeks after the invitational, I was the guest speaker at the annual Kids in Disability Sports banquet. I talked about my accomplishments from 2008 such as the solid showings at the state golf tournament and of course the Special Olympics NIT in Florida. In past banquets, I would be the one to get a trophy for my participation with the organization. This year I got to hand out KIDS sports bags to all of the participants in attendance that were getting their trophies. Speaking to an audience at the KIDS banquet made me feel like I was the voice for the group that I joined as a fifteen-year-old.

On Friday night of November 7, Mom, Dad, and I went to the Omni Parker House in downtown Boston again for the annual Red, White, and Bid, the wine tasting/silent auction benefit for Special Olympics Massachusetts. I did not bid on any items this year because I was saving my money. For the second straight year, I was the guest speaker. Before I read my speech, I congratulated Barack Obama for winning the presidential election earlier in the week. My speech was relatively the same as the one from the KIDS banquet. It was generally about my big year and also about Special Olympics. Once again I had the loudest applause of any in this benefit. That speech would go on YouTube. After my speech, I had people shaking my hand and telling me what a brilliant job I had done on the golf course. Later that night, I was given an official NFL football signed by New England Patriots linebacker Tedy Bruschi. Unbelievable! That football was another early birthday present for me.

On November 14, I attended a UMass–Lowell hockey game at the Tsongas Arena. The River Hawks played the Wildcats of New

Hampshire and went on to win 8–3. At the game I had another early birthday present. I won $209 on the fifty-fifty raffle. The guy who gave me my winnings said that I was one lucky man. It was actually the second time that I won on the fifty-fifty raffle.

On my twenty-second birthday I was given four gifts, but all of them were big. The first was when Memere gave me a $100 bill in the morning. In the evening, my dad gave me a box wrapped in newspaper catalogs. In that box were an authentic Jonathan Papelbon Red Sox home jersey, a navy blue Patriots long-sleeved shirt, and a box of twenty-four-karat gold Red Sox World Series championship coins plus a small sample of authentic infield dirt from Fenway Park. The night after my birthday, my brother Clint gave me a Boston Celtics championship DVD, a dark Red Sox T-shirt, and three packs of sports trading cards— two hockey, one basketball.

I ran two 5K road races in the last two months of 2008. The first was the Thanks-4-Giving 5K and then a five-miler at the Lowell Elks. Micky Ward ran that race that Thanksgiving morning. I didn't run a good race that day. My body just wasn't in it as I finished in at 25:08, good enough for twelfth out of twenty-seven in my age-group. On December 7, I took part in my second Special Olympics Jolly Jaunt. This time I went to the one held at Beverly Hospital in Danvers. Clint was there to run with me this time. It was a little snowy out there and I had never run in the snow before. I had snow flying in my eyes at times and I did not stop for water during the run. My legs and torso were cramping up as the last half of the race was uphill. Before the race, I told Clint that I would be lucky to finish the race in less than twenty-six minutes. I finished at a time of 25:07, almost the same time as the Thanksgiving race. My brother finished just a few seconds after me. I didn't think that I could best my brother that day because he was once a track star at the Voke.

The first person I hugged was my mother while Clint was feeling nauseous from all the running. Later on in the day, while I was in the tent, I took off my running jacket and sweatshirt and then a lot of steam was coming out of my body because my sweat was evaporating from a long race. It looked as though I had just finished flaming out. After that, I made a speech that Mom and I put together at pretty much the last minute. I said a thank you to some Law Enforcement officials that were at the Jolly Jaunt that day. After I was done, I gave out a trophy to the team with the most runners and two plaques to two individuals.

When the Boston Celtics won their seventeenth NBA title back in June of 2008, Kevin Garnett summed it up by saying, "Anything is possible!" That was how my whole year was summed up with those three words. It was the year in which I made two speeches that would make its way onto YouTube. I met a bunch of fascinating people such as Travis Roy, Chris Berman, Doug Flutie, and Nancy Kerrigan among others. I went to Arizona in the heart of the summer to discover a world that was far from ordinary, and I continued to get better at golf as I saw my personal bests fall one by one. I topped it all off by going to Florida to play golf for the first time and break 80 in eighteen holes for the first time. The year 2008 may have been the year the Patriots failed to complete their perfect 19–0 season when they lost to the New York Giants in the Super Bowl, but the Celtics ending their twenty-two-year-long championship drought made me feel a little better. It was also the year Michael Phelps won a record eight gold medals for swimming in the Summer Olympics in Beijing, and it was the year Americans elected an African American named Barack Obama as the forty-fourth president of the United States. Anything was truly possible in 2008. Then came 2009.

I remember the feeling when I was told that Tyler had special needs. At that point, the only thing I could focus on was his lack of possibilities . . . all I can say now is . . . anything is possible! Tyler has overcome each and every obstacle with thoughtfulness, tenacity, and courage.

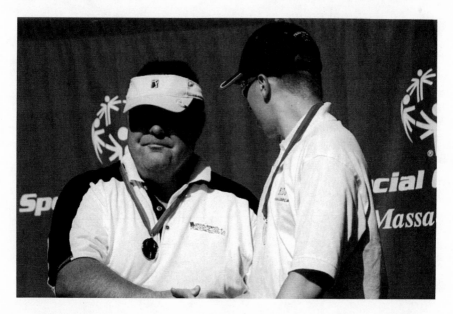

Shaking hands with Keith Peabody after winning my first
golfing gold medal at the state level for Special Olympics
Massachusetts on August 13, 2006.

My last day of work at Tyngsboro Public Library as I received my certificate of appreciation. (L to R: Library Director Randy Robertshaw, me, Mom, and Dad)

Running in my first ever ½-marathon all around the streets of Lowell October 15, 2006, at age nineteen!

Posing in front of world famous Harvard Stadium before the start of the Special Olympics "Let Me Be Brave" 40th Anniversary Gala in 2008.

Arizona: IN THE HEAT OF SUMMER!

Clint and I about to run in the 2008 Special Olympics Massachusetts "Jolly Jaunt" 5K road race in Danvers, MA.

2009: The Year of Personal Bests

THE YEAR 2009 BEGAN WITH the United States dragging its way out of its worst economic recession since the Great Depression. The year 2009 for me was when I found myself dragging my way through the busiest year of my life. And so early in 2009 I went back to college because with the shape the economy was in, I knew that I needed to get a college degree. I took two placement exams, one week apart from each other. I didn't feel like I did all that well on the first exam. After I wrote an essay about advancements in technology and answered twenty multiple-choice reading comprehension questions, I did some math problems. Then as I went to Intermediate Algebra, I had no clue. I was stuck. After four hours in the room, I quit as if I had failed. Mom said after the exam that I could not fail a placement exam.

I tried again and this time I took the second exam in the Disability Support Services office in the Lowell City Campus building. I took the same English exam that I took the week before this time with extended time and that was all I had to do. This time I felt like I did great. After the test I went to see Jeanne O'Connor in her office to discuss my classes for the spring semester. She went out and found a self-paced English course for me, and I decided to take it. Starting on January 21, the same day that Barack Obama was inaugurated. I was going to take two college courses in the spring 2009 semester at Middlesex Community College in Lowell: English Composition I and Computers for Technology. The Computers for Technology class was eerily identical to the Microcomputer Application class that I took last year. I had the same teacher from that same class the year before. I did not have to put pressure on myself to pass this course, but in English Composition I, I had to work really hard.

My first four weeks of the semester were confusing. One time in February as I was just getting my feet wet in college, I wound up getting sick with the flu. I did not throw up however, which is a good thing because I had not thrown up since 2002. Besides the bout with the flu, I was trying to get my work all straightened out. My slow start may have been possibly the result of the long layoff between college courses, but there were times when I thought I was getting it, but I really wasn't. For example, I turned in an argumentative essay through the computer and days later I went on my homework website and found out that my essay was flawed. I didn't know what to make of it at first because I thought I tried too hard to get this in return. I then went back to the Disability offices to see Jeanne O'Connor to book an appointment with a tutor there. She also showed me a room on the same floor as the Disability office called TRIO: Program for Student Achievement. She said that I could get help there and so I went there for tutoring. The people at TRIO were really helpful, and as the semester progressed so did I.

Outside of college, I was progressing as a public speaker. I had six speaking engagements in a span of two months from late February to the middle of April, and that was in the heart of my spring semester. In late February, I made my first two speeches of the year for the New Balance shoe company in Lawrence to help bring attract volunteers for Special Olympic events. I made the first one at the headquarters in downtown and the second one inside the cafeteria of the shoe factory outside the city. The second one was peculiar because I was speaking to an audience whose primary language is Spanish so there was an interpreter to help me out.

On the last Saturday of March, I went to this prep school near the Charles River in Cambridge called Buckingham Browne & Nichols to play in a unique basketball tournament with the KIDS group. The event taking place there was Bio-Ball, a basketball tournament benefitting Special Olympics. The school had a remarkable athletic facility with the games taking place on the basketball courts, and the skills competition taking place in an indoor area that is used for both tennis and ice hockey. Sixteen Special Olympic teams participated in this event along with the pharmaceutical and biotechnology companies sponsoring this event. The subtitle or motto for Bio-Ball was "the promise of a better tomorrow." Four hundred people were participating in this event and I got to speak to all of them during the opening ceremonies. I spoke about what I have done in 2008 and why Special Olympics is a very important organization. I got my usual standing ovation from a large crowd once again. Everyone liked what I said. Even the referees were also impressed by my speech. After I was done speaking to an enthusiastically raucous gymnasium, I shook hands with several CEO's of the companies sponsoring this tournament.

My team was paired with members of this company called Alnylam. My team only got to play the first and third quarters of each of the three games that we played. The Alnylam players played the second and fourth quarters. Basically the Special Olympic athletes were playing quarters 1 and 3, the biotech companies were playing the other two quarters. My team lost the first game but went on to win the other two games. After our basketball playing was over, we had lunch. Then we went inside the tennis center where the skills challenge phase of the Bio-Ball tournament took place. There were seven different kinds of challenges there—three-point shooting, half-court shots, dribbling, side-to-side chest passes, target passes, layups, and jump shooting. After the skills competition, Bio-Ball was over. It was a fantastic first time being at a prep school, speaking to a large crowd once again, and playing basketball.

March 31, 2009, was the day I went to Malden High School. Special Olympics was observing its Spread the Word to End the Word grassroots campaign. That day, I delivered a speech to a group of students who made a pledge not to use a certain word that offends people with an assortment of intellectual disabilities. The word is appropriately known as the R-word. This was my second speech since Bio-Ball, so I had to get it done and practice it in a hurry to get it right. This speech was about why people with autism are different than most other people and how some people judge those with autism as either being a genius or being mentally retarded. To put it in simpler terms, this speech was all about eliminating the R-word.

Two days after my speech, I saw myself in my predominately black attire with my gold medal around my neck in a news story on the World Wide Web at CNN.com. They showed me saying, "Using the R-word is insulting, disrespectful, and, quite frankly, ignorant." They also showed me urging people to "set an example to the next generation by eliminating that word from your vocabulary from this moment on." My mom was also in this story saying a couple of things, including being a mother of a person with autism for example. I said to this camera lady about how proud I felt about the kids at Malden high playing a part on recognizing people with disabilities as human beings because there are many people out there like me that deserve to be respected not mistreated. In a span of almost one whole year, I had two different speeches make the Internet. *Amazing!*

I made two more speeches in the month of April. On April 16, Mom, Dad, and I went to the Bank of America building in the financial district of downtown Boston. Over a year had passed since my legendary speech at Harvard University, but the people at Bank of America who were at the Let Me Be Brave Gala invited me at their headquarters to speak again. My speech was four pages long and it was generally about what I had done between the gala and the present time, my opinion about people with autism and many other intellectual disabilities, and why the world needs Special Olympics. After my speech, I shook so many hands that my right hand started to get so dry that it nearly bothered me every time it was squeezed. Nonetheless, I was glad to be in Beantown delivering an address to those who wanted to see me speak on the day when the Bruins played their first game of the Stanley Cup Playoffs.

A couple of weeks later, I went to Raytheon Headquarters in Bedford to deliver another speech. This time I was being filmed as part of an advertisement for Special Olympics and their upcoming Summer Games. Raytheon was sponsoring the Summer Games that year. I read the same speech in front of the camera. My speech was broadcasted to several Raytheon buildings in Eastern Massachusetts.

When Tyler delivers a speech, his true emotions come out. I'm not really sure why he is so comfortable delivering a speech to large crowds when most of us fear this challenge the most. I guess it's because he doesn't have to be concerned about the back and forth banter that is required in a normal conversation. He knows exactly what he wants to say and also knows that he won't be interrupted for the most part. On a few occasions, he has gone off script and quite frankly, it makes me nervous when he does that because I never know what he's about to say! Usually it works out for the best.

When May arrived, so did the final examinations for my two college courses: Computers for Technology and English Composition I. I breezed through the Computers final with very little problems. The next day I took the English final at the Disability offices at the MCC city building in Lowell. Thanks to the accommodations made by the people at Disability Support Services and with permission from my English professor, I had a limit of four hours to finish the final exam. My final exam essay was about how I respond or react to the news and what does the news mean to me. I typed for two hours and proofread for another hour. I made three printouts of my final exam and turned in the last printout. After three hours in this quiet room, my spring semester was over. I had worked extremely hard for almost four months, and in the end I earned *A*s in both my courses.

We are so grateful that Tyler is allowed to have this accommodation in college. This is the only accommodation that he has required thus far. The best part about Tyler going to college is the fact that he has learned to advocate for himself. He must make all his own arrangements for any accommodations that are necessary. He meets with advisors by himself and describes his challenges and works with the disabilities office to determine which accommodations will best suit his needs.

I played two rounds of nine-hole golf at Tyngsboro Country Club to begin the 2009 season with the Lowell General Hospital Golf League using my old clubs. In my first outing on April 27, I picked up where I left off from the invitational in Florida by making par on the first two holes of the course and later shot a 42 to begin the year. It was my lowest score to start a golf season. Next week, I shot a 46 on the same course and that was it for the clubs that I had used since 2003, the clubs that enabled me to get better at golf, and the clubs that I used to shoot a 79 in Florida. My clubs have gone through it all and now it was time for me to get a new and better set of clubs to take me to the next level.

After I shot the 42, Dad and I went to Stow Acres to get me club fitted. I went to their driving range to try out my clubs and then tried out a Cobra 6-iron. I noticed a distinct difference between the Cobra club and my club. Then I used a Cobra driver and compared it to my Nike Sasquatch. There too, was an obvious difference between the two drivers. I wasn't slicing the ball with the Cobra like I did with my clubs. I learned that the lie angle of my clubs was tilted toward the toe of the club head causing my ball to drift to my left. In the case of me, a left-handed golfer, my slices go left and my hooks go right. The Cobra club's lie angle was mainly in the middle, which would explain why my ball went straight with the club I tried out.

I love the fact that Tyler can understand what the pro at the course was explaining to him. Like many people, he is able to concentrate so well when the subject interests him.

After the club fitting, Dad and I went to their pro shop. I brought all of my gift cards that I got from the golf-a-thon and used them to purchase my new clubs. I was going to get a new driver, 3-wood, two hybrid clubs, and irons ranging from a 5-iron to a sand wedge. I was going to say goodbye to the Nike Sasquatch, the club that I got for Christmas in 2006, and the hybrid that I got at the golf-a-thon. As an incentive for getting new clubs at Stow Acres, Dad and I earned a free round of golf at Stow Acres. One week after getting fitted, Dad and I went back there to pick up my new clubs.

I had instant results using the new clubs. They made a significant difference in my game. I used them the next day when Dad and I played our free round of golf at the North Course of Stow Acres. I shot an 88 that day, but I made two birdies and five pars.

Two days after golfing at Stow Acres, Dad and I went to Mount Monadnock on a hiking trip with my dad's old coworker Dick Brown. It had been roughly ten years since I hiked up that mountain, and that was with the Gifford School on a rainy and foggy day in October of 1999. This time the weather was spotless, without a cloud in the sky. It was the first hike for us since another one of Dad's coworkers and one of his hiking buddies, Bill McDonald passed away. He died of complications from Alzheimer's disease back in January that year. This one was partly dedicated to Bill because we were all planning on spreading his ashes while making the hike up to Mount Washington later in the summer.

Our hike started at nine in the morning. The beginning of the hike was easy but bumpy and rocky. Then just like Gifford, it started to get steeper and more treacherous. I could see where Dad, Dick and I were and I could also see the top of Mount Monadnock. About an hour had passed since the hike started so we were making good time. The wind started to pick up now that we were headed closer to the top. It was a very warm day and the wind did not make the temperature any cooler. When I finally got to the top, the surface up there was all rocky, but what a view. I could see everything from the top of the mountain. We could not have picked a better day for a hike. While Dad was filming me with his digital camera, I said to him, "I love hiking."

During the hike I learned that Monadnock is the second most hiked mountain in the world to Japan's Mount Fuji. It is obviously the most hiked mountain in America, more than the world famous Mount Washington. On the way down, we didn't take the same trail we went up on. It was the least steep trail on the mountain otherwise known as the White Cross Trail compared to the White Dot Trail that we went up on. It took us two hours to get up and about an hour to get down. After the hike I was very tired and slept all the way until we got to Dick's house in Brookline, New Hampshire. My energy was all used up on that balmy Thursday. This hike up Monadnock was supposed to be a warm-up to the one up Mount Washington, but we didn't hike up Mount Washington at all in 2009.

Summer of 2009

THE SUMMER WAS A BUSY time and also a sad time for my family. On my dad's fifty-third birthday, his aunt Cora Marion passed away at the age of ninety-three. Her health had been failing and she had to go to a nursing home. My brother Clint, who had now become a Master Plumber, would move in to Cora's house. Her funeral was on June 2 and I was the pallbearer. I carried her casket, something I had never done before in any funeral.

Tyler did exceptionally well at being a pallbearer. He seems to like the structure of any type of service. He understands that death is part of life and he accepts the fact that as we get older it is inevitable that we all will pass.

After my spring semester was over, I enrolled in a summer online course for Middlesex Community College. I took United States History before 1865 from late May to early July. It was a unique course because I never took a class on the computer before. All I did was write essays and enter discussions with other students taking the course. I learned a lot about North America before the first settlements by the British in this land in the beginning of the seventeenth century. I also learned more about the American Revolution, the country's turbulent first several years, and the events that led to Civil War. I made the adjustment of doing homework on the computer and got an A on that course. My final exam was a long essay about the Kansas-Nebraska Act, and I got a 97 on it.

Many people have asked me why I didn't have Tyler sign up to get his degree participating in an online degree program. The simple answer is that I want him to be "connected" to people and ideas and experience different environments. I know that he would probably get good grades and finish his degree much earlier if he took an online degree program. But the fact remains he would be isolated and never learn to actually work face-to-face with people.

I made a couple more speaking engagements in the month of June. On June 11, I was invited to speak at the Knickerbocker Club in South Lowell to members of the Merrimack Valley Harley Davidson Chapter of Massachusetts and New Hampshire during their monthly meeting. They were once supporters of the Muscular Dystrophy Association in the past. This time, this group decided to name Kids in Disability Sports as their #1 charity of choice and so I came to speak about my time with the KIDS group in Lowell. They scheduled a bike run to benefit KIDS Inc. In that speech, I talked about my time with the KIDS group, told them they were making a difference in the lives of the children and adults who were stricken with disabilities by putting together this bike run, and used a quote from Jackie Robinson, saying, "One life is not important, except in the impact it has on other lives." After my speech, I had the loudest ovation of the whole meeting.

One week after the Knickerbocker Club speech, Mom, Dad and I went to the offices of Columbia Construction in North Reading. Columbia was the firm that was building the new Special Olympics Massachusetts Headquarters in Marlborough that time, and they invited me to do a motivational speech. I explained to them why they were doing this. I talked about overcoming obstacles to them and described my experiences with the Special Olympics. I told them that an obstacle is something that they had to deal with. After my speech, I was given a set of twelve Titleist NXT Extreme golf balls with the company logo on each ball. Then I was given an even bigger gift from the firm. It was a framed certificate for a free round of golf with two other guests at the TPC Boston Course in Norton, Massachusetts. The second round of the PGA Tour FedEx Cup Playoffs also known as the Deutsche Bank Championship takes place there every Labor Day weekend. It was the best gift that I could possibly hope for. If Vesper was the best course I played on last year, the TPC Boston Course was going to be the best course I will ever play on.

On Father's Day, Dad and I went to Gold's Gym in Chelmsford for the inaugural Big Kahuna 5K. The road race was named after the bar located inside the gym. I ran the race, Dad was the spectator. Two months earlier, I set a new personal best in a 5K road race in Groton when I finished in exactly twenty-three minutes and twenty seconds while enduring ninety-degree heat in late April. This race in Chelmsford was overcast and drizzly on that Father's Day. My goal for that race was to finish in between twenty-three and twenty-four minutes with the possibility of beating my time from the Groton Road Race.

Eighty-one runners participated in the Big Kahuna 5K. The first half of the race was uphill, and I made the most of it. My time after one mile was just over seven minutes. There was still a drizzle as I was struggling up the hill to the halfway point. The second half of the race was all downhill. After two miles of the 3.1-mile race, I had been running for 14:20. I was on pace to break my personal best. My legs were sore, it was a little wet, but I had to keep on going. Until I made the right turn onto the road that led to the gym, I did not look at my watch. Fifty yards before crossing the finish line, I passed a guy in a blue UMass–Lowell Recreation Center shirt. When I crossed the finish line, I stopped my watch at 22:19. I had just broken my personal best by one whole minute. I was exhausted, I was sick to my gut, but I was feeling more proud than exhausted and sick. I finished in thirteenth overall in the race, and second in my age-group. I won a silver medal and had my picture taken with the medal that I won. It felt amazing to have broken my personal best twice in two months.

Late June and most of July were not all that much fun as my dad and I were deprived of free time. Dad was working full-time at the luxury apartment in Chelmsford to fill in for his injured coworker and I was working more hours at Rick Reault's beekeeping business. I was also in the middle of wrapping up my online history course. I had also gone three weeks without going to Tyngsboro Country Club due in part to the weather. Until the three-week hiatus from Tyngsboro, I had just started to get my game into gear. I had shot back-to-back 39s on June 8 and 15 at Tyngsboro. I made the shot of the year on the first hole on June 15. I had this flop shot to the green fifty feet from the hole. It was almost like Tiger Woods on the sixteenth hole at the last round of the 2005 Masters. Once the ball landed, it was left of the flag and then all of a sudden it started to roll its way into the hole for an incredible birdie.

On June 29, Dad and I participated in the second annual Micky Ward Charities scramble golf tournament at Indian Ridge Country Club in Andover. We were with John Busby and Billy Sullivan again like last year. This year it rained worse than last year and we only played eleven holes. I didn't bring my best game there because I didn't have much time to practice. I did qualify for the $10,000 putting challenge. As soon as the rain stopped and the grounds were dry enough, the contest was on. I waited until later on when I decided to go. My putt was well read but I came up short of the hole.

At the clubhouse, there was a silent auction, raffle prizes, and a book signing by Micky Ward. That book was Micky Ward's autobiography called *Irish Thunder: The Hard Life and Times of Micky Ward*. It was written by Bob Halloran from WCVB-TV Channel 5. Halloran returned for the second annual tournament at Indian Ridge in 2009. I bought his book and had Micky and Halloran sign it for me. Bob wrote, "Tyler – Keep up the good fight!" And Micky wrote, "To Tyler, Best wishes, love you pal."

July 12 was the assessment round for the Special Olympics Massachusetts golf tournament. Mom and Dad took me to Mount Hood in Melrose, the ski area/golf course. For the third straight year I was playing eighteen holes with Keith Peabody. This time around I was going to play with another competitor. His name was Connor Daly from North Hampton, New Hampshire. He was sixteen years old, and like me, he was a left-handed golfer. My total score for the assessment round was 84. I went from playing my worst golf of the year to playing my best golf of the year in one day. It was like night and day, Jekyll and Hyde in Melrose. I had a great time playing with Keith and newcomer Connor. Connor was going to play in the SOMA golf tournament next month. This time the state tournament was going to take place at Stow Acres Country Club.

July was a very sad month for my family. On July 7 my uncle Harold O. Bell III died suddenly of a heart attack at the age of sixty-three. Before his funeral in Massachusetts on Saturday, July 18, there was a funeral that took place near the fire station he worked for in Pennsylvania. A lot of relatives and cousins and second cousins, and several other friends came to the Bay state to pay their last respects. The last thing I said to my uncle Harold before leaving for the church on the morning of the funeral was "Farewell, Uncle, I'll miss you, God bless." I was the pallbearer along with my brother Clint and my cousins Mark Ridgley and Dustin Deranian.

I rode with Mom and Dad and Clint to the church. Over there, my mom gave a stirring eulogy of her brother Harold. Mom described to the church full of people how nice Harold was to her and her five other sisters. For example, Harold was nice enough to bring my mom and her siblings with him to the beaches of New Hampshire while going out on one of his dates. I was impressed with the way Mom handled her emotions on the podium. She spoke very well in front of a large crowd during one of her hardest times in her life. Just as the church services were coming to a close, I got to carry Uncle Harold's casket into the car and rejoined my family. After that we drove all the way to the state line to Tyngsboro Memorial Cemetery. This was the place where I said my final goodbye to Uncle Harold "Mickey" Bell III. Mom thought that I was going to fall apart there but the truth was I had kept my composure all day. After saying farewell, we all went to Princeton Station for some food. I had a brief lunch and Clint had to leave early to attend a wedding up in Maine.

When I got home, I did some running on the treadmill. Then I went into the pool to wash the sweat off my body. I did not get into the pool at all in 2009 until the day before Harold's funeral. We had a little party out in the backyard patio with lots of company. It had all the makings of a full-scale family reunion that Saturday in July. Mark and I had a chipping contest, lots of food was being served until the sky went dark. It was like old times all over again. I had a joy being with my family members who were like old friends to me.

A couple of days after the funeral, I returned to work for the Registry of Deeds. I had just gotten a phone call from the Career Center of Lowell and they told me that they came up with the funds to bring me back to work at the registry for the duration of the summer. The people over there missed me so much because they liked having me around. Because of the economic hardship that America was going through that year, I wasn't able to come back there. Besides the invitational, I had a tough several months being away from work and being at home all the time. I went into a different office this time and I was scanning state and federal tax releases, state and federal tax liens, and death certificates. I was going to be all by myself for five hours a day, five times a week until the end of August.

During my free time, I would eat my own lunch, and read some books to pass the time. I quickly finished up the David Ortiz' autobiography called *Big Papi* and got started on Micky Ward's *Irish Thunder* during my breaks from work. The Micky Ward book had a lot of obscenities and F-words but it was a very accurate account of Ward's rise to the top of the boxing world. I learned a lot more about his personal and professional struggles and found that Micky even quit boxing on a couple of occasions. Somehow he came back to win a major professional boxing title and then had his three epic bouts with Arturo Gatti. A movie called *The Fighter* about the life of Micky Ward starring Mark Wahlberg was being filmed in Lowell that year.

Between Mount Hood and the Special Olympics state tournament at Stow Acres, I played at Tyngsboro Country Club four Mondays in a row. On July 13 the day after the round at Mount Hood, I continued to play grossly inconsistent golf. After shooting a back nine score of 36 in Melrose, I was off to my worst start at Tyngsboro all year. As I was about to make a quadruple bogey 9 on the fourth hole looking for my lost ball, my dad ditched me and continued the fourth and fifth holes without me. I had to finish the fourth hole and play the fifth all by myself. We never got this far apart on a golf course before. He never waited for me. He just kept on going on his own. He may have been trying to teach me a lesson, but I felt that he had gone too far at the time. When I got to the sixth hole, I wanted to take a swing at him, but that would have made it worse. But I chose to take it like a man and continue to golf. That day would have been over for me if I went out and unleashed my fury on my dad. I couldn't hurt him because he was my dad and I wasn't going to make this day any worse that it was. I responded by making my golfing do the talking as I made pars on the sixth and seventh holes. On the short par-4 eighth, my putt for birdie from ten feet went straight at the hole got. A par on #9 allowed me to finish the round with a 43.

Tyler is right when he says that his dad was trying to teach him a lesson. Like many golfers, sometimes Tyler takes his game too serious! If Ron had not walked ahead, I am sure that he would have taken Tyler off the course right there and ended that round of golf. It was far better to not react and let it play out. I am glad to see that Tyler felt abandoned because, quite frankly, sometimes I have felt as if he would never notice if I disappeared!

On August 1, the third annual Tyler Lagasse Scramble Golf Outing took place at Townsend Ridge. The 2009 version of my tournament was different than the first two. I was in a foursome with my dad, Rick Reault, and a gentleman named Skip Cotter. A lot of my friends came to my tournament. Gary Browning had brought his own foursome. Jaret

Foley and his family were there to participate, as was my dad's cousin who happened to live in Townsend. Paul Karrlsson-Willis and his wife Emma—a couple from England that we met in a Special Olympic fundraiser—were also in attendance. Twenty foursomes, or eighty participants, showed up that day, the largest turnout in the history of the Tyler Lagasse Scramble Golf Outing. Due to the economy, the price was lowered, and that resulted in this large turnout.

After the golf, Dad and I drove to the banquet, which took place at Townsend House. The clubhouse at the course was occupied because there was another tournament taking place there. The banquet took place inside a dining room at a local restaurant. The teams that finished in the top, middle, and bottom of the standings received their certificates from Townsend Ridge. I made a speech to the crowd and helped distribute the raffle prizes. In spite of the economic crisis and all the cutbacks, the third annual Tyler Lagasse Scramble Golf Outing was a downright success.

On Saturday, August 8, my family set forth on our seventh annual trip to Seabrook Beach. The next day, Dad drove me from the beach to Stow Acres for the 2009 SOMA August Games. To save money on account of the financial crisis, the games were shortened to just one day of events. The golf tournament taking place at Stow Acres was cut in half from thirty-six holes to eighteen holes for this year. I was going to be paired up with Keith Peabody and Nathan and Geoff Simonds, the pair that was in Florida last October.

A cameraman was there to film us teeing off on the par-5 first hole of the North Course. I was the last golfer in my group to tee off. I admit to feeling tension since I never golfed in front of a camera before. I hit a high pop up off the tee with the driver but drove the ball two hundred yards.

After a very long day at Stow Acres, I ended it on a high note. I capped off the back nine with a score of 44. My total for all eighteen holes was a 91. The greens may have kept me from lowering my score but in the end I earned my fourth state golf championship. New Hampshire's Connor Daly participated at Stow Acres and shot a 94, three strokes more than me. Connor would get the silver medal in my division.

After golf, while Dad and I were having a meal at the clubhouse, I saw myself on TV. They showed me teeing off on the first hole. I knew that a cameraman was there but I had no idea that I was going to be on TV that day. Robert Johnson, the SOMA president and CEO, was on TV, and he was quoted in the *Boston Herald* that day. Being on TV teeing off with my driver was a highlight bigger than the fourth gold medal in a row that I won. Because of my accomplishments on and off the golf course, the year 2009 was about to be one for the decade.

Two days after my state golf tournament, while I was in the middle of vacationing at Seabrook, Eunice Kennedy Shriver, the Mother of Special Olympics, died at the age of eighty-eight. Of course you have already read about the birth and growth of Special Olympics from the Let Me Be Brave chapter. She did so much to enrich the lives of people living with intellectual disabilities. Eunice had been sick for a while now and she was not well enough to be at the gala in Harvard back in April of 2008. Her loss was painful to not only the Shriver family and the Kennedy family, but to the Special Olympic family.

My picture from 2007 after I won the New England Invitational was on the front page of the *Lowell Sun* newspaper. The words with which I described Eunice were as follows: "Like Martin Luther King, Eunice had a dream, and just as Martin Luther King fought for civil rights, she fought for the advancement of people with disabilities. She dedicated her life to improving the quality of life for people like me. She had courage and perseverance, and she taught me courage and perseverance through sports." Those words were used on page 12 of the August 12, 2009, edition of the *Lowell Sun* and page B6 in the Metro section of the *Boston Globe* that same day.

Her death was on almost every news station in Boston. At Fenway Park after the first inning of a Boston Red Sox game, they honored Eunice Shriver and showed an image of her throwing out the first pitch at a Red Sox game some years ago. Robert Johnson made a speech about Eunice in front of the almost finished SOMA headquarters in Marlborough in front of several news cameras. Johnson would be on Channel 5 to speak again during a special on Eunice. Colin Davidson, a global messenger and fellow Special Olympian, was also on TV to say some words about Eunice. She is an irreplaceable figure in this world, and she will be missed. I never met her—I met her son at the gala—but my life wouldn't be the same without her. I'm glad that I am a part of Special Olympics, I'm glad that I have the chance to succeed at the many things that I am good at, and I am glad that I am writing about this. Eunice's brother Senator Ted Kennedy would pass away two weeks later.

Our family is very grateful for the contribution that Mrs. Shriver has made. We have met many remarkable people because of our participation in Special Olympics. It is not just a "one-day track meet." We have developed both personal and professional friendships and our lives have been blessed because of Mrs. Shriver.

The seventh vacation at Seabrook was not the best vacation yet, but it certainly was better than last year and perhaps the year before. We went out to eat at several restaurants like we did before. One time my parents took me to the batting cages near I-95. I had not hit a baseball in years so it felt good to be stepping up to the plate again. I also got to ride my bike around the neighborhood, jog along the shore, play some games with Mom, Dad, and Memere, and I got to read more of Micky Ward's book. One time I challenged Clint to a pistachio eating contest and beat him. I rated this vacation a B.

Dad and I played golf at Tyngsboro Country Club four more times in August as the season was winding down and college was coming around the corner. On the first two rounds in Tyngsboro since vacation, Dad had chances to beat me. In our first round together, he stumbled by making a 7 on the last hole and I beat him by four strokes, my 40 to his 44. Three days later we played at Tyngsboro again. My dad shot a 42, but he led by three strokes with three holes to go and two with two to go. But it took a birdie from three feet away on the eighth hole and a par on #9 to give me a score of 42.

Every once in a while, Ron beats Tyler at golf and I believe it keeps Tyler humble!

The summer of 2009 and the LGH Golf League season were coming to an end. I did not feel all that satisfied with the way the summer worked out. It was a boring yet eventful summer. Besides the vacation to Seabrook, my family did not do any spectacular things over the summer. Dad and I were just too busy working, and of course I was the pallbearer in two funerals this summer—the first for Aunt Cora and the other for Uncle Harold. My performance at the August Games at Stow Acres was mediocre to say the least even though I won a gold medal again. Dad and I didn't do enough eighteen-hole rounds of golf but by year's end, we would play at Tyngsboro a record twenty times.

In 2009 I worked harder than the year before. I took three college courses so far and got *A*s in all of them. I made a lot of money from the beekeeping business, the Registry of Deeds, and other side jobs here and there. I made more speeches in 2009 than I did in all of 2008. I set two personal bests at the 5K in this year alone. But on the golf course, thanks to the clubs that I got at Stow Acres, I was taking it to the next level, and I was already breaking 40 in nine holes on a regular basis. I was on TV hitting a golf ball, and I was in two newspapers mostly to express my condolences to the family of Eunice Kennedy Shriver. I may not have done well in the tournaments that I played in, but I was doing very well in the Lowell General Hospital Golf League.

September was the time for me to go back to school. I took two classes for the fall semester at Middlesex Community College in Lowell. I decided to major in liberal arts/life sciences concentration. Just like in the spring semester early in the year, I took two classes. I took environmental science with lab two days a week and a renewable energy class on Saturdays. I had never taken a college-level science course before and I didn't know what to expect. I wanted to help the environment any way I could since Cotting School and I believe that I could make a living and get a job doing so. Those two classes that I took were good starting points.

I was surprised when Tyler announced that he wanted to major in the environmental sciences. He is concerned with renewable energy. I think he will do well in that field.

Two days after the LGH season finale, Dad and I finally went on a big hike. It wasn't Mount Washington, but it was a big one in the heart of New Hampshire's White Mountains, called Mount Lafayette, with my dad and his friend Dick Brown. Lafayette was going to be my first five-thousand-foot hike and the biggest and longest one so far. I woke up at 5:30 a.m. and left the house at 6:15. We stopped at the rest area near Route 3 in Nashua to meet Dick and get up to the mountains in his car. Just before 9:00 in the morning we started our hike at the Cannon Mountain parking lot, went under I-93 and strolled into the woods. Mount Lafayette is blocked off by rocky hills from I-93. We took the Greenleaf Trail to the top, which was exactly 3.7 miles from I-93.

During our hike, we talked about that Monday night Patriots football game where they came back to beat Buffalo very late in the game. We also debated which were the best pancakes in New England and the best burger in New England. About an hour and a half into the hike we had good views of I-93. There was a hut over at one peak and we stayed in there for a while to use the restroom and purchase some bread. After that we continued on up to the top. I decided to go ahead of Dad and Dick and go from there. I laid myself down on a rock while I waited for the rest of my party. Then I kept on going until I reached the top. I was sucking wind on my way there. The altitude was getting to me but I was still going and I don't know what kept me going. Then after five-thousand-plus feet, I made it to the top.

It wasn't Mount Washington but it was as high as I had ever gone before on a hike. I was already having my lunch up there when the old timers arrived. There was a magnificent view of Franconia and the rest of the White Mountain wilderness. I had pictures of me taken, and then took a pair of pictures of Dad and Dick in front of a sign with Dad holding a picture of the late Bill McDonald. It would have been a more fitting tribute if we'd hiked up Mount Washington for Bill. We stayed at the top for an hour before we finally started out trek down Mount Lafayette.

On the way down we stopped at the hut for the last time. The hike began at 9:00 a.m. and ended at 4:15 in the afternoon. We traveled 7.4 miles on foot in seven hours. My feet were sore, my calves were tight by the time we came back to the parking lot. It was the biggest mountain I've ever hiked, it was the longest I've ever hiked, and it was the highest I've ever gone in the eastern half of the United States. I had a great time hiking with my father and Dick Brown.

One week after the hike up Mount Lafayette, Dad and I played eighteen holes on the Prairie Course at Green Meadow in Hudson. It was September 22, and Dad picked me up from Middlesex Community College in Lowell that day. We were originally supposed to golf at this new eighteen-hole course in nearby Dracut called Meadow Creek. We did get to the place but there was a tournament going on so we couldn't play there. Instead we agreed to go up to Green Meadow. We could have gone over to Tyngsboro Country Club to play eighteen there, but I haven't been to Green Meadow all year, and I've wanted to play there. Green Meadow is my favorite nearby place to golf eighteen holes. I shot a *78!* The score could've been less if I had made some more putts, but I was good enough to set another low mark.

On the day after I broke another one of my records at Green Meadow, a decision was made regarding the 2010 Special Olympics

USA National Games that were taking place in Lincoln, Nebraska. Two names were drawn to see who was going to be participating in Level 5 golf at the National Games, one was me and the other was Keith Peabody. The person that was going to Nebraska next July was me. I was more than thrilled. I was inspired to hear that I was going to compete on a national level again. The National Games were coming in ten months and I dedicated whatever time I had to prepare myself for it. I could not wait to go to the American Midwest to see what it is like over there.

Fall of 2009

ON THE DAY BEFORE MY third Special Olympics Golf-a-thon, Dad and I were supposed to go to Meadow Creek, the new course in Dracut for the Lowell General Hospital golf tournament, but Dad felt that the weather was too unsuitable for it. We did go to the Best Western Hotel in Marlborough for the pre-golf-a-thon get-together. I delivered a four-page-long speech to the crowd of more than twenty at the lobby. In my latest speech, I told them about how they made a difference in my golf game in 2009. I told them they were doing the right thing in giving back to Special Olympics and that I was going to Lincoln, Nebraska, to compete in golf for the upcoming USA National Games.

I had very little sleep between the reception and the actual golf-a-thon. We arrived at Stow Acres by 8:00 a.m. While I was practicing on the putting green, a familiar voice came to the green. It was Bob Montgomery, the former color commentator for Red Sox games, and backup catcher to Carlton Fisk during the 1970s. He reminds me of my grandfather, Harold O. Bell Jr. I remember as a little boy listening to him and Sean McDonough call Red Sox games on TV-38. I got so used to Jerry Remy that I kind of miss him being in the booth.

I was kind of nervous when I got to meet him. He seemed like a nice guy and he truly was. A lot of people around me said he was. Bob and I introduced ourselves and we challenged each other to a little putting contest. After that, Bob and I had our picture taken of just the two of us. I remember seeing Bob Montgomery at the Doug Flutie Tournament over a year ago. Later on at the golf-a-thon, I was given an autograph picture of Bob and in the picture was a message saying, *"To Tyler, great meeting you, good luck with all your future golf, Bob Montgomery."*

The plan for the 2009 Golf-a-thon was to have me play one hole with each of the foursomes that were out on the two Stow Acres courses. After that, I was to play a whole round with a foursome, and then something amazing was going to happen on the eighteenth hole of the South Course. Only nine teams of four participated in the 2009 Golf-a-thon, and I played one hole with each of them. This tournament was a "bramble" format, which was a scramble format with a twist. In this new format, the best ball is only in effect after the tee shots and after that the players can use their balls from where the best tee shot landed. The lowest score in each hole from any player in one foursome is counted.

Heidi, the volunteer from last year's golf-a-thon, drove me to the first foursome we saw. It was on the fourth hole of the North Course where Heidi, Dad, and I came upon the Canaccord Team with James Duncan, the man responsible for helping me get my new clubs. The fourth hole was a difficult par-4 with water to the left on the far end of the fairway. I helped make par on the fourth. After that I played with the ITG Canada Team on the long par-4, ninth hole. Emma Karrlsson-Willis was on the ITG Canada squad. My drive went out of sight to the left but the team made par anyway. Onto the fifteenth hole where we found Team International Assets, the team I was going to play with later in the day. They had two players, a golfer named Ted, and Eric Knudsen who had an outstanding drive. I didn't have a good showing on that hole.

I only had one birdie while shuttling to different foursomes. My lone birdie came on the par-5 sixth hole on the South Course while playing with the Vandham Corporation. I hit a stellar drive that was just yards from being the longest drive of this foursome. Two shots later, I hit a nice chip from the rough, I played my flop shot and got the ball high in the air and landed the ball to within a foot of the hole. I made the tap-in putt for birdie.

At five, there was a special minitournament called the Tyler Lagasse Golf Challenge. It took place on the par-5 eighteenth hole on the South Course. Nine competitors including me participated in the inaugural contest. I went last after of all the competitors teed off in order of their handicaps. I was a little nervous as I was about to tee off but I managed to find my comfort zone, maintain my focus, and hit the ball straight as an arrow and a long way. It was the second longest drive of the challenge. I was unable to cash in on my great drive as I duffed my ball with the 2-hybrid into the swamp in my futile attempt to make the green in two shots. There was a three way tie for first place and so the winner was decided by a chip-in and a putt-out. The winner of the inaugural Tyler Lagasse Golf Challenge was Paul Karrlsson-Willis, Emma's husband. I presented him with a very fabulous trophy. I didn't win my challenge but I would come away with something by the time the day was over.

There was an awards banquet going on inside the big room at Stow Acres. There was a slide show for the whole golf-a-thon with many pictures of me. I looked absolutely good swinging a club in one of those pics (short for pictures). During the dinner, I received a Callaway watch, $650 in Stow Acres gift cards, and I was awarded a trophy for being on the team that donated the most money during the golf-a-thon. At least $124,000 was raised during this event. One year into the most painful recession of our time, the 2009 Special Olympics Golf-a-thon was able to raise six figures. For the third year in a row, I had a blast being at Stow Acres in late September.

I am so grateful for all the time and effort that people put in for various charities. In this particular case, the charity of choice for this group of people was the Special Olympics. Tyler has met so many wonderful people since being involved in this organization. It is my hope that he, in turn, has demonstrated humility, confidence, and inspired people to overcome challenges.

After four years of golfing Monday afternoons at Tyngsboro Country Club with the Lowell General Hospital Golf League with my dad, in a year of personal bests and firsts, I was named the champion of the golf league for the first time ever. There was an end of season banquet going on at Ricardo's Café in Downtown Lowell one evening in early October. After a very large dinner that featured fried olives, salad, lobster ravioli, chicken parmigiana, and lots more, I was given a total of $55 in cash ($40 for finishing first in the 4 Clubs tournament with a gross score of 36, and $15 for getting closest to the pin on the ninth hole on the day I shot my personal best round of 36). Dad and I and the rest that were there for the dinner each got $30 gift cards to Golf n' Ski Warehouse. But my biggest award was this rectangular-shaped glass that read, "Best Golfer 2009, Tyler Lagasse, LGH Golf League." My golf handicap index for the year was 6.1, four points less than the next competitor,

Dave Kimball, the man who actually runs the golf league. My dad's handicap index was 20. It took me four long years to get to that special place in the league and I went through lots of changes during that time.

The month of November was a time of firsts. On the third day of that month, on my way home from class, Dad asked me, "Do you want to play some hockey tonight?" It came as a surprise to me because I heard about the new Dekhockey Center behind Gold's Gym in Chelmsford but I wasn't expected to play this year. The team that was captained by Rick Dupuis needed a player to fill out their roster. It was a yes or no question, and I decided to play that night.

The rink behind the gym had just been built over the summer. That area used to be a basketball court and a swimming pool. Dek hockey is similar to street hockey where there is no skating and a ball is used instead of a puck. You have to wear shin/knee guards, elbow pads, gloves, mouth guards, and a cup/supporter—you know, equipment normally used by hockey players. Helmets are optional in dek hockey. Dad got me some of the equipment at the dek hockey rink, I brought my own stick and two pairs of gloves with me—my work gloves and my black winter gloves.

I briefly played street hockey with Clint and his friends as a kid and a little floor hockey with the KIDS group four years earlier. At least I knew the game because I had been watching hockey for years, I just didn't play it that much. I arrived at the Dekhockey Center thirty minutes before my first game started. After putting my pads on, I gave this game a try. This game was harder than I expected. It was much different playing the game than watching it. I tried to hit the ball hard with my slap shot but I was pretty wild with my shot, sometimes I would shoot the ball out of the rink. There were six forwards, four defensemen, and one goalie completing the roster. My team's nickname was fittingly called the Bruins. I was on a team consisting mostly of middle-aged men. Some of them worked for the gym. Of course, Rick Dupuis was the owner. Even Micky Ward was on my team for a while. I played left wing on the second scoring line.

On the first shift of my first dek hockey game, I set myself in front of the net, I took a pass from a teammate who was behind the net, and just slapped the ball past the goalie and into the back of the net. I had just scored a goal on my first shot of the first shift of my first dek-hockey game! Unbelievable! We lost that game 5–2 but it was a good first experience for me. I learned that the rules of dek hockey were different than the game that was played on ice. Offsides and icing were different, high sticking was outlawed, but the quality of the game was good overall. I felt very tired after three ten-minute periods. That floor gave me severe lower back pains and I couldn't move my body without pain for a while. I went on to play a few more hockey games without ever scoring another goal again.

Tyler has been extremely fortunate to be asked to play in various leagues in our community. Each time he joins a team, we learn more about his challenges and are better able to address them. He looks forward to just "joining in," and I look for opportunities to discover or "uncover" obstacles that he may face and create new experiences that will help him lead a more independent, fulfilling adult life.

On November 13, Mom, Dad and I attended the Red, White, and Bid for the third straight year. This year we went to the House of Blues behind Fenway Park on Landsdowne Street. At least fifty items were being auctioned off, including a puck autographed by Bobby Orr. Several items were also being raffled off. This event was also a wine tasting but I didn't sample any alcoholic beverages. I was there to speak at this event for the third straight year. I spoke about my life, how it was affected by Special Olympics, what I am doing currently, and what I will be doing in the future. Even though being near Fenway Park made me nervous, I had a nearly flawless speech.

At this point, Tyler has gained confidence in his speaking ability. Many of the same people come each year to support Special Olympics. In fact, several people mentioned that they saw so much maturity in him as compared to the previous year. Sometimes it feels as if we aren't making any progress because we are too close to Tyler's challenge of autism. It is important for me to take the time to listen when people are giving me honest feedback regarding Tyler. I am always looking for ways to push Tyler forward, and I don't always need to do that. Sometimes I should just slow down and let the chips fall where they may. That is an easier task to say than to do!

Two days after the Red, White, and Bid, there was this open house at the Yawkey Sports Training Center, the new home to the headquarters of Special Olympics Massachusetts in Marlborough. There were about ten global messengers that showed up, including me, Michael Findlay, Colin Davidson, and Melissa Reilly. I arrived before the open house officially began so that I could be a part of the tour of the new facility.

Last month, Dad and I got to step inside the new building for the first time to tour the facility and to do a little interview about the upcoming National Games. On my second trip to the new place, I visited every room and office inside the building, the group was treated with snacks, water, and later pizza. I even saw an image of me speaking at the gala on a plasma TV early in the tour. I got to shoot some hoops at their basketball court. The key moment of the tour was when Jo Jo White paid a visit to the headquarters. I got a picture of him and he autographed it for me. He wrote, "Best Wishes from #10 Jo Jo White."

After the team meeting, I went into a conference room to be a part of the open house. Inside I watched an Internet movie about the Special Olympics, and I saw an image of myself at the gala in there. Inside the room, I finally met my golf coach for the National Games, Scott Ayres. He looked forward to having me on his team and we would see each other again on several occasions before the trip to Lincoln, Nebraska. Then I went inside this weight room to be with Colin Davidson and watch a little football. I also saw Keith and Marge Peabody there at the open house. I got myself two pairs of global messenger collared shirts, one long-sleeved and one short-sleeved, there. The open house was a total success. This building in my opinion was long overdue. It was named the Yawkey Sports Training Center after the people that owned the Boston Red Sox for seventy years. It was built during tough economic times. I had a wonderful time at the new SOMA headquarters that day.

SOMA Headquarters Grand Opening Gala

I WENT BACK TO THE new building on December 1 for the grand opening gala. I wore the gold medal that I won at the state golf tournament at Stow Acres. I made my twelfth speech in 2009 at the official opening of the Yawkey Center. This one was going to be the biggest speech of the year for me. Early in the gala, a self-portrait of Eunice Kennedy Shriver was unveiled on top of a staircase near the lobby of the building. Colin Davidson and Melissa Reilly were there to speak at the lobby during the first part of the gala. Denise Carriere was also there to speak inside the basketball court.

Later on in the party, all of the guests moved inside the basketball court. My family got to sit at the same table as the president and chief operating officer of Special Olympics International, Brady Lum. A couple of representatives from Columbia Construction, the firm that built the Yawkey Center, were on hand as well. There was a tribute to a gentleman named Donald Dowd, who established the Board of Directors for Special Olympics Massachusetts. Then it was my turn to speak. It was the longest speech of the year and longest since the Let Me Be Brave Gala in 2008.

I began by saying a few things about the recently deceased Eunice Kennedy Shriver who started the active lifestyle movement for people living with disabilities with inspiration from her sister. I told the audience that Eunice refused to believe that people with disabilities would not be accepted in the general society. I listed two examples of Eunice's vision, me, and the new Yawkey Sports Training Center where I spoke that night. I spoke of the new building and thanked the people for their commitment to the Special Olympics movement, telling them that this building is more than its physical characteristics. It represents the generosity of the people that built it. I also told the crowd about how Special Olympics was more than playing sports, my list of achievements from 2009 and that they were all possible on account of the supporters of Special Olympics, and how the Healthy Athletes Program helps improve the quality of life for people living with disabilities. I told them that I was never always good at golf and I didn't think that I would be golfing and making speeches for Special Olympics at age twenty-three. I gave the audience some advice about being on the road to greater things by saying never forget who *you* are, never forget where *you* came from, and never forget what *you* did to get to your current point in time. I wrapped it up by quoting Dr. Robert Anthony in his book titled *Think Big*, in which he said, "Winners are ordinary people with extraordinary determination." I told them they were all winners for contributing to Special Olympics and when they look back years from now, they'll think to themselves that they did the right thing because they believe in the abilities of people like me.

I was greeted with a large standing ovation after I was done speaking. I had pictures taken with global messengers and other Special Olympic athletes. The day after the gala, SOMA president and CEO Robert Johnson called my speech "stupendous" because my use of words was both astonishing and tremendous. I did feel like the main attraction that night in Marlborough.

December was the month to prepare for my final examinations. The fall semester of 2009 was the most arduous and demanding to date as I was taking my first meaningful steps toward an associate's degree in liberal arts/life sciences concentration. I spent most of the last month of the decade going over my notes, typing several pages with hundreds of words, making some printouts of my work, and making this solar power poster in my renewable energy course. My poster was based on three questions:

1) What is solar power?
2) Where is it used?
3) Why do we need it?

I also had to write a two page long essay about solar power. For extra credit, I typed in some current event reports. I also did a report on the

Copenhagen Climate Change Summit on the day when all of the world leaders came to an agreement to fix the global warming crisis. On my last renewable energy class, I graded my classmates' posters, and had to answer six questions as part of my final exam for this class.

On the day before the final exam for my environmental science class, I typed a four page essay. I took that final exam inside a conference room on the same floor as the disability offices instead of one of the offices there. It took me over two hours to get the whole test done. I had some trouble understanding some of the questions, but I felt that I got most of the questions right and believed that I did very well on the short answers and I was sure to have a good overall score. It was my first college-level science course. In September, I didn't know too much about environmental science, I never studied in a lab. As the year wound down, I got the hang of this and worked really hard to get an A minus in environmental science and an A in renewable energy. All those grades were the hardest earned since I came to college.

The year 2009 for me was a challenging year, but ready or not I was able to take that challenge on. Mick Jagger of the mega–rock band the Rolling Stones once said, "You can't always get what you want." Sure enough Mick Jagger was right. I didn't always get what I wanted this year. But I didn't let that stop me from setting several personal bests and trying really hard at being the best that I can be. Whether I am on the golf course, in the classroom, or behind a podium, it doesn't make any difference.

All year long, if not all my life, I had to overcome many challenges, face endless amounts of adversity, take numerous psychological slaps across my face, and paddle my way through this Phlegethon to earn my place in history. The year 2009 was a gateway year as the world was about to make its transition into a new decade. I can look back at the years between 2000 and 2009 as the decade of character because that decade was about showing character through thick and thin. I've had my share of ups and downs, wins and losses, positives and negatives, and somehow I lived through it all. Within those ten years, I went from winning two MVP trophies for the Cotting School basketball team to winning four straight state golf titles to being a bona fide global messenger.

Until 2009, I've never been this good on a golf course, I've never had to take this many college courses, and I've never had to make this many speeches for Special Olympics. That's why I called 2009 the year of personal bests. I've worked really hard to get my golf scores lower, to keep my grades high, and to nail my speeches. I've done more work than I could possibly imagine all year. In golf, I was the champion of the Lowell General Hospital Golf League and won the SOMA golf title for the fourth time. In college, I took five college courses and got *As* in four of them. Until 2009 I took four courses. By the end of the decade, I had made a dozen speaking engagements for Special Olympics, and two of them made the Internet.

2010: A Banner Year

THE SECOND DECADE OF THE new millennium started off with a bang. I celebrated the new year/decade running in a 5K at the Lowell Elks. Like the one on Thanksgiving, this event was a combination 5K/10K. Eight hundred runners were there to fight their own New Year's hangover and start off the New Year right. The races began at 11:00 a.m. I didn't run my best race like I did in several that I ran in 2009. I was trying to maintain a comfortable pace for all 3.1 miles. I was up after midnight watching the ball drop. I was thinking about pace instead of time. In the end, I finished the race at 24:53, a whole minute slower than at the same course weeks earlier. A few days after the race, I found out that I had finished in third place in my age-group. My streak of finishing 5Ks under twenty-four minutes ended at five races, but I came away with a medal and a significant achievement out of the race. Later in the day, the Boston Bruins played in the annual NHL Winter Classic at Fenway Park and beat the Philadelphia Flyers 2–1.

In the last week of January, I returned to Middlesex Community College to take two more college courses. I took United States History after 1865 and English Composition II on Tuesday and Thursday mornings. I had two very good teachers in the spring semester. Eventually I figured out what I needed to do to make it through the semester, and in the end I got As in both history and English.

I was in my first year with the Nashoba Shooting Stars in the winter of 2010. I would go to Nashoba Valley Ski Area in Westford twice a week for their practices. Late in the month of January, I competed in the assessment round of skiing at Blandford Ski Area all the way in the Berkshire Mountains of Western Massachusetts. It was a frigid cold day and I only did a pair of runs to get a gold pin for participation. I finished in second place overall after runs of 46 and 44.5 seconds. In the middle of March, our team got to participate in the Special Olympics State Winter Games at Wachusett Mountain. The weather was in stark contrast to the kind at Blandford. It was raining at Wachusett, which made the snow all slushy and as a result was going to have a major impact on the skiing performances of all of the participants—beginner, intermediate, and advanced alike. All of the events were crammed into one day because the rain was going to last all weekend. I did the giant slalom time trials, two slalom races, and the downhill race on this rainy day. I won a silver medal in each of the three events.

A week after the Winter Games, the Nashoba Shooting Stars wrapped up their skiing schedule up at Mount Sunapee. The Mills/ Golden Cup was taking place that day as was this winter picnic on the snowy base of the mountain next to the ski area parking lot. The whole team came up. There were foldable chairs, portable grills, lots of food, and some skiing. I participated in a pair of Mills Cup races with some of the members of my team. Becky from Cotting School and Melissa Reilly won the bronze and silver medals in the girl's overall division. I won the silver medal in the men's overall. Before that we had the team awards, where every member of the team got awards. I won the Best Form, Balance, and Agility Certificate, and Mom and Dad shared the Best First Year Coach Award. The last skiing of the year was fun and it was a good first year with the Nashoba Shooting Stars.

Also in March, I did a pair of big speeches. Mom took me to Winthrop High School east of Boston to speak at an assembly. Like last year when I went to Malden High School to make a speech to the students there, I attended the Spread the Word to End the Word event in Winthrop. There was a larger and more enthusiastic turnout than in Malden. Massachusetts Speaker of the House Robert DeLeo was in attendance that day. The whole auditorium was taking a stand against the R-word. I've never seen an atmosphere quite like it. When it was my turn to speak, I gave my views of the R-word to the audience. I made some comments about my life as well as my contributions and accomplishments to Special Olympics. A whole group of students were singing "My Wish" by Rascal Flatts and "That's What Friends Are For" by Dionne Warwick. I felt completely appreciated by these young people and pleased by their support at Winthrop.

On the Thursday night of March 11, I visited Cape Cod for the first time in twelve years. Cape Cod is normally a summer destination but I went there to speak in front of roughly a thousand members of the Massachusetts Association of Student Councils. They were holding their annual delegation at the resort and conference center in Hyannis, and they chose me to speak at the conference. They saw my Harvard Gala speech from 2008, and they wanted to show some support for Special Olympics. The size of the crowd in Cape Cod rivaled that of the one in Harvard. I did not disappoint. I did my job in front of the mostly teenaged 1,200 plus in attendance, and I got all of them on their feet. I had a couple of pictures taken with the student council members after the conference was over. I spent the night at the resort with my parents and returned home the next day.

Next week, I went to Buckingham, Browne, and Nichols in Cambridge to participate in the annual Special Olympics Bio-Ball Basketball Tournament. My team, Kids in Disability Sports, was teamed up with Alnylam again. Before the games started, I made a speech to all the athletes and biotech and pharmaceutical companies in attendance like I did last year. Essentially it was the same material from the previous Bio-Ball tournament but with new and added material. For the third time this March, I had an outstanding applause after one of my speeches.

There were twelve players that played for the KIDS group. One time we had to split up so that we could fill in for one team that was running late just for one game. I wasn't in enough shape to play well in Bio-Ball because I was turning my focus on skiing. My team did not win a single game at Bio-Ball. However, I was proud to be there to represent Special Olympics with the utmost dignity and respect.

After playing the games, I got to be on the radio for an AM sports radio station that was supporting Special Olympics in this tournament. I got to talk about the Boston Bruins and why they were slumping. I said hello to my brother Clint on the radio even though he didn't listen to that station. I explained on the radio how much of an impact my brother has made on me. I had enjoyed being on the radio for the first time.

After a lunch break, my team did the skills competition. Just like last year, I did some passing skills, some layups, free throws, three-pointers, half-court shots, and dribbling drills. I did not stay long after the skills competition. We did not stay for the championship game anyway. I said on the radio that the tournament was not about winning or losing, but to just be here for a cause. It was about having fun with your teammates and their teammates as well, meeting new people, and building friendships. I believe that being on the radio helped make this day better for me. Also my speech touched the hearts of the crowd at Cambridge once again. Both the speech and the radio appearance were the two biggest parts of the Bio-Ball tournament.

On the evening of Saturday, April 10, I went back to my old school from 1992 to 1999, the Community Therapeutic Day School in Lexington, for a little visit. Normally I would come every May for the annual alumni picnic, but this visit was different. The school was celebrating its thirty-fifth anniversary of its existence and its legacy of "history, health, and healing." I was one of the guest speakers of this special occasion. This was going to be my fourth speech of this young year.

There was a big silent auction inside two of my old classrooms. It had been ten years since I reentered my old classrooms, but I still remember going there as a kid. I got to reunite with some familiar faces there, therapists Nancy Fuller, Bruce Hauptman, and Alan Shapiro. Most of my old teachers were there, Michelle, Joanna, Linda, Bridget, Selene, Olivia, Priscilla and Steve. Dan the maintenance man was there, Daniel the psychologist was there, and Jan my favorite psychologist was there as well. My best CTDS friend Michael B. was there with his family. He was going to speak to a crowd inside the barn just like me. I went to CTDS that night with Mom and Dad and Denise Borghi. My brother Clint and numerous friends and relatives were also there.

The main event began when the sun went down. A series of speeches was kicked off with an introduction by Larry Hartmann. After that, Bruce, Nancy, and Daniel gave their sides of the story about history, health, and healing. Then Alan gave an emotional speech about his two families, one was his own and the other was CTDS. Then when he was fit enough to get himself together, he introduced the crowd to the three members of the CTDS alumni, Michael B. (CTDS class of 1999), Emma (CTDS class of 2005), and myself.

Michael's speech was one of a kind. He called CTDS his second home, how devastated he felt when he had to leave CTDS. He then went on to attend the Landmark School in Beverly for middle school and high school respectively, studied auto body and collision repair for a while but decided to study phlebotomy and became a medical assistant. He said that he spends time with people with autism ages eleven to fifteen at Seven Hills Charter School. I liked what he said very much and I believe he did a good job. After that, it was Emma's turn. She described history, health, and healing in her point of view. Then she and her father did a little musical performance, their rendition of Bob Dylan's "Forever Young."

Finally it was my turn to speak. I had a little trouble getting prepared to speak because I had to deal with this microphone wire that was wrapped around me in the beginning. I read the whole speech flawlessly but there were times when I went off script and other times when I inadvertently used humor to describe my experience at CTDS. There were some parts to my speech that were meant to be funny but the majority of the speech was supposed to reveal the serious side of CTDS. Still I made the crowd laugh more often than applaud for whatever the reason. I talked about how lost I was before coming to CTDS and how much I disliked special times and speech group. I may have used my body language and gestures to describe my CTDS experience better to the crowd. One time I was interrupted by Alan when he wanted to explain something to me. Toward the end of my speech, I unbuttoned my dress shirt and showed off my T-shirt from the 1999 CTDS Summer Program. I did the same thing earlier when Michael spoke. I got a big applause and big kisses from my dad and Alan. Michael said, "Ya bastard!" to me as I went back to my seat. It was like old times all over again. Near the end of the celebration, I almost got attacked by Alan, the one person who helped me all those year. It was the strangest night of the year coming back to my old school to rekindle old friendships and memories.

As soon as the weather and the grounds were suitable enough for golfing, Dad and I got on the links as soon as possible so that I could have enough golf practice in time for the upcoming Special Olympics USA National Games in July. We played our first round on April 13—the earliest that Dad and I have ever played before—at Tyngsboro Country Club. Right off the bat, I swung the club and hit the ball very well on my first shot of the year. It was a 2-hybrid off the tee that reached the white one-hundred-yard marker on the right side of the fairway. I did not look like a golfer that had been away from the game for six months. My second shot was to stay under an overhanging tree branch with a 5-iron. I actually got on the green from there and two-putted for par to begin the 2010 campaign. But the effects of the long layoff started to show and I took a triple bogey 7 on the second hole. I did recover on the third hole by making an eight-foot putt for a par and after back-to-back bogies on #4 and #5, I made par on #6 and #7, the latter of which I used a driver to get over the small pond. My last two holes were double bogies and I scored a 44 in my first round of 2010.

Nearly two weeks later, Dad and I went back to Tyngsboro for the start of the 2010 Lowell General Hospital Golf League season and my first title defense. After a bogey to begin the day, I went back to the hole I scored a 7 on and made birdie from seven feet. I made a par on the next hole, the long par-3 third. The next three holes were my worst of the day. But on the last three holes, I made par on each of them to finish the season opener with a score of 41.

National Games Training Camp

As APRIL WAS TURNING INTO May, I spent the weekend at DoubleTree Hotel in Westborough without my parents. I was one of many that were staying there on account of this Team SOMA (Special Olympics Massachusetts) training camp in preparation for the 2010 Special Olympics USA National Games. On day 1, the whole team went to the new Yawkey Sports Training Center for a little get together and a preview of what to expect at the National Games. My parents were there to take me to the hotel and we there for the preview at the Yawkey Center. Later on into the night, they left because parents were not allowed to be with the athletes during training camp. The whole team was at the basketball court for a few icebreaker activities. The whole team had to remember the four Ps to remind them of why they are here: PRIDE, PREPAREDNESS, PASSION, and PURPOSE.

After a slide show of the National Games, everyone on the basketball floor put away all the chairs and moved the small sets of bleachers to the side wall. We all played this game where each of the athletes asked questions to each other and if they said yes to those questions, the person who asked wrote their names down next to their question. After that we learned a new secret team handshake. The handshake starts when two people exchange hand slaps three times, followed by a fist bang, and concludes with both of them saying, "woo!" as both of the hand shakers sway back and wave their hands toward the side of their face. We all had to memorize it and practice it until we got it right.

Next, groups of athletes were separated in order of the sports that they were going to compete in to participate in this game called "suicide." The object of this game is to shoot a basketball into the hoop.

If a player misses the shot, that player must run down the basketball court and back with his team. If the shot goes in, then that player and his or teammates do not have to run. Members of the bowling team, the track and field team, the swimming team, the basketball team, the bocce team, the soccer team, the tennis team, and of course my team the golf team took part in the game. I shot for the golfing team and made the basket to "save my team's skins." After the Friday activities, I went to the hotel room to call it a night with my roommate Scott Merrill. Scott Merrill came to Port St. Lucie, Florida, for the 2008 Special Olympics Golf National Invitational.

The next day, I got up at 6:00 a.m. and started jogging at 6:30 with the whole team around the hotel parking lot. I took two loops around the hotel as the rest of them were either walking or jogging once around. I was obviously exhausted from all that running because I don't usually run in the morning. After the team run/walk, we all had our breakfast. After that I went into my golf clothes and joined my golf team for some practice that day.

My golf coach Scott Ayres took all of us to East Coast Golf Academy down Route 9 in Northborough. Two weeks earlier I made a visit there with my golf team and hit some golf balls off the artificial mats. This time around, my team hit balls off the grass on the other side of the driving range. I hit a lot of golf balls that day. Then I start to experiment with a new grip that I picked up during practice. I had just started golf a couple of weeks before training camp, but I thought my swing needed fixing because I was not all that satisfied by my playing. The golf professional had me switch my grip from an interlock to the more conventional golf grip with two hands forming two V shapes pointing directly to the club face. I did not hit my first ball that good at all, but as I swung with the new grip more, I started to get the hang of it. I first used my new grip on with the 7-iron. Using this new grip was somewhat like learning German but the more I learned it, the better I got.

After practice, my team went to the Yawkey Center for a little lunch. After that, we played nine holes of golf at Westborough Country Club. I was told that this course was hilly yet beautiful because coach Ayres was from the area. I tried out my new grip and hit my tee shot with it to the left. I duffed my second shot in an attempt to try and get back into play and would later finish the par-5 first hole with an 8. For the next few holes, I got better. On the third hole, a par-5, after a bad slice to the left, my 5-iron got me down the fairway and on my third shot I got on the green where I would two-putt for par. On the fourth hole, a par-4 dogleg left, I hit a great drive down the right side of the fairway only to finish with a two-putt bogey. Two holes later, on the par-4 #6, my tee shot went a little bit left, but I was able to get close to the green on my second shot, putt from the fringe and save par. After that, I would make a 5 on each of the last three holes. My final score for nine holes was 46, but given the fact that I was using my new grip and playing on a course that I never played on, I feel I did all right, and I had plenty of time to work on my swing with the new grip. After golf, we all went to this nearby Dairy Queen at Westborough Center. While I was enjoying my Reese's Peanut Butter Cup Blizzard, I was listening to a Boston Bruins playoff game against the Flyers on my MP3 device when Marc Savard scored the game-winning goal for Boston. I hugged the nearest person I could find from within my group as soon as the goal was scored. What a weird place to celebrate a Bruins playoff win. After taking game one, 5–4, the Bruins went on to win the next two games until their historic implosion at the hands of the Flyers a couple of weeks after the SOMA training camp.

After a brief stay at the hotel, I went to the Yawkey Center again for dinner and some team building exercises. Some group called TeamWorks was there to help supervise the team building activities. One of the exercises involved the whole team holding hands and walking around the basketball court to create this vortex. I also learned a few new high fives, including the "fishing buddies," where we picked a buddy and patted each other's forehands at the same time. I did the fishing-buddies thing with Mike Ciociolo, a golfer with Down's syndrome. Then several groups of eight had to construct a bridge made out of simply newspaper and tape. Our bridge did not pass inspection because it would not hold a shoe box. Later on at the Yawkey Center, there was a dance but I elected to go back to the hotel to watch the Celtics in the playoffs and get to bed for tomorrow.

May 2, Sunday, was the third and final day of the SOMA training camp. The morning was the same as the day before, up at six, run twice around the hotel, and breakfast. After that I went inside my room to read *The Glass Menagerie* for a while as part of my homework for English. Then I brushed my teeth, packed up my things and checked out of the hotel. Next, the whole team went back over to the Yawkey

Center. For about an hour, we all did a yoga session. It had been a while since I did yoga poses. The following poses I had done were the two warrior poses, the plank, the downward facing dog, the cobra, the sphinx, the spinal twist, and more.

After the yoga session, there was a talent show. Each team performed their own talents. As for me, I went and did something that I found time to practice on in my spare time. Like Tiger Woods in one of his Nike commercials, I bounced my ball with my sand wedge trying to keep the ball from hitting the ground. I did not attempt to swing at the ball in front of a crowd inside the big room. I bounced the ball exactly 145 times without hitting the ground. Everybody there was impressed with my talent. After that, it was time to go home. Just as I called my dad, he pulled into the parking lot. I told Mom and Dad all about my experience at training camp, about the handshakes, and this new golf grip. Going to the training camp was a start of something big for not just the golf team but the other teams in the upcoming National Games.

Hall of Famer and Golf in America

BEFORE I GET TO THAT one-week period in mid-May of 2010, let's go back to January of that same year. The year 2010 represented my eighth year of my involvement with Special Olympics. I have competed in basketball, golf, track and field, and have just completed my first year in alpine skiing. I have won numerous medals in each of the four sports that I have participated in. Then in the fall of 2007, I joined the Global Messenger Division of the Special Olympics and have made speeches to spread awareness and help raise funds for Special Olympics. Some of my speeches have made their way to YouTube and grabbed the attention of the Golf Channel. I was going to be filmed for a segment on their show *Golf in America* on the week of May 11–18.

Before I was going to be filmed, something very special happened to me earlier in 2010. Back in late January, I received a letter in the mail and read that I had been nominated for induction into the 2010 Special Olympics Massachusetts Hall of Fame class, athlete category. I was only twenty-three years old, and I did not think that I would receive such a nomination this soon. I was really surprised to have this happen to me. It was certainly an honor to be a nominee for the SOMA Hall of Fame this young in my life.

On Tuesday, March 16, when I was working out on the first floor at Gold's Gym in Chelmsford with my dad, I noticed something was not usual about this workout. As I was about to go upstairs, I found a group of people standing in the lobby. I thought to myself, *What's all this?* My mom was there. Andrew Dozibrin and his mom, Denise Mercier, were there. A couple of photographers, Terry Keilty and Martha Dove from Special Olympics, were there. Rick Dupuis, Micky Ward, and Keith

Henshaw from the gym were there. There were four balloons there as if a birthday party was thrown for me. Then Terry came to tell me that I have just been *inducted* into the Special Olympics Massachusetts Hall of Fame!

I said to myself' "Son of a gun!" as I was given the balloons and a congratulatory card. Before I knew it, I was getting flashed by photographer's cameras. I was posing for pictures with my family and the guys from the gym while my body was still sore from all that lifting. One week later, I would have my picture on the front page of the *Lowell Sun*'s sports section. Rick Reault also came to the gym to congratulate me. It was the most surprising day of my life. It was better than any birthday I've ever had in the past. Being a Hall of Famer is truly an honor. It means a lot to me, to my family, to the town of Tyngsboro, and to Special Olympics. I knew that all my work with Special Olympics was going to lead me to the Hall of Fame, but to be inducted at a very young age still came as a surprise. With all the medals I have won, with all the speeches I have made, I truly deserve it. I appreciate my induction and I will have a permanent place in Special Olympics Massachusetts history.

Ten years ago, I would never have dreamed of something like that to happen to me. Nobody within my family or associated with me would have expected all this to be possible. My twenty-three years leading up to my induction was no easy trip. I compare this trip to climbing to the peak of Mount Everest. Just think I went from not being able to tie my own shoe laces to hitting golf balls at least 250 yards down the fairway. I went from being so confused during a reading comprehension class at CTDS to making speeches using my own words in front of large crowds. I went from being wrapped up and held by my teachers to earning medals in four different Special Olympic sports. I went from being resistant to change to being a changed man myself. The Special Olympics Massachusetts Hall of Fame was only the latest in a series of steps in the right direction.

On Tuesday, May 11, I was all dressed up for a once in a lifetime occasion. My parents rented this small bus-sized party limousine to accommodate all of our guests. Mom and Dad, my brother Clint and his girlfriend, Memere, my two aunts and two uncles, my cousin Chantelle, Dick and Meg Brown, Rick and Sue Reault, and Gary and Michelle Browning all came. The 2010 Let Me Be Brave Hall of Fame Gala, as it was called, took place at Agganis Arena in Boston University. The arena was built in 2005 and is home to the Boston University Hockey Team.

When I went inside this facility, I was amazed by its storied history and impressed by all the pictures and memories and accomplishments made by the team. A lot of the greats played for BU, four members of the 1980 Miracle on Ice Team (Mike Eruzione, Jim Craig, Jack O'Callahan, and Dave Silk), Shawn McEachern, Mike Grier, and Chris Drury among others. I got to walk into the ice level with Nick Savarese through the same tunnel that the BU Terriers Hockey Team goes through. There was a big black stage in the middle of the floor with tables on each side. I ran up the stairs in my dress shoes to meet up with my entourage in this big club room to have some appetizers and drinks, and had pictures taken before the big ceremony. I had to stay in the room along with the other inductees so that we could all be introduced. Unbeknownst to me, one other member of the Cotting School class of 2005 was at the arena performing his musical instrument with his American Indian music group. It was Etienne! I didn't get to see him perform or see him that evening, but it was somewhat of a reunion.

I was among two other athletes (Michael Findlay and Melissa Reilly), three coaches (John Dempsey of North Attleboro, Lawrence's Phil Glendye, and Alec Levine of Hopkinton), three sponsors (Blue Cross Blue Shield of Massachusetts, Enterprise Rent-A-Car, and Raytheon Integrated Defense Systems), three Special Olympic families (the Davidsons, the Hellers, and the O'Keefes), the Bio-Ball Committee, Moynagh's Tavern, Lt. Rich Tavares (the Cape Cod police officer who ran around the track holding the flame of hope with Michael Jaxtimer-Barry in the 2008 gala at Harvard), and three volunteers (William Dockham, Lee Lamkin, and Dan Smith) being inducted that evening. I went out of the club room to get in line so that I can be introduced to the crowd. When my turn came, the announcer mispronounced my name as Taylor Lagasse. I showed no expression and just walked down the steps and headed to my table to meet my gang. If I did show expression the whole audience was going to think that I was insulted by the screwup.

The national anthem was sung by Candy O'Terry from Country 102.5 FM. After that, SOMA president and CEO Robert Johnson made a special tribute to Dr. Steven P. Perlman, professor of pediatric dentistry at the Goldman School of Dental Medicine at Boston University and founder of Special Smiles. Then dean Jeffrey Hutter came to speak more about Dr. Perlman. After that, Andrew Bearse, the Special Olympian and global messenger, came to speak about his experience with the organization. Andrew was from Vermont and competed in gymnastics for Special Olympics and the Junior Olympics. There was a video of him performing on the handle bars in one of his competitions. He was there for the global messenger training at the Yawkey Center earlier in January, and he was so enthusiastic when he spoke in front of the other global messengers. The last thing he said at the gala was "I am a champion!" He didn't get the same applauses as my speech at the last gala, but he sure did very well. After Andrew was done, Jim Braude and Margery Eagan of the talk radio station 96.9 FM and New England Cable News spoke about the campaign to eradicate the R-word from every dictionary around the world.

After dinner, there was a live auction conducted by Boston College alum Dan Flynn. In the middle of the auction, I went to the stage along with the other Hall of Fame inductees. The gala cochairs were members of Century Bank—the bank's founder Marshall Sloane and his children Barry Sloane and Linda Sloane Kay. I was to be given my formal induction and this large gold medal by Linda Sloane Kay and Robert Johnson. Linda described me as "a champion among champions," and after that, I accepted my induction and received the largest gold medal I would ever have. I did not give a speech. No other inductees were supposed to speak after being officially inducted. As soon as the inductions were concluded, I came back to my group and shook every hand I could find. It was like my graduation from Cotting School all over again only better than that.

I was only twenty-three years old, not nearly in the prime of my life, and already I have a permanent place in Special Olympics Massachusetts history. According to the program, I was described as "a great athlete and person, and moreover an outstanding advocate for SOMA." Also, I "remain humble and polite while also possessing confidence and pride in my achievements." Most importantly, I "exemplify superior sportsmanship, respect for rules of play, and a dedicated work ethic." This was a major step toward my manhood, but this event and this honor made me feel more than a man. I did what I could to stay as humble as possible, but this is by far the single greatest honor a Special Olympics athlete or associate could ever have. It's the single greatest honor I've ever had and could ever have. Not many things can be greater than this and I am proud to be in the Hall of Fame.

On May 15, a mere several hours after being stunned over the Bruins losing to the Flyers in historically humungous fashion—losing a 3–0 lead in both the series and the seventh game—I had to make a trip over to Stow Acres Country Club where my story for the Golf Channel's *Golf in America* was taking place. I was a little emotional from the night before but I had very little time to grieve. Jim Axelrod was going to do the interview with me and we were actually going to golf just one hole together. The production was going to be led by Paul Perrymore who happens to reside in the Philadelphia area, after what my Bruins had gone through. After me and my family introduced ourselves to Jim, Paul, and the rest of the crew, I went with Jim to the driving range to warm up, hit some balls, and actually give him some golf pointers. I showed him how I prepare for my shots and how I swing the club. The crew was actually filming me hitting some balls and so I had some butterflies in my gut with a camera hovering around me. All in all, I was able to swing my swing, make some contact and hit some balls long. More importantly, I handled being on camera very well.

Then Jim, the filming crew and I went to the first hole of the North Course, the exact same hole where I was filmed last year at the state tournament. Jim teed off first, and then it was my turn. This time with the camera parallel to my stance, I made better contact with the ball than last time, although my ball went a little right of the fairway. I used a 5-iron from the rough to get down the fairway and then got on the green on my next shot. In between shots, I gave Mr. Axelrod the "less is more" tip that Fred Wilkie gave me by telling him not to overswing the club. Jim followed up his nice tee shot with a fat second shot. I told Jim that there was nothing wrong with his swing. He just didn't make enough contact with the ball. He got on the green in only four shots. Both of us made bogey our only hole of the day.

After a brief time out on the course, we went into the function room inside the clubhouse for our conversation. I answered many of his questions that were not just limited to golf but life. I told Jim why I like the game by saying that it's a quiet and peaceful game and that you get to enjoy the outdoors for a change. I also said that public speaking is harder than playing golf because there are more people witnessing me speak than they are watching me golf. I explained whatever I could about my ever-confusing journey to where I am today and pointed out two people that have altered my life, Jaret Foley and John Navaroli. I asked the question "What do you say, Mr. La-ga-say?" to Mr. Axelrod because Mr. Navaroli taught me so much about character, and I try to show it as much as I can.

After I was done being interviewed, Mom and Dad were supposed to have their turns answering questions and explaining their sides of the story about me. Their interview was meant to take place in the porch of the clubhouse with me out of sight. Unfortunately the crew could not get everything set up the way they wanted. So they went to the Yawkey Center to do the interview there. While they were being interviewed, I spent nearly a whole hour in Nick's office using his computer and checking out the upcoming FIFA World Cup that was taking place in South Africa.

The next day the crew came to *my house* but Jim Axelrod was not there this time. I put on my golf attire to look presentable to the crew. There were stands and lights in my room! I was filmed reading my journal entries from when I won my first SOMA state title in golf, from when I did the half marathon and the duathlon. I got to show off my trophies from the KIDS group and Cotting School, my silver cup from the 2009 Golf-a-thon, my LGH Golf League champion glass, and my new SOMA Hall of Fame gold medal. I put on all my medals that I won from the SOMA state golf tourney one at a time starting with my first one in 2006. I had my journals and speeches laid out on the coffee table inside the living room so that they could be filmed while I went to the backyard to chip. Then I got to bounce my ball off my sand wedge and hit the ball in midair with it in front of the camera. It was the first time I was ever filmed doing one of my own golf tricks. Those two days were a lot of fun, I had a great time being interviewed and filmed.

My segment was aired on the season premiere of *Golf in America* on June 21. It all began when I asked the question "What do you say, Mr. La-ga-say?" They showed me giving tips to Jimmy Axelrod, preparing my shots, and swinging the club. My tee shot looked very good on camera, but I noticed I was overswinging at the driving range. They didn't show my parents in my segment, but they actually filmed CTDS's Bruce Hauptman saying that I was a "poster boy for autism" and that I would use "sign language to myself." They even showed a part of my speech from the 2008 gala at Harvard and my induction into the SOMA Hall of Fame. They showed me reading my journals, bouncing the golf ball with the sand wedge, and each of my four state gold medals in golf. My national television debut was living proof that people with autism and other special needs are just as similar as normal people.

After I got inducted into the SOMA Hall of Fame and got filmed for a show on the Golf Channel, I still continued to go where no Lagasse had ever gone before. Late in the spring semester, I had just received an invitation to join an elite honor society for students attending junior college and community college that have had advanced grade point average levels. This society was called Phi Theta Kappa, the initials of three Greek words—*phronimon, thumos, katharotes*, which mean "wisdom," "aspiration," and "purity." I was a little skeptical about joining such a group as this. But Faithe MacElliot and Aimee Rusman from the TRIO office convinced me to join and I did anyway. On May 25, 2010, I officially became a member of Phi Theta Kappa in Honors Night at the Bedford Campus of Middlesex Community College. This was right at about the time when I found out that I had *A*s in both U.S. History after 1865 and English Composition II. I was one out of 145 that had joined this society that evening. I waited in a long line to receive my certificate and have my white candle lit. After four long years of being a part-time college student and a strong commitment to my schoolwork, I was finally recognized for all my hard work in the classroom.

The Road to the National Games

IT WAS A CONTROVERSIAL MOVE for me to switch grips early in the golf season, especially with the National Games two months away. My dad said that my inconsistent and mediocre play was the result of the winter-long layoff between golf rounds, not my grip, but he let me use the new grip since it was up to me. And so I played the whole year with the new grip, which was the more conventional grip, where the gaps between my index fingers and thumbs formed a shape of a V pointing directly at the head of the club. I later rotated my left hand counterclockwise to more of a baseball grip because I felt that I would have more control of the club that way and I grew more accustomed to it while swinging the club.

We have encouraged Tyler to make his own choices about almost anything . . . including his golf grip. So many people believe that we pushed him to play golf. That statement couldn't be farther from the truth! Both Ron and I know very little about the game of golf. Simply put, we just see golf as an opportunity for Tyler to meet challenges head-on. In other words, we see golf as a tool for communication for Tyler. On many occasions, we reference golf whenever Tyler is faced with new challenges. It seems to give him a point of reference to draw on.

My first round with the new grip was on May 3 and I looked very good for most of the day at Tyngsboro Country Club in LGH Golf League action. My dad beat me by five strokes that day. It was embarrassing to say the least. I was still trying to adjust to my new grip but I was not making excuses. Golf is a crazy game sometimes. Whether you are an experienced golfer or just starting out, you are going to have holes once in a while like the one I had on #7 that day. When you do, you need to keep you composure and not let those bad shots get to you like that. You can't take your frustrations out on your clubs or the course, or else you are going to be sorry. Hopefully you can learn something out of that experience just as I did.

Just hours after the *Golf in America* crew wrapped up filming at my house on May 16, I had my first round of golf with the members of Team SOMA. I joined my coach Scott Ayres and the others at Mount Pleasant Country Club in Boylston (sorry, not the Mount Pleasant in Lowell). It was a nice eighteen-hole course, but we played nine holes since it was late in the day. I started out very promising by making par on the first hole, but I didn't make par or better the rest of the way. I was marred with inconsistency from the second hole on. I was hitting some good shots but there were times where I didn't execute those shots that well. It was also a matter of getting used to playing on another course that I never played before. In the end I would finish the round with a score of 48, a total of twelve strokes over par.

The next day, I went back to Tyngsboro looking to bounce back from the debacle the week before. My first five holes were still mediocre at best. A bogey on the last hole would give me a score of 42, an improvement of seven strokes from last week at Tyngsboro. One week after that, I would shoot a 41 at Tyngsboro.

On Memorial Day, May 31, there was no golf league so Dad and I went to Tyngsboro Country Club in the morning. I would finish the round by making my sixth bogey of the Memorial Day round. In spite of my six bogies, my final score was 39. I may have broken 40 in nine holes for the first time in 2010, but I still had a ways to go because I didn't feel that I have "turned the corner" just yet. There was still some room to improve with the nationals now weeks away.

As May was turning into June, I began to practice more and more on my game. Mom or Dad would take me to the driving range to hit balls off the grass in nearby Hudson, New Hampshire, at least once a week until the nationals in mid-July. The more I practiced, the better I seemed to get. I did a lot of golfing in the month of June. I had kept my own scores from thirteen of my rounds until the month of July. That is the most golf I've played in the first half of any golf season in each of the years that I've kept track of my scores for Special Olympics.

On June 4, Dad and I got invited to play golf at a very luxurious and very exclusive place. It was called the Golf Club at Turner Hill in the town of Ipswich, Massachusetts. Former Boston Bruin goaltender

Reggie Lemelin, and Baseball Hall of Fame closer Dennis Eckersley called the area home. Paul and Emma Karrlsson-Willis were members there. As a matter of fact, their house is located next to the eleventh hole of the golf course. They invited us to play eighteen holes with them that afternoon. Turner Hill is unlike any golf course I've ever played before. It's probably more difficult than Vesper Country Club in Tyngsboro. This place also has a driving range, a practice green, and a chipping area so I could warm up before I embark on an eighteen-hole journey.

For the first three holes, I had scores of 6–6–7. The first and third holes were par-4s, the second hole was a par-5 and the most difficult stroke hole on the course. I was still trying to adjust to another new course, which happened to be the most challenging of all the courses I've ever played before. I had some trouble getting myself into a rhythm but I was not making excuses. Golf is a game that tests your ability to deal with adversity. Sooner or later you'll be able to right the ship and who knows, you might be able to do better than you think. My total score for the front nine was a 47. A bogey on the par-3 eighteenth hole assured me a score of 49 on the back nine and 96 overall—I actually had the lowest score among my foursome. I lost five balls. Four of them came off the tee at holes 2, 7, 11, and 15. Considering this was the toughest course I've ever played on, at least I came away inspired. After golf, Dad and I had some dinner on the deck near the seventeenth and eighteenth holes. Dad and I had a great time spending the afternoon with the couple from England.

To me, the best part of golf for Tyler is the interaction between him and whoever he is playing with is what is most important. He is forced to converse with people and practice his communication skills. The benefit is the fact that on most occasions he gets to have a conversation with people that enjoy talking about the same subject . . . GOLF!

I participated in three scramble golf tournaments from the beginning of June to the National Games. On June 12, I played at Tyngsboro Country Club as part of a foursome of my dad, Rick Reault, and Gary Browning in a scramble tournament to benefit the Tyngsboro Legion Baseball Team. We played eighteen holes in murky weather that day—the first nine from the white tees and the last nine from the blue tees—and shot a team score of 66, four strokes under par. We made five birdies and a bogey as a team. I was responsible for four of my team's five birdies that day.

On the day after the scramble tournament at Tyngsboro, I ran in the Law Enforcement Torch Relay that started at the Middleton Police Department and ended at the State Police Barracks in Danvers. After finishing the 5K at a time of 23:39, I spoke about my induction to the SOMA Hall of Fame and going to the National Games in Nebraska. Then sometime in the middle of June, I ended up coming down with allergies. In spite of that, I kept on practicing my golf, spoke at Boston University in front of Team SOMA and the corporate sponsors supporting the team during our trip to Nebraska in July, and ran in the Big Kahuna 5K where I finished in twenty-fourth overall out of 106 runners and second in my age-group.

On June 27, I played the first nine of forty-five holes of golf over three straight days. Dad and I went to Tewksbury Country Club with the KIDS group that day and I shot a 42 on a par-33 course from the red tees, the shortest tees on the course. The next day, Dad and I went to Indian Ridge in Andover for the Micky Ward Charities scramble golf tournament. That day I played a role in setting up my foursomes first three birdies. Our final score was a respectable 66 and our best holes were the three birdies from holes 4–7.

On the day after the Micky Ward tournament, I went to the Overlook at the Nashua suburb of Hollis, New Hampshire. I went with Rick Reault to this tournament called the Tyngsboro Police Memorial. The golfing started between eight thirty and nine in the morning and it was already starting to get hot. I was responsible for the pars on the first and second holes. On #3, I wasn't any help at all, but we still made a par. Our best hole was the fourth hole as I smashed a brilliantly played driver and followed it up with a solid approach shot from 130 yards out with an 8-iron. After my attempt, Rick went out and nailed a thirty- to forty-foot putt for our only birdie of the day. A bogey on #5 put us back to two over par on the tournament. The last two holes were pars our final team score was a 73, two strokes over par. The score could've been higher if not for me.

Tyler receives so many accolades for his golf game, so I love it when he has to acknowledge the fact that someone else is responsible for a great shot at golf.

I played at Tyngsboro Country Club twelve times in 2010 before the National Games. Between the beginning of June and mid-July, I played there only five times. One week after shooting a 39 there on Memorial

Day, I went back there to shoot another 39, my first score under 40 in golf league play. Then for the next two weeks, I hit a pair of bumps on the road to the National Games. I was plagued with inconsistency on those two rounds with my dad. One week I had six bogies and two pars and shot a 44, and the next week I had five pars and two bogies and still shot a 43. On the day I shot the 43, I lost my cool on the fourth hole when my chip to the green went left on me and entered the water. I threw my club down on the ground in anger and that would have been the end of the round for me. But I finished the hole and made a quadruple-bogey 9.

It wasn't just my playing, it was my behavior on the course and the way I was handling adversity that mattered. I broke my promise to my mother about being a good sport when I threw my club. I have not been able to harness my anger and frustration all that effectively so far in 2010. So far it was a hard year for me as I was trying to meet my expectations after such a great year. Right now I just wasn't satisfied with my playing, and I knew I could do better because I've done better in the past. But my parents stressed sportsmanship over results, and so far I was failing to be a good sport. There were two things that I needed to work on before the National Games, my golfing and my sportsmanship.

On more than one occasion, we have stopped whatever we are doing, and packed up and called it a day! In other words, we have to show Tyler that we mean business and will simply go home because he is not behaving appropriately. We don't make a big scene, but he knows we mean business. In the end, it is what is best for Tyler. We have told him that as he grows into adulthood, his behavior or reaction will either work for or against him. I wish that he could self-monitor, but sometimes his emotions get the best of him.

On the first of July, I got to golf with Team SOMA one more time before the nationals. Dad and I went to Juniper Hill Golf Course in Northborough for nine holes. It was a thirty-six-hole course just like Green Meadow and Stow Acres. It was a wide open course for the most *part*. I spent all nine holes carrying my golf bag because I didn't bring my pull cart with me.

Again, we try to hold Tyler accountable for his actions. He was not pleased about this particular situation. However, he didn't think to rent a pull cart. Therefore, he needed to learn about responsibility and had to carry his clubs.

I only made one par that day, the par-5 third hole and I had to sink a putt from seven feet to do so. I made bogey on the other eight holes to shoot a not-too-shabby 43 in my first appearance at Juniper Hill, the fifth new course I've played this year.

I am sure that Tyler wanted to use the fact that he forgot his cart for his score that day. I do realize the need for Tyler to "keep things as predictable as possible." However, as I have mentioned before, I do not come "wallet size." Therefore, he needs to have new experiences—both positive and negative— to draw upon in order to move forward in his life.

There was no golf league taking place on July 5, but Dad and I went to Tyngsboro Country Club anyway. There were two heat waves going on, one coming from the air and the other coming from me. In July, when the weather gets hot, so does my game. After my first tee shot with a 4-hybrid went way left and on the other side of the trees, I managed to get on the green in two but I had this very long putt for birdie from fifty to sixty feet. I had not made this one spectacular shot all year and I didn't think I could make one out of this putt. My putt had good speed but the ball stayed to the right until it took a left turn with a couple of feet to go and was headed for the hole. The one big shot finally came on the first hole and that birdie served as a sign of things to come.

After a bogey on #2, I reached the green with the 3-wood on the long par-3, third and later made a crucial six-footer to save par. On #4 I found the sand from off the tee but I got out and later two-putted for bogey. I almost double bogied the fifth hole but still made a five-footer to put me at 2 over par. On #6, I took a bit of a gamble with a 3-wood off the tee and it paid off. The ball sat in the middle of the fairway with the green in sight. I used a 7-iron from over 150 yards, hit it good and made the fringe, twenty-five to thirty feet from the hole. I had a chance for my first ever eagle on the sixth hole and the second eagle on this course. I played my putt right to left and hit it firm, and like the first hole early in the day, I thought that I was going to miss right. Then the ball took this heavenly left turn and found the hole with the pin inside it. The ball went in when I nudged the pin. That eagle brought me back to even par. But a double bogey on #7 brought me back to two over par. My par on #8 and bogey on #9 allowed me to finish with a score of 38.

Still the birdie on #1 and the eagle on #6 were big confidence boosters for me heading into Nebraska.

Next week, I returned to play one more round at Tyngsboro before the National Games. After my slicing problems led to a triple bogey 7 to start the day, I made a 180 on the second hole by making birdie from the fringe twenty to twenty-five feet away, where the ball got lodged between the edge of the hole and the flagstick, just like on #6 the week before. After a bogey on the third hole where I had to make a putt from six to eight feet, I hit two great shots with the 4-hybrid and 3-wood to begin the fourth hole only to hit my third shot in the water hazard in my attempt to play it safe. After I finished the hole with a double bogey 7, Dad was really on me and said to me, "What were you thinking?" and "If you have a comfortable lead, play it safe. If you're behind in a close match, go for it."

The majority of time, Ron does not give Tyler any advice on his golf game. But sometimes I don't think that Tyler realizes every game is not a championship game. In fact, Tyler lives most of his life as if tomorrow will never come! Each day it seems as though everything—from the routine he uses to brush his teeth to the routine he uses to go to bed each night—cannot be changed. If for any reason it is changed, it seems as if it is the end of the world for Tyler.

I made par on the last two holes to finish the round with a score of 40. The negatives of that day were the first and fourth holes that ultimately prevented me from breaking 40. I actually set a record low for putts in a nine-hole round of golf that day with 12. But Dad and I had one more round of golf in us before it came.

On July 15, the day before I left my home to join my team in Boston, Dad and I went to Green Meadow up in Hudson to play on the more difficult Jungle Course. I started off slow, but on my third shot from just near the green, I made a great chip that put my ball at least a foot or two from the hole leading to a par. After bogies on the second and third holes, I used a 7-iron from 164 yards out on the elevated par-3 fourth hole and played the elevation to my advantage. I made the green from the tee box and two-putted for par. On #5, I used my driver and 8-iron to get to the green. My putt for birdie came up very short by eight feet, but I managed to make par. On the sixth hole, I barely got on in two shots with my driver and 7-iron. Since my birdie putt was long and uphill, I hit it firm because I felt the green was wet and slow.

My ball went past the hole, resulting in my second three-putt bogey. I would make bogies on the par-4 seventh and the par-3 eighth. Then on #9, the down and up par-5, I got on the green using driver, 3-wood, and gap wedge. I almost made a twenty-footer for birdie, and I almost missed a four-footer for par. Luckily the ball did a near 360 around the hole and went in to give me a score of 41 on the front nine.

After a par on #10 where I almost made birdie from at least thirty feet when I played a great putt only to see the ball go by the hole. I was twenty to twenty-five feet of the hole on the par-3 eleventh. My third straight chance at birdie was the closest I've ever come to making it. The ball started left then took a right turn before it rimmed out of the hole. So for the third straight hole, I had to settle for a par. After a bogey on the twelfth hole, the ugly ninety-degree dogleg left hole, Dad and I came upon the 538-yard, par-5 thirteenth hole, the longest and most difficult hole on the course. My drive drifted left on me but I had a good look at the green even though I was out of reach. My second shot, using a 3-wood, was "unbelievable" according to one of a pair of golfers that joined us on the third hole. I was able to get on in three shots and two-putt for my fourth par in the last five holes, seventh overall. The par-4 fourteenth was my worst hole as I made a double-bogey 6, but it turned out to be the only serious blemish of the day. The fifteenth hole was almost a mirror image of the fourteenth only this time I made a bogey. On the downhill par-3 sixteenth hole, I nailed a par putt from four to five feet after a good chip on. I then hit a nice drive off the tee at #17, barely made it in two but landed on the fringe. Like on the fifteenth and several other holes before, I failed to make a putt for par from under ten feet and instead made a bogey. The eighteenth was where I hit my best drive with the driver, down the right side of the fairway. My second shot was on an uphill lie and I used a 3-wood to hit my second of two great shots in a row. After that I would two-putt for par to finish with a 41 on the back nine and an 82 in eighteen holes, shattering my personal best at the Jungle Course in Green Meadow by eleven strokes. It was just the way I wanted to play, good consistent golf with the National Games just days away.

Tyler's description of his golf game is similar to the way he leads his life: full of detail and a distinct purpose for every facet of his life. He doesn't really know how to "chill out." He is the only person I know that will take written notes when watching TV shows or even commercials!

Nebraska: The 2010 Special Olympics USA National Games

ON THE FRIDAY AFTERNOON OF July 16, 2010, Mom and Dad drove me to Boston University to meet the whole delegation that was headed for Nebraska and the 2010 Special Olympics USA National Games. Fifty-one athletes along with five unified partners were going to compete in nine different sports in the largest sporting event in the history of the Cornhusker state. Seventeen staff members—fourteen coaches, a medic, the head of the delegation, and the assistant head of the delegation—were there to accompany the athletes to Nebraska. I would spend that night with my golf team at one of the dormitories off Babcock Street inside the campus of BU. Coach Scott Ayres, Jeffrey Bramley and his unified partner George Kent, Mike Ciociolo and his brother and partner Jim, and Scott Merrill were a part of the golf team. I said my goodbyes to my parents as soon as they were ready to leave.

Later in the afternoon, I joined a group of the delegation that took a big yellow bus from the campus for a tour of Fenway Park, two hours before game time. The Boston Red Sox were playing the eventual American League champion Texas Rangers that evening. We all arrived in time to see the 2010 Home Run Derby winner and Red Sox legend David Ortiz perform some batting practice from behind home plate! It was like a scene from *Field of Dreams*, when Kevin Costner was standing right on the sidelines across from all the baseball greats who were practicing. Then Carl Beane, the Red Sox public address announcer, was there to speak to us for a little bit while batting practice was still going on. We all got to walk on the warning track behind home plate, something that I've never done in my two tours of Fenway. I put some warning track dirt on the brim of my yellow Special Olympics Massachusetts hat to remind me of my home state and hoped that it would bring good karma and good luck.

Then we all took a walk through a tunnel under the seats. We made our way down the left field side of the park and got to visit the seats on top of Fenway Park's famed Green Monster. It was like climbing Mount Everest in Boston because not many people get to watch a baseball game from up there since there are so few seats on top of the large green wall. It was such a good view from the front row of the Monster seats. A couple of home run balls at batting practice went into the same section of seats where I was situated in. This area of Fenway Park is the Mount Everest of the whole ballpark. If not, it is the Mount Everest of baseball because nothing is better than this.

After the tour, I went with the team back to the dormitory, where there was lots of pizza delivered by Domino's Pizza. There had to be at least two dozen boxes of it in the room.

Again, Tyler is just as enthusiastic and descriptive about the number of pizza boxes. They seem to occupy just as much space and importance for him.

Afterward, there was a guest motivational speaker named Jimmy Pedro. He competed in the sport of judo at four Summer Olympic Games from 1992 to 2004. He won the bronze medal in the 1996 games in Atlanta and another bronze at the 2004 games in Athens, Greece, which makes him the most successful American in judo. Every SOMA athlete got to hold both of his Olympic bronze medals. He is the first and probably the only great American judo master, and he is from the Bay State.

Jimmy Pedro explained to us the rules of judo. It's like wrestling, but unlike most martial arts, there is no kicking and punching. He started taking questions after he was done talking about his career. I asked him a couple of questions. The first one was "Was there any times in which you fought your best fight and still didn't win and any times when you were not at your best and still won?"

He said yes. He explained something about not feeling up to a match and somehow finding a way to win and then not being able to win while being on top of your game. He summed up his answer by saying, "It's sports."

The next one was "What was the closest you have ever got to a war on the mat?"

He said there was a match in Hungary against a Russian competitor where he got head-butted so bad that his left eye was swollen shut. Judo is a sport where a single tournament of several matches takes place in only one day, so there is little time to rest between matches. One final thing Jimmy said to us about what to expect from the National Games was to "take in this experience because it is unlike anything you've ever seen before."

After the questions, he signed autographs for the many members of Team SOMA. I got an autographed picture of him in his blue judo uniform. I told him about the Fenway Park dirt on the brim of my hat. Then I went to the dorm room right away to get some sleep.

On Saturday, July 17, I woke up at three forty-five in the morning, took a quick shower, brushed my teeth, got into the clothes that I was supposed to wear, and made sure that I had everything packed. When everybody was ready, I got on the yellow bus that took us to Boston's Logan Airport. This was my third time flying out of the city of Boston, and this was my sixth time traveling by plane. Our scheduled flight was at 6:00 a.m., and we had to get there an hour before takeoff to get through security. We made a layover at one of the largest airports in the world—O'Hare International Airport—for a couple of hours. I went with the team through a sort of underground moving ramp as we went from one terminal to another. I looked up at the ceiling and saw all those crazy-looking lights with different colors. I found myself getting so lost in those lights that I spun around in a circle. It was a ridiculously long walk to get from one terminal to the next. Once we got to the other terminal, we found a Chili's and had breakfast there. Illinois was the fourteenth state that I've visited, and Nebraska was going to be the fifteenth. We took a smaller jet to Nebraska than the one we took from Boston to Chicago. I was listening to "Nebraska" by Bruce Springsteen and looking at the vast cornfields just before we landed at Lincoln Municipal Airport.

Tyler keeps track of every state he's been in, every venue he's visited, and anything else he can collect information on. It must be exhausting to live his life!

We got off the plane, and once we got inside the terminal, we saw many signs that read, "WELCOME TO LINCOLN." The airport was right next to the golf course where I was going to compete. The whole city was going nuts over the National Games. Everywhere I went, the Special Olympics atmosphere was great. I've never seen a big city support such an event so much. The Team SOMA delegation was split up into three groups and took three different planes from Boston to Lincoln. The whole delegation would spend the whole week at the Cather Hall dormitory inside the North Campus of the University of Nebraska–Lincoln, which was a little walk from the downtown area. The university is so large that there is another campus east of the city.

Later that day, I joined some members of Team SOMA to visit Memorial Stadium, the home stadium of the Nebraska Cornhuskers Football Team. That place truly was something else. It reminded me of this scene in the movie *Rudy* when Sean Astin walked inside Notre Dame Stadium. It was the largest sports venue I've ever set foot in. I didn't walk onto the field, but I was amazed by how big the place is from the inside. Besides the visit to the football stadium, the first day was all about settling in to our new home inside the campus and trying to figure out what to expect for the rest of the week.

I began my first full day in Nebraska by waking up at approximately 5:00 a.m. Sunday morning. When it was time for me to go to breakfast at this dining room inside Cather Hall, the place was packed with two long lines of people waiting to be fed. It was still early in the morning, but there was this large crowd waiting for at least half an hour just to get breakfast. After that, I left with the golf team at a quarter past six to catch the bus that would take me to my golf course. Jeffrey Bramley and George Kent were headed to Mahoney Golf Course on the east side of Lincoln, while I joined the rest of my golf team to Highlands Golf Course west of the city.

Highlands Golf Course is one the best golf courses in the state. The golf course had this nice clubhouse with a green roof. Outside there was a driving range and a putting green there so that I could warm up before each of my golf rounds. I played a nine-hole practice round after seven in the morning. Mom and Dad came to see me play that day, and it was the first time I saw them since last Friday. My coach Scott Ayres was my caddy for the day. As soon as I was all warmed up, I went to the first hole to tee off (unofficially) for the first time in Nebraska. The first hole was a par-5, and two shots in, it started to rain. We all took shelter in a nearby hut to stay dry. After the delay, which lasted some twenty minutes, I resumed playing and finished the hole with a par. I made par on the second hole from the regular tees, not from the tees where all the Special Olympic golfers were going to be playing off of during competition.

What a difference a few years and a LOT of therapy make! I can remember when a sudden change in weather would stop Tyler in his tracks. He would just shut down and not be able to do anything but either be held by Ron or me or just go to sleep. It's great that he can use strategies that he has learned from his teachers and therapists and "stay present" and participate in life.

I birdied two of the last three holes to finish with a score of 35, one stroke under par!

What a way to start the National Games. Even though it didn't count, it was the first time that I've ever shot under par in a nine-hole round of golf. It was my first time playing in Nebraska, and to be able to have a score like this in a place I've never been to before should simply be impossible to describe. And considering what I've gone through all my life, it was all the more special. In spite of my most recent accomplishment, I still had fifty-four holes to go just to earn something even more significant.

After the practice round, Scott Ayres and I checked out the other nine holes of the Highlands Golf Course to see what they looked like. Then after that, we went inside the clubhouse for a bite to eat. Next, I checked out the pro shop. I bought a yardage book so that I could get a clear understanding of the course when I play. I also bought three Callaway golf balls with the Highland logo on them and a red Nebraska hat with a ball marker magnet thing on the brim for my friend Cody Browning.

It's important for any athlete to get a look at whatever venue they are going to compete on. For an athlete living with autism, the venue includes the dining hall, the buses, the dorms, the bathrooms, etc.

Later on that Sunday, I got dressed up in my green tie-dyed T-shirt and khaki shorts along with the rest of my team. After we had our team picture taken outside the dorm, we proceeded to march in this July heat all the way to Bob Devaney Sports Center, where the opening ceremonies were going to take place. You wouldn't believe how many people came to this place and how many states were represented in the 2010 Special Olympics USA National Games. The athletes from Alabama were wearing those Bear Bryant checkerboard fedoras during their walk to the opening ceremonies. The Missouri delegation was wearing green shirts and those straw hats with a blue ribbon, and they were chanting, "Show me! Show me! Show me! MO! MO! MO!" as they were making their march. Team Maryland was wearing those crazy stuffed-crab hats. Forty-eight states and the District of Columbia were represented in the 2010 nationals. The host state Nebraska had the largest delegation and brought more athletes to the games than any state. It was remarkably incredible or incredibly remarkable. Either way, the atmosphere at Devaney Center was as festive as any event that I've ever been a part of. I've never seen anything like it. It had all the energy to be the best Special Olympics National Games ever.

My team made the walk through the blazing hot sun to the nice air-conditioned building. Each state entered the arena alphabetically, with Nebraska being the last state to enter. As my team was waiting in line, I saw Tim Shriver. I was right next to him, and I tried to get his attention, but I did not speak to him. Then when our delegation was called, I looked up at the Jumbotron and saw myself in a crowd of green tie-dyed shirts and said, "I love you!" to my parents as they were in attendance, witnessing the most historic moment of my life. It's one of the single greatest accomplishments a person can have, being able to represent your home state in the USA National Games for Special Olympics.

After every delegation found their seats, the opening ceremony was officially under way. There were musical performances by Jars of Clay and Michael Sarver. There were guest appearances by 2003 U.S. Open Tennis Champion Andy Roddick and his wife, the supermodel and actress Brooklyn Decker. I let out a scream when Roddick came onstage because Roddick is my favorite tennis player. Also standing right beside Decker was a Special Olympian named Edward Barbanell, who starred in the 2005 comedy *The Ringer*, starring Johnny Knoxville, who plays a guy that rigs the Special Olympics by posing as a man with intellectual disabilities. Barbanell—who has Down's syndrome—is also a remarkable advocate for Special Olympics. Golfer Phil Mickelson and gymnast Nadia Comaneci made appearances on the Jumbotron. Then Charles Cooper, the president and CEO of the 2010 National Games, and Brady Lum, the president and COO of Special Olympics International, came onstage together.

At the opening ceremonies, there were videos of a few particular Special Olympic athletes. One was done on a female golfer named Grace

Anne Braxton, from the state of Virginia, who had won numerous Special Olympic titles as well as many state amateur golf titles. Another was done on a fellow Team SOMA member named Matt Millett. One month before the National Games, Millett went all the way to South Africa, the site of the 2010 FIFA World Cup soccer tournament. Millett was the only United States representative to take part in the Unity Cup along with several other athletes with intellectual disabilities all over the world as well as many other soccer legends and celebrities. There was an image of him playing in South Africa that was seen by the sold-out crowd at the Devaney Center. Never before has an event dedicated to people with intellectual disabilities been taken this seriously. The whole crowd was into it, and it could not get any better than this.

Then the grand finale of the ceremonies occurred. A Special Olympics runner came inside with the official Special Olympics torch, called the Flame of Hope. Once the big torch was lit, the 2010 Special Olympics USA National Games was declared officially open. Then Tim Shriver came onstage near the end of the opening ceremony to encourage us to do our best for this week. "Be a Fan" was the slogan as well as the official song of the games. I had a blast witnessing firsthand an event that is meant to make you embrace the power of the human spirit. But I was going to be in for a magical ride that would take me beyond what I could possibly dream of.

Up until this point, Ron and I had never been away from Tyler for such a long period of time. We knew that Tyler was safe in every way. However, being physically safe and emotionally safe are two different things altogether. Tyler was really motivated to fully participate in the National Games. He had prepared by going on a "get to know you" weekend orientation earlier this spring. He had practiced with his coach and his team on several occasions. Now it was time to see if all this preparation would pay off. To be perfectly honest, I didn't really care about how he would do in the competition. I was more concerned about his ability to process his environment. It was time for him to show us just how far he has matured.

Round 1: On Monday, July 19, day 3 of my weeklong visit to Lincoln, Nebraska, I began my first of three rounds of National Games golf at Highlands Golf Course. This tournament is similar to the 2008 NIT in Florida, where fifty-four holes of golf are played over the course of three straight days. Just before my round began in the morning, I found this

$5 bill in the parking lot. I wanted to find the person who lost it and give the $5 bill to him or her, but I didn't know who lost it. So I kept it and have not spent it since.

It warms my heart to see that Tyler has empathy for other people. There are many people who describe people living with autism as having no empathy or real emotions. This is an example of how false that impression is.

In round 1, I was paired up with a female Level 5 golfer from Kentucky named Christy Nicole Farwell. Each golfer had their own assigned volunteer caddy. Those caddies were actually employees of a company named KPMG. My caddy was Doug, a resident of San Jose, California, who works for the KPMG headquarters in the Bay Area of San Francisco. My coach, Scott Ayres, did not see me play, but Mom and Dad did. The course layout was different for the games. Instead of naming the holes the same way as the course from 1 to 18, the 8th and 9th holes became the 17th and 18th holes, holes 10 through 15 were 11 through 16, and holes 16 to 18 were 8 to 10. The reason the holes were rearranged for the tournament was possibly because the course officials wanted the competitors to transition from hole to hole more efficiently.

Again, it shows so much psychological maturity on Tyler's part that he can adjust to changes when clearly he likes things to stay the same all the time. I credit that accomplishment not only to the hard work that Tyler does on a regular basis but to the many teachers, mentors, coaches, and friends who have helped him throughout his life.

There was an eight-thirty shotgun start for every participant at Highlands. I began my first hole on the fifteenth hole, which is the par-3 fourteenth at the Highlands. My first shot of the 2010 Special Olympics USA National Games was not spectacular at all. It was lousy, to put it mildly. My tee shot with the 6-iron was low and left. It was one of those jitters that tightened me up and made me feel too uncomfortable or too pumped. I would finish with a bogey on the first hole and the next two holes, the par-4 sixteenth and the par-3 seventeenth. I had some trouble getting into a rhythm early on, but after that, I would find my game.

I've watched enough golf to know that good golfers do well because they put the bad shots out of their minds and move on to focusing on the next hole and how to make that hole a successful one. That is what Tyler tries to do . . . albeit not always with successful results!

My fourth hole was the eighteenth hole, which was shortened from 376 yards from the white tees of the course to 233 yards for the National

Games. It was not as hot as I expected it to be, but I had to contend with this wind that was blowing right at me. I pulled out my driver and took my chances against the wind and this uphill hole. I was just hoping to at least get my ball in front of the green, and then I let out a furious swing. The ball was right where I wanted it to be, nice and straight, but a few seconds after I hit the ball, I heard this long stanza of clapping next to the green . . .

The reason for this long clapping was because my ball was within two to three feet of the hole. I didn't notice my ball until I got halfway through the fairway. I was stunned by what I had done. I had the easiest chance at an eagle than I've ever had before in my life and possibly ever will have. The pin was placed on the front side of the green, which helped my shot a lot. Of course I had to shoot into the wind, which made the shot to the green an adventure.

As soon as I had my ten-year-old TaylorMade putter in my hand and was near my Titleist Pro V1 ball with the five black dots forming the letter V on it, I was set to complete the best hole of my life, and complete it I did, with a good two- to three-foot putt. After making the putt, I picked up my ball out of the hole and raised two fingers in the air, signaling that I had made an eagle 2. It was my second eagle of the year and second on a par-4 hole. So far, it was the highlight of my round, the tournament, and the 2010 golf season. Only a hole in one can top what I did on my fourth hole at the 2010 National Games in Nebraska.

That hole is situated right in front of the clubhouse. Therefore, there were many spectators on that hole witnessing all the athletes compete. My favorite part of watching Tyler compete or give speeches is watching the faces of the crowd. So many people set the bar so low for people living with challenges or disabilities. It is fascinating to see their expressions when our athletes outperform at each level. Our athletes genuinely support each other and demonstrate sportsmanship at the highest level. One thing for sure, our athletes do NOT *have poker faces. You know, when watching them, how they feel about their individual play. They either brush it off or challenge themselves to get better.*

On the next five holes, I alternated pars and bogies (pars on the first, third, and fifth holes and bogies on the second and fourth holes). After my slow start, where I bogied the first three holes, I went even par for the rest of the front nine and had a score of 36 heading in to the back nine. On my tenth hole, the par-5 sixth hole, I made the green in three shots. I forget how long my birdie putt was, but I made my first birdie of the tournament. That birdie put me at -2 for both the round and the tournament.

Then I hit serious adversity for the first time in the tournament. On the par-4 seventh, I hooked my 3-wood into the large sand trap on the right. I did get out and made the front of the green, but I wound up having to make four putts for my only double bogey in Nebraska. My troubles continued on #8, a long par-4 that was a par-5 for this tournament. I hit an awful hook into the tall fescue near the bunker. It took me two shots to get back into play, and by the time I was finished, I had back-to-back sixes. On the par-5 ninth, after going left off the tee followed by a long wait, my second shot was so heavy, my ball traveled fifty yards. My third shot missed the green, but two shots later, I managed to save par. Considering my troubles on the previous two holes, it was a nice recovery.

On the tenth hole, which is a slightly narrow par-4, I hit probably the straightest shot I have ever hit with the driver in 2010. With the wind really starting to howl now, I somehow was able to reach the green in two. But I ended up missing the hole in my attempt at par and had to take a bogey. After a brief lunch break, I resumed my playing. I struggled on the eleventh, an uphill par-4 with bunkers, as I didn't get on the green until my fourth shot and made a bogey 5. On the par-5 twelfth hole, I did hit a nice drive just to the left of the fairway. On my second shot, using a 3-wood from over two hundred yards out, I hit the green on the left side. From there I was able to make an easy two-putt for my second birdie of the day.

The thirteenth hole was a par-3 with water in front of the green. I used my gap wedge to get my ball on the green. Unfortunately I ended up with a three-putt bogey. On the last hole, the par-4 fourteenth, I hit a splendid drive down the middle of the fairway. Two shots later, I had this long putt for birdie. My read could not have been more perfect, but my ball just bounced out of the hole on me. That could have been a tremendous ending to a great first eighteen-hole round in Nebraska. I did make my par and scored a 79 in the first round of the National Games.

After my round, Mom and Dad were so proud of me for playing well enough to shoot a 79. Before I left the course, I ran into Grace Anne Braxton, the golfer from Virginia who had just shot an 82 earlier in the day. She said that she saw me on the Golf Channel's *Golf in America*, and she told me that my segment was "absolutely perfect." In a year that has been so crazy in the sports world, I overcame a slow start and two bumpy holes to break 80 for the third time in my life. Coach Ayres and I went back to my dorm with Mom and Dad. When I got back to my dorm room inside the campus, I was sending text messages with a cell phone that took longer for me to type the letters in. I had lots of replies from back home in Massachusetts. Jaret Foley wrote, "Keep up the good work." Then he called me on my cell phone and told me, "Keep your cool"—keep my composure, in other words.

We were very proud of Tyler's performance on the course. But we were most proud of Tyler's composure and ability to make adjustments throughout the day. I loved the fact that Tyler was meeting new people and actually interacting with them. He found common topics to generate genuine conversations with people from all over the country. He looked so poised and so relaxed. This is what we have all been working for!

Later in the day, I joined my golf team to visit Olympic Town in downtown Lincoln. This was truly something else, a city embracing the National Games, and it was off the charts. Everywhere I went, there were Special Olympians everywhere with credentials plus many Special Olympic team pins decorating their lanyards. I went inside Pershing Auditorium to check out the Sports Experience. It was incredible. There were many games being played, Ping-Pong, football, billiards, volleyball, basketball, even bowling and golf on Nintendo Wii. There were many monitors with the Wii, and it brought the many Special Olympic competitors into a sheer frenzy. After that, we went outside to listen to concert music. I visited a merchandise tent there and bought a blue "Be a Fan" T-shirt and a National Games lapel pin. After that, it was time to get go back to my dorm, wrapping up another fun-filled day. I needed to get some sleep for the second round because it was going to be another long day.

Round 2: In the middle of the night, just hours before the second round began, a huge rainstorm ripped through the city of Lincoln, soaking the golf course. But there was going to be golf on Tuesday, July 20. Doug and his colleague Farhad from KPMG were my caddy and driver for this round as they were the day before. I was paired up with Andrew Williams from Tennessee that day.

Doug and Farhad were wonderful throughout the tournament. Both of them commented on what a gentleman Tyler was. For me, it was an opportunity to educate two more individuals to remember to focus on what our kids CAN do versus what our kids cannot do.

My first hole of the day was the par-3, thirteenth hole. I used my gap wedge to get on the green and two-putted for par to begin the round. Then on the fourteenth hole, I hit a slice off the tee and later two-putted for bogey. I would alternate pars and bogies for the first seven holes. My first three pars came from par-3s. I made bogey on the hole where I made my eagle in round 1.

After a par on the par-5 first hole, I used a 7-iron on the hole that was transformed from a par-4 to a par-3. I got my ball up in the air and stuck it on the green, resulting in a two-putt par. On the third hole, I got on the green in two shots, got close to the hole in my long birdie attempt, and finished the hole with my sixth par in the first nine holes of the second round. I made three pars in a row on holes 1, 2, and 3. My score at the halfway point was 36.

After a bogey on the par-3 fourth hole, Andrew Williams and I showed the nearby spectators what we were made of. Andrew went first on the par-4 fifth hole and reached the green from the tee. He would later make an easy two-putt for a birdie. I hit a solid shot that came pretty close to the green. I could've easily made birdie on that hole, but my chip on and birdie try were both short, and I had to settle for a seemingly disappointing par. On the next hole, the par-5 sixth, I followed up two promising shots with a third shot that was not a good one at all. I finished that hole with a bogey 6.

Then on #7, my tee shot went left of the fairway. Then after getting on the green on my next shot and being a little too aggressive on my birdie attempt, I sunk my putt for par from just under ten feet. On #8, I nearly lost my ball on the left side, but I found it in the tall grass. I got out of there with a 7-iron and made the green on my third shot. My two-putt for par gave me a total of nine pars on that day. My most disappointing hole came on the par-5 ninth hole, a hole where I felt that I could reach the green in two shots. I hit my ball off the tee with the driver and found the middle of the fairway. My second shot with my 3-wood in an attempt to reach the green in two shots went way left. I came up short on my third shot, got on the green in my fourth, and topped it off with two putts for bogey. Andrew made the green in two shots on that hole. Then I dodged danger on the tenth when I hooked my ball right, narrowly missing the big lake. Andrew's tee shot was perfect compared to mine. My second shot was surrounded by trees, but I did get close to the green somehow. In the end, I finished with yet another disappointing bogey.

I enjoy watching Tyler make terrific shots, but I must admit I prefer to watch what he does when he gets himself in hot water even more! I am always looking for opportunities for him to learn how to overcome challenges. I use golf as an example for many other situations for Tyler. He seems to respond well to those analogies.

After a long lunch break, I hit a marvelous tee shot down the fairway. I hit a good 7-iron to the green and two-putted for a hard-earned par. On the last hole, the par-5 twelfth, I hit my ball next to where I wanted to, the left side with a shot to the green. My second shot was a "lucky dog" shot according to one of the witnesses. My ball was destined for the bunker until it made a kind skip out of there and settled on the grass. On my third shot, my ball made a good bounce toward the hole and stopped five feet from it. I finished the second round with a birdie to score a 42 on the back nine. Overall I shot a 78 to match my personal best from last September at Green Meadow.

I believe I had played a second round that was far from spectacular. I had no big holes, but at least I had no double bogies or worse. I just didn't feel all that satisfied with the way I played. To me it was an ordinary round until my birdie putt on the last hole made it a round worth remembering. Golf can be a weird game. You may not seem to have played your best game, but somehow you play well enough to have the best performance yet. It's all a matter of consistency, playing your game no matter how boring it seems to others. I wasn't all that great in the second round. I didn't make a lot of shots. I didn't necessarily play as well as I hoped. But I still managed to shoot in the 70s for the second straight day. I actually had more pars (10) than bogies (7), plus I made the birdie on the last hole to help me match my personal best score in eighteen holes of golf.

Golf also affords Tyler the opportunity to reflect on what worked and did not work that day. Again, this strategy is used on many occasions for him. We have encouraged Tyler to reflect on what works and does not work in all kinds of situations, such as schoolwork, relationships, and employment.

I was lucky to finish the second round because on my way back to the clubhouse, a passing rainstorm wreaked havoc on the golf course. I was already enjoying my stay at Nebraska. I was doing the best I can out there, and I was hoping to do better in the last round. Regardless of the score and where I finish in the tournament, nothing can take away the memories from the National Games. I was blessed to have the support of my family and many friends, and I was making them proud not because of my playing but because of my positive attitude and good sportsmanship. My mom would always ask me before playing in any sport, "What's the most important thing?"

I would say, "Be a good sport and be respectful," which was exactly what I was doing. I had gone through a whole lot in 2010, starting with the "winter rust" and the grip changing. There were eighteen holes to play until it was all over. I had to play my game, keep my cool, maintain my focus, and enjoy the journey. It was just that simple.

Tyler is right when he says that I ask him that question before each tournament. It's part of our ritual. It seems to ground him and help him focus on the important things in life.

Round 3: To put it as fondly and as accurately as possible, Wednesday, July 21, was the third and final day of the individual eighteen-hole golfing competition at the Highlands Golf Course in lovely Lincoln, Nebraska. The weather in Nebraska began with murky skies and a solid amount of rain. Fortunately after a while, the rain did stop, the skies brightened, and golf proceeded with its normal schedule. The third and final round began at 8:30 a.m. as every golfer teed off from each of their respective tees. That day I was paired up with this twenty-one-year-old from York, South Carolina, named Scott Rohrer. Scott shot a Special Olympics record 71 in the first round two days earlier and followed that up with a 75 the next day. He had a lead on me by eleven strokes. Before we golfed, I told Scott, "Don't worry, you're going to win the gold medal today."

Ron and I have the utmost respect for Scott and his family. Our paths have crossed on many occasions, and each time, I am awed by that young man and his family. Both Scott and Tyler are similar in so many ways. It is a joy to see them paired up. They complement each other very well.

Scott and I teed off on the par-4 tenth hole. I went first and hit a marvelous drive down the middle of the fairway. My game plan was simple. Swing conservatively, keep the ball in play, and if you see a good birdie chance, take it. And if you can't make birdie, make par. Scott Rohrer did not start out all that promising as he pulled his drive left and into the tall grass. He found his ball after a long search, but he couldn't get out in his second shot or his third. He decided to take a drop, got on the green, and made a triple bogey 7. I made the green in two shots and two-putted for par. On the par-4 eleventh, I stayed in play, missed the green on my second shot, chipped on, and saved par, while Scott had to settle for bogey.

On the par-5 twelfth, the hole where I made birdie twice, I used my driver, 3-wood, and sand wedge to make the green. But unlike the first two rounds, I two-putted for par. On the par-3 thirteenth, I overshot the green with my pitching wedge as the flagstick was positioned on the back of the green. I then made a nice chip to get within inches of the hole and tapped in for yet another par. On the par-4 fourteenth, I was lucky to avoid the bunker on the right. Flirting with the bunker would cost me later on. I did get on the green on my second shot. As I was reading my birdie putt, I made a modified impersonation of PGA Tour regular Camilo Villegas. I almost made my birdie from fifteen to twenty feet out as my ball just skimmed the cup. I finished that hole with my fifth straight par to begin the day. Scott Rohrer meanwhile had made three pars in a row after his horrendous start. My streak of five consecutive pars ended with a bogey on the par-3 fifteenth hole, the hole where Scott made bogey.

Throughout this round of golf, several photographers and video crews began following Tyler and Scott. It was an incredible sight to see. I was concerned that it might throw their game off, but much to my surprise, it had no effect on either player. They seemed to ignore the extra golf carts and camera crews and go on as if they were just having a regular round of golf at a neighborhood course.

After cutting Scott's overall lead to 7, we had the same scores on the next four holes. Then on the par-4 sixteenth, the match began to tilt in Scott's favor. I hit a good drive down the center of the fairway, but Scott's drive was much better. He has tremendous power for a Special Olympic golfer, the best I've ever seen out of all the players I competed with. I hit my second shot too long, while Scott hit a beautiful second shot and had a much easier shot at a birdie than me. I was fifty feet from the hole, and I would later make bogey. Scott would nail his birdie putt with ease, and then he would get in the groove from here on out.

On the seventeenth, after shooting my tee shot on the par-3, I played a good bump and run to set up an easy tap-in par. Scott found the left side of the green but was able to save par on that hole. On the short par-4 eighteenth, I made the green from the tee with the driver, just like I did in the first round. Scott found the hill right next to the back side of the green. I would make my first birdie of the day, while Scott chipped on and made the next shot for his birdie. After nine holes, I had a score of 35, while Scott had a 37, and he was just starting to get on fire.

Scott and I had great drives on the first hole. Scott made the green in two, while I found the sand to the left of the green for the second day in a row. I did get out and was able to two-putt for par. Scott would make his third birdie in the last four holes. The second hole was where Scott finally came back to earth after going two strokes under par in a span of eight straight holes. I hit a nice approach shot with my 7-iron to get to within fifteen to twenty feet from the hole. My par on the second restored my two-shot advantage in the third round.

Then through holes 3 to 5, I went into a slump. My first two shots on the par-4 third hole got me to the green, but I three-putted for bogey. On the par-3 fourth, I finally made the green from the tee box but misread my putt for birdie and then blew my putt for par to the left. Once again I had to settle for bogey. The fifth was the worst hole of them all. My drive with the 3-wood went left and into the tall grass. I found my ball after an arduous search for it, but I had to take a stroke since the ball was unplayable. I would make my last bogey of the National Games on the fifth. Scott's three pars combined with my three bogies gave Scott a one-shot lead for the third round, but it would be short-lived.

On the sixth hole, Scott and I made identical first and second shots. We both got on the green in three, I two-putted for par, but Scott missed an easy putt for par and had to settle for a bogey. We were now tied up for the third round. The next hole was the short par-4 seventh hole. It was my best hole of the back nine. I hit this perfectly struck tee shot, just like I did on #18 in the first round and earlier in the day, and made the green. I was able to two-putt for my fifth and final birdie of the tournament. I got the lead back from Scott with two holes to go.

After we both made par in the eighth, we came to our last hole, the par-5 ninth. My tee shot went a little to the right, and I nearly found the bunker. Scott was able to outdrive me and had a clearer shot to the green. I was now faced with the most difficult decision of the tournament. I was either going to go for the green with the 3-wood, which would mean going over a bunker and some mounds, or use my 5-iron to play it safe, because it has been my best club all year. Since I was in the rough, I chose the 5-iron. I hit the ball very well, but I went a little more to the right than I wanted to and found my ball in a bunker to the right of the green. I got out of the sand all right, but I had this lengthy birdie putt in my way. My putt was downhill, and I hit my ball a little too firm with it. Scott meanwhile had a shorter downhill birdie putt of his own. If he makes it, he would at least clinch a tie with me for the third round and I would not beat him. Sure enough he made the putt from eight feet and capped off a remarkable round after a slow start. Now it was my turn to attempt a putt for par. It was an uphill putt from six feet out. It was also my biggest putt of the tournament. After many practice strokes, I stepped toward my ball and hit it.

As the ball was slowly rolling toward the hole, my life was flashing before me at the speed of sound. I wasn't sure if I could make this putt before I attempted it. Somehow I knew what to do. I had played this game too long to miss a big putt like this. That six-foot putt was twenty-three years' worth of hard work, determination, persistence, and perseverance. On the last hole in the last round of the 2010 Special Olympics USA National Games, the ball went into the hole. I made my par, and I finished in a tie for the lowest score of the third and final round. I didn't know it until I finished adding up my total score from all eighteen holes of the third round. By the time I did so, I found out that my back nine score was a 40. After adding the front nine score (35) to the back nine score (40), my combined score for both the front and back nines was a 75! After fifty-four holes over three days, I had just completed my best round of golf in the biggest tournament of my life.

As for Scott Rohrer, his final-round score of 75 was added to his 75 the day before and his 71 in the first round. I told him he was going to win a gold medal, and he did just that. I took the silver medal and had the second-lowest score among the twenty Level 5 golfers that competed in Nebraska. Scott Rohrer and I were the two best golfers that Special Olympics had to offer that week in July. Between the two golfers, there was no sense of animosity, no bitter rivalry, even though we were evenly matched and played a very close third round. We were just two young men playing golf, doing the best that we can. I did the best I could for all fifty-four holes of the tournament. Even though I won a silver medal, I felt a good sense of accomplishment with my 75 because I had to make the putt for par on the last hole to do so.

It's too bad that these two fine gentlemen don't live closer together. They bring out the best in each other. It is so much fun to watch them play golf. They clearly have a genuine respect for each other. In fact, after their round of golf, both Tyler and Scott were interviewed by the local TV station, and each one of them spent most of their interview time complementing the other's performance on the course. Again, I was watching the crowd during the interview and noticed several people reduced to tears!

For the fifth straight year, I've beaten my personal best. It has become a sort of a habit for me setting personal bests, especially doing them in places I've never been to before—at Cherry Hill in Amherst in the 2006 states when I shot an 86, in Connecticut at the 2007 Special Olympics New England Invitational where I shot an 82, and at the 2008 National Invitational in Florida where I shot a 79 in the second round. In the 2010 Special Olympics USA National Games, I had one double bogey, twenty-one bogies, twenty-six pars, five birdies, and of course the eagle in the first round. It was not the silver medal I won that made my trip to Nebraska worth remembering. It was the experience that I had there that mattered. I loved every minute of it. The people over there were nice and helpful, the course was well maintained, and the tournament atmosphere was second to none.

It would be so easy for Tyler to dwell on the fact that he didn't win the gold medal. I am so impressed that he is able to put the entire Special Olympics experience into the proper perspective—meeting new people, having new experiences, and focusing on being the best you can be.

I had texts from my folks back home after telling them about my 75. Jaret Foley said, "Wow, that's great. Three rounds in the 70s, nice job."

My brother Clint said, "Great job, bro."

Rick Reault called me to say, "That was wild, amazing."

If my score was not impressive enough, it was my maturity, my sportsmanship, and my composure. Coming into the National Games, I had trouble being a good sport. All year long, I faced many great challenges head-on. But the rewards for these challenges were even bigger than the challenges themselves—my hard work in college, my induction into the SOMA Hall of Fame, my invitation to Phi Theta Kappa, my segment on *Golf in America*, and now the three scores in the National Games: 79–78–75. My showing there the past three days was well deserved.

Now that I was done with my golf tournament, I had plenty of free time for the rest of the week. I chose to join Mom and Dad and go see some other sports that were taking place during the National Games. Hours after I finished golfing, I went to watch some bocce at Cook Pavilion in the heart of the campus. We got to see a match featuring a playing pair representing Team SOMA. After that we went out to eat dinner at a place called Misty's. Then we visited Olympic Town and went inside Pershing Auditorium to visit the Healthy Athletes concourse. I had my feet checked out by a doctor, and he said that I needed to see a foot specialist. You could not go anywhere in the city without running into a Special Olympic athlete or associate. They were brightening up the city, making Lincoln the hub of Special Olympics for a whole week.

On the fourth day of competitions, Thursday, July 22, I decided to spend the whole day with Mom and Dad. We all went to the outskirts of the city to this nice multisports facility called the Abbott Sports Complex, where tennis and soccer were being played. Andy Roddick did a tennis clinic over there at one point during the games. I went to see Marc Segerman of Hyannis play some tennis. After that we went to the soccer fields to see Team SOMA in the bronze medal game of the soccer tournament. The whole soccer team was based in the greater Worcester town of Shrewsbury. Matt Millett and Colin Davidson were on that team, and they went on to win the game and the bronze medal.

Then we went out to lunch at a place called the Village Inn, right next to the Super 8 hotel my parents were staying in. After that I got to spend some time at their hotel room so that I could write in my journal about my experience at the National Games.

Ron and I let Tyler choose what we should do for that day of visitation. We were surprised that he basically wanted to spend the day in our hotel room writing. I guess he just wanted some downtime. I can see where he needed some quiet time due to the fact that he was completely out of his normal routine.

Then we went to the Devaney Center to catch some swimming action. It was a really crowded and noisy place. Denise Carriere, the 2008 SOMA Hall of Famer whom I played basketball with, was competing in swimming. After that we went out to another restaurant in Lincoln called Lazlo's for dinner.

Friday was the last day of competitions for the 2010 Special Olympics USA National Games. That day I went with most of Team SOMA to see some powerlifting at Kimball Hall. There were squats, bench presses, and dead lifts, and some of the best could lift at least five hundred pounds. Tom McCarter was the only one from Team SOMA doing the powerlifting events that day. I got to see Mom and Dad for the last time before they took their own flight home.

After the event, we walked through downtown Lincoln to a nearly empty Olympic Town. It was a far cry from the carnival-like atmosphere of early in the week when Rock Band on Wii was being played and the Pershing Auditorium was filled to capacity with many games going on. We visited the basement of Pershing Auditorium to check out the Healthy Athletes area. I had my hearing checked and passed with flying colors. I then went to this FUNFitness area, where the physicians and volunteers tested my strength, balance, flexibility, and endurance, and I did very well on all of those tests. After that I went upstairs to a nearly empty auditorium. Almost everything from earlier in the week was gone. The things that helped pack the auditorium—the Nintendo Wii, the Ping-Pong tables, the billiard tables, most of the sports experience except for basketball and soccer—were gone.

After that I went with the golf team to a Buffalo Wild Wings in the downtown area for lunch. After that we went to this place called Nebraska Bookstore. As soon as we got inside, the electricity was out. All the lights to this place were shut off. I did some browsing for a while before I bought myself a University of Nebraska T-shirt and necklace. Before I paid for them, the power was back on.

Then I went back to my dorm room to pack my things up, including the stuff I got during my week in the city of Lincoln. I filled up my backpack, my luggage bag, and my golf bag for the flight out of Nebraska very early Saturday morning. I showered one final time in this public bathroom where there are eight sinks. The water in the showers kept alternating from hot to cold several times. I missed taking showers at home and taking them alone with nobody around. I missed 100 percent total privacy as well.

Later on that Friday, the closing ceremonies were going to take place. After nearly a whole week of Special Olympics competition, the largest sporting event in the history of the Cornhusker State was coming to a close. There is an old saying that "all good things must come to an end." One of the best things to ever happen to me was to be a part of a team that participated in the biggest National Games in Special Olympics history and to have played my best golf ever there. Just like in the opening ceremonies last Sunday, I wore my green tie-dyed Team SOMA shirt with the khaki shorts. Instead of taking the long walk from Cather Hall to the Devaney Center, the team took buses there.

It was a packed house that evening at the home court of the Nebraska men's and women's basketball teams. For one week only, the city of Lincoln, Nebraska, was the epicenter of the 2010 Special Olympics USA National Games. The closing ceremony coincided with the National Youth Rally, where thousands of the nation's youth committed themselves to support their peers with intellectual disabilities, similar to the Spread the Word to End the Word campaign. John Cappiello, the athletics coach for Team SOMA and team videographer, filmed some members of the team describing their experiences at the National Games. I declared to him on camera, "This is the best week of my life!" The closing ceremony festivities were a tribute to the sporting events that took place over the course of a whole week. The second ever Special Olympics National Games was nothing short of a success.

After the 2010 Special Olympics USA National Games were declared closed, I stayed with the team at the Devaney Center for at least an hour longer. Before the National Games began, each member of Team SOMA had a bag filled with Team SOMA pins. We would trade our pins for other Special Olympic state pins with other athletes and representatives. I collected at least thirty pins throughout my week in Nebraska. The games may have been over, but everybody did not want to leave. There were athletes from one state trading one thing for another with other athletes from another state. I received one of those "Mo Magic" straw hats from an athlete from Special Olympics Missouri.

How has this experience changed me? Well, for one thing, I have discovered that there are more people with an array of disabilities in this country than I can ever think of, and I saw it firsthand in Nebraska.

At the opening ceremonies, I learned about Grace Anne Braxton, the female golfer from Virginia. At the golf course this week, I got to meet her. She was absolutely impressed by my *Golf in America* segment, while I admired her swing and demeanor. She was one of three Level 5 female golfers who competed in Nebraska. She shot scores of 82–80–87, which were good enough for a gold medal in her division. What was more amazing is that she actually had the third-lowest combined score out of the twenty Level 5 participants that played in the National Games.

I marvel at Tyler's powers of observation. He is such a keen observer. Sometimes I think that skill is both a blessing and a curse for him. It is a blessing because he can recall so many different aspects of what he sees, hears, and experiences. It's a curse because he can get overwhelmed by these observations, and he doesn't always process these stimuli accurately. Therefore, his decision-making skills are not always reliable or safe for him.

Besides my personal best score and silver medal, there are still many things that I'll remember from my weeklong trip to Nebraska. I met a lot of fascinating people over there, such as Grace Anne Braxton, Jim Porter from Team Indiana, and Andrew Williams of Tennessee and his caddy/coach Paul Rodgers. There are also the people at Highlands Golf Course who made me and the other participants feel welcome. There are also the volunteers from KPMG Doug and Farhad, who caddied for me and drove me in the golf carts throughout all three of my rounds there. Of course I will remember Scott Rohrer, a fine competitor with a knack for the game of golf. He plays golf three days a week with his father down in a state that is generally a year-round golf destination. His abundance of golfing time served him well for the National Games, and he deserved to win the gold medal with the way he played. There are also the places I visited in Lincoln that I will remember and the campus, especially Memorial Stadium. I will also remember walking out of the tunnel with Team SOMA and into the arena during the opening ceremonies. And finally, last but not least, I will remember having my family and friends, who were right behind me ever since I began the golf tournament.

It was the biggest sporting event I have ever been associated with, and I feel so amazed by the spirit and abilities of all the athletes that came to Lincoln, Nebraska, in the summer of 2010. What each athlete had to go through to get there, what they had to endure to earn those medals, gives you a lump in your throat just thinking about it. More than three thousand athletes from all over America, including golfers from Alaska, came to this one place for one week. The memories made by the athletes, the coaches, the volunteers, and me will last forever. I'll never forget what it took for me to do what I did in Nebraska.

Since the closing ceremony took place in the evening, I did not get back to my dorm until 10:00. I only got five hours of sleep because I had to leave the campus in the wee hours of the morning with my golf team to catch the early-morning flight to Chicago. It was exactly 3:15 a.m. when I woke up. I had all my stuff packed, but I had to change out of the clothes that I wore at the closing ceremonies and put my dirty orange polo on like the rest of my group. I didn't want to wear a dirty shirt to the airport, but Scott Merrill told me, "You gotta wear it." So I had to open up my golf travel bag to get my dirty-clothes bag, where my orange polo was. I was so stressed out on account of having very little sleep that my mind wasn't thinking straight. I partially broke one of my fingernails trying to get my shirt out of my bag and nearly flipped out over it in front of my golf team. Lucky for me, I found it, closed up my bag even though I was in no mood of doing so, brought myself together, and proceeded to leave my dorm. It was not much of a fitting way to leave a place where you set your own personal best in the biggest tournament of your life.

Believe me, I heard all about the fact that Tyler had to wear a "dirty" shirt! He had only worn that shirt for a few hours the night before, and it was important for the team to wear the same outfits when they travel for safety and security purposes. Tyler is extremely cautious when it comes to personal hygiene, and I am sure this was quite a challenge for him.

I left with one-third of Team SOMA on a big yellow bus that was taking us to Lincoln Municipal Airport. I saw the beautiful city of Lincoln one final time, in the dark. It was tough to say goodbye to Lincoln and Nebraska, but I was looking forward to saying hello to Massachusetts and Tyngsboro. I just could not wait to get back home. My parents had already left for the Bay State the other day, and I couldn't wait to see them again. I arrived at the airport, only to learn that my flight to Chicago was cancelled. How's that for a rude awakening?

Stormy weather grounded our plane back at O'Hare Airport. There was a possibility that I would not come home until Sunday. I could not go back to my dorm room because we already checked out and our big yellow bus was long gone. Probably somebody up there wanted me to stay in Nebraska a little bit longer. Sometimes these things happen for a reason, even when you feel at your grumpiest and you want things to go your way. Life can be tough, but you have to pull yourself together until all the tough parts are over and done with. I remember at CTDS when the teachers would tell me to "pull yourself together" when people around me were crying, and with all this in my head, it was a tremendously tough job for me.

It is wonderful to know that Tyler can draw on past experiences, such as the ones he had at his former school, CTDS.

It was rough for me to be spending more time in Nebraska when I should be on a plane heading for home. Later on I grew to accept that it was going to be a little while before I was actually going home. While my golf coach Scott Ayres was trying to find another flight to Boston, I spent the whole morning at the airport occupying myself by listening to my MP3, taking a nap, eating a bagel, reading a magazine or newspaper, buying some more souvenirs for my family back home, having some snacks that my parents bought for me, writing in my journal, and just goofing around a little. I kept in touch with my family on my cell phone through text messages and calls. I was told to hang in there by Mom and Dad. Even Rick Reault came to my aid over the phone. There was so much time to kill that I could've gone golfing with the golf team at the Highlands since it was right next door to the airport.

Finally, we were able to book a flight to Boston with a stop at Denver. My coach had contemplated taking a bus over to Kansas City and flying from there to Chicago, where we could possibly spend the night before flying out to Boston on Sunday. It was hard to get twenty people on a plane on a weekend, but luckily we pulled it off. After calling Lincoln Municipal Airport my residence for nine hours, I left Lincoln and Nebraska for good at one o'clock Central Standard Time. Then after spending two minutes at the Denver Airport and being given a burger from McDonald's, I was on my way home.

At 7:30 p.m., my plane landed at Logan International Airport in Boston, Massachusetts, seven hours later than my original arrival. It was worth the wait. My parents were at the baggage claim waiting for me. I was gladder to see them than I was to be home. There was no place like home, and my home is in the Bay State. My trip was officially over, and I could finally move on with my life.

We feel very fortunate that Tyler likes to keep in contact with us. We are also lucky that he can entertain himself most of the time. I am grateful for text messaging because he always sends us a text or calls us if anything out of the ordinary happens and we are not right beside him. We were at the bottom of the escalator at Logan Airport when he arrived. He looked exhausted and hugged us as if he hadn't seen us for months! He really doesn't like it when his schedule changes for any reason whatsoever. The difference today is the fact that it doesn't take as long for him to recover from changes. He also has skills to help him process the changes that spontaneously occur

Dad, me, and Dick Brown on top of Mount Lafayette.

My favorite pose of me actually swinging a golf club. Picture
taken at Stow Acres during the 2009 Special Olympics
Massachusetts Golf-a-Thon.

Handing the trophy from the Tyler Lagasse Golf Challenge to Paul Karrlsson-Willis towards the end of the 2009 SOMA Golf-a-Thon.

Me in my blue gym clothes learning that I was going to be inducted into the 2010 Special Olympics Massachusetts hall of Fame. My friends from the K.I.D.S. group were there to share the celebration. The one in the black hoodie and blue shorts to the right of me is none other than the mighty champion boxer Micky Ward.

05/11/2010

Accepting the medal for my induction into the SOMA Hall of
Fame at Agganis Arena in Boston University...

… and accepting my induction into Phi Theta Kappa – all in the same month!

That picture sums up everything I did to get to that point in my life. Mom and I celebrating!

07/21/2010

Posing with my competitor and Gold medalist Scott Rohrer after medal ceremonies during the 2010 Special Olympics USA National Games.

And now a time to put my entire National Games experience on record.

After the National Games

Two days after my homecoming, I went right back to work on my golfing. Dad and I played at our home course of Tyngsboro Country Club for the first time since the National Games. My string of consecutive holes of bogey or better ended at 42, when I made double bogey on the second hole during the Red, White, and Blue Tournament. I finished the round with a score of 38, tying with my lowest round at Tyngsboro in 2010. It was a great start toward my upcoming SOMA golf tournament at Stow Acres in mid-August.

It was important to Tyler to get right back into his normal routine. It was also important to take his head "out of the clouds." Too much celebrity status isn't good for anyone.

On July 31, one week after the Special Olympics USA National Games, Paul Perrymore and his crew from the Golf Channel's *Golf in America* came to my house to do a follow-up on my story, called "Tyler 2.0." This time Jim Axelrod was also coming over to my house to see my family again. Mom and Dad would be interviewed, and the crew was going to do more filming of me golfing. Filming was going to last all day, starting in front of the "The Lagasses" granite sign in the front yard, where Mom, Dad, and I posed. Jim Axelrod soon came to our house for the first time. I showed Jim my room and all of my trophies and awards as well as my front-page pictures of all the Boston major sports titles inside it. Later on I asked Jimmy how he liked my house. He said, "I didn't like it. I love it." I wasn't interviewed at all that day. Mom and Dad were the only ones who were taking questions from Jim, while I was doing some chipping in my big backyard. After the interviews and lunch, Jim Axelrod had to leave us, but the filming crew stayed with us as we drove to Stow Acres for nine holes of golf on the North Course. Dad and I had been golfing for thirteen years, but this was the first time that Dad and I were ever going to be filmed while playing golf together. I started off nicely as a rolling camera was whizzing behind me. It's the exact same place where I was filmed at the 2009 SOMA golf tournament and the first *Golf in America* story back in May.

Highlights of the day included Dad making a thirty-foot putt for birdie on the second hole. Overall I was hitting the ball well with a wire on me. Later on the par-3, eighth hole, I hooked my shot well right of the green. I chipped my ball on the green, but I had an uphill putt for par from at least fifteen feet. With the camera right in front of me, and this is the only take, I got my ball to roll in the hole and let out a "boo-yeah!" and a "save by Tyler!" because it counted as a par save. I actually made six pars that day, and three of my par putts were used on the show. On the last hole when we walked down the fairway, Dad asked me what the score was, and I told him, "Last time I checked I was beating you." I shot a nine-hole Stow Acres record low of 40. Dad shot a 45. A couple of weeks after the filming, my second *Golf in America* segment was aired on the Golf Channel, with extra footage from my first broadcast and the new material, which included my silver medal at the National Games. I thought my second time in front of the camera was better.

It was really interesting working with the Golf Channel for Tyler's segment. It is amazing how much footage is necessary for a five-minute story! Tyler was so focused on his golf game that I don't think he even noticed that the cameras were following him around all day!

Mom, Dad, Memere, and I went to vacation in Seabrook for the eighth summer in a row one week before my SOMA state golf tournament. Every day was a beach day for my family thanks to spotless weather all week long at the Seacoast Region of New Hampshire. A couple of times I would ride my bicycle around the neighborhood, I would also take walks down by the ocean with Mom and Dad, and we would play this Phase 10 dice game. We would go out to eat every day at nearby restaurants. And of course we watched *On Golden Pond* as part of our summer family tradition.

Tyler is big on traditions. I'm not sure if I would categorize these things as traditions, but nonetheless he insists that we watch that movie each summer at the beach.

On August 15, I went to Stow Acres for the golf tournament in the 2010 SOMA August Games. Just like last year, it was a one-day eighteen-hole event. Unlike last year, I was going to play on the South Course instead of the North Course. I teed off just shortly before noon with Steve and Travis Cole, the unified partners from Shrewsbury. My overall score for eighteen holes was a not-too-shabby 85, six strokes better than the previous year. That 85 was good enough for my fifth consecutive gold medal in the SOMA golf championship. In a year of milestones, my fifth gold medal in a row was another significant one to add to my new book of medals.

I would go golfing seven more times for the remainder of the year. The day after the state tournament, I would set a season-low score at Tyngsboro Country Club with a 37. One week after that, I got to play eighteen holes at Long Meadow Golf Club on the Lowell-Tewksbury line with KIDS athlete Andrew Dozibrin, Fred Wilkie, and Fred's nephew. In misty conditions, I shot an 88. I would also play golf with my mom for the first time at Pine Valley Golf Links on August 28. Mom had just started taking golf lessons that year, and she used my old clubs. And as the summer to remember was coming to a close, I had just finished up my fifth journal and written my thousandth journal page since I started journal writing upon my Cotting School graduation in 2005.

On Tuesday, August 31, I went to LeLacheur Park with Mom, Dad, and Clint to see a Lowell Spinners game. But I did not just come for the game. I came to throw out the first pitch. It was also Mike Eruzione bobblehead doll night, and he, too, was going to throw the first pitch. Ryan Asselta of FOX 25 was there as well as Comcast SportsNet. I made my way to the infield grass, where I met Mike Eruzione, the former BU Terrier and hero of the famed Miracle on Ice 1980 United States Olympic Men's Hockey Team. I told him that I was a River Hawks hockey fan but that for one night, I was a BU Terrier. My pitch by the way, with a pair of National Games sunglasses and a gold medal around my neck, made it over the plate. Rizzo's was a little short of the plate. After that, I had my picture taken with him. We sat in the Fenway Booth near the press box behind home plate. Later on, my family was given a box of several bobblehead dolls. One of them was autographed by Rizzo himself. The Spinners lost 4–0 that night, but to shake hands with a person from the Bay State who thirty years ago lifted a nation when it needed it meant a lot to me.

Even though Tyler wasn't even born yet, he knows so many different facts about important dates in history. He was thrilled to meet Mike Eruzione.

Two days after meeting Mike Eruzione at LeLacheur Park, I finally made my long-awaited hike up Mount Washington in New Hampshire's White Mountains with my dad and Dick Brown. Early in 2010, our hiking companion Richard "Dick" Brown was working out at a gym when he went into cardiac arrest. But luckily for him, some trainers nearby came over to perform CPR and had their equipment ready and were able to revive him. Dad and I saw him at a UMass–Lowell hockey game not too long after his ordeal at the gym. I was so glad that he had survived. Once during the summer, I went hiking up Gunstock Mountain with Dad and Dick Brown, followed by a swim in Lake Winnipesaukee.

On the day before the hike up Mount Washington, we went down the zip line at the Bretton Woods ski area. I had no idea what to expect from my first zip line experience. I had a harness put around my body plus a helmet on my head. Then a lady drove me, Dad, and Dick on this Polaris four-wheeler to the top of the zip line. Dad and I went first with Dick watching from the top. I had to position myself like I was doing a cannonball into a pool. Then we took off down the zip line together. I was picking up speed while the line was so loud from my harness, grinding the wire above me. I went from going full speed down the line to an abrupt stop. I had difficulty hearing out of my left ear from all the noise of the zip line. Dick went next and made it down all right. Dad and Dick went down a second time while I stayed at the bottom. I decided that one ride down the line was good enough.

What I most admire about Tyler is the fact that he does try new things. He really tries to overcome his fears. And he is not afraid to feel uncomfortable. He really didn't like the noise the zip line was making, but he went for it anyway.

Thursday, September 2, 2010, was the day I added to my long list of highlights from 2010. The day started at 5:00 a.m. for me, Dad, and Dick Brown. Two hours later, we took the Tuckerman Ravine trail up to Mount Washington in the biggest hike of my life. This hike was dedicated to a dear friend of my dad and Dick Brown, William "Bill" McDonald, an avid hiker who would spend his spring breaks skiing down Tuckerman Ravine in his college days. In the beginning of the hike, I listened to the Guess Who and Blues Traveler on my brand-new iPhone. We started our hike at a quarter past seven in the morning. It took us two hours to get from the base to the Tuckerman Ravine lodge. The first half of the hike was somewhat easy but pretty rocky. After passing the lodge, we got a closer look at the ravine. It's different in the summertime compared to the winter. Dick said the snow would cover up a giant-sized rock in the winter. It does snow a lot, eight to nine months of the year. There was no snow to be seen that day, especially in the middle of a heat wave.

Then once we were in the bowl of the ravine, the trail got more treacherous, rockier, and steeper. It was home to the highest recorded wind speed on earth—231 miles per hour! We made it to the top of the ravine, but we had a ways up the mountain, 0.6 miles to be exact. Dad, Dick, and I were all tired, from our feet dodging rocks for three hours straight with some breaks in between. It was starting to get cloudy as we approached the peak, plus the wind was picking up, so I had to put on my windbreaker. Here I was, twenty-three years old, with my dad and Dick Brown keeping me company, finishing up a four-hour-long hike as my feet were already burning after all this walking. My shirt was wet from sweat, but I was almost finished with my uphill climb. I knew that I was nearly done when I saw this pavement from the Auto Road leading up to the top of the mountain. Once I set foot on this road, I gave my dad a big hug.

I was on top of Mount Washington! Emotionally and physically drained, I had to climb up a set of stairs to the observatory with cramped muscles from all that hiking. It was pretty windy up there, but inside the observatory, it was nice. I changed my shirt and had some chili and chips for lunch. I got an ornament and magnet at the gift shop. We spent an hour at the peak of the mountain taking pictures of each other. Then we checked out this hut—amazing to see it stand after all this wind and snow. Finally we had to go down.

On my way down, I got to spread Bill McDonald's ashes. Dad and Dick spread some on our way up. When I tried to spread the ashes, the wind just shifted and turned the ashes toward me. I got some of Will on me. Going down was just as difficult as it was going up. I put a lot of pressure on my calves that way. It took us at least three and a half hours to get to the bottom. By the time we got to the base, it was just before five. I must have had two gallons of fluid during the whole hike, but my body was simply begging for rest when I was done.

The Mount Washington hike was not only a culmination of a memorable summer. It was a tribute to a friend. I believe William is looking down on us and thanking us for going through such an ordeal to complete a big hike. May Bill rest in peace. It was a big hike for Dick Brown because he nearly died several months earlier while working out at his gym. Dad and I were not only thankful that he is alive. We were thankful to have him join us for the hike up Mount Washington. I was thankful to have him come to my SOMA Hall of Fame induction back in May. I was glad to have hiked up Mount Washington, and we all could not have picked a more perfect time to do it. At 6,288 feet, it was the biggest hike of my life. Hiking that mountain gave me a sense of courage and honor, and it made me feel that I was worth a lot more than I could imagine. So SOMA Hall of Fame, Phi Theta Kappa, *Golf in America*, Nebraska, the thousandth page, the first pitch at LeLacheur, and now Mount Washington to add to my list of highlights in 2010— what can I say? I mean, what *can* I say?

The summer of 2010 had come and gone, and as September came, it was time for me to go back to school for the fall semester. I took two courses that fall at Middlesex Community College. I took Intermediate Algebra at the Lowell Campus on Tuesdays and Thursdays, and I took Baseball: The American Experience at the Bedford Campus on Wednesday evenings. I had not taken a college-level math course in three years, and I was rusty from the start. I was able to gut it out all semester long, working even harder than I've ever had on any other course before, and when Christmastime was coming, I finished this course with a grade of A-. Meanwhile I was enjoying the baseball class. I took it because I wanted to appreciate the game a lot more. I did so well in that class that my teacher said that I should teach this class. I would eventually get an A on this course. I did a written report and a PowerPoint presentation of baseball and the '60s in my Red Sox uniform. Mr. Navaroli would have loved it and would have been proud of me.

I am glad that Tyler got to take an elective course that really interested him. He did seem to enjoy that class tremendously. Sometimes it was hard to tell though, because he would prepare for that course the same way he did for every other course that he took. On average, I would say that he devotes between ten to fifteen hours to studying per course.

As the summer was waning, I wrote an e-mail to Mr. Navaroli about what I have done in the five years after I graduated from Cotting School, especially what I have done in 2010. I had not contacted or heard from him since 2005, the year I graduated. On Labor Day Monday, as I was checking my e-mail on my new iPhone, Mr. Navaroli replied back to me. The man who wanted to hear what I had to say every morning inside the school library wrote this on Sunday, September 5:

Dear Tyler,

> *What do you say Mr. Lagasse? How were your raviolis, Mr. Navaroli? I was very happy to read your e-mail, but I was not surprised. I always knew you would do great things. It took me a while to answer your e-mail because I was on vacation spending time in museums and libraries. I continue to work at the Cotting School but I no longer teach periodic classes during the day, because the new administration won't let me. But I do teach after-school classes—the History of Baseball, the History of the Boston Red Sox, and the most popular one is the History of Rock and Roll: 1955–1980. I continue to be in contact with other Cotting School graduates, but you have far surpassed them in accomplishments. Continue to grow in knowledge and wisdom. Read good books and listen to the oldies station, talk and listen to family and friends, and believe in yourself and a higher power. I'm sure everyone at the Cotting School would love to see you sometime—especially me. I know that you will do good in your courses. With algebra first learn the basics. Best wishes for a successful and happy future.*

> *Sincerely,*
> *"Honest" John Navaroli*

That e-mail just lifted my spirits because I was a little anxious about returning to college that fall. John has a way of making one's day brighter. He helps give you a positive outlook on your life. He was there for me every step of the way since I was fourteen. I don't remember the first day that I met him, but as I grew up, John and I grew a little closer. His periodic classes had something to do with it, and it made my life richer. John and I had a lot in common. We both like sports, and we both like to listen to oldies and classic rock. I remember the sheets of lyrics that he handed to me and my classmates and the music that we listened to in his classes about character, war, and identity. Whenever I feel down, whenever I feel like it, I listen to my music to help cope with my problems. Five years after graduation, his words were still true—the challenges for me were great, but the rewards were greater.

We have been so blessed that Tyler has been surrounded by people who are willing to "go the extra mile." They have embraced Tyler's challenges and helped him reach heights that not too long ago would have seemed unattainable. They have made not only Tyler's life richer but my life as well.

On September 14, I got to go to TD Garden with my brother Clint to see my favorite music group perform live, called Rush. My brother kept asking me, "Why do you like Rush?"

I said to him, "I like the way they play their music. I like their lyrics, their melodies, their beats, and they have a way of raising my spirits— Geddy Lee, Alex Lifeson, and Neil Peart." It was my first arena concert ever. When "Spirit of the Radio" was being played, it was spectacular— unlike anything I've ever seen or heard before. I took my own picture with the stage in the background during the "concert hall" part of the song. What could be a more fitting beginning to a Rush concert?

They played other songs, such as "Freewill," "Limelight," "Red Barchetta," "Subdivisions," "YYZ," "Closer to the Heart," "2112," "Tom Sawyer," and more. Drummer Neil Peart did a fabulous drum solo during the concert. The last song we heard was "Far Cry" from their 2008 album *Snakes and Arrows*. Rush put on a great show that night for the folks in Boston. I got a T-shirt and a poster of the band from their Time Machine Tour. Clint and I left early to beat the raucous crowd while they all waited for them to come back and perform an encore. I had such a blast at the concert that I actually felt a blast hit my chest from above the stage.

Tyler LOVES music. Sometimes it can get a little out of hand though. He likes to ride in the car and look at himself in the side mirrors and lip-sync to the songs. It looks pretty odd, I must admit.

At the LGH golf banquet, I won the Best Golfer Award again. It was an honor to be league champion again. The 2010 LGH golf season would be the last for me and my father in that league. It was a joy to have spent five years being with the league and playing on my home course every Monday afternoon in the spring and summer months with Dad. Being in a golf league allowed me to work on my game, get out to the golf course at least once a week, and above all spend a lot of time with my dad.

I participated in two more scramble golf tournaments in September. I finally got to go to the new Meadow Creek Golf Club in nearby Dracut for the first time to play in an eighteen-hole scramble. Then I got to participate in the golf-a-thon at Stow Acres in my own foursome for the first time with Dad, Nick Savarese, and David Fatula. We played only thirty-two holes in murky conditions from 7:30 a.m. to 5:00 p.m. and made fourteen birdies and two eagles as a team. The 2010 Golf-a-thon raised tens of thousands of dollars. I even got to meet three former members of the Red Sox at the golf-a-thon—Jerry Moses, John Tudor, and Rico Petrocelli. For the second straight year, there was the Tyler Lagasse Golf Challenge on the eighteenth hole of the South Course. For one day, the participants of this event continued to display such compassion in the most extraordinary way possible. They were amazing in their effort to support Special Olympics, and they did not disappoint one bit.

In December of 2010, the city of Boston was in the bidding to host the next Special Olympics USA National Games in 2014. Mom and Dad picked me up from college, where I took my last Intermediate Algebra class, and took me to meet with Jennifer Maitland and Klete Squires from Special Olympics Massachusetts and members of the selection committee. I got to visit the golf course at Franklin Park, where the golfing would take place. The selection committee was there to visit, and I shook hands with them. Then I went to the JFK Public Library and Museum to see the exhibits.

Finally I went to the Yawkey Center to make a heartfelt speech to some dignitaries and the selection committee. Boston Red Sox radio commentator Joe Castiglione was the master of the ceremonies, and I posed for a picture with him and Melissa Reilly. But the main event was me. I gave a brilliant four-page speech about my accomplishments in 2010 and why Boston, Massachusetts, is the right place to host the games. It is where Eunice Kennedy Shriver was born and raised. It would be fitting to honor her memory if the games took place in her hometown. I personally felt that Boston was the right place to host the next National Games. Boston is America's education and intellectual center. It has a rich history in politics, athletics, and innovation. If not for Massachusetts, there would be no Thanksgiving, no basketball or volleyball, and no railroads or trolleys or subways. There would not be an America if not for the American Revolution, which originated in Massachusetts. Of course I had many cheers and applauses as soon as my speech was finished. I did my best to convince the committee to select Massachusetts as the city for the next National Games. Several months later, the 2014 Special Olympics USA National Games was awarded to Princeton, New Jersey. I was disappointed, but at least the games would be closer to my home state than last time.

On a scale of 1 to 10, the year 2010 felt like a perfect 10. Not everything was meant to be perfect that year, but for me it was a banner year. It was the year when I first competed in alpine skiing for Special Olympics. It was the year that I got inducted into the Special Olympics Massachusetts Hall of Fame and Phi Theta Kappa. It was the year I went on TV twice for *Golf in America*, the year I conquered Mount Washington, the year I won my second straight golf league title, and the year when I played nine holes of golf with Mom and Dad for the first time ever. But the one that will top off all of the things that have happened to me in 2010 will be that I went to Nebraska to compete in the Special Olympics USA National Games. Nobody could have asked for anything better than this. This year was a tribute to the hard work that I have endured all my life. After all the adversity that I've had to face and after all the pain that I had to suffer, I came up in a big way to have the best year of my life. It truly was worth it in the end.

Epilogue

THE YEARS AFTER THE 2010 Special Olympics USA National Games have been amazing, but that's a story for the next volume of my autobiography. For those who can't wait to know what I have been up to since 2010, here's a little sneak peek. I got to attend two championship parades, one for the Bruins in 2011 and one for the Red Sox in 2013. I would to travel to Iowa, Maryland, New Jersey, Maine, and Arizona to play the game of golf and meet many more fascinating people, but you will have to wait and see. Late in 2012, my mom was diagnosed with breast cancer, but after months of treatment and not without enduring enormous amounts of pain, she was declared cancer-free. In 2014, I would achieve my single greatest personal accomplishment to date. It took years to realize it, but it's something that I will save for another time. I promise you, my second volume is going to be amazing.

I can, however, mention the following: My mom still teaches cosmetology at Greater Lowell Technical High School in Tyngsboro. Recently she earned her master's degree in occupational education. My dad quit his maintenance technician job at the luxury apartment complex and is now semiretired and works at New England Beekeeping Supplies and Carlisle Honey with his longtime friend Rick Reault. My big brother Clint is now a master plumber and now resides in the state of Maine. In January of 2014, Clint announced his engagement to his girlfriend of a couple of years, Nicole. Clint and I have gotten along better now than ever before, and because of me, he is taking up golf.

As for me, I still live in the house in the hometown where I've lived in all my life with Mom and Dad, but I have more responsibilities now than I've ever had before. My duties around the house include cutting the lawn in the summer and shoveling snow in the winter, emptying the dishwasher, putting towels and my clothes in the washer and dryer, and fixing up my own meals. I still have my own room, with many pieces of memorabilia surrounding it. When I want to get away from everything that distracts or overwhelms me, I go to Memere's basement to study, journal, work out, listen to music, and watch movies. Doing that allows me to regroup and cope with whatever life throws at me.

When I'm not at home, I make several speeches a year to help spread awareness of autism as well as the Special Olympics. In the last few years, I got to speak to elementary school students in Needham during their Embracing Autism Week. The children there are so fascinating. They really take things like this to heart. I mean they ask such interesting questions to me. I would get lots of letters written by the students there, and they seem to understand what I have gone through and are willing to learn more about autism. It's such a heartwarming thing for them to do, reaching out to people like me.

Besides speeches, I work for the bee business in the spring months to put together hives and various other supplies and perform other jobs that come my way, such as cutting grass. I still run some 5K road races, but I don't run as much as I used to. I take part in some charity golf events to work on my game and get better at it. But as much as I want to be a golfer, I'm still a college student. To be the best student I can be, I must devote a lot of time to study. If I am ever going to move up in the real world, I have to sacrifice. I have to focus on the material and take it seriously so that bigger and better things will come my way.

While I continue to build my future, I try to reconnect with my past. I went back to the Community Therapeutic Day School for the 2011 alumni picnic but haven't been back there since. I still cannot believe that it has been years since my last day of school there as a twelve-year-old, but I still remember that day as if it were yesterday. I still keep in touch with some people from Cotting School, particularly Mr. John Navaroli, through some e-mails a few times a year. I do see other former Cotting students once in a while, particularly in the winter months, when I ski with the Nashoba Shooting Stars Ski Team. Elia Veloso comes over to get her hair done once in a while. I see Jared Turcotte and his dad regularly at UMass–Lowell River Hawks hockey games because we're all season ticket holders there.

I've also gone through many changes since 2010. I no longer play or follow basketball anymore because I turned my focus toward skiing, and deep down hockey is my favorite sport to watch on TV during the winter months. I'm no longer an avid baseball fan like I was when I was a kid, but I try to make my annual pilgrimage to Fenway Park to take in the beauty of the American pastime. I've gotten used to the gadgets of our time, such as the iPhone and iPad, and I never go a day without them. I use my iPad to make speeches now. I admit that my iPad (which I call Tyler 3.0) is more portable and uses up no paper at all compared to my speech book. I joined Facebook so that I can keep in touch with some friends (old and new alike) and post significant moments in my life.

I still face challenges daily, and I still have my struggles, some normal, some unique. I am reminded time and time again that life is not always simple and the world can be intolerable if not dangerous. Living in this world is one thing, but living in this world with autism is unlike anything you can imagine. From the words of a person with special needs, if I had taught you anything, here it is. If you thought that you had seen enough, if you thought that you had done enough, *THINK AGAIN*. There are sensitive people out there with real thoughts and real feelings, and I happen to be one of them. They are still people, but you have to handle them different from most other people. I am old enough to know that because I have seen it firsthand, and sometimes it has a strong effect on me. However, I have the tools to overcome my challenges. Sometimes a little inspiration from what I see, hear, and do goes a long way. I also try to remember that I am a blessed person with a family looking out for me, that I have lived a fascinating life, and I have done so much during that time and that it can't be taken from me. For that, I am grateful.

I live an unorthodox life. It's not the life that I asked for, I didn't want to live this life, I didn't want any part of this life, and nobody would want to live how I lived. It took me all my life to realize that I was no ordinary person and that I was different from everyone else. That did not mean that I was better or worse. When I look back now and see what has happened to me all those years, after all the hard work that I was forced to go through, after all the speeches I've made, after all the medals from the Special Olympics that I won, I look at them with a sense of pride. I'm proud of what I've done in my short lifetime.

If I had gotten into trouble, if I had made any mistakes, I paid for them and learned from them. But there is more to my journey, more to the path, and more to the story.

Each person has their own path to their destiny. In a perfect world, people take the conventional path and go to school in their hometowns, graduate high school in a class numbered in the hundreds, go to college to get a degree and get a good-paying job, get married, buy a house, and have children. But in reality, we do not live in a perfect world. In fact, there are those that take the road less traveled. I am one of those who took that road. My path was full of bumps, detours, traffic, obstacles, setbacks, and many forms of adversity. Did I let them stop me? No. Did I let them knock me down on my rear end and keep me there forever? No. Did it make a man out of me? Yes, but I had to decide whether to let all this make a man out of me or let all this pummel me into surrender. Sometimes there are things in this world that bother me, the little things that don't bother many but me, things that don't make any sense to me, things that I have no control over, and things that I just can't fight because I don't feel that these things are worth fighting for. I did not go to the same schools as most people do, I did not take the same roads to school as most people do, and most parts of my life did not turn out the way I expected. But somewhere in the thick of it all, I am helping others, I am an inspiration to people like myself, and I am living proof that people with autism can be as good as they can be in the real world as well as in their world.

There was a time when I could not go through a whole day without whining and crying. There was a time when I could not listen in meetings at school. There was a time when I could not adjust to the slightest bit of change at all. My mother used to ask me three questions:

1) Are you safe?
2) Are you loved?
3) Do you have choices?

They all sound corny to me, but they are all true. I might not feel this way, but I am even when I don't think I know it.

I'm not a child anymore, but that doesn't mean that I don't have dreams. I still hope to become a professional golfer someday. If that doesn't work out, then I'll try my hand working with the environment.

Ten years from now, I see myself as either an environmental scientist or a golfer. But until then I'll still be writing, drawing, and golfing every now and then. I can golf a little bit more with my mom, who had just started to take up golf at the age of fifty-two. With my help, she is better now than she was when she picked up the golf clubs for the first time.

Every time I walk onto any golf course, it's just me, my clubs, the smell of the grass that has been cut, the course, the game, and my thoughts. In sports, anything can happen, and golf is no exception. A single shot can make a big difference in the outcome of a golf round. You can have one bad hole and still have a good round. You can make one bad shot and still be able to make par or perhaps better. You can have your best round ever and still not be able to best the other competitor that you're playing against.

I don't want to think of myself as autistic. I don't want to be remembered that way—that's not my goal in life. I believe that I was put on this earth for something more, for a good purpose, to make a difference in the lives of other people. In the years after my graduation from Cotting School in 2005, I have done that, I do so today, and I plan to continue doing it in the future. I have done things that are so inspiring, even I could not have envisioned it before, and neither could my family. My life is more than my autism, my golf, and my speeches. It's my journey through certain stages both memorable and not so memorable. I consider myself really fortunate to be writing about it, because how often do people with autism and other intellectual disabilities write about themselves? I'm thankful that my life is right where it ought to be. It may not be a perfect life but—what I'm about to say is clichéd, and most of the people where I come from tend to use this five-letter phrase—"*it* is what it is." However, I am proud enough to say that the *it* is called the life of Tyler Hollis Lagasse. That is what I have to say for now.

Acknowledgments

WITHOUT ANY OF THE FOLLOWING, my story would not be possible. Frankly, the first group of people that I want to thank is Alan Shapiro, Nancy Fuller, Bruce Hauptman, and the rest of the Community Therapeutic Day School. You people were like a family to me. You kept me in line for all seven years, your rules had a profound effect on me, and they were there to help me develop into the person that I am today. Without you, I would still be in this prison for life without a glimmer of hope for parole.

I also want to thank Cotting School for making my high school experience an enjoyable one, for giving me more to learn as I was making my delicate transition from childhood into manhood, for helping me respect those with disabilities, and for making me into a better human being. If I hadn't gone to Cotting School, I would not know firsthand how people with disabilities live. You teachers and staff have done an exceptional job in my four years there. Mrs. Dorothy Clark, thank you for having me embrace Shakespeare and history with such films as *Macbeth*, *Taming of the Shrew*, *Julius Caesar*, *All Quiet on the Western Front*, *The Bridge on the River Kwai*, and *The Diary of Anne Frank*. You are the best teacher I've ever had.

Ms. Elizabeth Harkins, thank you for putting me to work time and time again so that you could get the most out of me. Every time after I was done with any homework assignment, you would always take me to a higher level each and every time. I learned more about the benefits and values of hard work from you than any other person besides my parents. When you were my teacher, I did not understand why I had to complete every assignment after working so hard to complete just one and then having another and then another. I understand now what you were trying to do to me then. If not for you, I wouldn't have taken up journal writing, much less write this book. You have a way with keeping me and the other students going. For that, I am very thankful, and I am putting this hard work into good use.

To the Merrimack Education Center, I want to thank you for giving me my jobs at Kimball's, Lowell General Hospital, and Tyngsboro Public Library. Those jobs have helped me develop new skills as well as enabled me to pay for my college tuition. To the people at my job sites, particularly Paul Shanahan from the hospital and Connie Spickler and Randy Robertshaw from the library, I want to thank you for making me feel comfortable and confident at my workplaces.

To the people involved with Kids in Disability Sports Inc.—Bruce Lucier, Fred Wilkie, and Denise Mercier, to name a few; to the members of Team Micky Ward Charities, particularly Rick Dupuis and Keith Henshaw from Gold's Gym Chelmsford and of course Micky "The Fighter" Ward himself; and to the associates of the Nashoba Shooting Stars Ski Team, I want to thank you all for enabling me to continue playing the sports that I love, for helping me get better at my sports all the time, and for letting me succeed in numerous Special Olympic events.

To the people of Special Olympics both in Massachusetts and the whole of the United States, I want to thank you for unlocking my potential as an athlete, a public speaker, and something more. Without you, I would not live my life with a certain degree of purpose or meaning. Without you, millions around the world would not have something to live for. Without you, I along with the general population of those with a medley of disabilities would not have the recognition and respect that we so deserve.

To the supporters and volunteers of Special Olympics, the participants of the annual golf-a-thon, particularly Paul and Emma Karrlsson-Willis, I want to thank you for your generosity and your donations toward Special Olympics. You are the ones that keep this organization running. Without you all, the many Special Olympics sporting events around the world would not be possible. The millions of people with physical and intellectual disabilities would still be left out and ignored. I am not the only one grateful for your kindness. The late Eunice Kennedy Shriver is, and so are the many Special Olympic athletes around the world. You are honoring Eunice's memory and improving the quality of life of athletes and especially myself.

To Richard Howe and Tony Accardi at the Registry of Deeds in Lowell, I want to personally thank you for getting me settled in at my office job at the registry. Thanks to you I became an able worker behind a desk, with a computer and scanner in front of me. Thanks to you, I was able to help out the town of Westford plenty.

To Lauren Seeley and Jeanne O'Connor at the Disability Support Services and to Faithe MacElliot and Aimee Rusman at the TRIO offices of Middlesex Community College, I want to thank you for helping me continue to succeed in the classroom. Because of you, I am a consistent *A* student. Lauren, I want to thank you for all the times that you have helped me with my courses. I owe you a lot. Aimee, I want to personally thank you for convincing me to join Phi Theta Kappa.

Jim Axelrod, Paul Perrymore, and the rest of the crew that were a part of the filming of my story on the Golf Channel's *Golf in America*, I want to thank you all for filming me and bringing my story to a national audience. I hope you liked our house.

To all my friends, relatives, and family members whom I have known all my life, I want to thank you all as well for your support of me. Rick Reault, I want to thank you for letting me work for you in your beekeeping company. You and the rest of your family have been great friends with my family all these years. Rick Reault Sr., I want to thank you for putting together my scramble golf tournament at Townsend Ridge from 2007 to 2009. It has meant so much to me and Special Olympics. Gary Browning, you have a phenomenal family, and like Rick and his family, it has been a joy having you around me and my family. I look forward to our many events and get-togethers for many more years to come.

Uncle Bob and Aunt Beth Lavoie, I appreciate your company. I enjoy spending some parts of summer at your camp by the lake in Salem, New Hampshire, as well as Thanksgiving at your house in nearby Windham. Bobby, I also enjoy attending the many UMass–Lowell River Hawks hockey games with you and your father and brother in the winter.

To Aunt Lauri and Uncle Craig Somers, thank you for being there for me throughout my childhood. Thank you, Lauri, for introducing me to miniature golf and taking me to the driving range in my childhood. Craig, thank you for letting me work for you in your home improvement business. I learned a lot from your trade. Good luck at college, Chantelle. Remember, college is a tough and daunting period in life, but when it's over, after you've finished it, you'll look back and say to yourself, "All this hard work was really worth it in the end."

Terry and Roger Marion and Denise Borghi, thank you for all of your support throughout my life. You were there for me during my childhood when I got to spend some Friday nights at your house, and you continue to be there for me today as I attend college. It's amazing to see that you are still here to watch me grow into manhood, and I am grateful for that. You are one of the best godparents one can ever have.

To Dick and Meg Brown, first of all I want to thank you for witnessing my induction into the Special Olympics Massachusetts Hall of Fame. Second, I want to thank you, Dick Brown, for accompanying me and my dad on our many hikes and ski outings in the White Mountains of New Hampshire. I wish that your friend Bill McDonald was with us on our hikes up Mount Lafayette and Mount Washington. I also wish that I could have gone up hiking with Bill and got to know him a little bit more. I am thankful that you survived your life-threatening thing at the gym so that you could be with me and Dad for my first hike up Mount Washington.

Then there are those who have made a significant impact throughout my childhood but are no longer here anymore. They are my grandfathers Harold Omer Bell Jr. and my pepere, Edmond Victor Lagasse. Grandpa Bell, I miss hearing you call me "pal," because you made me feel like I was your pal. Pepere, I miss playing cribbage with you and going out for ice cream with you after every one of my piano lessons. Both of you were really good people, really special people to me, and I wish that you were here right now to see me as the man that I am today, to see what I have done, and to see me be a winner on the golf course and in the classroom. Shirley Noval, I wish that you were still around to be my babysitter a little more so that we could enjoy listening to '60s music together. Uncle Harold, I miss you a lot. I enjoyed your company a lot with Aunt Joyce, and I enjoyed going to the same campground site as my grandparents at Hampstead, New Hampshire, when I was a young boy. I miss you, but I always remember you. My book is dedicated to you all, and may you continue to rest in peace.

Jaret Foley, I want to thank you for being a big part of my life. Thank you for getting me to understand the rules of golf. Thank you for being my best friend. Without you, my life would be empty, my life would not be worth living, I would not live with courage, and I would not have a role model to look up to. I'm glad that I decided to take up running and train for the half marathon so that we could see each other again in the fall of 2006. You are my hero and always will be.

Mr. John Navaroli, thank you for enlightening me and enriching my life with your wisdom. I also want to thank you for teaching me what character is all about. I live by that word, and I have an obligation and a reason to show what character is all about thanks to you. Finally, thank you for encouraging me to be an inspiration to others, especially those with autism and many other disabilities, whether they are physical or intellectual. You are the inspiration to my book.

Last but certainly not least, I want to thank my family—my mom Deborah, my dad Ronald, my big brother Clint, my grammy Effie Christine Bell, and my memere Lorraine—for all of their support from day 1. First, I want to thank Memere for taking care of me whenever Mom and Dad were still at work, for feeding me lunches and dinners on numerous occasions, for joining my family on our vacations to the New Hampshire Seacoast, for being a fine companion to my family, and for being there when we need you or when you need us.

Grammy, thank you for being around for so long, for being a good grandmother since the day I was born, for all the good times that we spent together, for seeing me graduate from Cotting School, and for seeing me grow up into the man that I've become.

Clint, thank you for turning your life around, thank you for being a better brother to me, and, most of all, thank you for being a better friend to me. I had great times going with you to Red Sox games, the Rush concert back in 2010, and the two championship parades in Boston. Thank you for bringing out the competitive spirit in me. It served me well in my Special Olympics events. I enjoyed watching you compete in baseball, basketball, swimming, track and field, and soccer. And finally, thank you for bringing Chief into your life, then Dooley and Ginger, and the love of your life, Nicole.

Mom and Dad, thank you for being Mom and Dad first of all. Thank you for never giving up on me. Thank you for finding the right schools. Thank you for telling me what is right and what is wrong. Thank you for finding the right people. Thank you for having Jaret become my babysitter. I cannot imagine my life without the both of you together.

I am lucky to have you as my mother and father. I don't know where I would be without you. Most parents with an autistic child would call it quits or would be torn apart. Thankfully with your unwavering faith, your abundance of character, and overwhelming support from our many friends and family members, you stayed together for me. And this is what you get in return: the story of the life of your son. What do you think of your boy now?

Well, it's difficult to put into words how I feel about the subject of autism now. Frankly, it isn't anything like I thought it would be. But then again, parenthood in general isn't anything like I thought it would be either! I share Tyler's sentiment regarding all the people he thanked. I am sure that both he and I will inadvertently leave someone out, and for that I am tremendously sorry. Please don't take it personally.

For me, I would like to thank my husband, Ron, for being there no matter what the outcome. I remember the day we received Tyler's diagnosis, and I remember breaking down in tears, and you were right there for me and said, "We'll figure this out." I know I came up with some pretty "crazy" ways of trying to reach Tyler. I can't believe you found the strength to support me and let me do some of those crazy ideas. You picked up the slack at home when I was doing research to find solutions for Tyler's challenges. You made sure our house ran smooth. You made everything seem effortless. More importantly, you never gave up on our future.

There have been many professionals who have played key roles in our lives. In particular, each member of the Community Therapeutic Day School in Lexington has provided guidance, hope, and a safe place for us to turn to. For that, I will always be indebted to you. I credit everyone there for having the patience to listen to me when I had nowhere to turn. You listened when I complained, whined, bragged, and celebrated over every little thing. You praised me when I did a good job and most importantly called me out when I wasn't doing my best to help Tyler. You helped me realize that it was OK to make mistakes. You taught me that through those mistakes, I would learn an even more important lesson—patience. Thank you for your continued support and your kind ways of reaching the unreachable.

To my family and friends, I don't know how you've stood by us all these years. You have made every accommodation anyone could have asked for. You've changed your schedules so that Tyler could be included in all your gatherings. You have accepted him for who he is.

Jeanne and George, thank you for taking care of Clint whenever we had to go see a new specialist for Tyler. Sometimes I felt that he was at your home with your boys more than he was at his own house! To your two sons, Josh and Zach, thank you for letting Tyler tag along and hang out with you. I know it wasn't always easy to have Tyler there, but you always made him feel welcome. To Rick and Sue, thank you for being there each week through the good days as well as the bad days. You are more than friends to us. You are part of our family.

Gary and Michelle, thank you for your kind ways of always reaching out to us. You have always included us in all your celebrations, and I can't imagine any holiday or summer without the Lagasse, Reault, and Browning families celebrating together. We've laughed together, cried together, but, most of all, "been there" for each other. For that, I am most grateful.

Rick and Sue, you are not just friends. You are part of our family. Our lives are forever intertwined. You have been so supportive of our entire family. We have laughed together, cried together and truly been there for each other. You have celebrated our triumphs and genuinely felt our challenges as if they were your own. I feel so blessed that we are able to not only be close friends, but live within walking distance from each other

Dick, Meg, Mary, and, in memoriam, Bill, thank you for your friendship and sharing so many wonderful memories with us. You have always included Tyler in every invitation. You have opened your homes to us for many vacations. Those have been wonderful times for not only Tyler but our entire family.

To our friends, the Foleys, thank you for sharing your son Jaret with us. He opened a whole new world to Tyler by introducing the game of golf to him. Without golf, I don't know how life would have turned out for Tyler. Molly and Tim Dolan, thank you for your upbeat look on life. Your enthusiasm to live each day to the fullest is infectious. You have listened when I complained that things were moving so slowly for Tyler. You reminded me that life was not a race and to take time to enjoy each moment before they are gone. You have always found a way to make me laugh whenever I was feeling down.

Mark and Stacy, thank you for being such good friends. I don't know how many times we called you at the last minute and said we were coming for an overnight visit because we really needed a break from the world of autism. You welcomed us and let us just relax and forget about those challenges, and before we knew it, we were recharged and ready for any new challenge we would face.

Lauri, thank you for always being there to take over whenever I didn't have anything left to give. You were one of the few people I would let take care of Tyler when I wasn't around. I knew that if I left him with you, he would be safe. Words can never express how indebted I am to you for that. You have taken him on all those silly field trips that I was not willing to take him to. He loves spending time with you because he can feel the love that you have for him. Beth, you and Bob have done so much for Tyler throughout his life. He loves going to the hockey games with Bob. He really loves the cookouts at your camp in Salem too. Beth, thanks for your quirky sense of humor. And most of all, thanks for "getting" my quirky sense of humor.

To my sister, Sharyn, I know that you moved away when I was only nine years old. You didn't really get a chance to see me "grow up." I want to thank you for showing me how to nurture my children. I learned how to nurture from you. I remember that it was you I would turn to as a little girl whenever I needed help. You were always there with a hug, guiding me so I wouldn't get hurt. Janice, thank you for teaching me that the sky is the limit. You taught me how to be independent and to create my own destiny. Suzanne, thank you for teaching me that it's OK for me to take risks. Without that, I may have chosen a very different path for Tyler. I would be remiss if I did not mention my big brother, Harold (may he rest in peace). You were such a kind, compassionate man. You were always ready at a moment's notice to help me out whenever I needed you.

To my son Clint, thank you for being a wonderful son, just the way you are. You make me proud each day, just being you. You are a kind, compassionate man, full of laughter and thoughtfulness. I know that it could not have been easy for you during your childhood years. Countless hours were spent attending meetings, finding programs, and just plain figuring it out when it came to Tyler. You had to put your feelings aside, just to keep the peace with your brother, and I know that must have been a tremendous burden for you. I am so proud of the man you have become. I know that you will be a wonderful father someday, and I look forward to being your son or daughter's memere.

Finally, I would like to thank Tyler for teaching me that life is full of opportunities if you are willing to do the work. I am in awe of your willingness to overcome just about anything. You set goals, you persevere, and you succeed. And you make it look easy! You work harder than anyone

I have ever met. You never let obstacles stand in the way of reaching your goals. You make me want to be a better person. Whenever I feel like giving up, I think to myself, What would Tyler do? *I know that you would never give up on anything. You would find a way. I think we could all learn from you. I know I have. You have been a gift from God sent to me, and for that, I am most thankful. You make me want to be a better mother, friend, sister, and teacher. In short, you make me a better person.*

Edwards Brothers Malloy
Thorofare, NJ USA
May 4, 2015